G000271136

# ORIGINAL BAVARIAN ꜰᴏʟᴋᴛᴀʟᴇꜱ
# A SCHÖNWERTH SELECTION

## A DUAL-LANGUAGE BOOK

# ORIGINAL BAYERISCHE VOLKSMÄRCHEN

# AUSGEWÄHLTE SCHÖNWERTH-GESCHICHTEN

## FRANZ XAVER VON SCHÖNWERTH

Translated by
**M. Charlotte Wolf, Ph.D.**

**DOVER PUBLICATIONS, INC.**
Mineola, New York

*Bibliographical Note*

*Original Bavarian Folktales: A Schönwerth Selection / Original bayerische Volksmärchen | Ausgewahlte Schönwerth-Geschichten,* first published by Dover Publications, Inc., in 2014, contains the original text of *150 East Bavarian Tales,* in German, collected by Franz Xaver von Schönwerth and published in a three-volume work, *Aus der Oberpfalz: Sitten und Sagen,* between 1857 and 1859, reprinted from standard sources, and accompanied by new English translations by M. Charlotte Wolf, Ph.D., who wrote, in addition, the Introductions and footnotes.

*Library of Congress Cataloging-in-Publication Data*

Schönwerth, Franz Xaver von, 1809–1886.
  Original Bavarian folktales – a Schonwerth selection = original Bayerische volksmarchen - ausgewahlte Schönwerth-geschichten / Franz von Schönwerth ; [translated by] M. Charlotte Wolf, Ph.D.
     pages cm.—(Dover dual language German)
  Summary: "This collection of 150 fables is the first dual-language edition of highlights from a three-volume scholarly work originally published in the 1850s. The Introduction contains critical commentary, in addition to background on Franz von Schönwerth and his legacy"— Provided by publisher.
  ISBN-13: 978-0-486-49991-8 (pbk.)
  ISBN-10: 0-486-49991-X
  1. Folklore—Germany—Bavaria. 2. Tales—Germany—Bavaria. 3. Bavaria (Germany)—Social life and customs. I. Title.
  GR167.B3S378 2013
  398.20943'3—dc23

                                                        2013027089

Manufactured in the United States by RR Donnelley
49991X02    2015
www.doverpublications.com

# CONTENTS

iii

x                           Contents

# ACKNOWLEDGMENTS

I would like to thank Janet Kopito, language editor at Dover Publications, Inc., for her excitement, guidance and advice throughout this endeavor. Furthermore, I owe thanks to Erika and Dr. Adolf Eichenseer of the *Schönwerth Society*, who shared with me stories of their adventures in the study of Schönwerth's life and work.

I want also to express my sincerest thanks to my husband, Martin Tobias, who diligently edited the manuscript, and also was my companion and photographer on a whirlwind tour of Schönwerth sites in the Upper Palatinate in the summer of 2012, while I was collecting background material for this book. And finally, I am grateful that Dover Publications, Inc., agreed to publish this project, because it gave me an opportunity to reconnect with the memories of my childhood in the beautiful landscape and the rich language of the Upper Palatinate.

*M. Charlotte Wolf, Ph.D.*
*Colorado, December 2013*

"Some day you will be old enough to start reading fairy tales again."
C. S. Lewis, *The World's Last Night: And Other Essays*

# Introduction

## Who Was Franz Xaver von Schönwerth?

In 1810, when Franz Xaver von Schönwerth was born in the town of Amberg in the Upper Palatinate, his family had been there already for about 100 years. Originally, the Schönwerths were French aristocrats, the Comtes de Bellisle,[1] who left France during the Huguenot exodus around 1685. Via Switzerland, they arrived in North West Bavaria, where they settled in the region known as "Mainfranken," roughly halfway between Frankfurt and Nuremberg, and changed their name to "Schönwerth."[2] His great-grandfather, Andreas Schönwerth, moved to the former capital of the Upper Palatinate, Amberg, around 1720. There he worked as a painter and decorator. Andreas's son Christian became so skilled in his craft as a painter that he received an honorable mention in the Amberg Chronicle of 1817, which stated, "Among the many artifacts that speak to his skill are two paintings in the St. Annaberg Church in the town of Sulzbach: one of the Holy Trinity and one of Saint Ignatius and Saint Xaverius."[3]

---

[1] Bellisle: French for "Beautiful Island."

[2] Alternative spellings were "Schönwörth" or "Schönwerd," with "Wörth" meaning "island in the river." (See also the reference to "Wurth" in Jacob and Wilhelm Grimm, *Deutsches Wörterbuch*, 16 vol. in 32 books, Leipzig 1971. vol. 30, col. 2324.)

[3] Roland Röhrich, *Das Schönwerth-Lesebuch: Volkskundliches aus der Oberpfalz im 19. Jahrhundert* (Regensburg: Pustet Verlag, 1981): 15.

Joseph Schönwerth, Franz Xaver's father, continued the family tradition. In 1807, his skill garnered him a position as an art teacher at the Royal Secondary School in Amberg, enabling him to marry and have children. In 1809, he married a fellow Amberg citizen, the daughter of a ship's chronicler, and Franz Xaver was born the following year. With both an artistic and a literary streak inherited from both sides of the family, Schönwerth was destined to become an artist himself.

Since the family suffered financial hardship despite his father's relatively high social standing as a professor at a secondary school, Franz enrolled as a student at his father's school. His budding talents as a writer and historian were mentioned in a report card from 1828, which stated, "He is first in Latin prose, history, and geography, and in creative writing he is number four . . . Overall, he is the second best student."[4] The eleven notebooks from his time as a secondary school student, in which he jotted down idioms and grammatical peculiarities of his native tongue along with important dates from history, reveal his passion for language, literature, and history which would become a lifelong vocation (Röhrich 18).

After graduating in second place from the philosophical division of the preparatory school in Amberg, he left his hometown and enrolled at the Royal Bavarian Academy of Architecture in Munich. However, after five semesters he switched gears and enrolled in law school. One of his friends tells us of Schönwerth's life as a college student, full of hard work and deprivations—nothing new for the son of a secondary school professor from a remote town in what was one of the poorest regions of Germany:

> As a student, Schönwerth, like many of his comrades in misfortune, had to earn his living by tutoring . . . but in addition to that he committed to two years of diligently studying history with Professor Görres.[5] Even in advanced age . . . he produced

---

[4] „In der lateinischen Prosa und in der Geschichte, nebst der Geographie ist er der erste, in den poetischen Arbeiten der vierte . . . im allgemeinen Fortgang der zweite." Röhrich 17.

[5] Joseph Görres, at that time professor for general history and the history of literature at the Ludwig Maximilian University, seemed to have made a lasting impression on Schönwerth.

his notes from these lectures which he had copied with tireless efforts.[6]

Schönwerth comments on this time in a similar vein: "I used the free time beside my studies to earn a living through private tutoring, since I did not receive any support whatsoever from my parents... due to their unfortunate financial situation."[7]

In 1837, he concluded his studies with the highest distinction. After five years as an intern, in 1842 he finally landed his first permanent employment with the government in Upper Bavaria. Though highly educated, he still earned less than a skilled journeyman.

But 1845 was a windfall year for Schönwerth. After recommendation by a high government official, he was appointed Private Secretary to His Royal Highness, Crown Prince Maximilian of Bavaria. In this capacity, Schönwerth not only dealt with Maximilian's extensive private correspondence, but also was responsible for providing daily updates on events in science and the arts. Soon, however, the Crown Prince charged him also with managing his private estate. Schönwerth proved very skilled in that area, as the following anecdote reveals: During the tumultuous uprising of March 1848, the royal family was forced to hide from the revolutionary masses who barricaded streets and threatened to storm palaces. Schönwerth, in a daring cloak-and-dagger operation, drove an open carriage disguised as a waste removal cart and containing the entire assets of the Crown Prince's family, jewelry and all, out of Munich. This netted him not only the Crown Prince's unreserved trust, but also, after King Ludwig

---

Görres was a famous university teacher and pioneer of political journalism in the German political culture in the revolutionary period known as "Vormärz" [See also Jon Vanden Heuvel, *A German Life in the Age of Revolution: Joseph Görres, 1776–1848* (Washington, D.C.: The Catholic University of America Press, 2001)].

[6] „Als Student musste Schönwerth, wie so viele seiner Schicksalsgenossen, mit Stundengeben seinen Unterhalt erwerben... lag aber auch nebenbei durch zwei Jahre fleissig dem Geschichtsstudium bei Görres ob, dessen unermüdlich nachgeschriebene Vorträge er noch in höherem Alter... vorwies." Johann Nepomuk Sepp, „Franz Xaver von Schönwerth," *Der Sammler: Beilage zur Münchener-Augsburger Abendzeitung*, no. 81 (1886): 2–5: 2f.

[7] „... dass ich die mir von meinen Fachstudien freigelassene Zeit dazu verwendete, um durch Privatunterricht meinen Unterhalt zu gewinnen, indem ich... von meinen Eltern bei deren eigenen misslichen Vermögensverhältnissen nicht die geringste Unterstützung genoss... " Röhrich 19.

I's forced abdication[8] and Crown Prince Maximilian's succession to the throne, a promotion to Royal Interior Secretary and Chairman of the Finance Ministry's cash office in the newly appointed king's cabinet in 1848. Just three years later, in 1851, Schönwerth was promoted again, this time to Principal Secretary of the Finance Ministry, and then again 18 months later to Senior Legal Secretary. Considering that Schönwerth had completed his internship as a legal clerk only ten years earlier, this was a surprising rate of career advancement.

## More Than the Brothers Grimm

Although Schönwerth's position as a high-profile government official left him little time for other ventures, he started to pursue his interest in folklore. In 1851, he began collecting material for what was to become his greatest endeavor: recording the customs and tales of his homeland by inquiring of folk from the Upper Palatinate who earned their living in Munich as servants and workmen.[9] In 1854, he conducted preparatory work for a survey of "items on which I would like to receive more information," which he sent out to informants such as priests and teachers in the Upper Palatinate.[10] In particular, Schönwerth was interested

---

[8] In an ironic intersection of the personal and the political, the downfall of King Ludwig I was brought about by an exotic dancer from Ireland, rather than by the historical conditions of a time characterized by revolutions in France, Italy, and many German states that resulted in political changes in many of these. While the proletarian masses in Paris, Frankfurt, and Berlin demanded equality and political representation, the Bavarian people were scandalized by the machinations of a scantily clad woman who had managed to command the attention of the king and with it the power to ransack the not inconsiderable budget of the Kingdom of Bavaria. When an enraged Bavarian mob took to the streets, they shouted, "The whore must go," and when the king did not heed it, they called successfully for his abdication. Jan von Flocken, „Die Stripperin und die Revolution," *Die Welt*, 29 June 2007, <http://www.welt.de/kultur/history/article984878/Die-Stripperin-und-die-Revolution.html>. Accessed 28 Oct 2012.

[9] Hans-Jürgen Becker, „Rechtshistorische Aspekte im Werk von Franz Xaver von Schönwerth," *Schönwerth: Mit so leisem Gehör gesammelt*, (Regensburg: Schnell & Steiner, 2011): 75.

[10] Heidemarie Sander, „Schönwerth, Franz Xaver von," *Neue Deutsche Biographie*, 23 (2007): 424 <http://www.deutsche-biographie.de/pnd118610236.html>. Accessed 28 Oct 2012.

to learn more about the language and lore of the Upper Palatinate to explore connections to Germanic traditions, much as Jacob Grimm had done in his monumental and famous work *Deutsche Mythologie*.[11] Schönwerth shared the enthusiasm of many of his Romantic peers for the scholarly exploration of German cultural traditions, and in addition he was deeply connected to his Eastern Bavarian homeland and its language and customs. He repeatedly expressed his worry that "new" lifestyles would have a lasting impact on the traditional way of life of the Upper Palatinate people, and he intended to collect the legends, fairytales, proverbs, customs, children's games and rhymes, songs, cuisine, magical practices, and legal traditions of his homeland, so as to preserve the memory of these for posterity.[12] But unfortunately, few of the surveys Schönwerth sent out were returned to him, and his enthusiasm flagged.

However, his efforts received a boost after his marriage in 1856 to Maria Rath, a woman from the Upper Palatinate thirty years his junior. Her father was only ten years older than Schönwerth and was a kindred spirit with similar interests in literature, history, and folklore. Maria became instrumental in her husband's research. It was in large part through her that Schönwerth gained access to a large body of fairytales, customs, and legends of the region where she grew up and of the surrounding areas. In 1857, Schönwerth managed to publish the first volume of the most comprehensive collection of folklore, the three-volume *From the Upper Palatinate: Customs and Legends*.[13]

Schönwerth said about his interest in his native Upper Palatinate and the people who called it home:

> The [native of the] Upper Palatinate is no Bavarian, no Franconian, no Slav. He is part of a different tribe which stands alienated

[11] Jacob Grimm, *Deutsche Mythologie*, 1st ed., Göttingen: Dieterich'sche Buchhandlung, 1835.

[12] Oberpfälzer Kulturbund e.V., „Schönwerth, Franz Xaver von." *Kultur der Oberpfalz,* 2011 <http://www.oberpfaelzerkulturbund.de/cms/pages/kulturderoberpfalz/dbeintrag_details.php?id=221>. Accessed 28 Oct 2012.

[13] Franx Xaver von Schönwerth, *Aus der Oberpfalz - Sitten und Sagen*, vol. 1–3, Augsburg: Rieger, 1857, 1858, 1859.

among its mighty neighbors. That may be why they give him a
disapproving look and, because he is not of their blood, assume
they are entitled to impute to him faults which he does not have,
reduce the good which is inherent in him to a minimum, and even
insinuate that his traditional loyalty is [to] inertia, an entirely im-
pure motive.... And as they do to the people, so they do to the land.
    It is said to be an inhospitable province and a terror for each
traveler who happens to be led there by misfortune. This testi-
ness of the surrounding tribes may well have its origin in the fact
that the [native of the] Upper Palatinate has always remained the
same, and [he] does not like to accept anything from unbidden
and foreign schoolmasters which, understandably, severely hurts
their amour propre.[14]

The collection received high praise from Schönwerth's benefac-
tors and from experts in the field of folklore; among them was King
Maximilian II himself, who sent a letter to Schönwerth stating:

I have received your interesting work on the customs and legends
of the Upper Palatinate, Volume I, with joy. You know how highly
I regard such much appreciated work in the field of ethnography
of my country and I am pleased to hear that critical reviews also
are very appreciative of your venture. Receive my obliged thanks
for your attention, and I remain with merciful disposition, Yours
Graciously, King Max. Munich, this 25th of June, 1857.[15]

---

[14] „Der Oberpfälzer ist kein Bajuware, kein Franke, kein Slave. Er bildet einen eigenen
Stamm, der fremd zwischen seinen mächtigern Nachbarn steht. Daher mag es auch kommen, dass ihn diese mit scheelem Auge betrachten, und weil er nicht ihres Blutes, sich
berechtiget erachten, ihm Fehler anzudichten, die er nicht besitzt, das Gute, das ihm in-
newohnt, auf ein unbedeutendes Minimum herabzumarkten, ja seiner althergebrachten
Loyalität einen ganz unlautern Grund, Trägheit... unterzustellen! Und wie dem Volke,
ergeht es dem Lande. Es soll ein unwirthbarer Gau sein und Schrecken für jeden Rei-
senden, den das Mißgeschick dahin führt. Diese Gereiztheit der Nachbarn hat wohl nur
darin ihren Grund, dass der Oberpfälzer eben bleibt, wie er ist, und von unberufenen
fremden Schulmeistern nichts annehmen will, was deren Eigenliebe begreiflicher Weise
empfindlich verletzt." *Sitten und Sagen*, vol. 2: 42–48.

[15] „Ihr interessantes Werk über die Sitten und Sagen der Oberpfalz habe ich mit Vergnügen entgegengenommen. Sie wissen, welch hohen Wert ich so schätzbaren Beiträgen zur
Ethnographie meines Landes beilege, und es freut mich, dass, wie ich höre, auch die
Kritik sich sehr günstig über Ihr Unternehmen ausgesprochen. Empfangen Sie meinen
verbindlichen Dank für Ihre Aufmerksamkeit, der ich mit gnädigen Gesinnungen bin,

The king was so impressed with Schönwerth's work that three times he granted him a leave of absence, which allowed the folklorist to return to his homeland to conduct field research and inquiries in person. In contrast with the procedures established by the Grimm Brothers, Schönwerth visited with his fellow natives to ask them about customs and tales of all kinds. During the three leaves of absence in the Upper Palatinate, he met with hundreds of ordinary people such as servants, cooks, farmers, and craftsmen.

Jacob Grimm, whose *Deutsche Mythologie* and *Kinder- und Hausmärchen*,[16] co-authored with his brother Wilhelm, had inspired Schönwerth in his research, also was full of praise for the work Schönwerth had undertaken. In a review of the second volume of *Sitten und Sagen*, Grimm explicitly referred to the echos of a Germanic mythical world of gods in these tales:

Dear Sir, Maybe you were able to take a look at the Leipzig Central Newspaper wherein I expressed my great joy over your collection from the Upper Palatinate and could not help but stress in particular the retelling of the legend of Wodan and Frija . . . Yours Humbly, Jacob Grimm, Berlin, Sept. 26, 1858.[17]

In that same review, Jacob Grimm expressed his high regard for Schönwerth's scholarly work, stating that nowhere in Germany had the collecting of tales been conducted with such thoughtfulness, comprehensiveness, and such a fine ear.[18] The tales published in *Sitten und Sagen* carry the reader off into a mystical and magical world populated with Giants, Dwarves, Ghosts, and

---

Ihr wohlgewogener König, Max. München, den 25ten Juni, 1857." Erika Eichenseer, ed. *Franz Xaver von Schönwerth zum 200. Geburtstag: Sagen und Märchen aus der Oberpfalz: Ein Leseheft*, Weiden: Spintler, Druck und Verlag, 2010.

[16] Jacob Grimm, *Deutsche Mythologie*, Göttingen: Dieterich'sche Buchhandlung, 1835. ---,--, *Kinder- und Hausmärchen*, Stuttgart: Deutsche Verlagsanstalt, 1812.

[17] „Verehrter Herr, vielleicht ist Ihnen das Stück des Leipziger Centralblattes zu Gesicht gekommen, worin ich vor einem Vierteljahre meine große Freude über Ihre Sammlung aus der Oberpfalz laut werden liess, und nicht umhin konnte, auf die... mitgeteilte Sage von Woud und Freid ganz besonderes Gewicht zu legen... Ihr ergebenster Jakob Grimm, Berlin 26. Sept. 1858." Jacob Grimm, „Besprechung der *Sitten und Sagen*, Teile 1 und 2" *Literarisches Centralblatt für Deutschland*, 21 (1858): 336f.

[18] See footnote 18: Grimm, *Literarisches Centralblatt*.

magical animals set in a landscape of forests, rivers, castles, and mountains.[19]

In 1859, shortly after the publication of the third volume of *Sitten und Sagen*, King Maximilian awarded Schönwerth lifetime nobility in acknowledgment of his work. Such high praise notwithstanding, the three-volume collection sold very poorly. Although Schönwerth at first continued with his collection activity—as a contributory letter dated March 13, 1863[20] illustrates—he became increasingly discouraged by the disastrous reception of his publications as time went on. Consequently, he abandoned plans for the publication of more material from his now vast collection of stories and folklore. Around 30,000 pages of collected material on the customs of the region, hand-written in the hard-to-read Sütterlin style of those days, went into storage. They were not touched again until their rediscovery in the early twenty-first century.

With his passion for the language and lore of his native region so severely squashed, Schönwerth now turned his interest to linguistics. In the last twenty-some years of his life, he published a few more works, not based upon his own first-hand research materials, but mostly upon the work of others. Among them is a publication on Bavarian and Upper Palatinian grammar,[21] an

---

[19] Anna Bergler, „Franz Xaver von Schönwerth - der oberfälzer Volkskundler,“ *Die Bayern-Blogger.* 4 August 2010, <http://www.bayern-blogger.de/franz-xaver-von-schonwerth-der-oberpfalzer-volkskundler-3255>. Accessed 20 October 2012.

[20] Excerpt from a letter of master nailsmith Jakob Grader from Neustadt in the Central Bavarian Forest, a short drive from the border with the Czech Republic: „Hochedelgebohrner, Gnädiger Herr, Sie wünschen Sitten, Gebräuche, Aberglauben und dergleichen zu erfahren... Es mag schon etliche 20 Jahre sein, dass ich als Landwehrmann zur 12then Stunde in der Christnacht patrolieren musste, da sah ich bei hellem Mondschein eine Frauensperson die Straße kehren. In welcher Absicht sie es getan hat, weiss ich nicht; es war trocken und hatte keinen Schnee.“ („Dear honorable, gracious Sir, You wish to learn of customs, traditions, superstititions, and such things... It may well have been some 20 years ago when I had to patrol the streets as a militia man during midnight on Christmas Eve and I saw a female sweep the streets in bright moonlight. I do not know what her intentions were, for it was dry and there was no snow.“) „Kulturfreunde Lokbkowitz, Neustadt a.d. Waldnaab,“ <http://www.lobkowitz.de/weitere_Infos_ueber_Lobkowitz/Schoenwerth.htm>. Accessed 20 October 2012.

[21] Franz Xaver Schönwerth, *Dr. Weinholds Baierische Grammatik und die oberpfälzische Mundart* (Regensburg, 1869).

essay on the Bavarian dialects with particular consideration of the Upper Palatinian,[22] and another on idioms and proverbs of the Upper Palatinate region.[23] He died in Munich in 1886, after an eight-year retirement.

In a peculiar twist of fate, the lives of Schönwerth and King Ludwig II of Bavaria, known as "the fairytale king," intersected in many ways. Among other things, Ludwig, the son of Schönwerth's longtime employer, King Maximilian II of Bavaria, was born the same year Schönwerth was appointed as Maximilian's private secretary. Although I can find no written record to corroborate this, it is safe to assume that young Ludwig was familiar with the passion for folktales of one of his father's closest confidants, and was encouraged in his love of mythology by Schönwerth's activities. A dedicated patron of the arts, King Ludwig later designed and commissioned the famous Neuschwanstein Castle, whose outstanding beauty inspired Cinderella Castle in Walt Disney's Magic Kingdom.[24] Schönwerth died three weeks before his king drowned in Lake Starnberg in May of 1886, and was thereby spared the pain of grieving over the shocking end of a kindred spirit and fellow lover of wondrous lore.

## The Folktale Renaissance

In March 2012, an article in the British newspaper *The Guardian* reported the news that a "collection of fairytales gathered by historian Franz Xaver von Schönwerth (1810–1886) locked away for over 150 years in an archive in Regensburg," in a remote region of Eastern Bavaria commonly known as the Upper Palatinate,[25] had been unearthed. Though the find was indeed

---

[22] Franz Xaver Schönwerth, „Johann Andreas Schmeller und seine Bearbeitung der baierischen Mundarten mit Bezugnahme auf das Oberpfälzische," *VOR*, vol. 28 (1872): 229 ff.

[23] Franz Xaver Schönwerth, „Die Sprüchwörter des Volkes der Oberpfalz in der Mundart," *VOR*, vol. 29 (1874): III ff.

[24] "Neuschwanstein Castle: Your Travel Guide to Neuschwanstein Castle in Germany," <http://www.neuschwansteincastle.net>. Accessed 28 October 2012.

[25] Victoria Sussens-Messerer, "Five hundred new fairytales discovered in Germany," 5 March 2012 <http://www.guardian.co.uk/books/2012/mar/05/five-hundred-fairytales -discovered-germany>. Accessed 28 October 2012.

sensational, it was not really news because the collection, comprised of thousands of pages covered in neat handwriting and stowed away in 30 ungainly boxes, had actually been discovered a few years earlier. In 2010, the 200th anniversary of Schönwerth's birthday, some of the tales discovered in these boxes were published in an anthology titled *Prinz Roßzwifl* (*Prince Dung Beetle*[26] in the local dialect). It took another two years for details of the discovery to spread to the English-speaking world via the article in *The Guardian*. The name Franz Xaver von Schönwerth had been virtually unknown both inside and outside of Germany up to this point, but the Schönwerth Society has received a flood of inquiries from all over the world[27] because now folklorists, scholars of German literature, and publishers alike are curious to learn more about the folktales and the man behind them.

As mentioned earlier, Schönwerth's main intent was to preserve the day-to-day traditions, beliefs, and customs of his native region, and the folk tales of the region were one part of that body of knowledge.[28] While he lived, he published only excerpts from his vast collection, in the previously mentioned *Sitten und Sagen*. The bulk of his work is still sitting in the archive waiting to be transcribed, "mined" for tales, and, eventually, published.

While Schönwerth's work received little attention from the broad public during his life, the judgment of the experts in those times was unanimously enthusiastic. Jacob Grimm in particular was intrigued by Schönwerth's collection of the lore of a people still largely untouched by rapidly advancing industrialization (such as the railways). Grimm's all-around positive review of Schönwerth's work (see footnote 18) may have resulted from his

---

[26] Franz Xaver Schönwerth, *Prinz Roßzwifl und andere Märchen*, ed. Erika Eichenseer, Regensburg: Verlag Morsbach, Dr. Peter, 2010.

[27] "Schönwerth International," <http://typo3.schoenwerth.de/index.php?id=11>. Accessed 28 October 2012.

[28] In the Introduction to *Sitten und Sagen*, Schönwerth spells this out clearly: "However, I was less interested in the tales, but more in the many little, inconspicuous expressions which tell the point of view of the people and preserve the relics of a pagan belief." („Doch waren es weniger die Sagen, wonach ich trachtete, als jene vielen kleinen unscheinbaren Sätze, in denen die Anschauungsweise des Volkes sich ausspricht und die Reste heidnischen Glaubens sich erhalten." *Sitten und Sagen*, vol. 1: 43.)

recognition of a kindred spirit in the much younger Bavarian, and it started a period of collaboration during the last five years of Jacob Grimm's life, from 1858 to 1863.[29]

While there were similarities between the literary approaches of the Grimm Brothers and Schönwerth, there were also distinct differences. The Grimms, for example, did not collect tales by contacting "everyday people," as Schönwerth did on several occasions, during lengthy excursions to the Upper Palatinate between 1859 and 1861 and by mailing out surveys to community leaders in the region. Rather, they consulted professional story-tellers like Dorothea Viehmann, who contributed dozens of tales to *Kinder- und Hausmärchen*.[30] Also, various Schönwerth scholars have pointed out that the tenor of his tales is much "rawer" than those of the [Grimms'] fairytales.[31] This is because the Grimms frequently softened the message of tales they thought too violent for children, while Schönwerth had tried to preserve the tone and flavor of Upper Palatinian in his tales:

> I recorded [the accounts] straight from the mouths of the people and tried to preserve the natural simplicity of their communications. The way people think and talk is not supposed to appear in a farmer's smock or in dress gloves, but in the Sunday finery of the country people.[32]

---

[29] Jacob's younger brother, Wilhelm, his closest collaborator, had died in 1859. That, and the fact that Jacob was himself advanced in age, may have motivated him to look for a fellow folklorist and linguist who could continue his work. According to a reliable source, Jacob Grimm wished for Schönwerth to retire from his government post and dedicate his entire time to research and scholarship. (See also Johann Nepomuk Sepp, "Franz Xaver von Schönwerth," *Der Sammler*: 4.)

[30] Bernhard Lauer, „Dorothea Viehmann und die Brüder Grimm. Märchen und Wirklichkeit," *Märchenspiegel: Zeitschrift für internationale Märchenforschung und Märchenpflege* 2/9 (1998): 36–42.

[31] Maria Tatar, "King Goldenlocks: A Newly Translated Fairytale," *The New Yorker* 2 April 2012 <http://www.newyorker.com/online/blogs/books/2012/04/a-brand-new-fairytale.html>. Accessed 2 November 2012.

[32] „Ich habe es vom Munde des Volkes weg geschrieben und mich bemüht, die natürliche Einfachheit in seinen Mitteilungen beizubehalten. Nicht im Bauernkittel, aber auch nicht in Ballhandschuhen, sondern im ländlichen Sonntagsstaate soll erscheinen, wie das Volk denkt und spricht." *Sitten und Sagen*, vol. 1: 36.

For years, Schönwerth sought out fellow natives from the lower income levels because he felt they had been less exposed to schooling, city life, and "literary junk" (*Sitten und Sagen*, vol. 1: 42) than their more educated counterparts. It took a lot of preparation and circumspection to get these simple people to agree to an interview, because often they suspected that they were being made fun of. In the preamble to *Sitten und Sagen*, in which he describes his research and method for collecting authentic material, he commented on the skill needed to "mine" his interviewees:

> Women and weavers of my homeland deigned to sit with me to be interviewed, usually in exchange for little presents and light refreshments, and they became quite forthcoming when I was the one to start talking in the native tongue. It takes great practice to tease out exactly that which is significant, and this [process] must not lack patience. Because these people cannot escape the feeling that an educated person is unable to take a liking to such "silliness," they instantly begin to harbor suspicions that one wants to pull their leg.[33]

And, whereas the Grimms' fairytales are not tightly regionally delineated, Schönwerth limited his collection activity strictly to his native region, the Upper Palatinate.

Therefore, the reader may notice substantial differences in both language and content between the versions of Schönwerth tales that appear in this dual-language book and those made popular by the Grimms. The Grimms' widely known tale "The Gallant Tailor" (German, „Das tapfere Schneiderlein"), which appeared in the 1857 edition of *Kinder- und Hausmärchen*,[34] is a good example that offers some sharp contrasts. In this collection, the tale

---

[33] „Weiber und Weber der Heimat ließen sich gegen kleine Geschenke und Bewirtung in der Regel gerne herbei, sich als Inquisiten mir gegenüber zu setzen und wurden ganz mittheilsam, wenn ich der Erste war, in der heimatlichen Mundart zu erzählen. Es erfordert große Übung, gerade dasjenige, worauf es ankommt, herauszufragen und an Geduld darf es nicht fehlen. Diese Leute können sich nämlich der Ansicht nicht entschlagen, dass ein Gebildeter unmöglich an solchen »Dummheiten« Gefallen finde und fassen sogleich Argwohn, dass man sie zum Besten haben wolle." *Sitten und Sagen*, vol.1: 37.

[34] Brothers Grimm, *Kinder- und Hausmärchen*, Reprint of the Great Edition of 1857, ed. Hans-Jörg Uther (Munich, 1996): 110–119.

is titled "The Tailor and the Giants" (German, „Der Schneider und die Riesen").[35]

In the Grimm version, the story begins with a detailed description of the purchase of sweet compote, tells of the flies that "landed on it in droves" (KHM 111), recounts the tailor's victory over the seven flies with one stroke (as the tailor tells it!), and concludes with a phrase that boasts of the tailor's "courageous deed" with the following words, "You are such a [tough] guy?[. . . ] The entire world shall hear of this!"[36] (KHM 111).

In Schönwerth's version, the tailor is a much humbler lad who, wandering about in the world, one day finds in the forest a red silk sash on which are the words "Seven with one stroke; who can match that?" which he picks up and ties around his waist."[37] The two stories then follow two obviously similar threads, but the Grimm version contains much more dialog, whereas the Schönwerth version is focused more on narrative. Also, in the Grimm version, the tailor survives by using his wits, whereas in the Schönwerth version the tailor supplements his wits with true heroism, and finally is encouraged by Divine Prophecy that he will win the battle against a heathen army.[38]

But like Schönwerth's *Sitten und Sagen*, the motivation for the publication of Jacob Grimm's *Deutsche Mythologie* and the Grimm Brothers' *Kinder- und Hausmärchen* was a shared focus on the importance of folk traditions, East Bavarian and German respectively. Both Schönwerth and the Grimms favored the preservation of everyday culture of rural and small-town Germans over Greco-Roman classical ideas, to keep alive traditions that reflected a Germanic folk-culture reaching back into a prehistoric past. The lasting legacy of their important nineteenth-century works was an increased appreciation for native culture, which contributed to a

---

[35] *Sitten und Sagen*, vol. 2: 280–288.

[36] „Bist du so ein Kerl? [. . .] Die ganze Welt soll's erfahren!"

[37] „. . . ein rotseidenes Band . . . auf dem die Worte standen: ‚Sieben auf einen Schlag, wer macht es mir nach.' Der Schneider hob es auf und band es sich um den Leib." *Sitten und Sagen*, vol. 2: 280.

[38] See also Christine Pretzl, „Enstehungsgeschichte und Varianten der Märchentexte bei den Brüdern Grimm und Franz Xaver von Schönwerth," *Schönwerth: Mit so leisem Gehör gesammelt*, Regensburg: Schnell & Steiner, 2011: 11.

leveling of class barriers and led ultimately to the creation of a German republic in the early twentieth century.

## Folktales: Fairytales, Myths, and Legends

Surveying contemporary pop culture, from movies to TV shows, online games, and novels, one cannot help but notice the proliferation of fantasy and wonder. When turning to the nineteenth-century works of the Brothers Grimm for inspiration, many screen writers and directors have taken great liberties with their literary models, for example by having Snow White and her mother both appear young and beautiful in *Once Upon a Time*, a TV show based upon postmodern adaptations of (primarily) Grimm fairytales.[39] Another contemporary TV show that uses fairytale motifs liberally is the much more sinister *Grimm*, whose protagonist is a police detective who discovers his creature-hunting ancestry, and therefore pursues supernatural rather than human predators.[40]

The origins of these tales of wonder are rather less lurid. The German word for fairytale, "Märchen," is derived from the Middle High German "maere," which means "news," "message," or "lore." This hints at the original function of folktales, in a time when few people were literate. Folktales served the purpose of information brokerage by reporting real events or packaging knowledge so that it was easier to understand, remember, and pass along; hence the term "folklore."

But in contrast to the cultural benefits of these oral traditions of Schönwerth's day, there was also a dark side. Of the 150 stories in this collection, almost one quarter (35) warn of the existential threats from just one hostile magical force: *women*, in a variety of guises such as Witches, Drudes, and Mermaids.

When women are not portrayed as evil in Schönwerth's stories, they are often portrayed as being particularly susceptible to being

---

[39] *Once Upon a Time* is an American fantasy-drama television series that premiered on October 23, 2011, on the American Broadcasting network (ABC). ["Once Upon a Time (2011– )," <http://www.imdb.com/title/tt1843230/>. Accessed 29 Jul 2013.]

[40] Grimm premiered on October 28, 2011, on the National Broadcasting network (NBC). ["Grimm (2011– )," <http://www.imdb.com/title/tt1830617/?ref_=fn_al_tt_1>. Accessed 29 Jul 2013.]

led astray. Many of the other stories outline the restrictions on women to help them evade the Devil and his agents: from courtship, as brides, when pregnant, as mothers, through to old age. Similar perceptions seemed to reign not only in the remote region of East Bavaria, but also in other areas of Germany. In fact, for several centuries southern Germany in particular was a hotbed of witch-burning in Europe. In Germany, the witchhunting mania (from about 1480 to 1750) more or less peaked in the years 1561 to 1670, but the last to be sentenced to death for witchcraft was Anna Schwegelin in the southwest Bavarian city of Kempten in 1775, just 35 years before Schönwerth was born in 1810.[41]

The numerous harsh, cruel, or brutal elements within the original tales, usually purged from contemporary versions targeted at young audiences, hint that many of these tales were intended to transmit cultural norms for how to lead one's life. Life experiences and values were first interwoven into simple parables and allegories and then developed into stories to be passed on from generation to generation.

Fairytales were shared with audiences of all ages and from all walks of life. The intention was to help all people avoid dangerous situations that a soul encounters during its lifetime, particularly the pitfalls of evil, and among them the dangers lurking in evil people who manage to appear benign. Listeners also learned that beauty can exist in good as well as evil people and often goes hand in hand with pride, as well as sometimes with innocence. They learned about the importance of being humble and content with one's station in life, and that work, diligence, and piety bring

---

[41] See also:

1. Johannes Dillinger, *"Evil People": A Comparative Study of Witch Hunts in Swabian Austria and the Electorate of Trier*, Studies in Early Modern German History, Charlottesville, VA: University of Virginia Press, 2009.

2. Peter Steinfels, *Historians and Scholars Produce New Picture of Witches and Witch Hunts, but Questions Remain*, New York Times, 22 Oct 2005, <http://www.nytimes.com/2005/10/22/national/22beliefs.html?_r=0>. Accessed 10 Aug 2013.

3. Hansjörg Strasser, Anna Schwegelin: der letzte Hexenprozess auf deutschem Boden, 1775 in Kempten, Kempten: Verlag für Heimatpflege, 1985.

4. Charles Mackay, *Memoirs of Extraordinary Popular Delusions and the Madness of Crowds*, <http://www.gutenberg.org/files/24518/24518-0.txt>, Accessed 8 Aug 2013.

lasting success. They learned that envy, jealousy, selfishness, and greed are major causes for injustice and bad luck; that loyalty, truthfulness, and compassion will often be rewarded; that love may conquer all obstacles; and that appealing to or being grateful to a higher power may result in magical or divine intervention.

Legends are somewhat different from fairytales, though there is definitely some overlap. A legend tends to be tied to a particular place and professes to be loosely related to historical facts (as with many of the castle tales, for example), whereas a fairytale is timeless and independent of any locale.

Myths link legends and fairytales, and add poetic elements. Myths tell of ancient beliefs and origins: Hulda and Frija, Wodan and his wild hunt, kings sleeping inside mountains while awaiting the return of glorious times. We can even find traces of the thoughts and perspectives of our prehistoric ancestors, as in the following passage from a ballad by Johann Wolfgang von Goethe, „Nun saust es und braust es, das wütige Heer, ins weite Getal und Gebirge" ("And now it dashes and roars, the mad army, into the vast valley and mountains").[42] Eerie and supernatural, it is reminiscent of the ghostly army of the Norse god Wotan.

In this collection of folktales, the reader will find examples of all three of those categories of tales of wonder. Schönwerth did not make precise distinctions between fairytales, legends, and myths. His primary interest lay in collecting folktales told by the common people of the Upper Palatinate. For Schönwerth, it was much more important that the informant who told the story was a native of the region, than to categorize the tale told to him.

Volume I of *Sitten und Sagen* tells about everyday life—birth, courtship, marriage, and death—followed by tales about the forces of natural Elements in Volume II. Volume III deals with the mythology of Death, Heaven and Hell, and the end of the world.

The sheer number of tales in *Sitten und Sagen* (a total of approximately 900 pages) forced me to be very selective. I have tried to structure the selection much as Schönwerth did, grouping the stories by themes, and have aimed the focus on the

---

[42] Johann Wolfgang Goethe, „Der getreue Eckart," *Die Fackel, Lesebuch für höhere Schulen*, Berlin: Vandenhöeck & Ruprecht, 1962: 86.

traditions of the Upper Palatinate people. Each thematic group is preceded by a brief introduction which attempts to provide some context for the tales that follow.

These tales come from an oral tradition. Accordingly, and following humbly in Schönwerth's footsteps, I have tried to preserve the "voices" of the people of Schönwerth's day, while carefully adapting his language to more modern usage and grammar, and avoiding both twenty-first-century idioms and slang, and anachronistic vocabulary. For example, I chose the more modern term "Frau" instead of "Weib," which is what Schönwerth commonly used. Also, I added footnotes to explain the German idioms and the origins of traditions.[43]

As well as preserving their "voices," I have tried to convey an important aspect of the cultural context of the tales. In print, it is customary to capitalize religious (and mythical) beings and places such as God and the Devil, and Heaven and Hell, either out of religious or cultural reverence, or as a show of respect for deeply held beliefs of others. But in the harsh lives of the folk of the Upper Palatinate, Witches and Mermaids, Giants and Dwarves, Ghosts and Poor Souls, et al., all seemed to them every bit as real as God and the Devil, and every bit as fearsome or at the very least, worthy of respect. So I have capitalized those entities, together with many other supernatural or mythical beings. In many instances, choosing whether or not to capitalize was problematic. For example, in some tales, Lucifer himself ("the Devil") is the protagonist; in others "minor" devils play their parts. I have attempted to capitalize appropriately. Since the "minor" devils are not capitalized, neither are the "minor"

---

[43] "Similar to 'Fräulein,' the word 'Weib' became derogatory and nowadays is used only* in the [polite] adjective 'weiblich' (English, feminine)... In any case, we know for certain that the word was used synonymously with 'Frau,' regardless of age and social or marital status. Negative connotations ... began around 1500..." („Ähnlich wie ‚Fräulein' hat auch das ‚Weib' ... im Laufe der Zeit eine Abwertung erfahren, es wird nur noch in dem Adjektiv ‚weiblich' ... gebraucht. ... Sicher ist jedenfalls, dass das Wort gleichwertig zu ‚Frau' ohne Rücksicht auf Alter, Stand und Heirat verwendet wurde. Eine negative Belegung ... findet sich etwa seit 1500..."). „Was steckt hinter ‚Frau', ‚Dame', ‚Weib' und ‚Fräulein'?" <http://www.wissen.de/was-steckt-hinter-frau-dame-weib-und-fraeulein>. Abgerufen 6 Aug 2013. [*In fact, "Weib" is today not considered derogatory in other words also, such as "Altweibersommer" and "Weiberfasching."]

angels. Of the Elements, Wind and Water in particular presented the problem that in some instances (as wind and water) they are a part of the everyday natural landscape, in other instances (as Wind and Water) they are told of as supernatural entities. I hope that readers will forgive me the instances where they would have made choices different from mine.

I made every effort to preserve the narrative structure, and streamlined the text in only a few places for ease of comprehension. Quite often, the reader will notice a change of style and tone of the source texts, due to changing narrators. Schönwerth avoided adapting the different styles in order to create a more uniform format for his collection, and I made an effort to preserve this diversity in my translations. Also, I tried not to interfere with Schönwerth's alternation between the present and past tenses in the middle of a tale, because I believe he was trying to reproduce the tale exactly as one would have heard it told in his day: perhaps over a glass of beer or wine in the parlor of his Munich residence, or beside a crackling fire on a dark and windy night, somewhere in the eerie Bavarian Forest . . .

The nineteenth century saw a growing interest in the tales and mores of the native people of Germany and many renowned ethnographers, folklorists, and writers, among them Ludwig Bechstein, Wilhelm Hauff, Benedikte Naubert, and Johann Wilhelm Wolf. But Franz Xaver von Schönwerth stands with the Grimm Brothers as one of the greatest. Without doubt, he was the most prolific collector of tales in the Upper Palatinate, his native region. However, while the Grimm Brothers are widely known as collectors and popularizers of fairytales, Schönwerth's broader contributions to this field have been largely forgotten. Fortunately, with the rediscovery of the Schönwerth manuscripts and the article in *The Guardian*, which alerted the world to this find, interest in Schönwerth's work has been revived. As a fellow Upper Palatinian, I hope that this book will further encourage the reading of these tales, both by English speakers in general and by students of German in particular.

*M. Charlotte Wolf, Ph.D.*
*December 31, 2013*

# Original Bavarian Folktales
## A Schönwerth Selection

A DUAL-LANGUAGE BOOK

# Original bayerische Volksmärchen

## Ausgewählte Schönwerth-Geschichten

# LOVE, MARRIAGE, AND CHILDBIRTH

The stories in this section tell of love, courtship, becoming a bride, marriage, pregnancy, and birth. The people of the Upper Palatinate saw themselves as being constantly surrounded by Evil. Even before birth a human being was already threatened by it. Schönwerth explains:

> When a human being enters this world as a child, he or she immediately enters into a fight with the sinister forces which seek to destroy the mother who gave life and the child who enters into it.[1]

And even later, in the most intimate and affectionate moments of adult life, humans are still threatened by the powers of the dark. In his Introduction to *Sitten und Sagen*, Schönwerth says about love, for example:

> If the time of engagement is, for all intents and purposes, the zenith of life and the path up to this point is an ascending one, there are nevertheless dark forces which drop their poisonous blight into this sunshine of joy: love is haunted by love sorcery.[2]

The stories in the following section illustrate this, often in a dramatic way.

---

[1] „Kommt der Mensch als Kind zur Welt, so tritt er augenblicklich in Kampf mit finsteren Mächten, welche die Mutter, so das Leben gab, und das Kind, so ins Leben hineintrat, vernichten wollen." *Sitten und Sagen*, vol. 1: 39.

[2] „Wenn der Brautstand die eigentliche Hochzeit des Lebens, bis dahin die Bahn eine aufsteigende ist, so sind es dunkle Gewalten, welche in diesen Sonnenschein des Glückes ihren giftigen Mehltau fallen lassen: der Liebe schließt sich der Liebeszauber an." *Sitten und Sagen*, vol. 1: 39.

## 1 Die jungfräuliche Braut

Es war ein Mädchen, welches Abscheu hatte vor der Ehe, der Kinder wegen, die sie nicht liebte, und schritt erst dann zur Ehe, als ihre Zeit um war; denn sie wurde wegen ihres Geldes gesucht.

Der Priester aber, dem sie vor der Trauung beichtete, behielt ihr die Sünde, weil durch ihr Verschulden sieben Wesen nicht zur Welt gekommen wären, und gebot ihr eine Fahrt nach Rom zum Papst.

So ging sie in Begleitung ihres Bräutigams zum Papst nach Rom, aber dieser strafte sie und sandte sie heim mit dem Befehl, stets allein auf dem Wege zu schlafen, und den Ungeheuern, welche ihr begegnen würden, nicht auszuweichen, noch über sie zu steigen.

Es legten sich aber drei fürchterliche Ungeheuer an drei Stationen in den Weg, das erste ein Bär, das letzte eine Schlange, und sie kniete sich vor sie hin, und umfing und küsste sie, und die Ungeheuer hoben sich aus dem Wege.

In der letzten Nachtherberge kam sie am Morgen nicht herunter; man sandte ein Kind hinauf, nach ihr zu schauen. Als dieses die Türe öffnete, sah es eine weiße Taube aus dem Bette auf zum Fenster hinaus fliegen. Man suchte in dem Bette nach, es waren nur mehr Gebeine drin. Das letzte Ungeheuer war in der Nacht gekommen, und hatte zur Strafe den Leib verzehrt; die Seele aber war gerettet.

## 2 Bis dass der Tod . . .

Ein Mädchen hatte sich mit ihrem Geliebten zu ewiger Treue verschworen; er fiel im Kriege, und sie begann ein neues Verhältnis. Da kam der Geliebte nachts auf einem weißen Schimmel zu ihr und entführte sie auf sein Grab, wo sie am Morgen entseelt gefunden wurde.

## 1 The Spinster Bride

There was a girl who despised marriage because of children, whom she did not love, and she first thought about marrying when her time [to conceive children] was up; for she was highly sought after for her money.

However, the priest who heard her confession before the wedding did not absolve her of this sin because it was of her doing that seven beings had not been born, and he ordered her to go on a pilgrimage to the Pope in Rome.

Thus, accompanied by her bridegroom, she set out for Rome to visit the Pope, but the latter, upon giving her a penance, sent her home, ordering her to spend the nights on the way alone, and neither dodge nor pass any monsters whom she were to encounter.

At three stations during her journey, however, three dreadful monsters got in her way; the first a bear and the last a Serpent; and kneeling down before them, she embraced and kissed them, and the monsters cleared out of her path.

At the last night's accommodation, she did not come down in the morning; a child was sent up to look for her. Upon opening the door, it saw a white dove flying up from the bed and leaving through the window. They looked in the bed; all that was left were bones. The last monster had appeared during the night and had eaten the body as a punishment, but the soul had been saved.

## 2 Till Death . . .

A girl had committed herself to being eternally faithful to her beloved; he died serving in the war, and she began a new relationship. One night, her former beloved appeared on a white horse and took her away to his grave where she was found dead in the morning.

### 3 Liebeszauber[3]

In Eschelkam stand ein Küfnergeselle mit einem Mädchen in trautem Verhältnis; er musste auf die Wanderschaft, bat daher das Mädchen um ein Andenken, und wäre es auch nur ein Haar von ihrem Haupte. Sie hatte aber gehört, man solle kein Haar hergeben, wollte indessen doch die Bitte nicht abschlagen und ging hinaus, um aus dem Milchsiebchen ein Haar zu nehmen, wofür sie ein goldenes Ringlein erhielt.

Es waren etwa drei Tage verstrichen, als sie eine unendliche Sehnsucht nach dem Geliebten ergriff: es war ihr, als sollte sie zum Fenster hinaus. – Auf einmal sah sie das Milchsiebchen zur Tür hereinkommen und zum Fenster hinausfliegen. Nun kam sie zur Ruhe. Der Geliebte aber wartete in einem entfernten Dorfe des Mädchens; statt dessen flog ihm das Siebchen zu. – Später gestand er, wie er zu einer Hexe gegangen sei und das Haar habe besprechen lassen, dass wer es getragen, ihm nachlaufen müsse.

### 4 Der Teufel als Freier I[4]

Es ging ein Mädchen täglich zum Grasen. Da gesellte sich ihr ein Mann bei und gestand ihr seine Liebe, und das Mädchen ließ ihn sich gefallen.

---

[3] „. . . um die Liebe oder Treue des geliebten Gegenstandes zu gewinnen. Es wird dazu unter gewissen Sprüchen ein Stück gebrauchter Kleider oder Haar in einem neuen Geschirr gesotten, so kommt über die spröde Person plötzlich die Liebe mit solcher Gewalt, dass sie dahin laufen muß, wo die Liebe gesotten wird, und zwar um so schneller, je stärker das Wasser im Topfe wallt; und kann sie es nicht erlaufen, muß sie sich zu Tode rennen; kein Hindernis auf dem Wege ist so stark, das nicht überwunden werden wollte." *Sitten und Sagen*, Bd. 1: 131.

[4] „Selbst der Teufel findet manchmal Gefallen an den schönen Töchtern der Menschen, und geht zu ihnen auf die Frei, wenn sie nicht selbst sich ihm anbieten. Insoferne hinter dem Teufel der alte Heiden-Gott versteckt ist, deutet es auf das Niederlassen der Götter zu den Menschen, wie denn durch das ganze Heidentum diese Sage geht. Teilweise ist es wohl nur der verzerrte Ausdruck der Hoffnung auf die Geburt des Sohnes Gottes durch die Frau." *Sitten und Sagen*, Bd. 1: 134.

## 3 Love Charms[5]

In the town of Eschelkam there lived a cooper's apprentice who was in an intimate relationship with a girl; he had to take to the road and so asked the girl for a keepsake, even if it were only [a lock of] hair from her head. She, however, had heard that one should not part with hair, but she did not want to deny his request and went outside to get a hair from the milking sieve, for which she received a little golden ring in return.

Three days had passed, when an immense longing for the beloved seized her; she felt as if she should leave right out the window.—All of a sudden, she saw the milking sieve enter through the door and fly out the window. After that, she calmed down. The beloved, however, was waiting for the girl in a village far away; instead, the sieve came rushing to him.—Later he admitted that he had visited a Witch who had put such a spell on the hair that wherever he took it, its owner was compelled to run to him.

## 4 The Devil as a Suitor I[6]

A girl went to cut grass every day. One day, a man joined her and confessed his love to her, and the girl gladly accepted it.

---

[5] ". . . in order to win the love or loyalty of the loved subject. For this purpose, one boils a piece of used clothing or hair in a new piece of cookware while uttering certain spells, and thus love befalls the resisting person,* suddenly and with such force that she* has to run to where the love is boiling, the faster [she* runs] the stronger the water boils in the pot, and if she* cannot get there, she has to run herself* to death; no obstacle along the way is so strong that she* wouldn't be able to overcome it." *Sitten und Sagen*, vol. 1: 131. (*German „die Person" may refer to either gender.)

[6] "Even the Devil sometimes takes a liking to the beautiful daughters of the human race, and he goes on a courtship, even if they don't offer themselves up to him. Insofar as the ancient pagan deity is behind the Devil, this hints at the union between gods and humans, which is a theme throughout all pagan beliefs. It may also be a distorted expression of the hope for the birth of the son of God through a [human] woman." *Sitten und Sagen*, vol. 1: 134.

Einmal graste sie wieder und hatte unversehens vom Kraut Wohlgemut und Widridad[7] mit aufgenommen. Wie sie nun beide auf dem Wege nach Hause waren, sah das Mädchen an ihrem Geliebten auf einmal Hörner und Geißfuß. – Sie erschrak zu Tode; denn sie hatte den Bösen erkannt; der aber wich mit den Worten: »Wohlgemut und Widridad, hat mich um mein fein Lieb gebracht.«

## 5 Der Teufel als Freier II

Ein Mädchen hatte unbewusst den bösen Feind zum Geliebten; einmal verriet ihn der Geißfuß, als der Mond gar so hell in das Kämmerchen leuchtete. Sie nahm daher das Kraut Wohlgemut und Grodlkraut und legte es unter ihr Kopfkissen, wodurch der Teufel abgehalten wurde, sich ihr zu nähern. Er entwich mit den Worten: »Wohlgemut und Grodlkraut, hat mich um mein fein Lieb gebracht!«

## 6 Der Teufel als Freier III

Ein anderes Mädchen konnte auf dem Tanzboden zu keinem Tänzer gelangen. Voll Zornes ging sie hinaus und rief: »Der erste, so mir begegnet, muss mein Schatz sein, und wärs auch der Teufel!«

Auf dem Wege nach Hause begegnete ihr ein schöner Bauern-bub, der sie fragte, warum sie so früh schon heimgehe. Sie sagte es ihm und er bot sich ihr sogleich zum Geliebten an, führte sie in den Saal zurück, tanzte mit ihr und besuchte sie seitdem öfter. So oft er aber kam, brachte er ihr drei Laibchen Brot mit, doch fehlte an jedem ein Scherzchen. Sie meinte, er vergönne ihr nicht alles, und fragte ihn daher, warum er ihr die Laibchen nicht ganz gebe. Er aber schwieg; denn er tat es nur, damit er für seine Gabe den Nutzen aus dem Hause zöge.

---

[7] Dem Volksmund nach sollen diese Kräuter Zaubersprüche oder sogar Magie abwenden. (Vgl. dazu auch Hans Meyer and Thomas Oppermann, *Handwörterbuch des Deutschen Aberglaubens*, Berlin: Walter de Gruyter & Co, 1941: 552f.)

One time she was out cutting grass again and, inadvertently, picked up some herbs, In Good Spirits and Stonecrop,[8] with the grass. As they both went home together, the girl noticed that her beloved sported horns and a goat's foot.—She was scared to death because she recognized the Evil One, who disappeared with the parting words: "In Good Spirits and Stonecrop made me lose my dearly beloved."

## 5 The Devil as a Suitor II

Unknowingly, a girl had taken the Evil Enemy as her beloved; one day his goat's foot gave him away when the moon shone brightly into the little room. Therefore, she took the herbs In Good Spirits and Wild Thyme and put them under her pillow, which prevented the Devil from approaching her. He fled away, saying, "In Good Spirits and Wild Thyme made me lose my dearly beloved!"

## 6 The Devil as a Suitor III

Another girl was unable to find a steady dancer on the dance floor. Full of anger, she went outside and cried out, "The first one I encounter will have to be my sweetheart, even if it were the Devil himself!"

On her way home, she encountered a handsome farmer's son who asked her why she was going home so early. She told him and, instantly offering to be her beloved, he led her back to the hall, danced with her, and after that visited her now and then. Every time he visited, he brought three little loaves of bread, each missing the heel. She complained that he didn't present her with all of it and asked why he did not give her the whole of each little loaf. But he stayed silent because he was doing it only to further his own purposes.

---

[8] Presumably, those were herbs used to ward off evil spells or magic. (See also Hans Meyer and Thomas Oppermann, *Handwörterbuch des Deutschen Aberglaubens*, Berlin: Walter de Gruyter & Co, 1941: 552f.)

Einmal bat er sie, ihn in ihre Schlafkammer zu lassen; sie willigte ein: doch wollte er anfangs nicht vor ihr die Treppe hinauf gehen; da sah sie den Geißfuß. Voll Schrecken rief sie: »Herr Jesus, das ist der Teufel!« »Ja wohl,« erwiderte dieser, »du hast mich verlangt.«

Damit war der Zauber gelöst; das Mädchen aber verlangte nicht mehr nach irdischer Liebe, sondern bereute in einem Kloster ihre Freveltat.

## 7 Liebesorakel[9]

Bei seinem Erscheinen legte der Geliebte einen Dolch auf den Tisch. Das Mädchen voll Angst barg ihn in ihrem Kasten. Wirklich wurde sie Braut des Erschienenen, und lebte ganz glücklich in dieser Ehe. Nach mehreren Jahren bedurfte man einer Kiste; man stürzte nun jenen Kasten, und es fiel der verborgene Dolch heraus. Der Gatte erkannte ihn sogleich für den seinigen, fragte seine Frau, wie sie dazu gekommen, und als sie es ihm gestanden, wurde er rasend über der Erinnerung an das, was er bei seinem Vorrufe alles erduldet, und erstach mit demselben Dolche erst seine Frau, dann sich.

Der Geliebte, welcher in dieser Weise gerufen wird, soll nämlich fürchterlich viel zu leiden haben. – Zu Tiefenbach erschien aber der Böse in Gestalt eines Jägers mit dem Geißfuß.

---

[9] „Am weitest verbreiteten ist aber das Bettbrett-Treten; jedes Mädchen in jedem Dorfe kennt es, oder hat doch davon gehört. Das Mädchen steht am Andreas- oder Thomas-Abende um elf Uhr nachts auf, zieht sich aus, kämmt die Haare rückwärts und kehrt das Zimmer hinter sich, das Gesicht gegen das Fenster, mit einem ganz neuen Besen, den sie zum Kehricht in den Winkel stellt. Dann zieht sie ein Kopfbrett unter dem Bett hervor, lehnt es gegen die Bettlade etwas schräge, stellt einen Fuß darauf und sagt folgenden Spruch:

Bettbred, I tritt di,
Laß mir erschein
Den Herzliebsten mein!

Um Mitternacht geht dann das Bild des Zukünftigen durch das Zimmer. Amberg. Einige behaupten, es sei der Geliebte leibhaftig. Andere dagegen meinen, es sei der Teufel in jenes Gestalt. Für die erste Meinung gebe ich eine Sage als Beleg." *Sitten und Sagen*, Bd. 1: 141f.

One day, he asked her to let him into her bed chamber and she agreed, but at first he did not want to walk upstairs in front of her, and then she saw his goat's foot. Full of terror, she cried out, "Lord Jesus, it is the Devil!" "Quite so," he replied. "You asked for me."

Upon that, the spell was broken, but the girl no longer desired earthly love, and repented her sacrilegious act in a nunnery.

## 7 Love Sorcery[10]

At his first appearance, the lover laid down a dagger on the table. The girl, terrified, hid it in her coffer. She actually became the bride of the one that appeared and lived quite happily in this marriage. After several years, a coffer box was needed; hers was overturned and the hidden dagger fell out. The husband immediately recognized it as his own and asked his wife how she had acquired it and, after she revealed it to him, furious at the memory of what he had had to endure when called forth to appear, stabbed to death first his wife and then himself with that same dagger.

It is said that the beloved who is called forth to appear in such a manner, suffers terribly.—In the town of Tiefenbach, the Evil One appeared in the guise of a huntsman with a goat's foot.

---

[10] "The custom of 'bedboard stepping,' however, is quite common; every girl in every village knows it, or has at least heard of it. Around eleven on the eve of St. Andrew's or St. Thomas's, the girl gets up, undresses, combs her hair backwards and, facing the window, sweeps the room behind her with a new broom, which she then puts into the corner along with the dust. Then she pulls out the headboard from under the bed, puts it up against the bedframe in an angle, puts her foot on it and says the following words:

Headboard, I step on you,
Make appear
The dearest love of my heart!

At midnight, the image of the future lover will appear in the room. Some believe that it is the lover personified. Yet others believe that it is the Devil in the lover's guise. For the first opinion, I give as proof the following legend." *Sitten und Sagen*, vol. 1: 141f.

## 8 Der Fluch der Schwangeren

Im Bruckerwalde ist ein Weiher, der verlorene oder verwunschene Weiher genannt, stets voll Fische; ehe man ihn abläßt, sieht man sie noch, ist aber das Wasser abgelaufen, wird keiner mehr gesehen.

Eine arme Frau mit einem Kinde unter dem Herzen bat einmal beim Ablassen um einen Fisch, vergebens; sie fluchte, es möge niemand mehr einen Fisch aus diesem Weiher essen: seitdem ist der Weiher verflucht.

Nunmehr sticht man dort Torf, da er in Wiese umgewandelt nichts ertrug.

## 9 Magische Kräfte der Frauen im Kindsbett I[11]

Eine Kindsmutter ging mit ihrem Kinde innerhalb der sechs Wochen auf das Feld. Da kam ein Gewitter, es blitzte und donnerte fürchterlich. Schnell riss die Mutter dem Kinde das Kleid, welches eine Kindbetterin gemacht hatte, vom Leibe und warf es weg. Augenblicklich wurde dieses vom Blitz getroffen.

## 10 Magische Kräfte der Frauen im Kindsbett II

Zu einer anderen, die vor der Zeit hinaus in den Hof gegangen war, kam ein Mann im grünen Rock, einen großen Scheibenhut auf dem Kopfe, und mit einem Geißfuß: »Wie weit geht denn dein Vorhang?« fragte er. – »So weit als mein Hofraum,« war die schnelle Antwort. »Das hat dir ein guter Geist eingegeben, denn sonst hätte ich dich zerrissen,« fuhr er die Frau an und verschwand.

---

[11] „Kleider, welche eine Frau im Kindbett gemacht, ziehen den Donnerkeil an. Man hütet sich daher, solche Kleider zu tragen." *Sitten und Sagen*, Bd. 1: 159.

## 8 The Pregnant Woman's Curse

In the forest of Bruckerwalde is a pond called the Lost or En-chanted Pond, which is always full of fish. One can still see them before it is drained, but as soon as the water has run off, none can be found anymore.

Once a poor woman who carried a child under her heart asked in vain for a fish when the water was drained; she cursed it by saying: may nobody ever again eat another fish from this pond; since then the pond has been cursed.

Now they cut peat there, as it does not yield anything else since it became a meadow.

## 9 Magical Powers of Women in Childbed I[12]

A young mother went out to the field with her child within six weeks [after birth]. Suddenly, a thunderstorm arose, with terrible thunder and lightning. Quickly, the mother tore off the child's clothing, which had been made by a woman in childbed, and threw it away. Instantly, the clothes were struck by lightning.

## 10 Magical Powers of Women in Childbed II

To another woman who had left the house before her time,[13] there came a man in a green coat, with a large round hat on his head and a goat's foot, who approached her and asked, "How far are you allowed to go?"—"As far as my courtyard reaches," was her quick response. "That was what a good spirit prompted you to say, otherwise I would have torn you to pieces," he snarled at the woman, and disappeared.

---

[12] "Clothes sewn by a woman in childbed will attract lightning bolts. People therefore will beware of wearing such clothes." *Sitten und Sagen,* vol. 1: 159.

[13] According to popular belief in some areas in the Upper Palatinate, a woman with a child under the age of six weeks is vulnerable to the powers of the Devil, especially as soon as she crosses the threshold to leave the house.

## 11 Der Tod einer Frau im Kindsbett

In Geigant bei Waldmünchen hat sich einmal eine gekämmt in den ersten drei Tagen ihres Kindbettes, an einem Feiertag, während alles in der Kirche war. Da trat ein Mann, einen Totenkopf auf, mit einem Kamm in der Hand, an das Fenster heran und sagte: »Weil du nicht glaubst, musst du es mit der Haut büßen.« Mit diesen Worten verschwand er. Die Frau aber bekam solches Kopfleiden, dass sie in etlichen Tagen starb.

## 11 Death of a Woman in Childbed

Once a woman in the town of Geigant near Waldmünchen combed her hair within the first three days of giving birth, on a holiday, while everybody else was in church. A man with a skull for a head approached the window, with a comb in his hand, and said, "Because you don't believe, you will have to pay with your hide." Having spoken this, he disappeared. But the woman developed such a headache that she died within a few days.

# MOTHERHOOD, DRUDES,
## AND CHANGELINGS

The Drude (or Drud) and the Changeling are supernatural beings that menace both animals and humans, as well as children. While the Drude literally takes away a living being's breath, the Changeling aspires to take a human child's place. Schönwerth summarized the fears they inspired: "The Drude as well as the Changeling are the threatening aspects [of Evil]."[1]

The word "Drude" is Middle High German or Gothic in origin, and used to mean either "to step on" or "to squeeze tightly." In these tales, a Drude is a possessed woman who is able to split off into a ghostly double, so to speak, indistinguishable from the real person. So is the Drude made of flesh and blood, or is she a ghostly double? She is both. She is one of those creatures of the dark that participate in the Wild Hunt. At night, she sneaks into the room of a sleeper (a man, child, or animal) through a crack around a door or window or through the keyhole. Then she sits on the chest of the sleeper and "besets" them. And of course, a woman thus enslaved by the Drude's curse hides that dark secret from those around her.[2]

In traditional European folklore, a Changeling is believed to be a possessed infant, foisted on a woman (often in childbed or suckling her baby) by a Witch, or the Devil, or some other

---

[1] „Drud und Wechselbutt sind die drohenden Gestalten." *Sitten und Sagen*. vol 1: 39.
[2] Leander Petzoldt, *Kleines Lexikon der Dämonen und Elementargeister*, 3rd ed., Munich: Beck, 2003: 53–54.

14

supernatural creature, usually in exchange for her own child. That danger can be averted only by baptism or other holy ritual.

How does one recognize a Changeling? It is said to cry a lot and devour huge amounts of food. Frequently, it is described as being misshapen.[3]

Motherhood is sacred, but also extremely vulnerable to Evil. The only protection against the menace of Evil was to surrender completely to the protection of the Church and to abide by its rules with exactitude. For the Devil never sleeps . . .

---

[3] D.L. Ashliman, "Changelings," 1997, <http://www.pitt.edu/~dash/changeling.html>. Accessed 18 Nov. 2012.

## 12 Geschichte vom Wechselbalg I[4]

In einer Rockenfahrt[5] waren lustige Dirnen beisammen. Da hieß es auf einmal: »Wer traut sich jetzt noch in tiefer Nacht zum Kalkofen bei Klessing?« Denn dort sollte es spuken. Eine rüstige Dirne erbot sich dazu und versprach, als Wahrzeichen einen Ziegelstein davon mitzubringen.

Glücklich dort angekommen, nahm sie einen Ziegelstein und tat ihn in ihre Schürze. Doch auf dem Heimwege wurde es lebendig im Fürtuch, und es schrie ein Kindlein daraus hervor. Das Mädchen erschrak zwar darüber, doch hatte sie Erbarmen mit dem kleinen Wesen und wollte sogleich damit in den Pfarrhof zur Taufe gehen.

Aber als sie durchs Holz kam, schrillerte es von einer Tanne herab: »Seppo, lass dich nicht wippeln, nicht wappeln.« – Darauf entgegnete das Kind ganz hastig in dem Polster, in den es die Dirne gelegt hatte: »O beileibe nicht!« – und war verschwunden.

## 13 Geschichte vom Wechselbalg II[6]

In Seebarn bei Neukirchen Balbini lag eine Bäuerin am dritten Tage im Kindbette. Man hatte ihr kein Mehl vom Boden heruntergebracht; sie ging also selbst hinauf, es zu holen, und ließ das Kind im Bette zurück. Wie sie herabstieg, hörte sie in der Küche ein Kind schreien; sie sah also durch ein Binkenloch der Tür in die Küche und bemerkte darin auf dem Boden ein Kind liegen, in dasselbe Kissen eingemacht, wie ihr eigenes. Da dachte sie:

---

[4] „Über die Natur des Wechselbalges herrscht bei Roding eine eigentümliche Ansicht. Hiernach ist der Wechselbalg ein Kind, das sich aus einem leblosen Körper entwickelt, und dann verschwindet, wenn man es am sichersten zu haben vermeint." *Sitten und Sagen*, Bd. 1: 192.

[5] „Rockenfahrt." In der Oberpfalz versammelten sich abends die jungen Frauen eines Dorfes zum Spinnen (Vgl. dazu auch Jacob and Wilhelm Grimm, *Deutsches Wörterbuch*, Band 14, Leipzig: S. Hirzel, 1854–1961). Oft kamen auch junge Männer hinzu und diese Treffen arteten in Zusammenkünfte von moralisch fragwürdiger Art aus, zumindest in den Augen der örtlichen Behörden. Zuzeiten schritten die Behörden ein, um Zusammenkünfte solcher Art für ungesetzlich zu erklären (Vgl. dazu auch „Rockenfahrt <http://www.rzuser .uni heidelberg.de/~cd2/drw/e/ro/cken/fahr/rockenfahrt.htm>. Abgerufen 12 Jul 2012.)

[6] „In der Gegenwart kommt solches freilich nicht mehr vor, nachdem der Pabst in Rom derlei Spukgeister gebannt hat." *Sitten und Sagen*, Bd. 1: 196.

## 12 Changeling Story I[7]

A number of merry young women had gathered for a distaff meeting.[8] All of a sudden, someone asked, "Who dares to go to the lime kiln by Klessing?" For it was supposed to be spooky there. A spry young woman volunteered for the job and promised to bring back a brick as proof.

After happily arriving there, she picked up a brick and put it in her apron. But as she wended her way home, something came alive in the apron, and a little child cried from inside it. Though the young woman was frightened by this, she took pity on the little creature and decided to go directly to the presbytery to have it baptized.

However, as she passed through the forest, from a tree a voice shrilled: "Seppo, don't let yourself be teetered and rocked."—After that the child, from a pillow that the maiden had placed it upon, replied quickly, "Oh, by no means!"—and vanished.

## 13 Changeling Story II[9]

In the town of Seebarn by Neukirchen Balbini there was a farmer's wife in her third day after childbirth. Nobody had brought her any flour from the attic, so she went up there herself to fetch it, leaving her child behind in bed. When she came down, she heard a child cry in the kitchen; she looked into the kitchen through a knothole in the door and noticed a child lying on the floor; it was wrapped in the same pillow as her own. She thought to herself,

---

[7] "About the nature of the Changeling, people in Roding have a peculiar belief. According to it, a Changeling is a child that developed from a lifeless body and disappears exactly at that time when one believes that its possession is most assured." *Sitten und Sagen*, vol. 1: 192.

[8] Distaff meeting, German "Rockenfahrt." In the Upper Palatinate, young village women used to meet to spin yarn together in the evening (see also Jacob and Wilhelm Grimm, *Deutsches Wörterbuch*, vol. 14, Leipzig: S. Hirzel, 1854–1961). Often, when young men joined them, these meetings developed into social gatherings of a somewhat questionable moral nature, at least in the eyes of the various local authorities. At times, governments stepped in to outlaw gatherings of such a nature. (See also "Rockenfahrt," <http://www.rzuser.uni-heidelberg.de/~cd2/drw/e/ro/cken/fahr/rockenfahrt.htm>. Accessed 12 Jul 2012.)

[9] "In our times, such occurrences do not happen anymore, since the Pope in Rome has banished all phantoms and Ghosts." *Sitten und Sagen*, vol. 1: 196.

»Ach, ich habe schon oft gehört, man soll das nicht anrühren, sondern auf die Bettstatt zugehen« – und wie sie zum Bett hinkam, lag ihr Kind unversehrt dort, wo sie es hingelegt hatte. Als sie es aber auf den Arm nahm, fing das Kind in der Küche fürchterlich zu schreien an, und es entstand ein solches Getöse, dass sie meinte, Küche und Kind müssten zersprengen. – Es war die Wechselbutte, welche zum Rauchfang hinausfuhr, und hätte die Bäuerin sie berührt, so wäre sie ihr statt des eigenen Kindes geblieben, zur Strafe dafür, dass sie in den Sechswochen vor die Tür ging, ohne den Segen der Kirche zu haben.

## 14 Geschichte vom Wechselbalg III

In Geigant lag eine Bäuerin am neunten Tage allein mit dem Kinde zu Bette. Auf einmal hörte sie etwas an der Tür herumwischen, wie wenn jemand die Schnalle nicht finden könnte; doch hielt sie sich still und kehrte sich zu dem Kinde, um sich mit demselben unter der Decke zu verbergen. Wie sie aber ihr Kind nehmen wollte, war das Kissen leer; vergebens suchte sie überall im Bette herum. Voll Angst und Schrecken fing sie zu rufen an, bis Leute kamen. Man suchte im ganzen Hause; endlich fand man es im Schuppen, ganz nackt, aber gesund liegen; es war ein Mädchen. Dieses lebt heutzutage noch, doch ist es so klein wie ein Zwerg, wenngleich sonst wohlgestaltet.

## 15 Geschichte vom Wechselbalg IV

Eine Frau lag in den Sechswochen. Da kam öfter ein ganz kleines Männchen herein zur Tür, und während es so dasteht, wächst es, dass es an der Decke anstößt; es duckt sich und der Rücken legt sich an die Decke an, das Gesicht aber auf das Bett der Mutter; allmählich wurde es kleiner und kleiner, bis es zu seiner ersten Gestalt zusammensank und drohend durch die Tür verschwand. Mit geweihter Ware vertrieb die Frau, die heute noch lebt, den Unhold.

"Uh-oh, I have often heard that one should not touch that, but approach the bed instead."—And as she arrived at the bed, there lay her own child, unharmed, where she had placed it. When she took it up into her arms, the child in the kitchen began to cry horribly, and the uproar that developed was such that she thought kitchen and child might be torn asunder.—It was the changeling, which was escaping through the chimney, and, had the farmer's wife touched it, would have stayed in place of her own child, as a punishment for her leaving the room within the six-week period [after childbirth] without having yet received the blessing of the Church.

## 14 Changeling Story III

In the town of Geigant, a farmer's wife rested in bed alone with her child on the ninth day after giving birth. All of a sudden, she heard someone brushing on the door, as if a person were unable to find the handle; however, she kept quiet and turned toward the child to hide with it under the covers. As she tried to pick up her child, the pillow was empty; in vain, she searched the whole bed for it. Filled with fear and terror, she started to call until people showed up. After they had searched the whole house, finally they found it in the shed, completely naked, yet lying there healthy; it was a girl. It still lives to this day, however, it is as small as a dwarf, but otherwise it is well-shaped.

## 15 Changeling Story IV

A woman was in the six-week period after childbirth. Once in a while a very tiny little man entered through the door and, standing there, grows and grows until it touches the ceiling, then ducks down and, with its back still touching the ceiling, rests its face on the mother's bed; gradually, it shrank smaller again until collapsing to its first size, and disappeared through the door with a menacing look. The woman, who still lives, banished the monster with holy objects.

## 16 Die Teufelstaufe[10]

Eine Schwangere konnte, als sie in Kindesnöten kam, nicht entbinden. Nun war eben ein Student in der Ferienzeit beim Bauer, und wie er von der harten Geburt der Frau hörte, bat er um die Erlaubnis, hineinsehen zu dürfen. Da sah er über der Gebärenden eine Spinne, und trug dem Bauer auf, sie herunter zu nehmen und ihr den rechten Fuß abzuhacken. Der Bauer tat so, und die Bäuerin gebar nun ohne Mühe. Als der Student nach Hause kam, hatte seine Mutter keine Hand. Der Student hielt das Kind über der Taufe; es war das siebente, die ersten sechs waren alle gestorben.

Der Geistliche wollte im Einverständnisse mit der Hebamme auch dieses Kind, wie die ersten sechs, im Namen des Teufels taufen. Das merkte der Student. Er ließ daher einen frommen Priester kommen, und das Kind blieb am Leben.

## 17 Sage von der Drud I[11]

Die Knechte der Hirten oder Hüter heißen Schäfer. Ein solcher Schäfer war einmal in einer Rockenstube; um zehn Uhr nachts gingen sie aus der Kunkl, und der Schäfer begleitete sein Mädchen.

---

[10] „Diese Sage geht durch das ganze Land, und daher muß ihr eine höhere Bedeutung zugeschrieben werden. Ich lege dem Ganzen die alte heidnische Taufe unter, die dem Christen der Gegensatz der Christlichen war. Es ist die Deutung . . . der heidnischen Sitte bei Einführung des Christentums, und daher so alt als diese." *Sitten und Sagen*, Bd. 1: 203f.

[11] „[Druden sind] übermenschliche weibliche Wesen, die auf den Menschen . . . heilsam oder verderblich einwirken können." Siehe auch Leander Petzoldt, *Kleines Lexikon der Dämonen und Elementargeister*, 3. Aufl. München: Beck 2003: 53–54.

„Die Drud tritt also in doppelter Tätigkeit auf, rächend und sühnend. Nicht minder erklärt sich auch, warum die Drud der Kindbetterin und ihrem Kinde so sehr nachstellt. Sie hatte als Priesterin wohl früher die Aufgabe, Mutter und Kind durch eine heilige Handlung zu reinigen. In ihrer Pflicht gegen die Götter sucht sie die Heiden dem alten Glauben zu erhalten, die Christen wieder herüberzuziehen. Wo sie Widerstand findet, zürnt, droht sie. Daher die Gefahr für Mutter und Kind, bis die Kirche durch ihre Weihe die Drohung unwirksam macht. War früher das Kommen der Drud ersehnt, so ist es nun gefürchtet. Dass unter der Drud aber auch ein höheres Wesen, ein Walkyre, zuletzt die Freyja zu verstehen sei, habe ich oben angedeutet . . . Walkyre und Katze gehören auch zur Freyja." *Sitten und Sagen*, Bd. 1: 231f.

## 16 The Satanic Baptism[12]

A pregnant woman, having a difficult labor, was unable to deliver [the baby]. It just so happened that a student on vacation at the farm, hearing of the tough time the woman was having giving birth, asked permission to look in on her. He saw a spider sitting just above her, and he asked the farmer to take it down and chop off its right foot. The farmer did as bidden, and now the farmer's wife was able to deliver her baby without any trouble. When the student came home, his mother was missing a hand. The student held the child at the baptism; it was the seventh; the previous six had all died.

The priest, in agreement with the midwife, wanted to baptize this child also in the name of the Devil, just like the other six. This the student noticed. He therefore sent out for a pious priest, and the child stayed alive.

## 17 Legend of the Drude I[13]

The herdsmen's servants are called shepherds. One such shepherd once was at a distaff gathering; at ten that night they all left the spinning-room, and the shepherd walked off with his girl.

---

[12] "This legend is known throughout the country, and it must thus be assigned a higher significance. I interpret the whole as the ancient pagan baptism, which is for Christians diametrically opposed to the Christian one. Its interpretation refers to the pagan customs in existence at the time of the introduction of the Christian rites, and as such is as old as they." *Sitten und Sagen*, vol. 1: 203.

[13] "[Drudes are] supernatural female creatures which may . . . have healing or ruinous effects on humans." (See also Leander Petzoldt, *Kleines Lexikon der Dämonen und Elementargeister*, 3rd ed. Munich: Beck, 2003: 53–54.)

"Thus the Drude assumes a dual function, avenging and expiatory. Of equal importance is the explanation for the fact that the Drude preys on women in childbed and their children. As a priestess in bygone times it must have been her task to cleanse mother and child through a sacred ceremony. Fulfilling her duty toward the gods, she tries to keep the pagans true to the old faith and return the Christians to it. Where she encounters resistance, she makes threats. Thus there is danger for the mother and child until the Church has rendered ineffectual the threats. While in olden times the arrival of the Drude was welcomed, it is now dreaded. I have already hinted above that the Drude can also be seen as a higher being, a Valkyrie, even Freya . . . The Valkyrie and the cat are also connected to Freya." *Sitten und Sagen*, vol. 1: 231f.

Beim Hinterhaus angekommen, stellte sie den Rocken umgekehrt an die Haustüre und ging hinein, indem sie den Schäfer bat, ja nicht an den Rocken zu rühren. Dieser aber, als er sah, dass der Rocken verkehrt dastand, stellte ihn gerade hin. Da kam das Mädchen heraus und sprach:

> Hättest du mir den Rocken nicht verrückt,
> Hätt ich das Kind in der Wiege nicht erdrückt.

Sie war nämlich hineingegangen, um ein Kind in der Wiege zu drücken; es war nach dem Drücken tot.

### 18 Sage von der Drud II

Ein anderes Rockenmädchen lehnte auf dem Heimwege an die Wand eines nahen Hauses ihren Rocken und ließ ihren Leib dabei stehen: die Seele aber ging hinein, um zu drucken.

Währenddessen zog ein Wanderer vorbei; der redete sie an, und da er keine Antwort erhielt, trat er auf sie zu und rührte sie an; sogleich fiel der Leib zusammen und war tot.

### 19 Sage von der Drud III

Ein Bauer fand sehr oft beim Aufwecken seiner Leute die Magd nicht im Bette; er hielt sie für leichtsinnig und dem Mannsvolk ergeben, und machte ihr Vorwürfe über ihre Aufführung. Sie aber entschuldigte sich damit, dass sie aufs Drücken aus sei; zum Beweise wolle sie als Fass in die Stube hereinrollen, unter der Bedingung, dass man sie nicht anrühre, noch anrede.

Sie tat es, aber einer der Knechte konnte sich nicht enthalten und rührte das Fass an; da war das Fass verschwunden und die Dirne lag tot auf dem Boden.

### 20 Sage von der Drud IV

Der Seidlbauer in Kirchenrohrbach hatte eine brave Dirne, aber alle Mitternacht stand sie auf und drückte den Drudenstein im Haselberg.

On arriving at the rear building, she placed the distaff upside down at the door and entered the house, while asking the shepherd not to touch the distaff, no matter what. He, however, seeing the distaff was placed there upside down, turned it the right way up. Whereupon the girl emerged from the house and said:

> Had you not my distaff touched,
> The infant I would not have crushed.

For she had entered the house to embrace the child in the cradle; it was dead from her crushing embrace.

## 18 Legend of the Drude II

Another distaff girl, on her way home, leaned her distaff against the wall of a nearby house and let her body also remain there: her spirit, however, went inside to crush.

During that time, a wanderer passed by; he started talking to her and, when he didn't receive a reply, walked closer and touched her; instantly, her body collapsed and she was dead.

## 19 Legend of the Drude III

Often, while giving his staff their wake-up calls, a farmer found his maidservant missing from her bed; he thought her flighty and too free with the menfolk and reproached her for it. But, she gave as an excuse her need for squeezing; as proof she promised to roll into the sitting room in the guise of a barrel, on condition that nobody would talk to or touch her.

That she did, but one of the menservants couldn't stop himself and touched the barrel; the barrel disappeared and the girl lay dead on the ground.

## 20 Legend of the Drude IV

A farmer in the town of Kirchenrohrbach had a good maidservant, except that she got up every night at midnight to crush the Drude's Rock in the Hazel Mountain.

Der Bauer verbot es ihr streng, sie aber erklärte ihm, dass sie nur dann frei werden könne, wenn er ihr erlaube, etwas im Haus zu erdrücken.

Mit des Bauers Wissen erdrückte sie sein Ross, und war nun frei vom Bann.

## 21 Sage von der Drud V

Ein Mann konnte der Drud nicht ledig werden. Als sie ihn immer ärger plagte, erzählte er es einmal im Wirtshause zu Rittsteig, wie er gar keine Ruhe von der Drud habe. Da sagte die Wirtin zu ihm: »Wenn sie wieder kommt, und du meinst, es geht die Türe auf, so rufe schnell: ›Komm morgen früh wieder, ich leih dir was.‹ So wird sie kommen müssen und du bist frei. Und kannst du sie nicht anrufen, wenn sie kommt, so tu es nach dem Drücken!«

Als er nun abends zu Bette lag, hörte er die Tür gehen, und in demselben Augenblick drückte es ihn schon, so dass er nicht mehr sprechen konnte. Wie aber das Drücken nachließ, rief er schnell: »Komm morgen früh, ich leih dir was!«

Am andern Tages lag er noch im Bett, da kam die alte Hausfrau, bei der er in der Miete war, im Unterrock, ein weißes Tuch um den Kopf, mit einer hölzernen Schüssel in der Hand, und bat ihn, ihr Asche zu leihen. Der Mann erkannte sogleich die Gestalt, die ihn seither so arg peinigte, stand auf, gab ihr die verlangte Asche, sagte aber dabei: »Gelt, des nachts kommst du nicht mehr?«

Da schüttete die Frau die Asche aus der Schüssel auf den Boden und ging zornig fort. Doch kam sie nie mehr nachts, und redete niemals mehr ein Wort mit ihm.

## 22 Sage von der Drud VI

Ein Schneider in Traunstein wurde sehr von der Drud geplagt; einmal riet ihm eine alte Frau, wenn sie wieder komme, solle er zu ihr sagen: »Komm morgen früh um drei Späne!« – Kaum war er zu Bette, so kam sie. Da sprach er: »Komm morgen früh um drei Späne!«

The farmer strictly forbade her to do that, but she explained to him that she would only be free if she were allowed to crush something in the house.

With the farmer's permission, she crushed his horse, and then was freed from the curse.

## 21 Legend of the Drude V

A man was unable to get rid of the Drude. When she bothered him more and more, he spoke of it at the inn in Rittsteig, about how he was unable to find reprieve. The innkeeper said to him, "When she comes again and you see the door open, quickly call out, 'Come back tomorrow morning and I will lend you something.' Thus she will have to come back and you will be free. And if you are unable to call to her when she arrives, do it after she is done crushing!"

As he now that evening lay in bed, he heard the door open, and felt the crushing that same moment, so he was unable to talk any more. But when the crushing subsided, he quickly called out: "Come tomorrow morning, I will lend you something!"

The next day, when he was still in bed, his old landlady, with whom he boarded, arrived in her underskirts, with a white scarf wrapped around her head and with a wooden bowl in her hands; she asked him to lend her ashes. In an instant, the man recognized the likeness of the one that had tormented him so much since; he rose and gave her the ashes she had demanded, saying, "You won't be coming anymore at night, will you?"

Thereupon the woman emptied the ashes from the bowl onto the floor and left angrily. But she never returned at night, and she never said a word to him again.

## 22 Legend of the Drude VI

A tailor in Traunstein was much bothered by the Drude; one time an old woman advised him to say, when the Drude returned, "Come tomorrow morning for three pieces of kindling!" No sooner had he gone to bed when she came. He said: "Come tomorrow morning for three pieces of kindling!"

Während er noch im Bette lag am andern Morgen, kam seine Nachbarin, die überhaupt schon allgemein als Drud und Hexe galt, und bat ihn um drei Späne. Da stand er auf und gab ihr deren vier, mit der Frage, was sie denn damit anfange: sie habe ja selbst mehr als er.

Die Frau aber entgegnete: »Heute säe ich Lein; weil mir aber der Flachs schon mehrere Jahre missraten ist, so hat man mir geraten, Späne zu entleiben, diese zu Asche zu brennen und die Asche unter den Leinsamen zu mischen, so werde ich Flachs bekommen.« Von nun an ließ sie den Schneider in Ruhe.

### 23 Sage von der Drud VII

In einem Hause zu Eslarn stand ein Bette; wer darin schlief, über den kam nachts die Drud.

Einer wollte dies nicht glauben und legte sich hinein, lehnte aber ehevor das geladene Gewehr vor sich hin. Zwei Bekannte wachten bei ihm.

Auf einmal fing er zu ächzen an und zu stöhnen und wurde ganz blau im Gesichte; aus Furcht, er möchte ersticken, riefen ihn die anderen bei Namen, worauf er sogleich aufsprang und das Gewehr durchs Fenster abschoss.

Er erzählte nun, er sei plötzlich wach geworden und habe gesehen, wie eine alte Frau mit grauen Haaren durch das Fenster auf ihn zukam und sich ihm auf die Brust setzte, sodass sie ihm den Atem nahm; er wäre sicher erstickt, wenn man ihm nicht gerufen hätte. Da sei die Alte zum Fenster hinausgewischt und er habe ihr nachgeschossen.

Nun stellte man die Füße der Bettlade auf Ziegelsteine, diese aber in ein Gefäß mit Wasser, und von nun an war Ruhe.

Der Ungläubige aber leugnete fortan nicht mehr, dass es Druden gebe.

While he was still in bed next morning, the neighborwoman, generally regarded as a Drude and Witch by everyone, arrived and asked for three pieces of kindling. He rose and gave her four, asking what she was going to do with them, since she already had more than he did.

Whereupon the woman replied, "Today I am going to sow linseeds; but since the flax has turned out badly for several years, someone suggested that I shred kindling, burn it to ashes and mix the ashes with the linseeds, and I will have [good] flax." From then on, she left the tailor in peace.

## 23 Legend of the Drude VII

In a house in Eslarn there was a bed, and whoever slept in it was visited by the Drude during the night.

One man didn't want to believe this and he lay down in the bed, but first he placed his loaded gun in front of him. Two of his acquaintances kept watch.

All of a sudden, he started to moan and groan and his whole face turned blue; worried that he might suffocate, the others called his name, whereupon he immediately jumped up and fired the gun through the window.

He told them that he had woken up and seen that an old woman with gray hair had come toward him through the window and sat down on his chest, robbing him of his breath; he would have certainly suffocated to death if they had not called his name. Then the old woman had disappeared quickly through the window and he had shot after her.

Then they placed the bed on bricks set in a tank filled with water and from then on there was peace.

The disbeliever, however, no longer denied the existence of Drudes from then on.

## 24 Sage von der Drud VIII

Einen Bauer auf der Dürr drückte die Drud. Da ging er zum Hexenbanner, gewöhnlich der Schinder,[14] um Hilfe. Der gab ihm ein Kräutlein und einen Zaum. So fing er die Hexe in Gestalt eines Rosses, legte ihr den Zaum an und führte sie in die Schmiede zum Beschlagen.

Am andern Tage lag die Frau des Nachbarn im Bette, mit Hufeisen an Händen und Füßen.

## 25 Mutterkuss

Eine Bäuerin, welche in der Hoffnung war, trug sich immer mit dem Gedanken, dass sie das Kind, wenn sie es zur Welt gebracht, umbringen müsse. Sie beichtete dieses öfter dem Priester, aber die beängstigende Anfechtung verließ sie nicht.

Da erlaubte ihr der Priester, das Kind zu töten, unter der Bedingung, dass sie es zuvor küsse. Wie sie zur Entbindung kam, küsste sie dem Befehl gemäß das Kind. Die Mutterliebe war aber mit dem ersten Mutterkuss so stark über sie gekommen, dass ihr dieses Kind von nun an das teuerste wurde.

## 26 Muttersünde I

In der Gegend von Tiefenbach war eine Bäuerin, welche von jeher kein kleines Kind leiden konnte. Endlich gebar sie selbst, aber sie hasste das Kind ihres Leibes.

Einmal war sie eben beschäftiget, als das Kind hungerte und nach der Brust der Mutter weinte. Die harte Frau aber achtete es nicht, sondern arbeitete fort. Desto ärger schrie das Kind. Da nahm es die grausame Mutter und legte es voll Zorn mit dem Fluche an die Brust: »Da trink dir alle Teufel hinein!«

---

[14] Schinder oder Abdecker waren jene Personen, die mit der Beseitigung und Verwertung von Tierkadavern beschäftigt waren. (Vgl. dazu Eike Pies, *Zünftige und andere alte Berufe, mit 222 zeitgenössischen Illustrationen und Zunftwappen*, 3. Aufl. Wuppertal: E. und U. Brockhaus, 2005: 10.)

## 24 Legend of the Drude VIII

A farmer from Dürr was crushed by a Drude. He asked for help from the local spell-breaker, commonly the knacker,[15] who gave him a herb and a bridle. Thus he captured the Witch in the form of a horse, bridled her, and led her to the blacksmith to be shod.

The next day, the neighbor's wife was found in bed with horseshoes on hands and feet.

## 25 A Mother's Kiss

A farmer's wife, who was pregnant, was always thinking of killing the child after she had delivered it. This she confessed to the priest on several occasions, but the terrifying temptation did not leave her.

So the priest gave her permission to kill the child on condition that she kissed it first. When she had delivered the child, she kissed the child as ordered. With the first kiss, however, motherly love seized her so strongly that from that time on this child was the dearest thing to her.

## 26 The Sins of a Mother I

Somewhere around the town of Tiefenbach there was once a farmer's wife who had never liked little children. Finally she gave birth herself, but she hated the child of her own womb.

Once she was busy with something when the child became hungry and cried for the mother's breasts. The hard woman, however, did not heed this, but kept working. The child cried harder and harder. Full of anger, the cruel mother put it to her breast uttering the curse, "As you drink, enter, all ye devils!"

---

[15] A knacker was the person who took care of horses and other domestic animal cadavers. (See also "knackers' yard," *Longman Dictionary of Contemporary English* <http://www.ldoceonline.com/dictionary/knackers-yard>. Accessed Jul 16, 2012).

Sogleich fing das Kind, kaum acht Tage alt, zu lachen an und zwickte beim Trinken den Mund so fest zusammen, dass ihm die Brustwarze im Munde blieb. Es hatte auch so viele Kraft bekommen, dass es in den Fatschen[16] nicht mehr zu halten war, sich am ganzen Körperchen erbärmlich zerfleischte und am dritten Tage starb. Allgemein hieß es, dass das Kind besessen gewesen; auch sollen bei seinem Verscheiden mehrere schwarze Vögel, gleich Amseln, von ihm weggeflogen sein.

Ein Jahr darauf wurde die Frau wieder Mutter, sie konnte aber das Kind nicht zur Welt bringen, sondern starb in den Wochen, und als man ihren Leib öffnete, hatte das Kind keine menschliche Gestalt.

## 27 Muttersünde II

Ein böses Frauenbild hatte schon drei uneheliche Kinder, als sie Hochzeit machte; das eine warf sie ins Wasser, das andere grub sie in den Mist, das dritte versteckte sie im Wald unter einem Ziegerhaufen.

Am Hochzeitstag trieb der Hirt aus gegen den Wald hin; da hörte er ein Kind weinen und sprach vor sich hin: »Ich höre dich wohl, aber sehe dich nicht, weiß auch deine Mutter nicht!«

Da erwiderte das Kind: »Meine Mutter hat mich daher gelegt und mit Ziegernadeln zugedeckt! Das erste hat sie ins Wasser getragen, das zweite hat sie in Mist eingraben, mich hat sie hierher gelegt und mit Ziegernadeln zugedeckt. Meine Mutter hat heute Hochzeit, trägt einen grünen Kranz, und hat doch schon drei Kinder eingraben; erbarm dich meiner, nimm mich auf deinen Arm, trag mich in das Wirtshaus hin, und setz mich auf den Tisch, weil die Braut meine Mutter ist.«

So nahm der Hirt das Kind, und trug es in das Wirtshaus in den Hochzeitssaal und setzte es nackt auf den Tisch. Da fing

---

[16] Fatsche, vom Lateinischen *fascia* (Binde, Wickelband), war eine Kindertragemethode, die das Wachstum der Gliedmaßen fördern sollte, indem das gesamte Kleinkind, besonders aber Arme und Beine, so mit Bändern umwickelt wurde, dass es sich kaum bewegen konnte. (Vgl. auch Alfred Fuchs, „Volkskunst,“ *Der Landkreis Freyung-Grafenau*, Hrsg. Paul Praxl, Freyung: Verlag Freyung-Grafenau, 1982: 279–292.)

Immediately, the child began to laugh, even though it was only eight days old, and clamped its mouth together so hard while drinking that the nipple stayed in its mouth. Also, it had become so strong that the swaddling was unable to contain it, and it mutilated itself so brutally that it died three days later. The common opinion was that the child was possessed; also, several black birds resembling ouzels[17] were said to be seen flying off when it passed away.

A year later, the woman became a mother again, yet she could not give birth to the child, but died during pregnancy, and when they opened her womb, they saw that the child did not possess human form.

### 27 The Sins of a Mother II

A wicked woman already had three children out of wedlock before she married; the first she threw into the water, another she buried in dung, and the third she hid in the forest under a pile of twigs and branches.

On her wedding day, a shepherd was herding in the forest when he heard a child cry, and he said, "I hear you very well, but I cannot see you, and I don't know your mother either!"

Thereupon the child replied, "My mother placed me here and covered me with tree needles! The first one she carried into the water, the second she buried in dung, she placed me here and covered me with tree needles. My mother is celebrating her wedding today and she wears a green wreath; and yet already she has buried three children; have mercy on me, take me on your arm and carry me back to the inn and put me on the table, because the bride is my mother."

So the shepherd took the child and carried it to the inn, into the wedding hall, and placed it naked onto the table. Thereupon

---

[17] *Turdus merula,* also known as blackbird.

das Kind wieder zu reden an: »Grüß Gott, Grüß Gott, Ihr Hoch-
zeitgäst, weil die Braut meine Mutter ist. Mein Brüderl hat sie
ins Wasser tragen, mein Schwesterl hats in Mist vergraben. Pfei-
fer, pfeifts auf den Dusch, es ist der Braut ihr Nagerlbusch.«

Da schwur die unnatürliche Mutter: »Wenn ich die Mutter
soll sein, so sollen alle Teufel mich holen ein!« und der Teufel
kam und zerriss sie vor aller Augen.

## 28 Warum die Kinder nicht schon von Geburt an laufen können

Als Eva das erste Kind gebar, war unser Herrgott nicht weit entfernt. Er rief ihr daher zu: »Eva, lass dein Kind zu mir herge-
hen!« Die Mutter aber erwiderte in Besorgnis, das Kind möchte
sich etwas tun: »Ach, Herr, es ist ja noch ganz schwach.«

»Nun, so lass es,« entgegnete ihr der Herr; »doch soll von nun
an weder dieses, noch ein anderes Kind, so lange die Welt steht,
vor einem Jahre gehen können.«

the child started talking again, "May God be with you, may God be with you, dear wedding guests, because the bride is my mother. She carried my little brother into the water, and she buried my little sister in the dung. Piper, pipe your fanfare; it is the bride with her bush of little nails."

Upon which the unnatural mother swore an oath: "If I should be that mother, may all devils carry me off!" And the Devil appeared and tore her apart in front of everyone's eyes.

### 28 Why Children Cannot Walk from Birth

When Eve gave birth to her first child, our Lord was not far away. He called to her, "Eve, let your child walk to me!" The mother, however, replied in her anxiety that the child might harm itself: "Oh Lord, it is still so very weak."

"Well, let it be then," the Lord replied, "but henceforth neither this one nor any other child, so long as the world remains, shall be able to walk before a year has passed."

# PREMONITIONS, GHOSTS, AND
# POOR SOULS

The people of the Upper Palatinate were forever at the mercy of weather, political upheavals and wars, famines and epidemics, as well as lacking news media, reliable weather forecasts, and doctors. Therefore, out-of-the-ordinary animal behaviors and celestial signs often seemed to foretell impending doom or even death. So they tried anxiously to recognize these signs in time, and then enlist divine assistance in hope of preventing the worst. Reality, however, showed that the worst could not always be prevented. A child of the Upper Palatinate himself, Schönwerth was familiar with tales of magical animals, Birds of Death, signs which appeared to be sent from Heaven, and also tales of the torment of the Poor Souls and spirits who could not find peace until they had atoned for their crimes.

In his introduction to *Sitten und Sagen*, Schönwerth describes the ever-haunting fear of Judgement Day thus:

> And when a human being has arrived at the turning point from which he is supposed to step outside of this world, after he has completed his task well or badly, it is the uncertainty of his future destiny, the fear of a judge and a penance, which fills the departing son of the Earth with trepidation.[1]

---

[1] „Und steht der Mensch an dem Wendepunkte, wo er hinaustreten soll aus dieser Welt, nachdem er seine Aufgabe gut oder übel gelöst hat, so ist es die Ungewißheit des künftigen Schicksales, die Furcht vor einem Richter und einer Strafe, welche den scheidenden Erdensohn mit Bangen erfüllen." *Sitten und Sagen*. vol 1: 39f.

## 29 Der Totenvogel[2]

Der Bauer und sein Knecht von Berg bei Windisch-Eschenbach,
einer Einöde, gingen ins Holz; sie schlugen einen Baum; da lockte
der Totenvogel: »Mit, mit, mit!« Der Bauer hörte es und sagte
zum Knechte: »Horch, der Totenvogel ruft; stirbt eins aus der
Freundschaft!« der Knecht aber hatte nichts gehört. Sie sägten
nun den zweiten Baum um; im Fallen erschlug er den Knecht.

## 30 Todesahnungen und den Tod vorhersagen I

Eine Frau war in Kindsnöten und das Bett gegen das Fenster
gerichtet. Da sah sie am Himmel ein feuriges Schwert, während
sie einen Knaben gebar. Sie erschrak und dachte, was wohl aus
diesem Knaben werden solle. Dieser erschoss auch als sechzehn-
jähriger Bursche um Geld einen Bauer, welcher seine Tochter vor
zudringlichen Liebhabern sorgsam zu verwahren pflegte. Durch
den Meineid derer, die ihn gedungen, und welche schwuren, dass
er um die verhängnisvolle Zeit bei ihnen gewesen, entging er der
Strafe und verließ seine Heimat.

Schon 74 Jahre alt, kehrte er endlich zurück und wurde von
der Gemeinde erhalten, da er gar nichts hatte. Aber nichts ist
so fein gesponnen, es kommt dennoch an die Sonnen. Denn
nicht lange, so entwendete er aus dem Hause, wo man ihn be-
herbergte, eine große Summe Geldes während der Kirchenzeit.
Er ging damit in den Wald, um es zu vergraben. Da ihn aber
die Kirchengänger auf diesem Wege gesehen hatten, wurde er
verhaftet, und weil er den vor sechzig Jahren verübten Mord
gestand, mit dem Schwere vom Leben zum Tod gebracht.

---

[2] „Auch Toten-Eulerl, Grauvogel, Sterbvogel genannt, ein kleiner grauer Vogel, ruft
gewöhnlich Abends unter Gebetläuten von einem Baume oder dem Dache herab und
setzt sich dann ans Fenster; sein schneller Ruf ist: »mit, mit, mit«, und wo er ertönt,
stirbt Jemand." *Sitten und Sagen*, Bd. 1: 270.

## 29 The Bird of Death[3]

A farmer and his manservant from a mountain by Windisch-Eschenbach, in the wilderness, went into the forest; as they cut down a tree, the Bird of Death beckoned: "[Come] with, with, with!" Upon hearing this, the farmer said to his manservant, "Listen, the Bird of Death is calling; one of our friends will die!" The manservant, however, had not heard anything. Then they sawed down a second tree; as it fell, it killed the manservant.

## 30 Premonitions and Predictions of Death I

A woman was in labor, her bed facing the window. There she saw a fiery sword in the sky as she gave birth to a boy. She was terrified and wondered, what will become of this boy? Indeed, when he was a mere lad of sixteen he shot to death, for money, a farmer who carefully kept his daughter away from pushy suitors. Because of the perjury by those who had hired him and who said, under oath, that he had been with them at the fatal time, he escaped his sentence and left his native home.

Finally, at the age of 74, he returned and was supported by the community because he had no possessions or money whatsoever. But nothing is so finely spun that it can escape the Sun. For not long after, he stole a large sum of money from the home where they housed him, while people were at church. He carried it to the forest to bury it. However, because the churchgoers had seen him on his way there, he was arrested, and because he confessed to the murder committed sixty years ago, was executed by the sword.

---

[3] "Also known as Little Owl-of-Death, Graybird, Deathbird; a little gray bird, which usually calls from a tree or rooftop when the evening prayer bells chime, and then sits down at a window; its quick call sounds like, '[Come] with, with, with,' and where it is heard, someone dies." *Sitten und Sagen*, vol. 1: 270.

### 31 Todesahnungen und den Tod vorhersagen II

Auf dem Donnersberg bei Oberviechtach hauste ein Schneider. Dieser war einmal auf der Stehr und arbeitete bis tief in die heilige Christnacht, während die Leute alle schon in die Mette gegangen waren.

Wie er nun fertig war, machte er sich gerade unter der Mette nach Hause, und als er einige Zeit gegangen war, kam ein gläsernes Fass daher, spiegelnd wie der feinste Kristall, bis vor seine Füße. Er fürchtete sich und wollte umkehren; aber auch da rollte das Fass vor seine Füße.

So entschloss er sich, lieber den Weg nach Hause fortzusetzen, und das Fass ging immer vor seinen Füßen her, und er sah in demselben mehrere Totentruhen und Männer daneben, welche er gar wohl kannte, da sie zur Zeit noch am Leben waren; auch sah er sich selbst bei dem letzten Sarge stehen.

Nun ergriff ihn solche Angst, dass er besinnungslos niederfiel, und Leute, die von der Mette heimkehrten, ihn nach Hause bringen mussten. Krank legte er sich zu Bett und alle, die er durch das Fass gesehen, starben noch im selben Jahr – der letzte, der starb, war der Schneider.

### 32 Todesahnungen und den Tod vorhersagen III

Die Fischerin von Weiding war das fünfte Mal im Kindbett; und während der Kirchzeit am fünften Tage, da sie gerade in der Küche saß, um zu kochen, kam ein kleines, grünes Männchen mit grünem Hütlein herein und sagte zu ihr: »Im zehnten Kindbett musst du sterben.« – Wirklich starb sie beim zehnten Kind am Kaiserschnitt.

### 33 Todesahnungen und den Tod vorhersagen IV

Zu dem Müller von Schönau wurde der Pfarrer gerufen, um ihn, den schwer Kranken, zu versehen. Auf dem Wege mit dem Mesner und dem Boten wollte er auf dem Steg über einen Bach gehen, der der Mühle das Wasser abgab, als sie den Müller darauf stehen sahen, die Haue auf der Schulter, als ob

### 31 Premonitions and Predictions of Death II

On Thunder Mountain near the town of Oberviechtach there lived a tailor. He once visited the Stehr farm and worked until late on Holy Christmas Eve, while everyone else was attending Midnight Mass.

When he was finished, he set off for home just as Midnight Mass was underway, and after he had walked for some time, a glass barrel, polished like the finest crystal glass, rolled up to his feet. He became frightened and wanted to turn around; but again the barrel rolled up to his feet.

So he decided he better continue on his way home, and the barrel always rolled along before his feet, and he saw inside of it several coffins and men beside them, all of whom he knew very well, since presently they were still alive; also, he saw himself standing beside the last coffin.

At this he was seized by such terror that he fell to the ground senseless, and people returning from Midnight Mass had to help him home. He lay down in bed feeling sick, and all of those whom he had seen through the barrel died in the same year—the last to die was the tailor.

### 32 Premonitions and Predictions of Death III

A fisherwoman from the town of Weiding was in childbed for the fifth time; during Mass on the fifth day, while she was sitting in the kitchen getting ready to cook, a little green man with a little green hat entered and said to her, "When you are in childbed for the tenth time, you shall die."—And indeed, she died, while delivering her tenth child by Caesarean section.

### 33 Premonitions and Predictions of Death IV

A priest was called to the miller of Schönau to administer to him, the gravely ill man, the last rites. On the way, accompanied by the sacristan and the messenger, he wanted to cross a footbridge over a creek which provided water for the mill, when they saw the miller on it with a pick on his shoulder, as if

er zum Wasserrichten gehen wollte. Als sie ihn zu grüßen ge-
dachten, voll Verwunderung, dass man sie zu einem Gesunden
rufe, verschwand er. Sie setzten gleichwohl ihren Weg fort, kamen
zur Mühle und erfuhren, dass er vor einer Viertelstunde gestorben sei. Es war dies um die Zeit, wo er ihnen erschienen. Seitdem sieht man ihn öfter auf der Brücke.

## 34 Der Höllenbube in Hirschau

Eine Bauerndirn ging zur Erntezeit mit ihrem fünfjährigen Kind
zwischen zwei Getreidefeldern, um den Schnittern das Mittages-
sen zu bringen; das Kind blieb manchmal zurück, um Kornblu-
men aus den Feldern zu pflücken, und die Mutter achtete nicht
viel darauf. Auf einmal aber war der Knabe verschwunden und
kehrte nicht wieder, soviel man auch nach ihm suchte.

Zehn Jahre später ging die Dirne desselben Weges in gleichem
Geschäfte, da stand der Knabe auf derselben Stelle, wo sie ihn verloren und erzählte, wie er vor zehn Jahren den Blumen nachgegan-
gen sei, habe er plötzlich vor einem großen Tor gestanden, und unter demselben ein alter Mann, der ihm freundlich winkte und ihn
fragte, ob er nicht bei ihm bleiben wolle; er solle es gut haben, Essen und Trinken zur Genüge, jeden Tag sechs Kreuzer[4] Lohn, und
jedes Jahr ein neues paar Schuhe; zu tun habe er nichts als das Tor
zu öffnen, so oft in der Kirche eine Leiche ausgeläutet werde; doch
dürfe er die Vorübergehenden nicht fragen, woher sie kommen, und
nicht nachschauen, wohin sie gehen. – So sei er nun geblieben und
habe in dieser Zeit viele Bekannte aus Hirschau vorbeigehen sehen,
zuletzt den Herrn Pfarrer; da konnte er sich nicht mehr halten,
und blickte ihm nach und sah nun eine Stube, und in dieser hatten
alle Platz gefunden, welche vor ihm vorübergegangen waren, vom
ersten bis zum letzten. Am andern Tage kam aber der Greis, der
ihn gedungen, und kündete ihm den Dienst auf mit den Worten:

---

[4] Kreuzer [mittelhochdeutsch kriuzer]; vom 13. bis 19. Jahrhundert in Süddeutschland,
Österreich und der Schweiz verbreitete, ursprünglich silberne Münze mit zwei aufge-
prägten Kreuzen, später Münze aus unedlerem Metall von relativ geringem Wert. (Siehe
auch: *Duden Universalwörterbuch* <http://www.duden.de/rechtschreibung/Kreuzer>.
Abgerufen 16 Jul 2012.)

he were about to go work on the watercourse. When they tried to greet him, surprised that they had been called to a healthy man, he disappeared. They continued on their way regardless and, upon arriving at the mill, learned that he had died a quarter of an hour earlier. It was about the same time he had appeared to them. Since that time, he has been seen now and then on the bridge.

## 34 The Hell's Boy from Hirschau

A farmer's maidservant, on her way to the harvesting with her five-year-old child, was walking between two cornfields to carry lunch to the reapers, and the child hung back once in a while to pick cornflowers from the fields, but the mother did not pay very much attention. All of a sudden, the boy disappeared and did not return, no matter how much everyone searched for him.

Ten years later, the woman walked the same path on the same business, and there was the boy in the very same place where she had lost him, and he told her how he had looked for flowers ten years ago when suddenly he found himself standing before a huge gate under which stood an old man who beckoned to him in a friendly way, asking him whether he wanted to stay with him; he would be comfortable there, would have food and drink aplenty, six German kreuzers[5] every day for wages, and every year a new pair of shoes; all he had to do was open the gate every time the death knell pealed in the church; however, he was not allowed to ask the passersby from whence they came nor look where they were going.—So he stayed, and since then had seen many acquaintances from Hirschau pass by, most recently the priest; he was unable to resist, and looking down the path after him, noticed a room which held all those who had passed by him, from the first to the last. Next day, the old man who had hired him came and terminated his employment with the following words,

---

[5] German kreuzer, from Middle High German *kriuzer*, named for the cross marking them; a small coin of silver and later of copper used in Austria, Germany, and Hungary from the 13th to the mid-19th centuries. (See also *Merriam Webster Unabridged* <http://unabridged.merriam-webster.com/noauth/mwlogin.php?return=/cgi-bin/unabridged?va=kreutzer>. Accessed 16 Jul 2012).

»Weil du das Gebot übertreten, das ich dir gegeben, hast du deinen Lohn; ziehe hin, wo du hergekommen bist!« – Der Mann lebte noch in dieser Zeit, war nicht traurig, lachte aber nicht, sprach wenig, hatte nicht viel Umgang, und sagte nur Vertrauten, was er gesehen, darunter der Mutter der Erzählerin.

## 35 Geister, Gespenster und arme Seelen I

In Strahlfeld ging eine Häuslerstochter[6] wallfahren zum »Haubrünl«, eine Frauenkirche bei Roding. Unterwegs kam sie aber an einem Wirtsaus vorbei, in welchem Tanzmusik war, trat ein, fand Gesellschaft und tanzte den ganzen Nachmittag. Darnach ging sie heim. Doch bald wurde sie krank und starb. Nun ging sie als Geist im Hause um; weil aber in dieser Familie große Zwieträchtigkeit war, so litt sie es nimmer darin, und sie zeigte sich nun an einem Berge in der Nähe. Da ging ein Schneider etwas angestochen von Neunkirchen heim; er sah sie und redete sie an. Da eröffnete sie ihm, dass er sie erlösen könne, wenn er wallfahren ginge für sie, und das Geld zu einer heiligen Messe pfennigweis zusammenbetteln wollte.

Er tat es, und während der heiligen Wandlung zeigte sich ihm der erlöste Geist in der Kirche; er kniete allein in einem Stuhl und rief immer, ob denn niemand den Geist sehe, der ganz weiß vor ihm stehe. Dem Schneider wurde unwohl, der Angstschweiß stand ihm auf der Stirne, bald darauf starb er.

## 36 Geister, Gespenster und arme Seelen II[7]

Wo man von der Seemühle nach Weiding geht, ist ein Weiher, bei welchem viel gesehen und gehört wird, insbesondere ging einer um ohne Kopf. Da führt einmal nachts der Weg einen Betrunkenen vorbei. Auf der Wiese schreit einer: »Wo soll ich ihn hintun?«

---

[6] Häusler: Dorfbewohner, der bei einem anderen zur Miete wohnt. (Siehe auch: *Duden Universalwörterbuch* <http://www.duden.de/rechtschreibung/Haeusler>. Abgerufen 16 Jul 2012.)

[7] „Diese Sage ist eine der verbreitetsten in der Oberpfalz, und nahezu jedes Dorf behauptet, dass die Geschichte in seiner Gemarkung vorgefallen sei." *Sitten und Sagen*, Bd. 1: 302.

"Since you disobeyed the order which I gave you, here you have your wages; go back to whence you came!"—To this day [when the story was retold], the man was still alive; he was not sad, but did not laugh, spoke little, did not keep much company, and told only his closest confidants what he had seen, among them the narrator's mother.

## 35 Ghosts, Spirits, and Lost Souls I

In the town of Strahlfeld a cottager's daughter[8] once went on a pilgrimage to the "Haubrünl," a church dedicated to Our Lady, close to Roding. On her way there, she came to an inn where she heard dance music, entered, found company and danced all afternoon. After that, she went home. But soon after that, she fell sick and died. Then she haunted the house as a Ghost; however, because there was so much strife in the family, she could suffer it no longer and began to haunt a mountain nearby. A tipsy tailor on his way home from Neunkirchen noticed her and spoke to her. She disclosed to him that he could redeem her soul if he went on pilgrimage on her behalf, while begging penny by penny for the cost of a Mass.

That he did, and during Holy Transsubstantiation the redeemed spirit showed itself to him in church; he knelt in a pew by himself and kept calling out whether anyone else could see the Ghost, who stood all-white before him. The tailor began to feel unwell; cold sweat appeared on his forehead, and he died soon thereafter.

## 36 Ghosts, Spirits, and Lost Souls II[9]

As one walks from the Lake Mill to the town of Weiding, one finds a pond where much has been seen and heard, particularly a headless man who haunted the place. One night, a drunken man passes by. On the meadow, a man yells out, "Where should I put it?"

[8] Cottager: a person who lives in a cottage, usually renting rather than owning. (See also *Merriam Webster* <http://www.merriam-webster.com/dictionary/cottage>. Accessed 21 Nov 2012).

[9] "This legend is one of the most common in the Upper Palatinate, and almost every town claims that this story happened within its bounds." *Sitten und Sagen*, vol. 1: 302.

Er trug einen Markstein auf der Schulter, den er früher verrückt hatte. Darauf erwiderte der Betrunkene beherzt: »Narr, tu' ihn hin, wo du ihn genommen!« »Herr, vergelts Gott, jetzt bin ich erlöst,« sprach der Geist und verschwand. Der Betrunkene wurde ganz nüchtern.

Diesen Geist hatten schon viele gehört, niemand aber hatte gewagt, ihn anzureden.

### 37 Geister, Gespenster und arme Seelen III[10]

Ein Bauer ging auf den Markt. Auf dem Wege musste er über ein Brückchen. Da stand ein kleiner Knabe, der ihn bat, ihn doch hinüber zu tragen, da er gar so wasserscheu wäre.

Der Bauer hob ihn also auf und nahm ihn auf seinen Rücken. Währenddem nieste der Kleine. Der Bauer sagt: »Helf Gott!« – ebenso musste er auf der Mitte und am Ende des Brückchens niesen, und jedesmal sagte der Bauer sein »Helf Gott.« Wie er dieses das drittemal gesagt hatte, rief der Kleine: »Vergelts Gott, du hast mich erlöst. Schon viele haben mich getragen, beim erstmaligen Niesen auch ›Helf Gott‹ gesagt, aber nur du hast mir dreimal Gottes Hilfe gewünscht. Hättest du mich diesmal nicht erlöst, so wäre dir eine Kuh gefallen, welche du in deinem Garten eingegraben hättest. Aus der Stelle wäre ein Baum gewachsen, aus diesem Baume wären Bretter geschnitten und aus diesen eine Wiege gemacht worden, und das erste Knäblein, das darin gelegen, würde mich erst erlöst haben.« Dann sagte er ihm noch viel Unglück, unter anderem dreimaliges Abbrennen,[11] voraus und verschwand.

---

[10] „Gleich große Verbreitung, wie die vorgehende, hat diese Sage vom dreimaligen Niesen und Helfgott. Merkwürdig ist auch der Zug in diesen Sagen, dass den Menschen, der eine arme Seele erlöst hat, Unglück an Leib und Gut zum Lohn trifft, so als wären Leiden ein vorzügliches Geschenk." *Sitten und Sagen*, Bd. 1: 303.

[11] Im Oberpfälzischen kann „abbrennen" auch bedeuten, dass jemand bankrott geht.

He bore a milestone on his shoulder, which he had unlawfully moved sometime earlier. Thereupon the drunken man replied valiantly, "Fool, put it back whence you took it!" "Sir, God bless you; now my soul is redeemed," the Ghost said, and vanished. The drunk became stone-cold sober.

This Ghost had been heard by many before, but nobody had dared to speak to him.

## 37 Ghosts, Spirits, and Lost Souls III

A farmer went to market. On his way, he had to cross a little bridge. There stood a little boy who asked him to carry him across because he was afraid of the water.

So the farmer picked him up and carried him over on his back. While doing so, the little one sneezed. The farmer said his "Bless you!"—The boy sneezed in the middle and at the other end of the bridge also, and every time the farmer said his "Bless you." After he had said this for the third time, the little one called out, "Thank God, you redeemed my soul. Many carried me across, and also said "Bless you" when I sneezed the first time, but only you wished me God's blessing three times. If you hadn't redeemed me, one of your cows would have fallen, which you would have buried in your backyard. At that spot, a tree would have grown from which boards would have been cut and a cradle would have been made from them, and the first little boy who would have lain in it would have redeemed me." Then he told him of many more misfortunes still to come,[12] among them three bankruptcies [or, burnings of his farm],[13] and disappeared.

---

[12] The legend of sneezing thrice and Bless You is a common one. "The motif that a person who redeems a Poor Soul will be struck by misfortune to himself and his goods as a reward, as if suffering were an exquisite present, is a strange thread in these legends." *Sitten und Sagen*, vol. 1: 303.

[13] In Upper Palatinian, "Abbrennen" may mean "bankruptcy" or "burning down of a building."

## 38 Tiermagie[14]

Ein Knecht ging während der Mette in den Stall um zu horchen, was die Pferde sich erzählen werden. Da sagte ein Pferd zum andern: »Bin ich froh, dass diese harte Woche – sie war eine ganze Woche, ohne Feiertag dazwischen – vorbei ist.« – Dieses aber erwiderte: »O nein, wir bekommen es in dieser Woche noch viel härter.« – »Warum dieses, es sind ja die Christtage,« meinte das erste. »Ach,« schloss das Zweite, »ich muss zum Arzt, du zum Priester reiten in der Nacht, und alle beide müssen wir den Bauern auf den Friedhof führen.« – Und es geschah so.

## 39 Geister, die Tiere necken I[15]

Ein Wirt in Spalt hatte zwei schöne Schimmel im Stalle; diesen waren gar oft über Nacht Mähne und Schweif in so viele kleine Zöpfchen geflochten, dass am Morgen alles zusammenhelfen musste, dieselben wieder auseinander zu bringen. Man ließ die Nacht über im Stalle wachen, sah und hörte aber nichts; gleichwohl waren am Morgen die Zöpfe vorhanden. Einer, der an einem Quatembersonntage[16] geboren war, sah die Hexe, eine Frau aus Spalt, auf den Rossen reiten.

---

[14] „Aber auch als weissagende Tiere gelten die Pferde zur Zeit noch; durch die ganze Oberpfalz geht der Glaube, dass die Tiere im Stalle, Pferd und Rind, in der Weihnacht um die zwölfte Stunde reden und die Zukunft verkünden. Die Sage hierüber ist überall dieselbe." *Sitten und Sagen*, Bd. 1: 326.

[15] „Noch ein anderes Vergnügen finden diese neckischen Geisterchen darin, dass sie Mähne und Schweif in eine Unzahl kleiner Zöpfchen flechten, die man mit vieler Geduld und Mühe lösen muß. Selbst das Futter wird nicht verschont; sie flechten kleine Strohriegerln davon. Wo das Schragerl einkehrt, soll Glück weilen; gleichwohl sehen es die Leute nicht gerne im Stalle seine Behausung aufschlagen, weil das Vieh zu sehr davon geplagt wird. Was hier von den Pferden, gilt auch vom Rindvieh in Stalle, dem der Schweif in Zöpfchen geflochten wird." *Sitten und Sagen*, Bd. 1: 327f.

[16] „Quatember: Man versteht darunter jeweils den Mittwoch, Freitag und Samstag von vier Wochen im Jahr, die ungefähr mit dem Beginn der vier Jahreszeiten zusammenfallen und die man in Rom seit dem 8. Jahrhundert als ‚Quattuor tempora' (vier Zeiten) bezeichnet." (Siehe auch *Steyler Missionare* <http://www.steyler.eu/svd/medien/zeitschriften/stadtgottes_DE-CH/2010/2010_11/quatembersonntag.php>. Abgerufen 17 Jul 2012.)

## 38 Magical Animals[17]

During Christmas Eve Mass, a manservant slipped out to the stable to listen in on what the horses were telling each other. There, one horse said to another, "I am so glad that this hard week—it was a whole week, without a Holy Day—is over." Whereupon the other replied, "Oh no, this [coming] week is going to be much harder." "Why is that, after all, it will be Christmas," the first one wondered. "Ah," concluded the second. "I must go to the doctor's, you must ride to the priest in the night, and we both will have to lead the farmer into the graveyard."— And so it came to pass.

## 39 Ghosts and Spirits that Tease Animals I[18]

An innkeeper in the town of Spalt had two beautiful white horses in his stable; many a night their manes and tails had been braided into so many little braids that in the morning everybody had to pitch in and help undo them again. They set up a night watch in the stable, but heard and saw nothing; nevertheless, in the morning the braids were there. A man who had been born on one of the Quatember Sundays[19] had seen a Witch, a woman from the town of Spalt, riding on the horses.

---

[17] "Also, horses are still known as animals that are able to foretell the future; in the entire region people believe that animals kept in the stable, horses and cattle, are able to talk at midnight on Christmas Eve, and predict the future. The legend is the same everywhere in the region." *Sitten und Sagen*, vol. 1: 326.

[18] "Another pastime of these teasing little Ghosts is that they braid the mane and tail into innumerable little braids which have to be undone with a lot of a patience and work. Even the food is not safe; they braid it into little straw loaves. Where the 'Schragerl' enters, there is said to be happiness; even so, people don't like it when it takes up its home in the stable because the animals are much bothered by that. What is said about horses is also true for cattle in the stables, whose tails will be braided in little braids." *Sitten und Sagen*, vol. 1: 327f.

[19] "The pattern followed in modern times was est[ablished] in the 11th century: Wednesday, Friday, and Saturday after (1) 1st Sunday in Lent; (2) Pentecost; (3) Holy Cross Day, September 14; (4) St. Lucia's Day, December 1." (See also Erwin L. Lueker, Luther Poellot and Paul Jackson, *Christian Cyclopedia*, Concordia Publishing House, 2000 <http://cyclopedia.lcms.org/display.asp?t1=q&word=QUATEMBER>. Accessed 17 Jul 2012.)

## 40 Geister, die Tiere necken II

Der Klosterwirt zu Neumarkt hatte erst vor acht Jahren einen wunderschönen Falken; drei Nächte nacheinander war ihm die Mähne geflochten in mehr als hundert Zöpfchen, welche bei Tag sich von selbst auflösten. Das Pferd stand jedesmal voll Schaum und zitterte an allen Gliedern; ein Knecht hielt Wache, sah aber nichts.

## 41 Magische Rinder I[20]

Zu Oberrohr bei Falkenstein hatte ein Bauer in einer Raubnacht[21] im Stalle gelauscht; er hörte, wie der Stier zu sprechen anfing und den baldigen Tod seines Herrn verkündete. Davon erschrak er so, dass er wirklich bald starb; vor seinem Tode verordnete er aber, dass der Stier, der gesprochen, seine Leiche fahre; wo er stehen bleibe, soll eine Kapelle auf seine Kosten gebaut werden. Als nun der Stier wirklich stehen blieb, wurde an der Stelle, seinem Verlangen gemäß, eine Kapelle, dem heiligen Quirin zu Ehren, erbaut; davon heißt sie St. Quer.

## 42 Magische Rinder II

Die Mutter der Erzählerin, aus Letten, hatte eine verzauberte Kuh, und suchte dagegen bei einer Abdeckerin Hilfe; sie musste dieser an drei abnehmenden Freitagen je eines von folgenden drei Stücken, ein neues Haferl, unglasiert, vom Hafner, ein

---

[20] „Wie das Pferd gehört das Rind zu den weissagenden, ausserdem auch zu den weisenden Tieren. – Um die zwölfte Stunde der Christnacht reden die Ochsen im Stalle: sie verkünden die Zukunft; der Bauer horcht daher unter dem Barren. Auch zählt es zu den Gespenstertieren; besonders sind es die Striche am südlichen Böhmerwalde, wo Kälber und weisse oder schwarzgefleckte Stiere nachts den Wanderer schrecken." *Sitten und Sagen*, Bd. 1: 332.

[21] „Es gibt gewisse Nächte, in welchen die bösen Geister und böse Menschen die Macht haben, vom Vieh den Nutzen zu rauben . . . Die Raubnächte gehen mit dem Advente an, und zwar mit dem Andreasabend, und dauern bis zum Walpurgisabend . . . In diesen Nächten wird dem Vieh im Stalle sehr zugesetzt." (Stephan Gröschler, „Die Rauhnächte—Mythos und Brauch (2)." *Kraftvolle Orte: Kraftvolle, mystische und geheimnisvolle Orte*, <http://www.kraftvolle-orte.de/2011/12/die-rauhnaechte-mythos-und-brauch-2>. Abgerufen 21 Nov 2012.)

## 40 Ghosts and Spirits that Tease Animals II

Just eight years ago, the innkeeper at the monastery inn in Neu-markt had owned a magnificent brown-gray horse; three nights in a row its mane had been braided into more than one hundred little braids that came undone by themselves the next day. Every time, the horse stood with its mouth foaming and trembling in every limb; a manservant kept watch but saw nothing.

## 41 Magic Cattle I[22]

In the village of Oberrohr near Falkenstein, a farmer was eaves-dropping in the stable during one of the Robber's Nights;[23] he heard the bull begin to talk and proclaim the imminent death of its master. Upon this he became so frightened that indeed he soon died; but before his death he ordered that the bull who had spoken was to carry his corpse; where it stood still, a chapel was to be built at his expense. So when the bull actually stopped, a chapel was built there in accordance with his wishes, dedicated to Saint Quirin; thus it is named St. Quer.

## 42 Magic Cattle II

The narrator's mother, from the town of Letten, owned a be-witched cow, and sought relief againt the spell from a knacker woman; she had to bring her on three Fridays of the waning moon each of the following: a new little unglazed pot made by a potter, a

---

[22] "Like horses, cattle belong to the group of animals that predict and also foretell.—At the twelfth hour during Christmas Night, the oxen talk in the stable; they predict the future; the farmer listens therefore, sitting up in the rafters. Cattle are found also among the Ghost ani-mals, especially in the region at the southern end of the Bohemian Forest, where calves and white or black-spotted bulls frighten wanderers at night." *Sitten und Sagen*, vol. 1: 332.

[23] "There are certain nights in which evil spirits and people have the power to rob animals of their usefulness . . . The Robbing Nights start with the Advent, to be more specific with St. Andrew's Eve and last until Walpurgis Night . . . On these nights, the ani-mals in the stables will be bothered mightily." (Stephan Gröschler, "Die Rauhnächte—Mythos und Brauch (2)," *Kraftvolle Orte: Kraftvolle, mystische und geheimnisvolle Orte* <http://www.kraftvolle-orte.de/2011/12/die-rauhnaechte-mythos-und-brauch-2> Accessed 21 Nov 2012.)

Stück Seife vom Seifensieder, und drei Ellen ungebleichte Leinwand bringen. Das drittemal ging sie mit der Abdeckerin noch
vor der Sonne ungesprochen zu einem laufenden Wasser und
warf die drei Stücke überrücks hinein, dass sie fortschwammen.

Als sie nach Hause kehrte, war der Zauber gewichen und die
Kuh gab gesunde Milch. Die Abdeckerin hatte ihr auch angebo-
ten, die Hexe, welche es getan hatte, kommen zu lassen; dieses
lehnte die Bäuerin ab.

piece of soap made by a soap boiler, and three cubits of unbleached linen. On her third visit, she went with the knacker woman, without talking, to some running water before the sun rose and threw the three pieces over her shoulder so that they would float away.

When she returned home, the spell was lifted and the cow gave good milk. The knacker woman had offered also to conjure up for her the Witch who had done it; the farmer woman declined this.

# WITCHES AND THEIR FAMILIARS

The people of the Upper Palatinate detested and feared women whom they took for Witches, because they believed them to be out to destroy both their physical and their spiritual well-being. Etymologically speaking, a Witch was a woman with occult knowledge or knowledge of healing plants, but with Christendom on the rise, the old pagan beliefs and their followers were demonized.[1] In traditional folklore, therefore, a Witch was always equipped with magical powers, and was usually a baneful female in league with the Devil and his demonic minions. Often, animals such as ravens, black cats, and also Dragons (or Serpents) became "familiars" (associates) of Witches and were rewarded for their devotion with their own magical powers.

The exact origin of the German word "Hexe" (English, Witch) has not been clarified; it is possibly a combination of the Old Germanic word for fence (or hedge) with the Old Norwegian word for "elf" or "evil spirit." Possibly this alluded to an evil spirit apparently sitting on a hedge.[2]

---

[1] Gernot L. Geise, „Die weisen Frauen: Als Hexen verunglimpft, niemals rehabilitiert," *EFODON-SYNESIS* 11/1995. <http://www.efodon.de/html/archiv/geschichte/geise/hexen.html>. Accessed 17 Nov 2012.

[2] Origin and meaning of the word Hexe are not clear. The word may be a variation of the old German word *hazussa* which means "hedge woman." In that interpretation, a Witch is a supernatural being sitting on a fence or hedge. This would make sense from a historical perspective, since in the Middle Ages a fence or hedge separated a town and its residents from the surrounding forests. The fence was the barrier between humans

Schönwerth was intrigued by the widespread belief in the unrelenting malevolence of Witches:

> Hostile forces come forth where a human makes his home and they fight them over this space. This provided motivation [for me] to discuss the traditional folklore views of Witches who even seek to rob humans, after all their work and toils are completed,[3] of the pleasure of their labor, the benefits of their domestic animals, the fruit of their fields.

His collection provides numerous examples of the genre.

---

and demons. (See also Denise Hofmann, *Die Hexe in ausgewählten Märchen der Brüder Grimm*, Master's Thesis, Books on Demand GmbH, Norderstedt, Germany, 2009: 5).

[3] „Feindliche Kräfte stehen auf, wo er sich heimisch macht, und wehren ihm den Raum. Dieses gab Anlaß zur Besprechung der volkstümlichen Anschauungen von Hexe[n] . . . , welche den Menschen am Ende seiner Arbeit und Plage noch um den Genuß des Lohnes, den Nutzen vom Vieh, die Frucht vom Felde zu bringen trachten." *Sitten und Sagen,* Bd. 1: 40.

## 43 Hexengeschichten I[3]

Ein Schneider war auf der Stehr und sah, wie die Bäuerin zum Buttern herrichtete und dergleichen tat, als wolle sie das Weihwasser und geweihtes Salz hineintun. Sie hatte aber über der Türe ein Büchschen, und langte hinein und schmierte den Butterstecken. Während des Butterns sagte sie immer ganz still für sich hin:»Aus jedem Haus einen Löffel voll,« und so immer fort. Der Schneider aber hatte genau achtgegeben, und als die Bäuerin hinausging, nahm er schnell von der Salbe und steckte es ein.

Als er nach Hause kommt, sagt er zur Frau:»Frau, richt mir zum Buttern her!« Diese aber meinte, sie habe nichts als ein wenig eine Milch.»Tu's nur her,« erwiderte der ungeduldige Schneider,»und das Butterfass dazu!« Er nahm nun seine Salbe, schmierte den Butterstecken, fängt zu buttern an und spricht dabei immer:»Aus jedem Hause eine Schüssel voll.«

Als er fertig war, reichten die Schüsseln und Töpfe nicht mehr zu, sie mussten die Schäffel nehmen, und da auch diese nicht langten, zu den Nachbarn gehen und Geschirr entleihen. Ist nicht lange angestanden, so kommt schon der Böse und hat das Buch, und da soll der Schneider unterschreiben. Der sagte:»Ist recht!« schreibt aber den Jesus Namen ein. Da konnte der Böse das Buch nicht mehr fortnehmen, und im Buche sind alle Hexen und Hexenmeister gestanden. All diesen konnte der Böse von nun an nicht mehr an, denn er hatte das Buch nicht mehr.

---

[3] „Hexen sind gottlose Frauen, welche mit dem Teufel gegen Verschreibung ihrer armen Seelen in Bund treten, um mit dessen Hilfe dem Nächsten zu ihrem Vorteil oder auch bloss aus Rache und Bosheit zu schaden. Dieser Schaden trifft vorzüglich das Zug- und Nutzvieh, und darunter vorzugsweise die Kühe, welchen sie den Nutzen oder die Milch nehmen." *Sitten und Sagen*, Bd. 1: 363.

## 43 Legends of Witches I[4]

A tailor visited the Stehr farm and saw how the farmer's wife made preparations for churning butter and acted as if she intended to add Holy Water and salt. But she had a little can above the door, and reached into that and greased the butter sticks. During the churning, she kept repeating quietly, "From each house a spoon full," and so on and on. The tailor, however, had paid close attention, and when the farmer's wife left the room, he quickly took a sample from the ointment and put it in his pocket.

When he arrived home, he said to his wife, "Wife, prepare everything for churning butter!" She, however, said that she only had a little milk left. "Just give it to me," the impatient tailor replied. "And the butter churn too!" He then picked up his ointment, greased the buttering stick and starts churning, saying again and again, "From each house a bowl full."

When he was done, there were not enough pots and pans, so they had to resort to their tubs and, as these weren't enough either, they had to go to their neighbors and borrow dishes from them. It did not take long before the Evil One comes along and brings with him the Book, and asks the tailor to sign. The tailor said, "All right!" but wrote there the name of the Lord Jesus. Thereupon the Evil One was unable to take the Book away, yet in the Book were the names of all the Witches and Warlocks. Henceforth, the Evil One was no longer able to wield power over them because he no longer had the Book.

---

[4] "Witches are godless women who enter into a pact with the Devil by committing their souls, in order to harm their neighbors, with the help of the Devil, to their own advantage or simply out of revenge or wickedness. This harm targets primarily the domestic animals, and preferably the cows from whom they take their benefits, or their milk." *Sitten und Sagen*, vol. 1: 363.

## 44 Hexengeschichten II[5]

Auf dem Aichhof zwischen Velburg und Hohenfels wurde vor alten Zeiten einmal eine Bäuerin mit ihrer Tochter als Hexe verbrannt.

Beide waren nämlich der Hexenzunft einverleibt und fuhren alle Nacht auf einem Besen durch den Schornstein auf den Blocksberg. Der Knecht hörte davon und versteckte sich in der Küche, um dahinter zu kommen. Wie nun die Bäuerin und ihre Tochter meinten, alles schliefe im Hause, kamen sie in die Küche, nahmen einen Besen, bestrichen mit einer in der Ecke verborgenen Salbe Stirne und Besen, und flogen dann zum Schornstein hinaus.

Als der Knecht dieses sah, wollte er auch versuchen, wie denn das Ding wäre; aber kaum hatte er die Salbe an Stirne und Besen gebracht, als es ihn wider Willen hinaushob und auf den Blocksberg trieb. Die Bäuerin und ihre Tochter ergrimmten, wie sie ihren Knecht herankommen sahen, und verwandelten ihn in einen Esel, den sie laufen ließen.

So fing ihn ein Bauer und verhandelte ihn an einen Müller, bei dem er nun mehrere Jahre arbeiten musste. Zufälligerweise hörte er aber eines Abends, als er auf der Weide in der Nähe von Frauen graste, diese Märchen erzählen, und eine sagte unter anderm, dass, wer von Hexen verzaubert sei, sich damit helfen könne, wenn er am Antlasstage einer reinen Jungfrau das geweihte Kränzchen vom Haupte reißen könnte. Der Esel merkte sich dieses,

---

[5] „Die Hexe läßt sich, wenigstens in ihrer ursprünglichen Erscheinung, als Priesterin der heidnischen Gottheit erkennen. Vor allem hat aber der Kampf zwischen Christentum und Heidentum auf die Gestaltung des Begriffes der Hexe eingewirkt. In ihr zeigt sich Nachklingen heidnischer Götterverehrung selbst noch zu jener Zeit, wo das Christentum schon den Sieg auf seiner Seite hatte, und das Heidentum nur mehr im Geheimen bestehen konnte. Daher fährt die Hexe nachts, wenn die Christen schlafen, zu dem Opferfeste, dem Teufel oder Heidengotte dargebracht, an den heiligen Ort, wo das Opfer stattfinden soll. Solche Orte heissen Blocksberg, von Block, dem Altare von Stein oder Baumstämmen auf Anhöhen errichtet. Der Altar ist ein einziger Felsenblock. Wo ein solcher Ort ist, darf man auf eine alte Opferstätte raten. Sie liegen im Walde verborgen, nach alter Sitte; später hielt diese Lage das neugierige Auge ferne. Das Opfer ist aber ein gemeinsames des Volkes, daher kommen viele Hexen zusammen; die Zeit, wo es gefeiert wird, eine heilige und regelmässig zu dreimal im Jahre, zu Anfang, Mitte und Ende Winters. Kein Heidenfest ohne Opfer, Mahl und Tanz. Daher das Hexenmahl, der Hexentanz." *Sitten und Sagen*, Bd. 1: 390f.

## 44 Legends of Witches II[6]

On the Aich Farm, between the towns of Velburg and Hohen-fels, in olden times there were a farmer's wife and her daughter who were burnt as Witches.

In fact, both were sworn members of the Guild of Witches and rode all night on a broomstick, through the chimney and on to the Block Mountain.[7] The manservant heard of this and hid in the kitchen to find out details. When the famer's wife and her daughter believed everybody in the house to be asleep, they entered the kitchen, took a broom, greased their foreheads and broomstick with an ointment hidden in a corner, and then flew up the chimney.

When the manservant saw this, he also wanted to try it, to see what would happen; but no sooner had he applied the ointment to forehead and broom than he was involuntarily lifted up and swept off to the Block Mountain. The farmer's wife and daughter were enraged when they saw their manservant approach, and they turned him into a donkey which they let run away.

Thus, he was caught by a farmer and sold to a miller, for whom he had to work for several years. By chance, one evening when he was grazing in a pasture close to some women, he overheard them recounting tales and one said among other things, that if someone were spellbound by Witches, he could undo the spell if, on Holy Thursday, he were able to snatch a little holy wreath from the head of a pure virgin. The donkey took note of this

---

[6] "At least in her original shape, the Witch can be understood as priestess of a pagan deity. The struggle between Christianity and paganism most decidedly affected the development of the concept of the Witch. In it, we can see echoes of the pagan worship even in those times when Christianity had already won the battle, and pagan traditions were able to survive only in hiding. Hence the Witch rides to the festival of sacrifice at night, when all the Christians are asleep, to the sacred site where the sacrifice is going to take place, to conduct the rites dedicated to the Devil or the pagan deity. Such sites are called Block Mountain, denoting a block or altar made of rock or logs built on hilltops. The altar is one slab of rock. Where one finds such a site, one can guess that there had been an ancient sacrifical site. They are hidden in forests, according to an ancient custom; later that helped them escape detection. The sacrifice is a common feature of the people, thus many Witches gather; the time when it is celebrated is sacred and regularly celebrated three times a year, at the beginning, middle, and end of winter. [There is] no pagan festival without sacrifice, a meal, and dance. Hence the Witches' Meal, the Witches' Dance." *Sitten und Sagen*, vol. 1: 390f.

[7] Witches' Mountain.

und biss am nächsten Frohnleichnamstage einem kleinen Mädchen den Kranz vom Kopfe weg; in demselben Augenblicke gewann er seine vorige Gestalt.

Seine Feindinnen klagte er aber bei Gericht an, und beide wurden verbrannt. Doch war nicht Ruhe; denn ihre Geister gingen um und neckten die Leute im Hofe so lange, bis der Knecht ihre Gebeine von der Richtstätte nahm und in geweihte Erde vergrub.

### 45 Hexengeschichten III

In dem kleinen Orte Haag, bei Tiefenbach, hatte ein Bauer eine Bauerntochter aus Stegen geheiratet. Kaum war sie einige Tage dort, so konnte keine einzige Bäuerin des Ortes mehr Schmalz machen. Die neue Frau aber, obwohl sie nur zwei Kühe hatte, trug jeden Marktag mehrere Pfund davon zum Verkaufe, weshalb sie bald allgemein in der Umgegend in dem Rufe einer Hexe stand. Sie ging auch nie zur Kirche, solange sie lebte.

Man hat sie öfter ganz nackt in einer Wiese eine Hand voll Kräuter sammeln sehen. Wenn sie Butter machte, war sie nackt, die Haare fliegend. An Walburgi brachte sie die ganze Nacht nackt beim Vieh im Stalle zu; es waren zwar nur zwei Stücke drin, doch löste sie jährlich für verkauftes Schmalz an 200 fl.

Einmal hat sie einem Bäcker, mit dem sie wegen eines Fahrtweges in Streit geriet, die ganze Wirtschaft verheert, und dieser konnte ein paar Monate lang kein ordentliches Brot zusammen bringen, bis er mit geweihten Sachen dem Zauber ein Ende machte, und die Hexe zwang, sich am andern Morgen ihm zu zeigen.

Auch als Wetterhexe hatte sie Ruf. Einmal entstand ein heftiges Gewitter bei starkem Winde; ihr Nachbar sah sie eine Stunde vorher aus dem Hause gehen. Da warf er, als ein arger Windstoß daher kam, ein spitzes Messer in die Luft hinauf. Das Wetter hörte sogleich auf, aber die Frau hatte ein Auge verloren.

Nach ihrem Tode ging sie um und arbeitete vorzüglich in den Milchgeschirren herum. Ein Kloster-Geistlicher las sie in eine zinnerne Flasche hinein, und vertrug sie auf den Schwarzenwührberg.

and, on the next Feast of Corpus Christi, with his teeth he snatched away a wreath from the head of a little girl; instantly he regained his previous form.

He accused his enemies before a court of law, and both were burned to death. However, that was not the end of it; for their Ghosts were still haunting and teasing people in their former home until the manservant moved their bones from the execution site to consecrated ground.

## 45 Legends of Witches III

In the hamlet of Haag, near the town of Tiefenbach, a farmer had married a farmer's daughter from Stegen. No sooner was she there for a few days, then not a single farmer's wife in the hamlet was able to make butterfat anymore. The new wife, although she owned only two cows, took several pounds of it for sale on Market Day, and so she soon acquired the reputation around the neighborhood of being a Witch. Also, she never went to church as long as she lived.

She was now and then seen standing in a meadow completely naked, gathering a handful of herbs. When she churned butter, she was naked, with her hair flying. On Walpurgis [Night], she spent the entire night in the stable naked, with the animals; in it were only two cows but she earned 200 gulden each year, with the butterfat she sold.

Once she completely destroyed a baker's business because she had quarreled with him over a footpath, and he was unable to bake good bread for a couple of months until he put an end to the spell with the help of holy objects, and forced the Witch to reveal herself the following morning.

She had a reputation as a Weather Witch as well. One day, a fierce thunderstorm with a strong wind developed; her neighbor saw her leave the house an hour before the storm. As a terrible gust of wind approached, he threw a sharp knife up into the air. The [stormy] weather ceased immediately, but the woman had lost an eye.

After her death she haunted [the house], and most particularly the milking harnesses. A priest from a monastery sealed her [spirit] into a tin flask using incantations, and then abandoned her on Schwarzenwühr Mountain.

## 46 Hexengeschichten IV

Die Mutter der Erzählerin, aus Neumarkt, erfuhr an sich selbst Folgendes: Sie half einer alten Frau von Haag nach Neumarkt ziehen; auf dem Wege ging die Alte voraus und ließ wie unbedacht ein Stück Brot fallen; das hob die Frau auf und aß es; aber sie konnte nicht mehr weiter; sie hatte die Fraisen.[8] Man brachte sie also nach Neumarkt hinein, und, weil die Alte im Rufe der Hexerei stand, wurde der Geistliche gerufen. Dieser ließ im Strohsack nachsuchen, und man fand in jedem Ecke desselben angebrannte Zündhölzer, Besenreiser und Stopsel. Der Geistliche befahl, alles sorgfältig herauszunehmen und ins Feuer zu werfen. Da kam die Alte, und bat um Gotteswillen, sie nicht ganz zu verbrennen, sie wolle es nicht mehr tun.

## 47 Hexengeschichten V

Eine Bäuerin, unweit Neukirchen B., hatte ein sechzehnjähriges Töchterlein, welches bei der jungen Dirne schlafen musste. Diese war aber eine Hexe und unterrichtete das Mägdlein in ihrer Kunst und fuhr mit ihr aus zu ihren Versammlungen, wo es bei Musik und Tanz recht lustig herging. Die Dirn war gut im Haus gelitten, weil alles unter ihrer Hand zu gedeihen schien.

Einmal ging das Töchterchen auf Besuch zur Baderin des Ortes, und hörte diese klagen, dass sie so wenig Milch von ihren Kühen erhalte. Dem, meinte das Mädchen, sei leicht abzuhelfen, man solle ihr nur ein Tischtuch geben. Sie legte nun das Tuch über eine Asenstange,[9] so dass die vier Zipfel herabhingen

---

[8] ‚Freis/Freis,‘ allgemein (Empfindung von) Gefahr(en), Furcht, Bedrängnis empfunden, oft als Plural verwendet. Jacob und Wilhelm Grimm, *Deutsches Wörterbuch*, 16 Bände (1854–1960) <http://woerterbuchnetz.de/DWB/?lemid=GF08540>. Abgerufen 18 Jul 2012.

[9] „Ase, Spännase, ein in Bauernstuben zu sehendes, oben um den Ofen laufendes hölzernes Gestell . . . auch Stange, worauf die Holzspäne, (die Spänne) gelegt werden, die Asenstange in noch ungemauerten Bauernhäusern." Lorenz von Westenrieder, *Handbuch des deutschen Aberglaubens (Glossarium Germanico-Latinum vocum obsoletarum primi et medii aevi: Imprimus Bavaricarum)* München: Verlag J. Zanglianis, 1816: <http://books .google.com/books?id=hZVEAAAAcAAJ&pg=PA26&lpg=PA26&dq=was+ist +eine+asenstange&source=bl&ots=pGG0Ts3KXu&sig=Hem3ePPZJC66SAgJRFyp VS2n-JU&hl=en&sa=X&ei=9jYHUMOFEYeu8AT2s43-CQ&ved=0CEgQ6AEwAw#v =onepage&q=was%20ist%20eine%20asenstange&f=false>. Abgerufen 18 Jul 2012.

## 46 Legends of Witches IV

The following happened to the narrator's mother, from the town of Neumarkt: she was helping an old woman move house from Haag to Neumarkt; on their way, the old one went in front and dropped a piece of bread, as if by accident. The mother picked it up and ate it, but could go no further; she was overcome by fear. They took her to Neumarkt and, because the old woman was reputed to be a Witch, the priest was called. He had her straw mattress searched, and they found on each of the four corners burnt matches, broom-twigs, and corks. The priest ordered everything to be carefully taken out and thrown into the fire. Then the old woman appeared, imploring, for God's sake, not to burn her completely; she would do it no more.

## 47 Legends of Witches V

A farmer's wife living near Neukirchen B. had a daughter of sixteen who had to share her bedroom with the young maidservant. The latter, however, was a Witch who taught the maiden her craft, and also took her to her gatherings where there was much merry music and dance. The maidservant was well-liked in the house because under her touch all seemed to thrive.

One time, the little daughter went to visit the town barber's wife and heard her complain how little milk her cows gave. That, the girl said, would be easy to fix; just give her a tablecloth. She then placed the cloth over one of the rods that were part of the wood-drying frame above the hearth, so that the four corners of the cloth were

und fing an einem derselben zu melken an; es dauerte nicht lange, so wurde ein Weidling voll. Nun wollte sie aufhören. Die Badersleute aber drangen in sie, fortzumelken, obgleich sich das Mädchen wehrte, weil bei längerem Melken die Kuh im Stalle umstehen müsse. Sie melkte also fort, und die Kuh fiel im Stalle.

Jetzt wurden die Eltern gerufen, und die Tochter gestand unbefangen ein, was sie von der Dirn gelernt habe. Zu Hause fand man das Buch, in welchem die Namen derjenigen eingezeichnet waren, die sich als Hexen dem Teufel verbündet hatten.

So wurde die Dirn auf dem Scheiterhaufen verbrannt, dem Mägdlein aber zu Tode Ader gelassen.

## 48 Hexengeschichten VI

In der Nähe von Cham, seitwärts Holzkirchen, ist ein Berg, Blocksberg genannt. Von diesem Berge geht in der Walburginacht um die zwölfte Stunde der Hexenritt aus und endet Morgens bei Gebetläuten.

Einmal gingen mehrere Musikanten von Holzkirchen, wo sie aufgespielt hatten, in dieser Nacht heim; ihr Weg führte sie den Blocksberg vorbei; unten schon hörten sie Musik. Sie gingen den Berg hinauf, statt aber auf eine Ebene zu kommen, stiegen sie auf einen Baum.

Die Musikanten stiegen hernach auch herunter. Wie sie nach Hause kamen, waren sie ganz verkratzt und erkrankten; der eine davon starb. Einige hatten von Holzkirchen her noch Kirchweihnudeln in der Tasche; diese hatten sich in Rossäpfel verwandelt.

## 49 Hexengeschichten VII

Zur Zeit, wo es noch Bären gab, war zu Rittsteig ein Bärenjäger. Einmal in der Walburgisnacht ging er aus auf Bären; da geriet er unversehens in ein Steingespreng, in welchem er sich nicht mehr aus kannte; auch erschien ihm die ganze Gegend fremd, obwohl er darin auf seinen früheren Jagden oft herumgestreift hatte.

hanging from it, and began milking; it was not long before they had a little bucketful [of milk]. Then she wanted to stop. The barber and his wife, however, urged her to go on milking, though the girl protested because the cow would fall over dead in the stable. So, she continued milking, and the cow collapsed in the stable.

Now they called her parents, and the girl innocently admitted all she had learned from the maidservant. At home they found the Book, in which were shown the names of those who had as Witches allied themselves with the Devil.

So the maidservant was burned at the stake, but the maiden was put to death by bloodletting.

### 48 Legends of Witches VI

Close to the town of Cham, by Holzkirchen, there is a mountain called Block Mountain. From this mountain, Witches ride out at midnight on Walpurgis Night and return in the morning when the church bells toll.

One time on this night, several musicians returned home from Holzkirchen, where they had played; their way back led them past the Block Mountain, and soon they heard music. They walked up the mountain, but instead of arriving at level terrain, they climbed a tree.

Afterwards, the musicians climbed down again. When they arrived home, they were all scratched up and fell ill; one of them died of it. Some of them still had pastries [baked for a Holy Day] from the country fair in their pockets; these had turned into horse apples.

### 49 Legends of Witches VII

In the time when bears still roamed the land, there was a bear hunter in the town of Rittsteig. Once he went bear hunting on Walpurgis Night; he strayed unexpectedly into a stony place where he no longer knew his way; also, the whole area seemed strange to him, even though on his earlier hunts he had explored it often.

Nach langem Herumirren kam er endlich auf einen schönen freien Platz, in dessen Mitte ein blaulichtes Feuer matten Schein warf. Er ging darauf zu, und wie er näher kam, sah er einen ungeheuren Hund auf den Hinterbeinen sitzen, und rings um das Feuer viele kleinere Tiere, die er nicht erkennen mochte. Auch hörte er Musik, ohne Musikanten zu gewahren. In einem großen Kreise aber tanzten eine Menge weiblicher Wesen mit fliegenden Haaren einzeln herum. Beherzt, wie er war, ging er gerade auf sie los; der Hund aber gab einen Laut, worauf alles verschwand. Er wollte nun sehen, ob das Feuer keine Glut hinterlassen habe, fand aber nur einen schwarzen Haufen, von dem er nicht wusste, was es sein sollte, und ein weißes Tuch mit eingemerktem Namen. Er wusste auch, wem es gehöre; denn der Name lautete gerade auf jene Frau seines Ortes, welche im Rufe stand, eine Hexe zu sein.

Er behielt dieses aber bei sich und sagte niemanden etwas, bis die Frau starb. So oft sie ihm begegnet war, hatte sie ihm ganz sonderbare falsche Augen gemacht.

Der Mann aber starb, es ist noch nicht lange her, mehr als hundert Jahres alt.

## 50 Hexengeschichten VIII

Es war eine Bäuerin, welche die Hexenkunst verstand. Jedesmal um Mitternacht machte sie ihr Haar. Einmal sahen ihr die neugierigen Knechte durch das Schlüsselloch zu. Da saß die Bäuerin, ihren Kopf auf dem Schoß und die Haare kämmend; statt dessen hatte sie den Kopf eines Geißbockes auf. Hernach nahm sie die Spindel zur Hand, um zu spinnen. Die Spindel aber war so groß, wie ein Wischbaum,[10] und der Asper[11] gleich einem Mühlstein.

---

[10] Wischbaum: lange Stange.
[11] Asper, auch: Spinnwirtel, -windung.

After much wandering, finally he arrived at a beautiful open space, and in the middle of it there was a fire whose flickering bluish light threw faint shadows. He walked towards it and as he got closer, saw a huge dog sitting up on its hindlegs and numerous small animals, which he did not recognize, around the fire. Also he heard music, without any musicians to be seen. But in a large circle, there were many female beings dancing by themselves, with their hair flying. Being courageous, he walked straight towards them; but the dog made a sound, upon which everything disappeared. He then wanted to see if the fire had left no glowing embers, but found only a black heap of something he knew not what, and a white kerchief with a name embroidered on it. He knew also to whom it belonged; for it was the name of that woman in his village who had a reputation as a Witch.

But he kept this to himself and told nobody until the woman died. Every time she had met him, she had looked at him with strange, deceptive eyes.

Yet when the man died—it has not been that long—he was over a hundred years old.

## 50 Legends of Witches VIII

There was a farmer's wife who practiced witchcraft. Every midnight, she did her hair. One time, some curious manservants watched her through the keyhole. There sat the farmer's wife, with her head in her lap, combing her hair; she wore the head of a billygoat instead. After that she picked up a spindle and began spinning. The spindle, however, was as big as a hay-lashing pole[12] and the top whorl was as big as a millstone.

---

[12] German "Wischbaum," used for lashing hay onto a hay trailer.

## 51 Hexengeschichten IX

Eine Bäuerin war in der Hoffnung. Da kam zu ihr eine alte Nachbarin, die als Hexe im Rufe stand, und trug sich als Gevatterin[13] an; denn das Kind sei ein Mädchen. Die Bäuerin aber fürchtete die Frau, und getraute sich nicht, es abzuschlagen.

Als nun die Bäuerin wirklich mit einem Mädchen niederkam, wartete sie der Nachbarin, weil diese versprochen hatte, schon selber zu kommen, wenn es Zeit zur Taufe sei. Sie kam auch richtig. Das Kind wurde getauft und der Kindbettschmaus gehalten. Nach demselben nahm die Gevatterin Abschied, und hieß die Sechswöchnerin einkehren.

Diese ging also, wie sie es nur vermochte, zu ihr auf Besuch. Sie läutete an der Tür; da war der Glockenzug eine Schlange. Sie stieg die Treppe hinan, da tanzten Besen und Ofengabeln mitsammen auf der Stiege. Wie sie an der Stubentür war, sah sie durch das Gutzerl,[14] dass die Gevatterin ihren Kopf im Schoße habe und Läuse suche. Erschrocken stieß sie einen Schrei aus. Das hörte die Gevatterin, setzte ihren Kopf schnell auf und ging ihr entgegen. »Nun Gevatterin, es freut mich,« sprach sie, »dass Ihr Wort haltet und kommt; geht nur herein und setzt euch zum Essen.« Mit diesen Worten setzte sie Speisen auf den Tisch, und lud nochmal ein, zuzulangen, mit den Worten: »Gevatterin esst, Gevatterin trinkt, Gevatterin seid gern da!«

Die Bäuerin aber erwiderte furchtsam: »Mag nicht essen, mag nicht trinken, bin auch nicht gern da!«

Hexe: »Warum?«

Gevatterin: »Ja, mir ist halt allerhand begegnet, wie ich herging.«

Hexe: »Was denn?«

Gevatterin: »Zum ersten, wie ich läutete, ringelte sich eine Schlange an die Glocke hinan.«

Hexe: »Ach, das war ja nur der Zug zu meiner Glocke.«

---

[13] Gevatterin, hier abwechselnd im Sinne von „Taufpatin" und „Schwester" oder „gute Freundin" benutzt.
[14] Gutzerl, auch Türspion.

## 51 Legends of Witches IX

A farmer's wife was expecting a child. An old neighbor woman, who had the reputation of being a Witch, visited and offered to be a godmother of the child; [she did this] because it would be a girl. The farmer's wife was frightened, but feared the woman and dared not refuse.

When the farmer's wife indeed delivered a girl, she awaited the neighbor woman because the latter had promised to come without fail when it was time for the baptism. She came as promised. The child was baptized, and the childbirth feast began. After that, the godmother bade farewell and invited the new mother to visit after six weeks had passed.

The young mother thus went to pay a visit as soon as she was capable of doing so. She rang the doorbell—the bell pull was a snake. She climbed the stairs—there were a broom and some spit forks dancing together. When she arrived at the sitting-room door, through the peephole she saw that the godmother[15] had her head on her lap, and was searching it for lice. Startled, she let out a scream. The godmother heard that, quickly put her head back on [her shoulders], and walked towards her. "Well, sister, I am delighted that you kept your word and came to visit; just come inside and sit down to eat." With these words, she placed the food on the table and invited her again to help herself, with the words, "Sister, eat; sister, drink; sister, be glad to be here!"

The farmer's wife, however, replied timidly, "Don't want to eat, don't want to drink, and I don't feel glad to be here!"

The Witch: "Why?"

The farmer's wife: "Well, I encountered all kinds of things on my way here."

The Witch: "What, then?"

The farmer's wife: "First of all, when I rang, a snake curled up to the bell."

The Witch: "Oh dear, that was just the bellpull for my bell."

---

[15] The German "Gevatterin" can mean both "godmother" and "sister," the latter both in a literal sense and in the sense of meaning "close female friend."

Gevatterin: »Zum zweiten haben auf der Stiege Besen und Ofengabeln mit einander getanzt.«

Hexe: »Warum nicht gar, das waren mein Knecht und meine Dirn, die haben immer etwas miteinander.«

Gevatterin: »Nun, wie ich vor der Stubentür stand, sah ich, dass Ihr den Kopf herunter hattet und Läuse suchtet.«

Da fuhr die Hexe auf und schrie sie an:

»Friss, oder ich zerreiß dich«—und zerriss sie.

## 52 Hexengeschichten X

Es waren einmal zwei Schwestern, und die eine davon hatte ihre Wohnung weit weg im Walde aufgeschlagen, weil sie eine Hexe war. Die andere aber wusste nicht, dass jene eine Hexe sei, und ging, sie im Walde zu besuchen.

Wie sie an den Wald kommt, begegnet ihr ein Wagen mit Totenköpfen beladen. Sie ging vorüber in lauter Angst.

Im Walde stieß sie auf einen zweiten Wagen, voll Totenbeine; sie fürchtete sich noch mehr, ging aber doch ihres Weges fort.

Als sie nun zum Haus im Walde kam, war ein großer Düngerhaufen da, und darauf rauften sich zwei Mistgabeln herum. Sie eilte vorüber, um in die Stube zu kommen; hier sah sie aber eine Frau sitzen, welches einen Totenkopf aufhatte, und sich mit einem Geißfuß kämmte.

Erschrocken über diesen Anblick, wollte sie die Tür schließen, um schnell diesen unheimlichen Ort zu verlassen; aber die Schwester hatte ebenso schnell Totenkopf und Geißfuß weggeworfen, kam ihr freundlich entgegen und nötigte sie, hereinzutreten und sich zum Essen niederzusetzen. Sie konnte aber nicht essen; da fragt die Hexe, warum sie nicht esse.

Schwester: Ach, ich bin noch voll Angst und Schrecken; denn als ich in den Wald kam, begegnete mir ein Wagen voll Totenköpfe.

Hexe: O du närrisch Ding, das waren ja meine Dorschen; iss nur!

Schwester: Ich kann nicht essen, denn als ich weiter im Walde ging, stieß ich auf einen Wagen mit Totenbeinen.

The farmer's wife: "Second, I saw the broom and the spit forks dance together on the stairs."

The Witch: "Why not—those were my man- and maidservants; they always have something going on with each other."

The farmer's wife: "Well, when I was at the door to the sitting room, I saw that you had taken your head off and were searching it for lice."

Whereupon the Witch rose up and screamed at her,

"Eat, or I will rip you apart"—and ripped her apart.

## 52 Legends of Witches X

Once upon a time there were two sisters, and one of them had made her home far away in the forest, for she was a Witch. The other one, however, did not know that she was a Witch and went to visit her in the forest.

When she arrived in the forest, she encountered a cart laden with skulls. She went past it, terribly frightened.

In the forest, she came across a second cart, full of bones; she was frightened even more, but continued on her way.

When she arrived at the house in the forest, there was a big dung heap, and on top of it two pitchforks were fighting. She hurried past them to get to the sitting room; where she saw a woman sitting, wearing a skull, and combing her hair using a goat's foot.

Terrified by this sight, she wanted to close the door so that she might quickly leave this unearthly place, but, just as quickly, her sister had discarded the skull and the goat's foot, then approached her in an amicable manner, compelling her to enter and sit down for a meal. However, she was unable to eat anything; whereupon the Witch asked her why she was not eating.

The sister: "Oh dear, I am still so full of terror and fright; for when I arrived in the forest, I encountered a cart full of skulls."

The Witch: "Oh, you silly thing; those were only my beets; eat now!"

The sister: "I cannot eat, for when I continued on my way through the forest, I encountered a cart full of bones."

Hexe: O, du dummes Ding, das waren ja meine gelben Rüben; iss nur!

Schwester: Ich kann nicht essen.

Hexe: Warum nicht.

Schwester: Ich kann nicht, denn wie ich zum Hause kam, rauften zwei Mistgabeln auf der Düngerstätte.

Hexe: Das waren ja meine Mägde, sei nicht dumm und iss!

Schwester: Ich kann nicht.

Hexe: Warum?

Schwester: Als ich in die Stube trat, sah ich jemanden sitzen mit einem Totenkopf.

Hexe: O du Närrische, das war ja mein Mann. Iss jetzt, oder ich fress dich!

Schwester: Bist du eine Hexe?

Hexe: Ja, ich bin eine Hexe und zerreiße dich.

Bei diesen Worten fuhr sie auf die Schwester zu und wollte sie erwürgen, als drei Jäger, die im Walde sich verirrt hatten, hereintraten.

Sogleich schoss einer davon auf die Hexe, und diese fiel tot nieder. Die andern aber durchsuchten das Haus, nahmen das Wertvolle zu sich und wollten eben fortgehen, als die Mägde hereinkamen, welche von der Hexe in Mistgabeln waren verwandelt worden, nun aber durch den Tod derselben ihre Erlösung gefunden hatten.

## 53 Hexengeschichten XI

Eine Hexe beichtete ihren Stand einem Klostergeistlichen, erklärte ihm aber auf Abmahnen, dass ihren Versammlungen die Muttergottes leibhaftig anwohne; er möge sie nur bei der nächsten Ausfahrt begleiten, so könne er sich selber überzeugen.

Es setzte sich daher der fromme Mann am bestimmten Tage mit der Hexe in einen Wagen, und beide fuhren dahin durch die Luft über Berg und Tal. Da hörte er Geläute, der Wagen senkte sich und stand in Mitte einer prachtvollen Kirche, angefüllt mit einer zahllosen Menge. In der Tat wandelte auch die Mutter Gottes leibhaftig auf dem Altare herum, voll Glanz und Schönheit. Doch meinte der Pater, für eine Mutter Gottes wäre sie doch etwas

The Witch: "Oh, you foolish thing; those were only my carrots; eat now!"

The sister: "I cannot eat."

The Witch: "Why not?"

The sister: "I cannot, for when I arrived at your house, there were two pitchforks fighting on the dung heap."

The Witch: "Those were only my maidservants; eat and don't be stupid!"

The sister: "I cannot."

The Witch: "Why?"

The sister: "When I entered the sitting room, I saw someone sitting there, with a skull.

The Witch: "Oh, you foolish thing, that was only my husband. Now eat, or I will eat you!"

The sister: "Are you a Witch?"

The Witch: "Yes, I am a Witch and I am going to rip you apart."

With these words, she ran at her sister, intending to strangle her, when three huntsmen entered who had lost their way in the woods.

Instantly, one of them shot at the Witch, and she fell dead to the floor. The others, however, searched the house and took all the valuables, and were just about to leave when the maidservants, who had been turned into pitchforks by the Witch but now through her death had found their release, came into the house.

## 53 Legends of Witches XI

A Witch confessed her condition to a priest at a monastery, but when reproved, explained to him that the Mother of God appeared in the flesh at their gatherings; he might simply accompany her on her next ride, so that he could see for himself.

Thus, on the day chosen, the pious man sat down in a cart with the Witch, and they both rode thither through the air, over mountains and valleys. Then he heard bells tolling, the cart descended and came to a halt in the center of a magnificent church that was filled with a countless crowd. And indeed, the Mother of God, in the flesh, was promenading on the altar, full of splendor and beauty. The Father mused, however, that she was dressed somewhat too

zu üppig und verführerisch gekleidet, sprang auf den Altar und hob ihr ein bisher verborgen gehaltenes Kruzifix mit den Worten unter die Augen: »Bist du die Mutter des Herrn, so sieh hier deinen Sohn!«

Da erlöschten wie mit einem Male sämtliche Lichter, und dichte Finsternis und Grabesstille lagerten ringsum. Der Pater stieß sich an rauhen Steinen, und als es gegen den Tag ging, befand er sich im Gemäuer eines Galgens.

### 54 Von Katzen I[16]

In der Oberpfalz befindet sich auf dem Lande die Düngerstätte mit der Odlhöhle vor der Tür des Hauses; so auch vor dem Wirtshause zu Oberzell.—Der Nachtwächter hörte einmal vor der zwölften Stunde, als er im Orte zum Ausrufen ging, ein ungewöhnliches Heulen, Miauen und Klagen, als wenn tausend Katzen beisammen wären und sich herumbalgten. Neugierig ging er dem Lärmen nach, bis er sie vor dem Wirtshause traf; da nahm er seinen Wächterspieß und schlug unter die Katzen. Über dem Lärmen waren aber auch die Leute aus dem Wirtshause aufgestanden, um nachzuschauen, was es gebe; da erblickten sie eine Menge Katzen, meistens rote, obwohl im ganzen Orte keine von solcher Farbe war, und mitten unter ihnen den Nachtwächter, der um Hilfe rief.

Als sie aber hinzukamen, lag er schon tot in der Odlhöhle und zwei der Katzen auf ihm, welche sich flüchteten, da es eben zwölf Uhr schlug. Der Nachtwächter wurde leblos herausgezogen.

Allgemein glaubt man dort, dass es Hexen gewesen, welche den Mann, der sie beleidigte, umgebracht.

---

[16] „Überhaupt finden sich Katzen gerne mit Hexen zusammen; sie sind die eigentlichen Hexentiere. Man scheut sie deshalb, und da in den Raubnächten die Hexen besondere Gewalt haben, setzt man die Katzen in dieser Zeit vorsorglich nach Gebetläuten vor die Haustür." *Sitten und Sagen*, Bd. 1: 358.

lavishly and seductively for the Mother of God, jumped onto the altar, and raised up to her eyes a crucifix that had been hitherto concealed, with the following words: "If you are the Lord's Mother, behold here your Son!"

Thereupon all at once all the lights went out, and total darkness with the silence of the grave ensued. The Father stumbled against rough stones, and when daylight appeared, he found himself inside the walls of a gallows yard.

### 54 Of Cats I[17]

In the Upper Palatinate, one finds in the countryside that the dungheap together with the cesspit is located in front of the entrance to the house; as it was in front of the inn in the town of Oberzell—The night watchman once heard, just before midnight as he walked around town announcing the hours, an unusual howling, meowing, and wailing, as if a thousand cats had gathered and were tussling with each other. Curious, he followed the noise until he arrived at the inn; there he took his watchman's spear and used it to club the cats. Because of all the noise, people had arisen from the inn to see what was going on; there they saw a crowd of cats, mostly red ones, even though there were none of that color in the whole town, and in the midst of it all the night watchman, shouting for help.

But when help arrived, he was already dead in the cesspit, with two of the cats of top of him, which escaped just as the clock struck midnight. The night watchman was pulled out, lifeless.

Popularly, it is believed there that Witches had murdered the man who had offended them.

---

[17] "In general, cats enjoy the company of Witches; they are the original Witch animals. People shy away from them for that reason, and since in the Robbing Nights Witches assume special powers, as a precaution cats are put out of the house after the evening prayer tolling." *Sitten und Sagen*, vol. 1: 358.

## 55 Von Katzen II

Ein Geistlicher hielt sich einen Kater; groß und schön war sie seine einzige Freude, daher auch bei dem Essen stets mit auf dem Tische zu Gaste.

Eines Abends wurde der Geistliche zu einem Kranken gerufen. Als er in der Nacht wieder heimkehrte, sah er in einem Stadel vor dem Dorfe Licht und hörte Musik. Er ging drauf zu, was sah er? Sein Kater saß da und geigte, andere Katzen aber sangen und tanzten.

Als es wieder Essenszeit wurde, war der Kater der erste auf dem Tische; da sagte der Pfarrer, indem er ihn streichelte: »Kodl,[18] Kodl, wo bist du gestern gewesen?« Er hatte aber die Worte noch nicht aus dem Munde, als die Katze schon zum Fenster hinaus war und sich nicht mehr sehen ließ.

## 56 Von Katzen III

Ein Bürger aus Neustadt ging nachts von einem Dorfe nach Hause; auf dem Wege sah er in einem Felde Katzen in Frauenkleidern an einem Tische Mahlzeit halten; er trat hin und wurde von ihnen mit Kücheln beschenkt. Des andern Tages, als er zu Hause aufstand, gedachte er der Gabe; er langte die Kücheln aus seinen Taschen heraus, und siehe, es waren Kuhfladen.

## 57 Von Katzen IV

Bei einem Müller sprachen öfter Mühlknechte, die keinen Platz hatten, um Arbeit zu; so viele aber hineingingen, kam keiner mehr heraus, und allgemein hieß es, die Müllerin sei eine Hexe. Da kam auch einmal ein Mühlknappe, um Arbeit zu suchen; er war aber gewarnt worden, und als er schlafen ging, nahm er ein geweihtes Licht brennend zur Seite, einen Säbel zu Kopfhaupten. Als es elf Uhr schlug, sprangen drei Katzen, eine schwarze, eine graue, eine weiße, auf den Tisch. Eine sagte zur andern: »hau das Licht ab!« aber es konnte keine hinan, denn das Licht war geweiht.

---

[18] Kodl: oberpfälzisch für „Kater."

### 55 Of Cats II

A priest had a tomcat; large and beautiful, it was his only joy, and so he was always a guest on the table during meals.

One evening, the priest was called to an ill man. When he returned home that night, he noticed lights in a barn outside the village and heard music. He went closer, and what did he see? His tomcat was sitting there, playing the fiddle, and other cats were singing and dancing.

When the time for the next meal had come, the tomcat was the first on the table and the priest, while stroking him, asked, "Oh tomcat, tomcat, where were you yesterday?" The words had hardly left his mouth when the cat jumped out through the window and was seen no more.

### 56 Of Cats III

One night, a citizen of the town of Neustadt was on his way home from a village; on the way he saw in a field there were cats in women's clothing sitting at a table, sharing a meal. He stepped closer and was given pastries by them. The next day, when he woke up, he remembered the gift; he reached into his pocket and, lo and behold, they were cow pies.

### 57 Of Cats IV

At a certain miller's abode, miller's servants who had no employment often asked for work; but however many went in, none of them left, and it was common opinion that the miller's wife was a Witch. Once a miller's apprentice arrived, seeking work; but he had been warned, and before he went to sleep, he placed a burning holy candle by his side, and a sword at the top of his head. When it struck eleven o'clock, three cats jumped onto the table; one black, one gray, one white. One said to the others, "Extinguish the light!" but none could get near it, for the candle was holy.

Da wollte die Weiße mit aller Gewalt hinhauen; der Knappe aber nahm seinen Säbel und schlug ihr die Pfote ab, worauf alle drei zum Fenster hinaus flüchteten.

Am nächsten Morgens ging er zum Müller hinunter, der sich freute, ihn zu sehen, und dann hinausging, um bei der Müllerin Suppe für ihn zu bestellen. Doch bald kehrte er mit den Worten zurück: »Ich weiß nicht, was die Frau hat; sie liegt noch im Bette und gibt mir keine Antwort.« »Das glaube ich wohl,« erwiderte der Knecht, »geh nur wieder hin zu ihr und schau unter das Bett!« Da tat es der Müller, und die Müllerin hatte nur eine Hand und das Bett war voll Blut.

### 58 Eine Drachengeschichte[19]

Am Kirchweihsamstag in Neubäu sah man eine Weberin, die im Verdachte der Hexenkunst stand, den Drachen im Schwarzenwührberge bestellen. Kaum war sie zu Hause, so kam er in Gestalt einer roten flügellosen Schlange so groß wie ein Wischbaum[20] über den Kamin des Häuschens dieser Frau und fuhr sich ringelnd hinein. Nach langem Verweilen sah man ihn wieder herausfahren; er hatte ihr Schmalz zum Küchelbacken gebracht.

Diese Frau betete nie, machte kein Kreuz, konnte niemanden in die Augen schauen, wurde in der Beichte auch niemals losgesprochen. Sie ging nur nachts um Futter. Immer verkaufte sie Schmalz, und hatte doch nur eine Kuh. Dieses Schmalz ergab dem Käufer nicht. Auf dem Miste vor ihrem Hause sah man gar oft von jenen Fladen, gelblich weiß und in der Größe hölzerner Teller, welche der Drache speien soll, als Überreste seines Raubes.

Wo man solche Fladen sieht, geht es nicht recht zu.

---

[19] „In enger Verbindung mit der Hexe, als ihr Helfershelfer, steht der Drache." *Sitten und Sagen*, Bd. 1: 393.
[20] Vgl. auch Fußnote 12, Seite 65.

Thereupon the white one wanted to jump onto it with all its might, but the apprentice took his sword and cut off its paw, whereupon all three fled out the window.

On the next morning, he went down to the miller, who was pleased to see him and then stepped out to order soup for him from his wife. In a little while he came back, however, with the words, "I do not know what is wrong with my wife; she is still in bed and does not reply to me." "I can well believe that," replied the apprentice. "Just go back up to her and look under the bed. That is what the miller did, and the miller's wife had only one hand and the bed was full of blood.

## 58 A Dragon Tale[21]

On Parish Fair Saturday in Neubäu, people saw a weaver, who had the reputation of practicing witchcraft, invite the Dragon from the Schwarzenwühr Mountain to her house. No sooner was she home when he arrived in the shape of a red, wingless Serpent, the size of a hay-lashing pole, above the chimney of the woman's little house, and wriggled down into it. After a long visit, it was seen flying out again; it had brought her butterfat to make pastries.

This woman never prayed, never crossed herself, was unable to meet anybody's eyes, and also never received absolution in the confessional. She went out for fodder only at night. She was always selling butterfat, yet she had only one cow. This butterfat yielded the buyer nothing. On the dungheap in front of her house often one could see those flat cakes, yellow-white and large as wooden plates, which the Dragon spews up as remants of his robberies.

Where one sees such flat cakes, something is not right.

---

[21] "Closely connected to the Witch is the Dragon, her accomplice." *Sitten und Sagen*, vol. 1: 393.

# THE ELEMENTS:
## EARTH I—FRUITS OF THE EARTH

From time immemorial, the fruits of the Earth have been of the utmost importance for humanity. As in ancient times, fruits and vegetables, bread, dairy products, fish, and meat, were still the basic components of food for the people in the Upper Palatinate in Schönwerth's time.

In the Upper Palatinate particularly, though, the ground was rocky and hard and did not yield much besides potatoes, beets, and barley, so farmers had to struggle with the soil to end up with full stomachs. That struggle made the people always ready to suspect hostile forces behind pestilence and adverse weather (such as drought, flooding, hail, ice storms, and frost), as Schönwerth points out:

> Earth was given to man in subservience by the Lord; its produce and products, earned by him by the sweat of his brow, are supposed to feed and clothe him . . . However, even here the Enemy intrudes: whatever man intends to create, he always feels that he has to wrestle, fight, and win in order to generate it.[1]

---

[1] „Die Erde wurde von dem Herrn der Welt dem Menschen in Dienstbarkeit gegeben: ihre Erzeugnisse, im Schweiße des Angesichts gewonnen, sollen ihn nähren und kleiden. . . . Aber auch hier drängt sich der Feind ein: was auch der Mensch schaffen will, immer fühlt er, dass er ringen, streiten, siegen müsse, um es hervorzubringen." *Sitten und Sagen*, Bd. 1: 40.

## 59 Geschichten von den Früchten der Erde: Brot[2]

Es war eine Frau, dessen Kind sich verunreinigt hatte; die Frau, übermütig, reinigt es mit Brot. Da erschien ihr ein Engel von Gott gesendet, und strafte sie ob des Frevels, und er ging hinaus auf den Acker, wo die Ähren von der Erde auf wuchsen, und fing eine Strupfe der Ähren und begann von unten nach oben zu streifen. Da fiel die Frau auf die Knie und bat den Engel um Schonung, wenn auch nicht für sie, möge er doch so viel am Halme stehen lassen, dass Hund und Katze davon bekommen könnten. Da erbarmte sich der selige Geist und hielt oben an der Spitze des Halmes inne, und seitdem wächst die Ähre nur oben am Halm.

Seitdem wird aber auch von dem ersten Brot der neuen Frucht das erste Stückchen dem Hunde und der Katze des Hauses gegeben.

## 60 Geschichten von den Früchten der Erde: Rüben[3]

Von Alten-Veldorf ging ein armes Ehepaar aufs Rübenstehlen, sie mit der Kürm auf dem Rücken, er mit dem Schubkarren. Der Schubkarren ist aber nicht geschmiert gewesen, und knarzte bei jedem Umgange des Rades: »afs Roubmsteln, afs Roubmsteln.«[4]

Als sie nun an dem Rübenacker angelangt waren, stellte er den Schubkarren nieder; das Geräusch hatte aber einen Hasen, der gerade hier in der saß, aufgejagt. Das gute Ehepaar hielt den Hasen für den Feldhüter, packte schleunigst zusammen und machte sich quer über den Bifang[5] davon, während der Schubkarren auf der holperigen Bahn um so mehr knarzte: »I ho koiñ Roubm, I ho koiñ Roubm.«[6]

---

[2] „Das Brot ist Gabe Gottes, und darum in Ehren zu halten . . . Brot hat überhaupt die Kraft, den Zauber zu bannen." *Sitten und Sagen*, Bd. 1: 403.

[3] „Wenn man im Herbste des Weges geht, so steht es einem frei, zur augenblicklichen Stillung von Hunger oder Durst, eine oder die andere Rübe aus dem nächsten besten Rübenacker auszuziehen; daher der Reim: Eine: ist keine/ Zwei: ist erst eine/ Drei: sind frei Vier: sind lieb/ Fünf: ist ein Dieb." *Sitten und Sagen*, Bd. 1: 409.

[4] Umgangssprachlich; auf hochdeutsch: „zum Rübenstehlen, zum Rübenstehlen."

[5] „Bifang ist eine altdeutsche Bezeichnung (von befangen: umfangen, einschließen) für ein eingefriedetes Feld, gewöhnlich ein schmales Ackerbeet." *Enzyklo Online Enzyklopädie* <http://www.enzyklo.de/Begriff/Bifang>. Abgerufen 20 Jul 2012.

[6] Umgangssprachlich; auf hochdeutsch: „Ich hab' keine Rüben, ich hab' keine Rüben."

## 59 Tales about the Fruits of the Earth: Bread[7]

There was a woman whose child had soiled itself; the carefree woman cleans it up with bread. An angel, sent by the Lord, appeared and punished her for the sacrilege; going out to the field where the ears of corn grew from the Earth, he took hold of one of the ears of corn and started to strip the stalk from the bottom up. The wife, upon this, fell to her knees and begged the angel to spare them, even if it were not for her, but that he might leave enough on the stalk for the dogs and cats to have to eat. The blessed spirit had mercy and stopped stripping right at the top of the stalk, and since that time, ears of corn only grow on the top of a stalk.

Since then, the first little piece of the first loaf of broad of a new harvest is fed to the dog and cat of each house.

## 60 Tales about the Fruits of the Earth: Turnips[8]

From the town of Old Veldorf, a poor married couple went to steal turnips, she with a back carrier, he with a wheelbarrow. Since the wheelbarrow was not greased, however, it squeaked with every rotation of the wheel: "Let's go steal turnips, let's go steal turnips."

When they finally arrived at the turnip field, he set down the wheelbarrow; however, the noise made a rabbit that had been sitting there leap away with a start. The good couple took the rabbit for a field guard, packed up everything immediately and made off across the enclosed[9] field, while the wheelbarrow squeaked even louder on the bumpy path: "Ain't got no turnips, ain't got no turnips."

---

[7] "Bread is a gift of God, and thus must be honored . . . In general, bread has the power to dispel magic." *Sitten und Sagen*, vol. 1: 403.

[8] "Walking about in the fall, custom allows one to pull out one or another turnip from the next best turnip field to quench one's immediate hunger or thirst; thus the rhyme: One is none/ two is one / three are free / four are dear / five—you are a thief!" *Sitten und Sagen*, vol. 1: 409.

[9] "[usually passive] ~ sth (in / with sth) to build a wall, fence, etc. around sth: The yard had been enclosed with iron railings. The land was enclosed in the seventeenth century (= in Britain, when public land was made private property)." *Oxford Advanced Learners Dictionary* <http://oald8.oxfordlearnersdictionaries.com/dictionary/enclose>. Accessed 10 Nov 2012.

### 61 Geschichten von den Früchten der Erde: Klee[10]

Zu Hochau, bei Waldmünchen, tanzte einer wunderbar auf dem Seil, und die Zuschauer waren vor Entzücken außer sich. Da kam eine Dirn des Weges, eine Kürm mit Gras auf dem Rücken, unter welchem sich vierblättriger Klee befand. Diese fing zu lachen an, und rief aus: »Sind doch die Leute so närrisch und schauen hinauf, während der Mann auf der Straße geht.« Darüber erboste der Seiltänzer und machte durch seine Künste, dass es der Dirne schien, als ginge sie tief in Wasser; sie hob daher ihre Kleider auf, und alle Umstehenden begannen zu lachen.

Nach einer andern Lesart sagte die Magd: »Es geht ja nur ein Hahn auf dem Seile.«

---

[10] „Wer vierblätterigen Klee unverdanks gefunden bei sich trägt, sieht alle verzauberten Sachen und kennt die bösen Leute." *Sitten und Sagen*, Bd. 1: 410.

## 61 Tales about the Fruits of the Earth: Clover[11]

In the town of Hochau, close to Waldmünchen, a man was dancing wonderfully on a tightrope, and all the onlookers were besides themselves with rapture. A maidservant came along, carrying a back carrier laden with grass amongst which there was also a four-leaf clover. She began to laugh and called out, "People are really foolish, looking up while the man is walking on the street." Infuriated by this, the tightrope artist put a spell on her so that it appeared to the maidservant as if she were walking in deep water; she therefore lifted up her skirts, and all the onlookers began to laugh.

According to another version, the maidservant said, "That is just a rooster on the tightrope."

---

[11] "If you, by chance, find a four-leaf clover and carry it with you, you will be able to see all enchanted things and recognize evil people." *Sitten und Sagen*, vol. 1: 410.

# THE ELEMENTS:
## LIGHT—THE SUN AND THE MOON

Schönwerth awards the highest place in the natural order of things to the Sun and the Moon:

> Accordingly and rightfully so, Light appears to be the highest Element, and as such it already enjoyed divine worship with the pagan people of ancient times. For the Germanic people, light is personified by these two large celestial bodies that divide off time, the Sun and the Moon, and is thus separated into a female [half] and a male half of the godhead of light.[1]

Almost all peoples have myths that tell of the Sun and Moon. They are described as brother and sister, or husband and wife, or rivals or collaborators, or just good friends. In some tales they symbolize genders, in others, authority. All the tales acknowledge their coexistence; many seek to explain a supposed mutual dependency. Several of Schönwerth's stories about the Sun and the Moon have this mutual dependency as their theme.

But beyond symbolism, the Sun and the Moon affect people's lives directly. They have magical powers; the Sun shines its light

---

[1] „Licht erscheint sonach mit Recht als das höchste der Elemente, und hat als solches schon bei den heidnischen Urvölkern göttlicher Verehrung genossen. Dem Germanen verkörpert sich das Licht in den beiden großen Gestirnen, welche die Zeit abteilen, in Sonne und Mond, und wird somit in eine weibliche und in eine männliche Hälfte der Lichtgottheit gespalten." *Sitten und Sagen*, vol. 2: 12.

on crimes, and the Moon awakens longing in human hearts. Also in Schönwerth's collection, we learn about "The Man in the Moon" and the moonstruck virgin, and of girls and women who, with varying results, spin or attempt to spin lunar threads.

## 62 Die Hochzeit von Sonne und Mond

Sonne und Mond sind Frau und Mann. Als sie Hochzeit hielten, tat der Mond, der stets als etwas kalt und langweilig gilt, in der Brautnacht der feurigen begehrenden Braut nicht zur Genüge: er hätte lieber geschlafen. Das verdross die Sonne und sie schlug dem Manne eine Wette vor, dass, wer von ihnen zuerst erwachen würde, das Recht haben solle, bei Tage zu scheinen: dem Trägen gehöre die Nacht. Würden sie beide zugleich wach werden, sollten sie fortan nebeneinander am Himmel glänzen. Da lachte der Mond gar einfältig vor sich hin: er ging die Wette ein, weil er nicht glauben wollte, dass er verlieren könne, und lachend schlief er ein.

Davon hat er das Lachen behalten. Die Sonne aber ließ der Ärger nicht lange ruhen; schon vor zwei Uhr wach, zündete sie der Welt das Licht auf und weckte den frostigen Mond, und hielt ihm ihren Sieg vor und zugleich die Strafe, dass sie nun nie mehr eine Nacht mitsammen verbringen würden.

Darum habe sie die Wette gesetzt und mit einem Eid bekräftigt, dass sie gebunden sei und nicht schwach werden könne. Seitdem leuchtet der Mond bei Nacht, die Sonne bei Tag.

Die Sonne aber reute bald der Schwur, den sie in der Hitze des Zornes getan; sie liebt ja den Mond. Und auch dieser fühlt sich immer zur Braut gezogen: er hielt ja die Wette für Spiel, für Neckerei, und Scherz war es, dass er sich so kalt gezeigt. Daher möchten sich beide gar gerne wieder vereinen. Sie kommen sich auch öfter näher und treffen manchmal zusammen; es ist dieses die Zeit der Sonnenfinsternisse. Weil sie aber mit gegenseitigen Vorwürfen beginnen, keines die Schuld der Trennung tragen will, so geraten sie hintereinander zum Streite; doch keines wird Herr. Die Zeit, welche ihnen zur Versöhnung geboten ist, läuft ab, und es kommt die Stunde wieder, wo die Sonne ihrem Schwur gemäß wandern muss. Blutrot von Zorn macht sie sich auch auf den Weg. Hätten sie nicht gestritten, wären sie vereiniget worden. Bis der Zorn sich legt, vergeht wieder geraume Weile, erst eine neue Finsternis zeigt an, dass sie sich wieder getroffen. Aber immer wieder wird diese Zeit nicht benützt.

## 62 The Marriage of Sun and Moon

The Sun and the Moon are husband and wife. When they married, the Moon, who has always been thought of as acting a bit cold and boring, did not satisfy the hot and desiring bride; he preferred to sleep instead. This annoyed the Sun, and she offered her husband the following bet: whichever one would awake first should have the right to shine during the day; to the lazy one would belong the night. Should they awaken at the same time, then they would shine side by side in the sky for all eternity. Thereupon the Moon smiled to himself in a silly manner; he agreed to the bet not willing to believe that he could lose it, and he fell asleep, smiling.

From that, the Moon kept his smile. The Sun, however, was restless because of her anger; awakening before two o'clock, she lit the lights for the world and woke up the frosty Moon, presenting him with her victory and at the same time with the punishment—that they would nevermore spend a night together.

That is why she formulated the bet and affirmed it with an oath so that she would be bound by it, and not relent. Since then, the Moon shines at night and the Sun during the day.

However, the Sun soon regretted the oath she had made in the heat of anger, for she really loves the Moon. And the latter also always feels drawn to his bride; indeed, he had taken the bet for a game, for banter; and had pretended to be cold in jest. Thus, both would like very much to reunite. Often they come closer and sometimes even meet; these are the times of eclipses. But because they start reproaching each other and neither wants to accept blame for the separation, they end up quarreling; however, neither one is the winner. The time that is allotted to them for their reconciliation runs out, and again the hour arrives when the Sun, according to her oath, must continue her journey. Crimson with anger, she goes on her way. If they had not quarreled, they would have been reunited. Until her anger has abated, considerable time will go by once again; only the next eclipse will show that they have met once more. But again and again, that time is not used.

So ist die Sonne immer heiß vor Liebeszorn: manchmal aber, wenn sie so allein wandelt, sieht sie ihr Unrecht ein: dann weint sie blutige Tränen und geht blutrot unter.

Aber auch der Mond empfindet Trauer und Leid, dass er zur Sonne nicht kann; darum nimmt er ab, bis er zur kleinsten Sichel wird; wird er nach und nach voll, so hofft er; ist er aber voll, sieht er sich getäuscht und nimmt wieder ab. – Von seiner unglücklichen Liebe ist er weich gestimmt: daher sein Licht so mild und melancholisch. Daher klagen ihm auch unglücklich Liebende ihr Leid.

### 63 Die Sonne sieht alles[2]

In Wersberg erschlug ein Wirt seinen Gläubiger, einen Juden, an einem abgelegenen Ort. Umsonst hatte der Jude ihm gedroht, es werde, wenn auch keines Menschen Auge die Tat gesehen, doch die Sonne den Täter verraten. Der Wirt lachte nur. Lange Zeit blieb der Mord unentdeckt. Eines Morgens aber lag der Wirt im Bette, als die Sonne gar herrlich durch die Fenster der Kammer hereinblickte. Da fing er für sich hin zu lachen an. Seine Ehehälfte bemerkte dieses und fragte um die Ursache, und wurde in ihrer Neugierde um so dringender mit Fragen, je weniger ihr Mann dem Wunsche entsprechen wollte. Nach langem Bitten endlich erhielt sie das Geständnis der Tat.

Bald darnach gerieten die beiden Gatten über eine Kleinigkeit in Streit. Der Mann droht der Frau, sich an ihr zu vergreifen. Da entfuhren der Unbedachtsamen die Worte: Willst du mir es auch machen, wie du dem Juden getan?—Dieses wurde gehört und führte zur Entdeckung und Bestrafung des Mörders. –

---

[2] „Ein anderer Überrest der göttlichen Verehrung der Sonne liegt in der Sitte, dass der Landmann, wenn er früh Morgens auf dem Wege sich befindet und die Sonne aufgehen sieht, den Hut abnimmt. In der Sonne ist ein Auge, welches auf die Erde niederschaut und alles sieht: von ihm gehen die Strahlen aus, welche der Sonne den leuchtenden Glanz geben . . . Dass die Sonne alles sieht, liegt im Sprichworte: ‚es ist nichts so fein gesponnen, es kommt dennoch an die Sonnen.'" *Sitten und Sagen*, Bd. 2: 51.

Thus the Sun is hot with angry love; but sometimes, when she wanders all alone, she realizes her injustice; then she weeps bloody tears and sets, crimson.

However, the Moon also feels sorrow and pain that he is unable to meet with the Sun; he therefore wanes until he is the smallest of crescents; while he waxes, he is hopeful; as soon as he is full, he feels deceived and starts waning again.—His unhappy love makes him softhearted; thus his light is mild and melancholy. And therefore unhappy lovers complain to him about their sorrows.

## 63 The Sun Sees Everything[3]

In the town of Wernsberg, an innkeeper slew his creditor, a Jew, in a secluded spot. In vain, the Jew had threateningly told him that, even if no human eye had seen the deed, the Sun would betray the perpetrator. The innkeeper simply laughed. For a long time, the murder remained undiscovered. One morning, the innkeeper was lying in bed, when the Sun shone quite splendidly through the window into the bedchamber. Thereupon, he started laughing to himself. His better half noticed this and asked for the reason, and the more her curiosity made her insistent, the less her husband wanted to meet her request. After she begged him for a long time, she finally received his confession of the deed.

Soon thereafter, both spouses began to argue over a trifling matter. The man threatens to harm his wife. Imprudently, the following words escaped her: "Do you want to do to me what you did to the Jew?" Someone overheard this and it led to the discovery and punishment of the murderer.

---

[3] "Another remnant of divine Sun worship can be seen in the countryfolk's custom of raising their hats to the Sun upon setting out for their journeys when seeing the Sun rise. Inside the Sun there is an eye which looks down on Earth and notices everything: the rays that give the Sun its radiant shine originate from this eye . . . That the Sun sees everything is expressed in the saying, 'Nothing is so finely spun that it can escape the Sun.'" *Sitten und Sagen*, vol. 2: 51.

## 64 Die Bäuerin und der Mond

Eine Bäuerin hatte in Gewohnheit, die Samstagnächte fleißig bei Mondschein zu spinnen. Da warf ihr der Mond einmal sechs Spindeln zu mit dem Gebote, sie binnen einer Stunde voll zu spinnen. Die Frau war aber klug und spann um jede Spindel nur einen Faden, und als der Mond um zwölf Uhr wieder kam, lagen die Spindeln mit einem Faden auf dem Boden. Der Mond hob sie auf und sagte:»Das ist dein Glück, dass du auf diesen Gedanken kamst; aber lasse es dir gesagt sein: Der Tag gehört dein, die Nacht mein.«

## 65 Die Spinnerin im Mond[4]

Die Tochter eines armen Beamten wurde zur Doppelwaise. Um ihrem Bräutigam einige Aussteuer zuzubringen, trat sie als Kammermädchen in Dienste. Man ließ ihr aber keine Zeit, an ihrer Ausfertigung zu arbeiten, und so spann sie nachts für sich bei Mondlicht, insbesondere in den Samstagnächten, in welchen man ohnehin nicht spinnen soll. Dabei machte sie das Fenster auf. Immer freundlicher schien der Mond herein, immer weicher wurde sie. Die Blässe erhöhte ihre Schönheit. Oft wurde sie darüber von ihrer Frau getadelt und spottend die Spinnerin im Monde gescholten. Sie aber fühlte sich immer mehr vom Monde angezogen: denn der Mond zieht alles an sich, besonders Mädchenherzen, weil er selber so unglücklich in seiner Liebe zur Sonne ist.

Einmal schlief sie ermattet von des Tages Mühen ein und träumte, sie werde in den Mond hinübergetragen. Als sie erwachte, befand sie sich wirklich im Monde. Sie ist nun die Spinnerin im Monde, und noch sieht man sie darin mit dem Rädchen.

---

[4] „Der Mond zieht alles an sich, bringt alles in Bewegung." *Sitten und Sagen*, Bd. 2: 62.

## 64 The Farmer's Wife and the Moon

A farmer's wife had the habit of spinning industriously by the light of the Moon on Saturday nights. Once the Moon tossed her six spindles with the request to fill up all six of them with thread within an hour. The woman, however, was cunning and spun only one piece of thread around each spindle, and when the Moon returned at twelve o'clock, the spindles lay on the floor, with one piece of thread on each. The Moon picked them up and said, "It is fortunate that you had this idea; but let it be declared to you: the day is yours, the night is mine."

## 65 The Spinstress in the Moon[5]

The daughter of a poor civil servant became a double orphan. To acquire some dowry for her bridegroom, she started working as a chambermaid. However, she didn't have time to work on her bridal ensemble, and so she began to spin alone by herself every night in the moonlight, particularly on Saturday nights, when one is not supposed to spin at all. While spinning, she opened the window. The Moon shone inside, friendlier and friendlier, and she became softer and softer. The paleness improved her beauty. Often, her mistress rebuked her over this and, mockingly, chided her as "Spinstress in the Moon." She, however, felt drawn to the Moon more and more, for the Moon draws everything to it, particularly the hearts of maidens, because he is so unhappy himself over his love for the Sun.

Once she fell asleep, worn out by the day's toils, and dreamed that she was carried up to the Moon. When she awoke, she was indeed in the Moon. She is now the Spinstress in the Moon, and one can still see her there with her little spinning wheel.

---

[5] "The Moon draws everything to it, sets everything in motion." *Sitten und Sagen*, vol. 2: 62.

Der Rocken nimmt mit dem Mondeswechsel ab und zu, aber immer bleibt noch etwas Flachs daran. Sie darf mit dem Rocken nicht zu Ende kommen. Ist einmal der Flachs alle gesponnen, geht die Welt unter. Manchmal ist der Rocken sehr dick angelegt. Da wird die Spinnerin müde beim Spinnen und ihr Köpfchen neigt sich und ihre Haare streifen an des Flachses Haar, wodurch der Mond verdunkelt wird. Dann ist Mondsfinsternis. Aber sie wird es bald inne und fährt zurück: daher endet die Mondsfinsternis oft so plötzlich. Manchmal spinnt sie gedankenlos ihre langen Haare mit hinein, und wenn sie es empfindet durch den Schmerz, den das Einlaufen des Haares in das Rädchen verursacht, so hat sie zu tun, es zu lösen; dann dauert die Finsternis länger.

Als die Sonne am Morgen darnach aufging, wurde sie überrascht, ein Mädchen im Monde zu sehen; sie glaubte dieselbe glücklich in Liebesglück, weil sie das Köpfchen so sinnig zur Arbeit neigte. Auf einmal hörte sie den Bräutigam der Maid um sein Liebchen klagen. Er war vor Klagen matt im Walde niedergesunken und entschlafen, als sie Abends beim Niedergehen die Erde streifte und ihn mit auf und zu sich empor nahm. Beim Auf- und Untergange der Sonne erkannte er aber seine Braut im Monde, und diese ihn, und beide waren voll Sehnsucht nach einander. Das sah auch der Mond zu seinem neuen Schmerze; die Sonne war ihm untreu geworden und auch die Maid, die er bei sich hatte, wollte seiner nicht gedenken. Nicht selten weint er dann. Die Zähren, welche er vergießt, sind die abschießenden Sterne, die Sternschnuppen. Wo sie auffallen, findet man einen Kreuzer, der nie weicht, so oft man ihn auch ausgibt, oder ein Zettelchen, welches in Versen die Zukunft des Finders enthält.

## 66 Der Mond im Brunnen[6]

Eine Dirn holte zum Einmachen des Brotes Wasser aus dem mondbeleuchteten Brunnen. Als sie gebacken und eingeschossen hatte,

---

[6] „Man soll auch nicht da Wasser schöpfen, wo der Mond sich spiegelt: man schöpft sonst den Mond mit. Die Mädchen giessen das so geschöpfte Wasser wieder aus, und holen es lieber an anderer, dunkler Stelle." *Sitten und Sagen*, Bd. 2: 63.

As time passes, the distaff fills and empties with the changes of the Moon, however, there is always some flax remaining. She is never allowed to finish with the distaff. When the time comes that all the flax has been spun, the world will end. At times, the distaff is very full. Then the Spinstress becomes very tired, her little head sinks down, and her hair touches the flax threads, whereupon the Moon turns dark. That is when we have lunar eclipses. However, she soon notices and, startled, pulls back; thus a lunar eclipse often ends so rapidly. Sometimes, unaware, she spins her long hair up into the distaff, and when she notices it by the pain caused by her hair being pulled into the little wheel, she has to untangle it; then the eclipse lasts longer.

When the Sun rose the morning after this had happened, she was surprised to see the girl in the Moon; she had thought that same girl to be happily in love because her little head had been bent so devotedly over her work. All of a sudden, she heard the maiden's bridegroom lamenting for his little love. He had sunk down in the forest and fallen asleep, weak with lamentation; when she touched the Earth while setting in the evening, she picked him up and lifted him up to her. During the risings and settings of the Sun, he recognized his bride in the Moon, and both were full of longing for each other. This the Moon noticed with renewed sorrow; the Sun had become unfaithful to him, and even the maiden whom he had with him gave him no thought. He often cries then. The tears which he sheds are the shooting stars, the falling stars. Where they strike the ground, one finds a coin that never leaves, however often one spends it, or a little scrap of paper bearing verses that foretell the finder's future.

## 66 The Moon in the Fountain[7]

A maidservant once fetched water for making bread from the moonlit fountain. When the bread had risen and she had baked it,

---

[7] "One is not supposed to ladle water where the Moon is reflected; otherwise one will scoop up the Moon along with it. The girls will pour away water they collected in such a manner and prefer to fetch it from another, darker location." *Sitten und Sagen*, vol. 2: 63.

da ist der Mühlbach abgerissen, durch den Backofen gedrungen und hat gerade jenen Laib hinausgeflötzt, in welchen der Mond hineingebacken war. Als nun der Laib einige Zeit auf dem Wasser daherschwamm, erweichte der Teig und der Mond schaute heraus. Sogleich entstand starker Nebel und hob den Mond wieder an den Himmel.

## 67 Die Mondbraut[8]

Einem Dirnlein schien der Mond immer in das Fenster, wenn sie zu Bette ging und erhellte das Kämmerchen fast mit Tageshelle. Das Mädchen war schön und der Mond verliebt. Der Geliebte des Mädchens aber war ein reicher Bauernbursche, der es nicht redlich meinte und sie zu Fall zu bringen suchte. Einmal führte er sie zum Tanze, da drang er in sie, ihm das Kämmerchen zu öffnen, und in der Verwirrung und Aufregung sagte sie ihm zu. Um keinen Verdacht zu erregen, ging sie früher heim. Als sie eintrat, schien aber der Mond gar so schön in's Zimmer, und als sie zu Bette ging, war es ihr, als ob er immer näher käme, und zuletzt hart vor dem Fenster harre, traurig mit den Augen ihr zuwinkend. Da kam der Geliebte; sie hieß ihn aber wieder fortgehen; denn der Mond scheine ja gar so helle herein und gerade auf das Bettchen; er könne ja wieder kommen, wenn es dunkel wäre. Doch so oft er wiederkehrte, immer schien der Mond in die Kammer. Wohl ärgerte er sich weidlich darüber und fluchte dem Monde, sein böses Ziel konnte er nicht erreichen.

Da nahm er sie zur Frau und der Mond schien nicht mehr in die Stube, und herzlich dankte ihm das Mädchen, dass er ihrer Keuschheit gewartet und sie zur ehrlichen Frau gemacht habe.

---

[8] „Das Mondlicht gehört den Geistern; da tanzen sie auf den Wiesen . . . Daher ist es dem Menschen untersagt, im Mondschein zu tanzen, besonders verschlungen . . . Der Mond beschützt auch die Keuschheit der Mädchen." *Sitten und Sagen*, Bd. 2: 64.

all of a sudden the mill stream broke its banks, flooded into the baking oven, and washed out the very loaf into which the Moon had been baked. After the loaf had been swimming on the stream for a while, the bread dough softened, and the Moon peeked out of it. Then and there, a thick fog developed and lifted the Moon back up into the sky.

## 67 The Moon's Bride[9]

The Moon always shone through a young girl's window as she went to bed, and brightened her little chamber almost as if it were daylight. The girl was beautiful and the Moon was in love. The girl's beloved, however, was a rich farmer's son, who did not have honest intentions and sought to bring about her downfall. One time, he took her out to a dance and pressed her to open her little chamber to him, and in her confusion and excitement, she agreed. In order not to arouse suspicion, she went home earlier. When she entered her bedchamber, the Moon shone so prettily into it, and when she laid down, it seemed to her as if it came closer and closer, and finally, it stayed right outside her window, winking at her with sad eyes. Then her beloved arrived; she, however, sent him away again because the Moon seemed to shine so brightly into her room, and directly onto her little bed; he could come back if it became dark. But every time he returned, the Moon was shining into her chamber. No doubt, he was thoroughly angry over this and cursed at the Moon, but he was unable to attain his wicked goal.

Thereupon he took her as wife and the Moon shone into the room no more, and the girl thanked the Moon heartily that he had watched over her chastity and made an honest wife of her.

---

[9] "The moonlight belongs to the spirits; they dance in it, on the meadows . . . Thus it is forbidden to humans to dance in the moonlight, particularly when dancing intertwined . . . The Moon also guards the virtue of maidens." *Sitten und Sagen*, vol. 2: 64.

## 68 Die faule Tochter I

Eine alte Frau hatte eine faule Tochter, die wollte nicht gerne spinnen. Darüber wurde die Mutter böse und verwünschte sie in den Mond, wo sie nun ewig spinnen muss. Weil sie aber das Garn nicht zum Weber bringen kann, lässt sie es in die Lüfte hinausfliegen. Im Herbste, wenn es Altweibersommer ist, sieht man die Spinnfäden überall herumfliegen; diese kommen von der Spinnerin im Monde.

## 69 Die faule Tochter II

Eine ist gewesen, die hatte eine Tochter, welche sie zu keinem Tanze gehen ließ: dafür sollte sie nur recht fleißig spinnen. Als aber einmal die Alte fort war, ging das Mägdlein gleichwohl zum Tanze. Die Mutter kommt heim, sucht die Tochter und findet sie beim Tanze. Im Zorne verwünschte sie das eigene Kind in den Mond hinein, und die Windsbraut kam und riss sie hinauf. Da muss sie nun spinnen und ihr Gespinnst sind die Herbstfäden, das Herbstgespunnst; wenn diese Fäden fliegen, ist der Altweibersommer, und man sagt dann: die Spinnerin erntet.

## 70 Die Alte im Mond

Im Monde sitzt eine alte Frau, die flechtet einen Korb, und daneben sitzt ein großer Hund, der lauert, bis die Alte mit dem Korbe fertig wird, und wenn er sieht, dass sie bald zu Ende kommt, rappt er dar und reißt den Korb zusammen; zerreißt er den Korb, wird Mondsfinsternis. Doch nicht ganz darf der Hund den Korb zerreißen, sonst geht die Welt unter.

## 71 Herr und Frau Mond

Im Monde ist wirklich der Bauer, welcher, als er noch auf Erden lebte, alle Feiertage auf seiner Wiese Stauden ausgrub. Als er starb, kam er zur Strafe in den Mond.

### 68 The Lazy Daughter I

An old woman had a lazy daughter who did not like to spin. Thereupon the mother became angry and cursed her into the Moon, and there she has to spin forever. Since she is unable to bring the yarn to the weaver, she lets it fly off into the air. In the fall, when Indian summer has arrived, one can see the gossamer threads flying around everywhere; they come from the Spinstress in the Moon.

### 69 The Lazy Daughter II

There was an old woman who had a daughter whom she did not allow to go to any dances: instead, she was supposed to spin industriously. Once, when the old woman was out and about, the maiden went to a dance nonetheless. The mother returns, looks for the daughter, and finds her at the dance. Angrily, she cursed her own child into the Moon and a Whirlwind came and swept her up. There she has to spin, and her strands are the autumn threads, or fall gossamer; when these threads are floating, it is Indian summer and they say: the Spinstress is harvesting.

### 70 The Old Woman in the Moon

In the Moon an old woman sits, weaving a basket, and sitting beside her is a large dog, waiting for the woman to finish with the basket, and when he sees that she is close to finishing, he leaps up and tears the basket apart; when he has torn it up, there will be a lunar eclipse. But the dog is not allowed to tear up the basket completely, or the world will come to an end.

### 71 Mr. and Mrs. Moon

In the Moon there really is a farmer who, when still alive on the Earth, dug up shrubs on his grassland on every Holy Day. After he died, he had to go into the Moon as punishment.

Schon zu seinen Lebzeiten trug er den Namen Mond, und seine Frau und Alle, die ihm kannten, hießen ihn so. Sie waren kinderlos. Als er nun krank wurde und vermerkte, dass er sterben müsse, redete er sich mit seiner Frau darüber ab, dass er sie nach dem Tode abholen solle.

Als er daher starb, kam er nachts vor das Fenster seiner Frau und klopfte. Sie stand sogleich auf, schaute hinaus, erkannte ihren Mann und fragte: »Bist du es, Mond?«—Der erwiderte: »Ja, ich bin der Mond auf der Welt gewesen und bin es noch, und muss es in Ewigkeit sein. Willst du mit, so ziehe dich nur warm an, denn bei mir ist es kalt.« Sie zog sich also an, nahm Holzschuhe und ihren Pelz und ging mit ihm.

Seitdem scheint der Mann vor, die Frau nach Mitternacht, und weil diese warm gekleidet ist und einen Pelz anhat, der keine Kälte annimmt, so fällt, wenn sie scheint, alle Kälte auf die Erde, und daher kommt es, dass die Kälte nach Mitternacht stärker ist als vorher. Ferner ist die Gestalt im Monde nach Mitternacht viel dicker und traubiger ist, als vorher, dieses kommt von den dicken Kleidern der Frau. Endlich werden Träume, nach Mitternacht geträumt, viel seltener wahr, als jene vor Mitternacht: denn die Gesinnung der Frau ist viel veränderlicher als die des Mannes.

## 72 Der Sohn im Mond

Wie die Mutter ihre Tochter, verwünscht auch ein Vater seinen Sohn in den Mond, aber aus einem anderen Grunde. Ein Bauer wurde nämlich ungehalten, dass seine Frau ihm so viele Kinder zur Welt brächte, und als ihm das siebente, ein Knabe, geboren wurde, verwünschte er es in den Mond. Der Knabe wuchs zum schönen Jungen heran und kam auch richtig in den Mond, und muss nun dort ackern, bis ihm Erlösung wird.

Already, while still alive, his name was Moon, and his wife and everyone who knew him called him thus. They were child-less. Then when he fell ill and realized that he was going to die, he talked about that with his wife, and about that he should collect her and take her with him after his death.

After he had died, he arrived at her window during the night and knocked. She rose at once, looked outside, recognized her husband and asked, "Is it you, Moon?"—He replied, "Yes, I was the Moon before, and I still am, and will have to be for all eternity. If you wish to come with me, put on only your warm clothes, for it is cold in my place." Thereupon she dressed, took her wooden shoes and her fur coat, and went with him.

Since that time the man shines before and the wife after mid-night, and because she is dressed warmly and wears a fur that does not embrace the cold, all the cold seems to fall on Earth when she shines, and thus it is that the cold after midnight is greater than it is before. Also, the shape of the Moon is much big-ger and seems more rugged after midnight compared to before, which is due to the wife's heavy clothes. Finally, dreams dreamed after midnight will come true much less often than those dreamed before midnight, for the wife's way of thinking is much more changeable than that of her husband.

## 72 The Son in the Moon

As the mother wishes her daughter into the Moon, so does the father wish his son into the Moon, but for a different reason. For a farmer became angry that his wife gave birth to so many children, and when the seventh child, a boy, was born, he wished it into the Moon. The boy grew up to be a handsome boy and really did arrive in the Moon, and now he must plow there until his redemption.

# THE ELEMENTS:
# FIRE, WIND, AND WATER

Three Elements, Fire, Wind, and Water, delivered many benefits through their interactions with the people of Schönwerth's time, but brought with them yet more uncertainties. Fire had obvious benefits (warmth in winter, cooking, metalworking), but could destroy when it raged out of control. Wind, which could not be seen coming or passing by, could cool and dry in summer's heat, or it might blow down trees and houses. Water was ubiquitous in numerous and often inexplicable guises as solid, liquid, and vapor. It could be steam, fog, dew, rain, hail, ice, and snow, sometimes clear but sometimes obscure or reflective, sometimes moving (as in rivers), sometimes still (as in lakes), and often creatures lived in it. Moreover, the Elements must have been noticed interacting in mysterious ways; Wind stirs up Water and fans Fire—but Water extinguishes Fire.

Small wonder that in folklore, Fire, Wind, and Water were believed to have magical powers and so, like the Sun and Moon, often they were personified as Fiery Men, Jack-o'-lanterns, the Whirlwind, Water Men, et al. All those magical beings had frequent interactions, sometimes friendly, sometimes hostile or even murderous, with the people of the Earth who, as the tales relate, had to rely upon their quick-wittedness, skillfulness, and strength of faith in order to stand their ground against these supernatural entities.

Schönwerth elaborates on this context thus:

Fire is naturally associated with Light; like Light, it appears in dual form . . . as both celestial and subterranean Fire. . . . Air is depicted as the native territory of mythical creatures . . . in the Wild Hunt, and also in giant creatures such as the Wind and his family. . . . Water is the mythical Element because it is so richly represented in myth and legend, for example in the radiantly beautiful Mermaids, who experience the utmost joy and misery in their love for the sons of Earth. From the Water the children come and the unpurified souls of the departed return to this Element for the purpose of redemption in the shape of tiny little fish.[1]

---

[1] „Mit dem Licht ist naturgemäß das Feuer verbunden: auch dieses tritt . . . in einer Zweiteilung auf, als himmlisches und unterirdisches Feuer . . . Die Luft zeigt sich als Tummelplatz mythischer Wesen . . . im wütenden Heere, dann riesiger Naturen, wie im Winde und seiner Familie. . . . Das Wasser [ist] das mythische Element, so reich ist es in tiefgehender Mythe und Sage vertreten, [z.B. in] den in Schönheit strahlenden Wasserfrauen, welchen in der Liebe zu den Söhnen der Erde höchstes Glück und Unglück zuteil wird. Aus dem Wasser kommen die Kinder und in dieses Element kehren die nicht gereinigten Seelen Verstorbener zur Läuterung in Gestalt kleiner Fischchen zurück." *Sitten und Sagen.* vol. 2: 12f.

## 73 Der feurige Mann[2]

Der Urahn des Erzählers hatte gar oft Kohlen zu fahren vom Ranahof nach dem Hammer Loidersdorf bei Ensdorf. An heiligen Zeiten kam der feurige Mann im Walde zu ihm hin, und schüttelte sich, dass die Funken davon flogen. Dann redete ihn der Kohlenbrenner an: »Wie, geh' her und zünde mir!« und warf ihm drei Heller—denn es muss eine ungerade Zahl sein—vor die Füße als Lohn hin, worauf der Geist ihm den ganzen Weg entlang zündete.

Manchmal erlaubte sich der Mann einen Scherz und schalt den Geist: Geltenscheißer, oder: Blecharsch! Da rugelte er ihm auf und er musste ihn tragen, so lange der Weg dauerte, und so schwer, dass er vermeinte, Himmel und Erde liege auf ihm. Doch konnte er ihn vertreiben, wenn er die heiligen Namen aussprach.

Der feurige Mann sah aus von vorn wie ein anderer Mensch, hinten war er ausgemöltert, Gesicht und Leib waren schwarz, die Augen feurig; er trug ein ganzes Kleid, Goller und Hose aus einem Stücke, auf dem Kopfe einen Hut. Er konnte sich himmelhoch machen, aber auch ganz klein, wie denn die feurigen Männer an heiligen Abenden auf Weichselbäume hüpfen. War er gezahlt, so musste er zünden.

## 74 Der Landsmann

Ein Bube fuhr aus der Mühle heim und sah den Landsmann. In großer Furcht darüber setzte er sich vor das Mühlgitter und betete. Die Ochsen zogen ihren Schritt fort. Je mehr aber der Knabe betete, desto näher kam der Geist. Zuletzt und zuläng machte er sich sogar auf das Mühlgitter. Da fluchte der Bube: Ui Teufel, wie heiß!—»Hättest du nur noch ein Vaterunser gebetet,

---

[2] Auch: Landsknecht oder Landsmann. „So heissen die feurigen Männer in gewissen Gegenden, vorzüglich oben am Böhmerwalde. Sie zeigen sich in finsteren Nächten und halten sich neben den Wäldern auf; sowie ein Wanderer des Weges einherkommt, sind die etliche Schritte hinter ihm, und leuchten ihm nach Hause, bald groß, bald kleiner werdend. Man darf aber dabei kein unlautres Wort ausstossen, nicht fluchen und schimpfen, sonst verschwinden sie. Für das Heimleuchten zahlt man sie mit drei Brotbröseln, Pfenningen oder Hellern. Neustadt." *Sitten und Sagen*, Bd. 2: 97.

## 73 The Fiery Man[3]

One of the narrator's ancestors frequently carried coals from the Rana Farm to the hammer-mill village of Loider near Ensdorf. On Holy Days, the Fiery Man met him in the forest, shaking himself so that the sparks flew. Then the charcoal maker addressed him, "Hello, come hither and light my way!" and threw three coins—for it had to be an odd number—at his feet, whereupon the Ghost made light for him the whole way.

Sometimes, the man allowed himself a joke and scolded the Ghost, calling him a molten metal farter or a tin arse! Thereupon the Ghost climbed on his back, and he had to carry him the whole way and he was so heavy that it felt as if he were burdened with both the Earth and Heaven. However, he could drive it off by invoking holy names.

From the front, the Fiery Man looked like any other man, in the back he had a melted-out concavity, his face and body were black, his eyes fiery; he wore a full body garment, with shirt and pants made in one piece, and on his head a hat. He was able to stretch himself as high as the sky, but also [make himself] tiny, for example on Holy Evenings, when the Fiery Men hop up into sour cherry trees. After he was paid, he had to start a fire.

## 74 The Man-at-Arms

A young lad was on his way home from the mill and saw the Man-at-Arms. Terrified, he sat down against the fence by the mill and prayed. The oxen continued to pull the cart along. But the more he prayed, the closer came the apparition. Finally, it even climbed onto the fence and stretched out there. Thereupon the lad swore, "Oh, Devil; how hot!"—"If you had said one

---

[3] Also, Man-at-Arms or Countryman. "That is what the Fiery Men are called in certain places, most often at the north end of the Bavarian Forest. They show themselves in dark nights and stay close to the forests; as soon as they see a hiker coming along, they follow closely and light his way home, growing larger and smaller. You are not allowed to utter any mean words, no cussing or ranting, otherwise they will disappear. For lighting the way home, one pays them three breadcrumbs, pennies or coins. Neustadt." *Sitten und Sagen*, vol. 2: 97.

so wäre ich erlöst gewesen«—war der Schmerzensruf des geisterhaften Wesens.

## 75 Irrlichter[4]

Einer von Breitenwün bei Velburg ging nachts ziemlich ange-
trunken vom Jahrmarkte heim. Auf dem Wege hüpften Lichtlein
vor ihm einher, und besonders drei hielten sich ganz in seiner
Nähe und umtanzten ihn, weshalb er ihnen zurief: »Wenn ihr
mir leuchtet, dass ich heimfinde, bekommt jedes einen Taler.«[5]
Freudiger hüpften die Lichter vor ihm her; bis der Mann an
seinem Dorfe war. Da sagte er: »So jetzt könnt ihr wieder heim,
ich brauche euch nicht mehr.«—Die Lichtlein aber gingen nicht
heim, sondern stets vor ihm her, bis zum Hause und von da in
die Stube, und leuchteten dem Bauer in das Bett, und leuchteten
so lange bis er einschlief. Und so geschah es jede Nacht und
als es dunkelte, waren sie um ihn. Nun baute er eine Kapelle
am Dorfe und stiftete ein ewiges Licht. So als dieses das erstemal brannte, ließen sich die Lichtlein nicht mehr sehen.—Das
Kapellchen steht heut zu Tage noch, aber das ewige Licht ist
ausgegangen.

## 76 Geschichten vom Wind I[6]

Eine Christenfrau verirrte sich im Walde und kam zu einer
einsamen Hütte, wo sie die Frau um Nachtherberge ansprach.
Diese aber wollte sie nicht behalten; wenn der Menschenfresser
heimkäme, würde er sie sogleich schmecken und auffressen.

---

[4] „Unter den Irrlichtern versteht das Volk geisterhafte Wesen, meistens arme Seelen,
welche der Erlösung harren. Sie sind im Kleinen, was die feurigen Männer im Großen. . . .
Wer sie sieht, darf sie nicht beschreien, sonst wird er irre geführt, noch weniger verhöh-
nen." *Sitten und Sagen*, Bd. 2: 98f.

[5] „Am Ende des 15. Jahrhunderts begann man in vielen deutschen Ländern mit der Prä-
gung von großen Silbermünzen. Wurde diese neue Großsilbermünze anfangs noch als
‚Guldengroschen' bezeichnet, setzte sich etwa ab dem Jahre 1520 immer mehr der Name
‚Thaler' durch." „Die Geschichte des Talers." *Germany Cash* <http://www.germanycash
.de/taler/taler.html>. Abgerufen 23 Jul 2012.

[6] „Der Wind ist ein Riese und Christenfresser." *Sitten und Sagen*, Bd. 2: 107.

more 'Our Father,' I would have been redeemed," the ghostlike creature cried out in pain.

## 75 Jack-o'-Lanterns[7]

A man from the village of Breitenwün near Velburg went home one night from the country fair, rather drunk. On the way, little lights were bobbing along before him, and three in particular kept very close to him, dancing around him, whereupon he called out to them, "If you give me light so that I may find my way home, I will give each of you a Taler."[8]

Even more merrily the little lights bobbed along before him until the man reached his village. Then he said, "Now you can go home again; I don't need you anymore."—However, the little lights did not go home, but went in front of him, to his house, and from there into his sitting room, and they lighted the farmer's way to bed, and they kept glowing until he fell asleep. And so it happened every night; as soon as daylight faded, they were around him. Then he built a chapel in the village and paid for an eternal flame. As soon as it burned for the first time, the little lights were no longer seen.—The little chapel still stands today, but the eternal flame has gone out.

## 76 Tales of the Wind I[9]

A Christian woman lost her way in the forest and arrived at a lonely cottage where she asked the woman for lodging for the night. The latter did not want to keep her, however, for upon the Man-Eater's return, he would instantly smell her and eat her.

---

[7] "Jack o' Lanterns are commonly thought of as ghostlike creatures, mostly Poor Souls, who are awaiting redemption. They are like Fiery Men in miniature . . . When you see them, you are not allowed to talk loudly to them, much less ridicule them, otherwise you will be led astray." *Sitten und Sagen*, vol. 2: 98f.

[8] "Any of numerous silver coins issued by various German states from the 15th to the 19th centuries." "taler," *Merriam Webster* 23 July 2012 <http://www.merriam-webster .com/dictionary/taler>. Accessed 23 Jul 2012.

[9] "The Wind is a Giant and devourer of Christians." *Sitten und Sagen*, vol. 2: 107.

Die Christenfrau meinte zwar, in der Küche würde er sie nicht finden: es war aber dort gerade am gefährlichsten, weil der böse Mann zum Kamin hereinkommt, und sie zum Kamin hinausreißen und verzehren würde. So ließ sie sich in der Hühnersteige verstecken.

Da brummte und sauste es um die Hütte, und der Wilde kam herein und schrie: »ich schmecke Christenfleisch!« Die Frau aber redete es ihm aus, es wäre nur eine zugeflogene Henne, die sie in die Hühnersteige gesperrt habe. Der Wilde aber wollte nun die Henne sehen: da zeigte sie ihm in der Hühnersteige die in eine Henne verwandelte Christenfrau. »Das ist dein Glück!« sprach er und gab sich zufrieden.

Der Wilde war aber der Wind und seine Frau war eine Hexe, und die Christenfrau musste eine Henne bleiben und die Hexe hauste von da an mit dieser Henne.

## 77 Geschichten vom Wind II

Eine Frau, Namens Selamena, war mit ihrem kleinen Kinde ob ihrer Schönheit so stolz geworden, dass sie sich U.L. Frauen gleich achtete und sogar versuchte, gen Himmel zu fahren. In Mitte des Weges aber zwischen Himmel und Erde wurde sie gestürzt und von ihrem Kinde getrennt. So schweben nun beide in der Luft. Die Mutter ruft im heulenden Sturmwinde nach ihrem Kind, das sie nicht findet, aber in seinen wimmernden klagenden Tönen, dem winselnden Winde, vernimmt. –

## 78 Warum der Wind vom Meere her weht

Bei Erschaffung der Welt war der Wind schon persönlich auf der Welt und hatte auch eine Frau. Beide waren aber sehr dick, und der Mann hatte überdies einen Bart so groß, dass er dreimal um den dicken Leib herumging. Ungeachtet dieser Dicke konnten sie durch jeden Spalt, jedes noch so kleine Loch mit großer Leichtigkeit hindurch. Doch müssen sie schon lange auf der Welt gewesen sein, weil es zu ihrer Zeit, wie jetzt, Grafen, Fürsten und Könige gab.

Though the Christian woman was of the opinion he would not find her in the kitchen, in fact it was the most dangerous there because the evil man enters down the chimney, and he would snatch her out through the chimney and eat her. So she agreed to be hidden in the chicken cage.

A humming and swishing around the cottage ensued; the savage entered, crying out, "I smell Christian flesh!" The wife, however, talked him out of it; it was only a chicken that wandered into the house, that she had locked up in the chicken cage. The savage then wanted to see the chicken, so she showed him the Christian woman, whom she had transformed into a chicken, in the chicken cage. "You are lucky," he said, and was satisfied.

The savage, however, was the Wind and his wife was a Witch, and the Christian woman had to remain a chicken and the Witch lived with this chicken from then on.

### 77 Tales of the Wind II

A woman named Selamena had grown so proud of her own and her little child's beauty that she likened herself to Our Dear Lady, and she even tried to enter into Heaven. Halfway between Heaven and Earth, however, she was pushed down and became separated from her child. Therefore, now both float in the air. In the howling Wind of the storm, the mother calls out for her child which she cannot find yet still can hear, in the plaintive wailing of the whining Wind.

### 78 Why the Wind Blows from the Sea

At the Creation of the World, the Wind was already there in person, and also he had a wife. Both were very fat, and moreover, the man had a beard so long that it wound around his fat body three times. Despite their corpulence, they could squeeze through each gap and even the tiniest hole with the greatest ease. Anyway, they must have been already in the world for ages, because there were counts, princes, and kings in their day, just as there are now.

Nun lebte auch ein Graf, der konnte den Wind nicht leiden und äußerte sich oft sehr beleidigend über denselben. Eines Tages ging er in seinem Walde spazieren, und als er so ging, kam ihm eine alte dicke Frau in den Weg. Als der Graf ihrer ansichtig wurde, fragte er sie: »Wer bist du, woher kommst du, wohin gehst du, warum bist du so dick?« Die Frau erwiderte: »Ich bin die Windin, welche du nicht leiden kannst.« »Wo hast du deinen Mann?« fragte der Graf weiter. »Den sollst du gleich sehen!« war die Antwort. Dabei hub sie zu blasen an und führte den Grafen in einem Augenblicke zu dem gläsernen Berge, wo sie ihn niedersetzte und warten hieß. Dann zwängte sie sich durch eine Spalte des Berges, und nicht lange, so kam ein ungeheuer dicker Mann heraus, mit einem Barte, der dreimal um den dicken Leib herumging. Dieser näherte sich dem Grafen und sprach zu ihm: »Kennst du jetzt den Wind, über den du so oft geschmäht hast?«—und schlug ihn dann mit einer Rute, worauf der Graf sogleich in Stein verwandelt war. Doch sah und hörte er auch als Stein alles, was um ihn her vorging und in dem gläsernen Berge geschah. Jeden Tag sah er Leute aus allen Ständen ankommen und zu Stein werden; er erfuhr auch, dass diese Steine zehn Jahre so stehen mussten und dass nach dieser Zeit die Vornehmen gebraten, die Geringen gesotten wurden, worüber er in große Angst geriet.

So waren zwei Jahre vergangen. Da gedachte er, wie heute sein Geburtstag sei und dass seine treue Gattin, wenn sie um sein Los wüsste, gewiss alles aufbieten würde, ihn zu befreien. Kaum hatte er es gedacht, so kam ein sonderbarer Vogel, den er noch nie gesehen, setzte sich auf seinen Kopf und ließ aus dem Schnabel einen Ring, den Ehering seiner Gattin, und ein Zettelchen fallen. Sogleich stand der Graf in seiner menschlichen Gestalt da und las, dass er sich sofort aufmachen, und dem Vogel folgen solle, wohin er immer fliege.—Der Vogel flog und der Graf ging ihm nach und kam vor ein Schloss, das ganz voll Feuer war. Der Vogel flog mitten in das Feuer hinein, der Graf aber getraute sich nicht, ihm dahin zu folgen und blieb außen stehen. Nach einiger Zeit kam ein reichgeschmückter Fürst heraus, nahm den Grafen bei der Hand und führte ihn unversehrt mitten durch die Flammen in einen prächtigen Saal, in welchem gleichfalls eine Menge steinerner Figuren standen.

There once was a count who didn't like the Wind, and he often made insulting remarks about him. One day he went for a walk in the forest and as he was doing so, an old, fat woman appeared in his path. When the count saw her, he asked, "Who are you, where do you come from, where are you going, and why are you so fat?" The woman replied, "I am the wife of the Wind whom you find insufferable." "Where is your husband?" the count continued to ask. "You shall see him soon!" was the answer. Thereupon she began to blow and, in a blink of the eye, carried the count to the Glass Mountain, where she put him down and told him to wait. Then she squeezed through a cleft in the mountain, and it was not long before an immensely fat man appeared with a beard wound three times around his fat body. Approaching the count, he said, "Do you now recognize the Wind, whom you have vilified so often?"—and then struck him with a wand, upon which the count immediately turned into stone. However, even made out of rock he saw and heard everything that went on around him and in the Glass Mountain. Every day, he saw people from all social ranks arrive and be turned into stone; he learned also that these rocks had to stay that way for ten years and that, after this time, the nobles were to be roasted and the commoners were to be boiled, which put him in great fear.

Two years had passed by in this way. He thought about how it was his birthday today and that his faithful wife would certainly do everything she could to set him free if she knew of his fate. Scarcely had he thought it when a strange bird that he had never seen before arrived and landed on his head, and dropped from its beak a ring, his wife's wedding band, together with a little slip of paper. Immediately, the count stood there in his human form and read that he was to set off at once and should follow the bird, no matter where it should fly.—The bird flew and the count followed him and arrived at a castle that was completely filled with Fire. The bird flew right into the middle of the Fire, but the count dared not follow it and remained standing outside. After a while, a richly adorned prince emerged, took the count by the hand and led him through the flames unharmed into a magnificent hall in which also stood numerous stone figures.

Da sagte der Fürst: »Weißt du, ich habe dich erlöst und aus der Gewalt des Windes gerettet; denn es wäre dir sonst ergangen wie allen anderen, welche am gläsernen Berge versteinert stehen. Ich war wie du in Stein verwandelt, bin aber nun befreit durch den Feuergeist. Siehst du diese Gestalt von Stein«—und damit deutete er auf eine Bildsäule hin –»es ist ein verwandelter König: ihn wird der Wassergeist erlösen.«

Kaum hatte er diese Worte vollendet, so kam ein Vogel geflogen, ein Zettelchen im Schnabel, und setzte sich auf den Kopf des Steinbildes, und sogleich fing dieses sich zu rühren an und bald stand der König vor den Beiden da.

Auf dem Zettel aber stand geschrieben, dass jeder von den Dreien einen Wunsch tun könne, nach der Größe der drei Stücke, in welche sie den Zettel zerreißen sollten. Da wünschte sich der Graf so dick zu werden als er wolle, und der Fürst, so weit zu sehen als er wolle, und der König, so hoch zu werden, dass er bis an die Sterne reiche.

Nun führte sie der Fürst, der so weit sehen konnte, durch einen unterirdischen Gang hinaus und bemerkte draußen im gläsernen Berge Scharen von Bewaffneten, an der Spitze den Wind, am Ende die Windin, und als er in die Höhe schaute, erblickte er eine Unzahl bewaffneter Vögel. Da machte sich der König so lang, als er es brauchte und holte die Vögel, einen um den anderen, herunter, und die beiden anderen erschlugen sie.

Der Fürst aber sah nun wieder, wie der Wind mit seinem Heer den gläsernen Berg verließ und gegen sie anzog. Und es wurde den Dreien recht bang um ihr Leben: denn es fehlte nicht viel mehr auf elf Uhr nachts, und wenn diese geschlagen, wussten sie, dass der Wind über sie Gewalt habe.

Da machte sich der Dritte so dick als er es vermochte und tat den Mund weit auf, und der Wind und sein Heer und die Windin zogen alle in den Mund hinein, und als die Windin eingezogen war, rief der, welcher so weit sah: »den Mund zu!« und der Graf schloss den Mund und hatte nun Wind und Heer und Windin in seinem Leibe, so dass ihm ganz übel wurde. Der aber, welcher so weit sah, führte ihn an das Meer und hieß ihn niederknien und alles, was seinen Magen so sehr beschwerte, in das Meer speien.—Und er tat so, und Wind und Heer und Windin versanken im Meere.

The prince said, "You know, I redeemed you and rescued you from the violence of the Wind, for otherwise you would have suffered the same fate as all the others who stand petrified at the Glass Mountain. Like you, I was turned into stone, but I am now released by the Spirit of Fire. See you this figure of stone?"—and with that he pointed at a statue—"He is a transformed king: the Spirit of Water will redeem him."

No sooner had he finished these words, when a bird came flying, a slip of paper in its beak, and landed on the head of the stone likeness, whereupon immediately it began to move, and soon the king stood before the two of them.

On the paper it was written that each of the three could make a wish, in accordance with the sizes of the three pieces into which they should tear up the slip of paper. Whereupon the count wished to become as fat as he wanted, the prince to see as far as he wanted, and the king to grow so tall as to reach up to the stars.

Now the prince, who could see so far away, led them out through an underground passage, and noticed outside, on the Glass Mountain, legions of armed men with the Wind at their head, and the Wind's wife at their rear, and when he looked up into the sky, he saw a myriad of armed birds. Thereupon the king stretched out to become as tall as he needed and fetched the birds down, one by one, and the other two slew them.

But the prince looked again and saw how the Wind had started leaving the Glass Mountain with his army, and was marching toward them. And the three began to fear mightily for their lives because it was almost eleven o'clock at night and they knew that, once the bell began to toll, the Wind would have power over them.

Thereupon the third one grew as fat as he could and, opening his mouth wide, sucked in the Wind, his army and the Wind's wife too, and as soon as he had drawn in the Wind's wife, the one who was able to see far called out, "Close your mouth!" and the count closed his mouth; and now that he had the Wind and the army and the Wind's wife inside his body, he became very queasy. However, the one who had the gift of seeing far led him to the sea and told him to kneel down and spew everything that weighed so heavily on his stomach into the sea.—And that is what he did, and the Wind and the army and the Wind's wife sank into the sea.

Seit dieser Zeit ist das Meer so unruhig und kommen alle Winde vom Meere her.

## 79 Geschichte vom Gewitter

Es waren ein paar alte Leute, welche sehr fromm lebten und den Armen gerne mitteilten. Da kam einmal eine arme Frau vor die Tür und bat um Almosen. Die guten Leute hießen sie hereingehen und reichten ihr ein Stück Brot. Beim Hinausgehen sah aber die Frau ein Kind im Bette liegen, ging darauf hin, besah es und kündete den Eltern an, dass diesem ein großes Unglück bevorstehe, indem es vom Blitze erschlagen würde. Doch wolle sie für das Stückchen Brot nebst einem Vergelts Gott noch einen guten Rat erteilen; so oft das Mädchen beim Blitzen beten werde: »Und das Wort ist Fleisch geworden und hat unter uns gewohnt,« werde das Wetter ihm nicht ankönnen. Die Eltern ließen nun ihr Kind dieses Gebet fleißig verrichten, sagten ihm aber erst den Grund, als die Jungfrau Neigung zu einem jungen Manne gefasst hatte. Nun nahm sie den Schleier. Einmal aber zog um ihr Kloster ein arges Gewitter sich zusammen, drei Tage wütete es und verheerte die ganze Gegend. Da baten die Klosterfrauen die Jungfrau, sie möchte doch lieber sich opfern, als so viele dem Unglücke preisgeben: sie werde damit Gott ein angenehmes Opfer bringen. Die Jungfrau bereitete sich nun vor für das Jenseits, und als es wieder blitzte, unterließ sie ihr Gebet und sogleich wurde sie vom Blitze getroffen.

## 80 Geschichte vom Regenbogen[10]

Der Teufel brauchte einmal einen Zirkel, um seine Hölle zu bauen, fand aber keinen. Da ging er zu einem Engel, des Herrgotts Werkmeister, und bat sich einen Zirkel aus, um den Bogen für seine Hölle zu ziehen. Der Engel nahm den Zirkel vom Himmelsbogen und warf ihn dem Teufel hinunter. Der aber wusste nicht

---

[10] „Auf einen Regenbogen folgt Regen drei Tage lang, oder Schnee . . . Zwei Regenbogen auf einmal deuten auf schönes Wetter, und der Regen, der dabei fällt, ist sehr fruchtbar . . . Viele Regenbogen, viele Regen." *Sitten und Sagen*, Bd. 2: 130.

Since that time the sea is restless and all the winds come from the sea.

## 79 A Thunderstorm Tale

There was once an old couple that lived piously and happily shared with the poor. One day, an old woman came to their door and asked for alms. The good people asked her to enter and gave her a piece of bread. Upon leaving, the woman saw a child lying in bed, approached it, looked at it, and announced to the parents that there was going to be a great misfortune in that it would be killed by lightning. However, in exchange for the little piece of bread, she would give them a "God Bless" and a piece of good advice; if every time there was lightning the girl would pray, "And the Word was made flesh, and dwelt among us," the weather would not be able to harm her. From then on, the parents had their child recite this prayer diligently, but did not tell her the reason why until the young woman developed an affection for a young man. Then she took the veil. One time, a severe thunderstorm developed around her convent; it raged for three days, devastating the whole region. Thereupon the nuns begged the maiden to sacrifice herself rather than to abandon so many to misfortune; she would thereby offer God a pleasing sacrifice. Therefore the maiden prepared herself for the afterlife, and when the lightning started again, she refrained from saying her prayer and at once was struck by lightning.

## 80 A Rainbow Tale[11]

Once the Devil was in need of a pair of compasses to build his Hell, but did not find one. Thereupon he went to see an angel, God's master-workman, and asked for compasses in order to draw a circle for his Hell. The angel took the compasses from the Heavenly Arch and threw them down to the Devil. He, however, did not know

---

[11] "After a rainbow, there will be three days of rain or snow . . . A double rainbow predicts good weather, and the rain that comes with it is very fertile . . . Many rainbows, much rain." *Sitten und Sagen*, vol: 2: 130.

mit ihm umzugehen, und ersuchte den Engel, ihm zu zeigen, wie er denn das Werkzeug handhaben solle. Da stellte der Engel den goldenen Zirkel auf und machte auf das Gewölk einen Halbkreis, welcher in den sieben Regenbogenfarben glänzte. »Halt,« rief der Teufel, »jetzt kann ich es schon selbst,« und griff nach dem Zirkel, um den Kreis zu vollenden. Er vermochte ihn aber nicht zu halten und nicht zu drehen. Der Zirkel fiel um und dem Teufel auf die Stirne und schlug ihm ein Horn. Seitdem hat der Teufel ein Horn und der Regenbogen nur einen halben Ring.

## 81 Geschichte von den Tauperlen

Die Tauperlen sind die Tränen der gefallenen Engel, der jüngeren nämlich und unerfahrnen, welche unwissend dem Luzifer gefolgt sind. Nun weinen sie jeden Morgen und Abend; ihre Tränen fallen als Tau zur Erde; sie dürfen nämlich vor und nach der Sonne fliegen, und sehen noch auf kurze Zeit den Glanz ihrer Tränen in der farbigen Pracht des von der Sonne beschienenen Taues, damit sie daran erinnert werden, wie auch sie einst geglänzt haben. – Am Morgen, wenn die Sonne kommt, verbergen sich die Geisterchen in den Schoß der Frauenmäntelchen und sehen da noch ihre Tränen glitzern und blitzen, bis diese auch hier von der Sonne aufgezehrt sind. Dann aber müssen sie sich in ihre Räume zurückziehen zwischen Himmel und Erde und dürfen erst wieder fliegen, wenn die Sonne untergeht.

## 82 Geschichte vom Schneeglöckchen

Als Unser Herr Alles erschaffen hatte, Gras und Kräuter und Blumen, und ihnen die schönen Farben gegeben, in denen sie prangen, machte er zuletzt auch den Schnee und sagte zu ihm: »Die Farbe kannst du dir selbst suchen, denn du frisst ja so Alles.« – Der Schnee ging also zum Gras und sagte: »Gib mir deine grüne Farbe,« dann ging er zur Rose und bat um ihr rotes Kleid, dann zum Veilchen, und wieder zur Sonnenblume, denn er war eitel und wollte eine schöne Jacke haben. Aber Gras und Blumen lachten ihn aus und schickten ihn seines Weges. Da setzte er sich zum Schneeglöckchen und sagte betrübt:

how to use them, and asked the angel to show him how the tool should be handled. Thereupon the angel positioned the golden compasses and drew in the clouds a semi-circle, which shone with the seven colors of the rainbow. "Stop," the Devil called out, "I can now do it by myself," and reached for the compasses to complete the circle. However, he was unable to hold them or rotate them. The compasses fell over and hit him so hard on the forehead that they raised a horn there. Since that time the Devil has a horn and the rainbow only a semi-circle.

## 81 A Tale of Dew Drops

The dew drops are the tears of the fallen angels, of those younger and inexperienced ones who, in their ignorance, followed Lucifer. Now they cry each morning and evening; their tears fall onto the Earth as dew, because they are permitted to fly [only] before sunrise and after sunset, and can thus behold for a short time the sparkle of their tears in the colorful splendor of the dew illuminated by the sun, so that they are reminded of how they also once shone.—In the morning, when the sun comes up, the little spirits hide away in the middle of the Lady's Mantle flowers and there they can see their tears glisten and flash until those too are consumed by the sun. But then they must retreat into their space that is between Heaven and Earth and are permitted to fly again only when the sun goes down.

## 82 Legend of the Snowdrop Flower

After Our Lord had created everything, grass and herbs and flowers, and given them the beautiful colors in which they are resplendent, also He created the Snow and said to it, "You may choose your own color, because you eat everything anyway."—So, the Snow went to the Grass and said, "Give me your green color," then he went to the Rose and asked for her red dress, then to the Violet and then to the Sunflower, because he was vain and wanted to have a beautiful coat. But the Grass and the flowers laughed at him and sent him on his way. Thereupon he sat down by the Snowdrop and said unhappily,

»Wenn mir niemand eine Farbe gibt, so ergeht es mir wie dem Winde, der nur darum so bös ist, weil man ihn nicht sieht.« Da erbarmte sich das Blümchen und sprach bescheiden: »Wenn dir mein schlechtes Mäntelchen gefällt, magst du es nehmen.« Und der Schnee nahm es und ist seitdem weiß; aber allen Blumen bleibt er feind, nur nicht dem Schneeglöckchen.

## 83 Als der Schnee zu Mehl wurde

Ein Taglöhner, dem es sauer wurde, sein täglich Stück Brot zu gewinnen, murrte oft über unseren Herrgott bei seiner strengen Arbeit, am meisten aber dann, wenn Schnee fiel und das Arbeiten noch mehr erschwerte; dieser sei doch zu gar nichts gut, und nicht einmal von Gott erschaffen worden, weil er weder im Paradies noch in der Arche Noe war. Einmal war er wieder im Walde, um Holz zu fällen, als der Schnee in dicken Flocken niederfiel. Fluchend suchte er Schutz in einer Felsenhöhle. Kaum ruhte er hier einige Augenblicke, so stand ein Engel vor ihm und fragte ihn, warum er gar so oft des Teufels gedächte, so selten aber unsers Herrgottes. Da meinte der Taglöhner, Unser Herr denke auch an ihn nicht, und darum könne er nicht gut Freund mit ihm sein. Der Engel fragte nun, was denn Gott tun solle, damit er zufrieden wäre; und der törichte Mensch wünschte, dass statt des Schnees Mehl vom Himmel falle. Und sofort fiel das Mehl in dicken Wolken herab, und die Leute kamen und sammelten es und hatten nun Brot genug und arbeiteten nicht mehr. Als aber dem einen das Haus abbrannte und dem anderen eine Mauer einfiel, und weder Zimmermann noch Maurer Hand oder Fuß rühren mochte, kam es dahin, dass die Leute wie bei Erschaffung der Welt in Höhlen wohnen und zuletzt von Wurzeln und Kräutern leben und nackt wie die ersten Ahnen gehen mussten. Die wilden Tiere vermehrten sich und Hecken und Dornenbüsche, Gesträuche und Wald wucherten da empor, wo ehedem blühende Fluren und Wohnstätten waren. In diesem Elende erkannte nun auch der Taglöhner die Torheit seines Wunsches und seinen Übermut, an der Weltordnung Gottes meistern zu wollen. Tief erschüttert sprang er von seinem Lager auf, um den Engel aufzusuchen, und – erwachte.

"If nobody gives me a color, then it will go with me the same as with the Wind, who is so disagreeable only because one does not see him." Whereupon the little flower took pity on him and said humbly, "If you like my simple little mantle, you may take it." And the Snow took it and henceforth has been white; however, he remains an enemy to all flowers, except for the Snowdrop.

### 83 When Snow Turned Into Flour

A day laborer, who was peeved over having to earn his daily bread, often grumbled at Our Lord when doing his hard work, but most often when snow fell and made his work even harder; he decided that snow was good for nothing at all, and had not even been created by God because it had existed neither in Paradise nor in Noah's Ark. One time he was out in the forest again to fell trees, when the snow came down in thick flakes. Cursing, he sought shelter in a cave. He had rested there for hardly a few moments when an angel stood before him and asked him why he thought so often of the Devil, but so rarely of Our Lord. Because, the day laborer replied, Our Lord was not thinking of him either and therefore he could not be good friends with Him. Then the angel asked, what would God have to do so that he would be satisfied, and the foolish fellow wished that instead of snow, flour would fall from the sky. And immediately, flour fell down in thick clouds, and the people came and gathered it up, and now had enough bread and therefore worked no more. However, when one man's house burned down and another's wall collapsed, and neither carpenter nor bricklayer would stir either hand or foot, it came about that people had to live in caves, just as they had done at the time of the Creation of the World, and finally had to live on roots and herbs and go naked, like their first ancestors. The wild animals multiplied, and hedges and thornbushes, shrubbery and forest grew out of control where once there had been thriving fields and villages. In this misery, the day laborer recognized now the foolishness of his wish, and also his arrogance to want to improve upon God's ordering of the world. Deeply shaken, he jumped up from his bed, in order to seek out the angel and—awoke.

Er trat hinaus vor die Höhle und Schnee lag vor seinen Füßen. So warf er sich auf die Knie und dankte dem Herrn, der ihn in einem Traumgesichte belehrt hatte, und fortan war er mit seinem Schicksale zufrieden.

## 84 Wie die wilde Jagd entstand[12]

Zu Zeiten Karls des Großen wurden sie uneinig der Religion halber. Der Ritter von Blocksburg nahm heimlich eine sehr schöne Försterstochter zur Ehe und wurde darüber verfolgt. Da rief er die Geister der Hölle zu Hilfe und wurde nun zum Ritter der Hölle. Daher ist die wilde Jagd entstanden.

## 85 Der Graf von Natternberg und die Wilde Jagd

Der Graf und die Gräfin von Natternberg fuhren alle Samstage und Sonntage auf die Jagd und schonten nicht der Fluren des Landvolkes. Da wollte sie einmal der Teufel mitsamt dem Berg und dem Schloss darauf, in dem sie wohnten, in die Donau werfen: er lud alles auf einen Schubkarren und führte es dem Strome zu, als man in Deggendorf läutete; da musste er weichen. Seitdem steht der Natternberg mit seinem Schlösschen hart an der Donau, und sieht man noch jetzt unten am Berge die beiden Schubkarrenbäume hervorstehen. Das gräfliche Ehepaar aber muss nach seinem Tode zur Strafe für sein wildes Jagen jede Woche in der Samstag- und Sonntagnacht als Nachtgload[13] fahren. Sie sitzen in einem Wagen, mit vier Rappen bespannt, eine Meute Hunde voran, welche feurige Zungen ausstrecken und winselnd heulen. Der Zug geht immer denselben Weg, niemals zurück, von einem Holze bei Pfatter hinter Wolfersdorf hinum wieder in's Holz. Früher fuhr das Geisterpaar auch über des Pfarrers Äcker

---

[12] „Die wilde Jagd ist der böse Feind mit seinen Teufeln . . . der die Verdammten . . . und die Armen Seelen jagt, und alles mitnimmt, was ihm auf der Erde widersteht. Der Anführer des Zuges ist der böse Feind, der an der Spitze reitet. Alle Jäger, Edle und Gemeine, welche die Saaten des Landmannes in ihrer wilden Lust verheerten, wurden von diesem verflucht, und sind nun in das Wilde Heer aufgenommen." *Sitten und Sagen*, Bd. 2: 147.

[13] „Nachtgload," oberpfälzisch für „Nachtgeleit."

He stepped out in front of the cave, and snow lay at his feet. So he sank to his knees and thanked the Lord, who had taught him [a lesson] in a dream, and from that day forward, he was content with his destiny.

## 84 How the Wild Hunt Began[14]

In the days of Charlemagne they were having a dispute over religion. The Lord of Block Castle secretly took a woodsman's very beautiful daughter as his wife and was persecuted for it. So he called upon the spirits of Hell for help and thus became a Knight of Hell. That is how the Wild Hunt was created.

## 85 The Count of Natternberg and the Wild Hunt

The Lord and Lady of Viper Mountain went hunting every Saturday and Sunday, and they did not spare the fields of the farmers. One time, the Devil wanted to throw them into the river Danube, along with the mountain and the castle on its top in which they lived: he loaded everything into a wheelbarrow and took it to the river; when the bells in Deggendorf tolled, he had to retreat. Since that day, Viper Mountain with its little castle stands right by the Danube, and one can still see the two wheelbarrow trees protruding at the foot of the mountain. After their deaths, as punishment for their wild hunting, the noble couple had to ride out in the Wild Hunt every Saturday and Sunday night. They sit in a carriage drawn by four black horses, a pack of hounds in front with fiery tongues outstretched and howling whiningly. They always take the same path, never returning that way, starting from a forest near the town of Pfatter, past Wolfersdorf, and then back into the forest again. The ghostly couple used to ride across the priest's fields also,

---

[14] "The Wild Hunt is the Evil Enemy with his Devils, who hunts the damned and the Poor Souls and sweeps along everything that resists him on Earth. The leader of the troop is the Evil Enemy who rides in front. All hunters, noblemen, and commoners, who destroyed the farmer's crops in their maniacal delight, were cursed by him, and are now part of the Wild Hunt." *Sitten und Sagen*, vol. 2: 147.

und am Morgen sah man die Straße in der Furche. Das verdross den Herrn, und er ging einmal hinaus und stellte das nachtfahrende Paar und befragte es, warum sie nicht auch wie andere ehrliche Leute auf der Landstraße oder im Hohlwege blieben, und verbot ihnen das Abweichen vom Wege. Da bekannte der Graf, ein großer, schwarzer, bartiger Mann, was er im Leben verbrochen und wie er bis zum jüngsten Tage so fahren müsse.

## 86 Wasserriesen

In einem Dorfe an einem großen Wasser gab es einmal lauter schöne Mädchen, dass alle Welt Freude daran hatte, und sie wurden immer schöner, je öfter sie vom Baden im Wasser heimkehrten. Das hörten die Mädchen aus anderen Orten und sie zogen aus allen Gegenden herbei, und nahmen ein Bad im Wasser. Da sie aber sehr garstig waren und auch nicht lange unter dem Wasser bleiben konnten, wie die Mädchen des Dorfes, wurden sie nicht schöner, ja viele ertranken im Wasser. Nun blieben die fremden Mädchen zwar aus, dafür aber meldeten sich Freier aus allen vier Himmelsgegenden. Alle Mädchen des Dorfes hielten an einem Tage Hochzeit. Gegen den Morgen hin, der darauf folgte, gab es aber fürchterlichen Lärmen. Alles lief zusammen. Jeder Bräutigam zog seine Braut an den Haaren herum, und stieß und schlug sie, so lange er es vermochte; dann lief er davon.—Es hatte sich befunden, dass die Mädchen nicht recht beschaffen, insbesondere beschuppt waren. Da kam der Richter mit seinen Knechten und besah sich die Bräute und befahl einen Scheiterhaufen zu errichten, um auf diesem die Fischweiber insgesamt zu verbrennen. Als die Flammen schon loderten, schlug das Wasser am Dorfe hohe Wellen und es streckte sich ein ungeheuer großer Kopf daraus hervor, der spie Wasser wie ein Walfisch und löschte das Feuer, und auf dem dicken Wasserbogen gingen die Bräute wie auf einer Brücke vom Holzstoß hinüber an's Wasser und in den Rachen des Wassermannes hinein wie in ein großes Tor.

Seitdem baden keine Mädchen mehr in diesem Wasser.

and in the morning one could see their path across the furrows. The priest took offense and one time went out to confront the night-traveling pair, and asked them why they did not stay on the country road or in the ravine, like other decent people, and forbade them to venture from the road. Thereupon the count, a big, dark, bearded man, confessed the crime he had committed when alive, and how he must ride like this till Judgement Day.

## 86 Water Giants

In a village by a large body of water there once lived beautiful girls such as made all the world rejoice, and they grew more and more beautiful every time they returned home from bathing in the water. When the girls from other localities heard this, they moved to this village from all over, and bathed in the water. However, since they were very ugly and were incapable of staying under the water for a long time, as the village girls did, they did not grow more beautiful; many of them even drowned in the water. So then the foreign girls stayed away, it is true, and instead suitors from all four quadrants of the heavens presented themselves. All the village girls held a one-day wedding. But as the morning that followed approached, a dreadful uproar ensued. All the villagers quickly gathered together. Each bridegroom pulled his bride about by her hair and pushed and pummeled her as long as he was able to, then he ran away.—It turned out that the girls were not created the right way; in particular, they were covered in scales. Whereupon the magistrate arrived with his officers and examined the brides, and ordered a pyre be constructed on which to burn all the fish women together. When the flames were already blazing, tall waves surged from the water by the village, and an enormously large head stretched up from it, spouting water like a whale and extinguishing the fire, and the brides walked on the big arc of water as if it were a bridge, from the woodpile over to the water and into the mouth of the Water Man, as if it were a large gate.

Since that day, no girl bathes in this water anymore.

## 87 Wasserzwerge[15]

Die Bewohner eines Schlosses im Walde waren sehr der Jagd ergeben. Einmal kamen sie während des Jagens an einen kristallhellen Waldbach, der an einer Stelle ganz sonderbar aufwallte und eine Art Wasserglocke bildete. Sie wunderten sich darüber und stießen mit einer Eisenstange an der Stelle hinunter. Da hörten sie Kindergeschrei und ein Zwerg fuhr zornig empor auf die Wasserfläche und verwies den Jägern ihren Übermut: sie hätten jetzt in den Palast der Zwerge ein Loch gestossen, das Wasser dringe ein und habe schon mehrere ersäuft; nur schnell sollten sie mit derselben Stange Etwas zum Verstopfen der Öffnung hinabreichen. Da steckte einer der Jäger seinen Goller[16] an die Stange und fuhr damit zur selben Stelle hinein. Aber der Zwerg brachte ihn voll Ungeduld wieder herauf, denn er war zu groß für das Loch, und bat nur um eine handvoll Haare aus dem Pelze des Gollers. Man willfahrte ihm und zufrieden fuhr er wieder hinunter.

Voll Staunen entfernte sich die Gesellschaft, und ging denselben Bach entlang. Da sahen sie einen anderen Zwerg auf dem Wasser daherhupfen, und tanzen, und mit seinem Hütchen spielen, das er immer in die Höhe warf und wieder fing. Sie fragten ihn, wie es denn da unten bei ihm aussehe. Er sprang nun zu ihnen hin und erbat sich Lohn, wenn er es gesagt habe. Sie waren dazu gerne bereit, und er erzählte ihnen nun, dass die Zwerge unter dem Wasser lebten, gerade so, wie die Menschen auf der Erde, und dieselben Wohnungen mit Zimmern und Gängen unter dem Wasser hätten, nur etwas kleiner, dass ein Mensch nicht darin zu wohnen vermöchte. Sie hätten aber Mangel an Speise. Würde man ihnen täglich etwas Nahrung bereit stellen, wären sie mit Vergnügen bereit, im Schlosse bei der Arbeit zu helfen,

---

[15] „Sie heissen allgemein nur Wassermännlein und sind geisterhafte Wesen, doch nicht rechte Geister, weil sie sonst nicht so viel mit den Menschen, deren Gesellschaft sie lieben, verkehren könnten. Die Männer fühlen sogar oft Liebe zu reinen menschlichen Jungfrauen . . . Hervorzuheben ist noch die Abhängigkeit, in welcher sich dieses kleine elbische Volk den Menschen gegenüber befindet, indem sie Mangel an Speise haben und diese von den Menschen erbitten." *Sitten und Sagen*, Bd. 2: 179–181.

[16] Goller: arch. für „(Pelz)-Kragen."

## 87 The Little Water Men[17]

The dwellers in a castle in the forest were devoted hunters. Once, while out hunting, they happened upon a crystal-clear forest stream, which bubbled up quite peculiarly at one place and formed some kind of a water bubble shaped like a bell. They puzzled over this and poked down into that place with an iron rod. Thereupon they heard children screaming, and a Little Water Man surged angrily up to the water's surface, scolding the hunters for their arrogance because they had poked a hole into the palace of the Little Water Men; water was coming in, and already several had drowned; quickly, with the same rod, they should just reach down [with] something to plug the hole. So one of the hunters fastened his [fur] collar to the rod and drove it into that same place. But the Little Water Man impatiently brought it back up, because it was too big for the hole, and asked for only a handful of hair from the fur of the collar. They complied with his request and, satisfied, he went down under the water again.

The party left, filled with amazement, walking along that same stream. Whereupon they saw another Little Water Man hopping on the surface of the water, and dancing, and playing with his little hat, which he threw up into the air and caught again and again. They asked him what it looked like down there at his dwelling. He skipped up to them and asked to be paid, if he told them. They readily agreed to that, and he told them that the Little Water Men lived under the water the same way humans lived above ground, and that they had the same dwellings with rooms and hallways under the water, only somewhat smaller, so that a person would be unable to dwell there. But they had a shortage of food. If people were willing to supply a little food on a daily basis, they would gladly help with the work in the castle, and also

---

[17] "They are commonly known as Little Water People, and they are ghostlike creatures, but not real Ghosts, otherwise they would be unable to conduct that much business with the humans, whom they love. Indeed, their men often feel love for young human women. Also noteworthy is the dependence on humans these little elfish people experience, in that they have a shortage of food which they ask for from humans." *Sitten und Sagen*, vol. 2: 179–181.

und auf der Jagd vor ihnen herzugehen und so viel Wild zu zeigen, dass sie dessen genug bekämen. Auch die Waldfrevler würden sie zur Anzeige bringen.—Der Schlossherr sagte es zu und die Zwerge hielten ihr Wort.

## 88 Das Burgfräulein bei den Wasserzwergen

Ein Burgfräulein ging mit ihrer Amme am Wasser spazieren. Da tanzte vor ihren Augen ein spitzes graues Hütchen auf dem Wasser. Die Amme sah aber Nichts. Sie ging nun öfter an's Wasser und immer näher tanzte das Hütchen heran und war zuletzt vor ihren Füßen. Nicht lange und das Hütchen setzte sich ihr auf den Kopf. Nun ging sie einmal allein herab aus dem Schlosse an's Wasser, und wieder setzte das Hütchen sich ihr auf den Kopf, und da sie nahe am Ufer stand, glitten ihr die Füße aus, und sie sank hinab in die Fluten. Da aber nahmen sie die Zwerge auf und pflegten ihrer auf das Sorgsamste. Der König verliebte sich sogar in die schöne Jungfrau und bot ihr seine Hand an. Als er mit seinem Antrage zurückgewiesen wurde, bat er die Maid, sie möge nur bei ihnen bleiben: er wäre schon zufrieden, wenn er sie sehen könne. Und nun ließ er ihr einen großen herrlichen Kristallpalast bauen, und ging immer um denselben herum, nur um die Jungfrau zu sehen. Jeder ihrer Wünsche wurde erfüllt. Doch begann sie bald Langeweile zu haben und sich wieder auf die Erde zurück zu sehnen. Auf ihr Verlangen brachten ihr die harmlosen Zwerge sogar das Hütchen, mit dem sie herabgefahren war. Sie setzte es schnell auf, und so gleich war sie am Lande, bedeckt mit dem schönsten Perlenschmucke, den ihr der Zwergenkönig zum Geschenk gemacht hatte.

## 89 Der Fluch der Wasserzwerge

Die Besitzer eines Edelhofes hatten in alter Zeit einen Vertrag mit den Wassermännchen abgeschlossen, dass diese die kleinen Fische, welche beim Steigen des Wassers in die offenen Aushöhlungen der Steine getrieben und beim Fallen darin zurückgelassen würden, für sich nehmen dürften. Der Vertrag wurde treu gehalten, und die Letzte des Stammes erlaubte ihnen sogar zeitweise auch in dem großen Wasser zu fischen.

to walk before them during a hunt, and to show them so much game that they would have plenty of it. And, they would also bring the forest poachers to light.—The lord of the castle agreed to this, and the Little Water Men kept their word.

## 88 A Noble Damsel Living Among the Little Water Men

A noble damsel and her wet nurse were strolling by the water when she saw, before her very own eyes, a little gray pointed hat dancing on the water. But the wet nurse saw nothing. From then on, the damsel went more and more often to the water, and the little hat danced nearer and nearer to her, until at last it was right at her feet. Not much longer and the little hat sat itself on her head. Now, she went down by herself from the castle to the water and again, the little hat perched on her head and, since she stood close to the bank, her feet slipped and she sank down into the torrents. But the Little Water Men took her in and tended her most carefully. The king even fell in love with the beautiful maiden and offered his hand in marriage. When his offer was turned down, he implored the maid just to stay with them; he would be content if he were able only to see her. Then he had a big fabulous crystal palace built for her, and often walked around and around it just to see the maiden. Every one of her wishes was granted. However, soon she began to feel bored and yearned to be back above ground. At her request, the harmless Little Water Men even brought her the little hat by which she had been transported there. Quickly, she put it on and instantly was back on land, covered with the most beautiful pearls, which the king of the Little Water Men had given her as a present.

## 89 The Curse of the Little Water Men

In olden days, the lord of a manor had entered into an agreement with the Little Water Men that the little fish that were washed into the rock pools on the shore when the water rose, and left behind there when it fell, should be theirs for the taking. The agreement was kept faithfully, and the last of the [noble] lineage even allowed them, occasionally, to fish in the main body of of the lake.

Nun zogen aber andere Herren auf, welche den Zwergen feindlich gesinnt waren; insbesondere waren es die ungezogenen Jungen, welche in ihrem Übermute die kleinen Wasserlachen ausschütteten oder die Fischchen verdarben. Da schickten die Zwerge Gesandte an den Edelherrn, um sich über den Treubruch zu beschweren. Der aber fertigte die kleinen Leute mit Hohnlachen ab und die bösen Buben trieben es nun ärger denn zuvor. Nun trat eine neue Gesandtschaft der Zwerge vor den Burgherrn und führte diesmal eine ernstere Sprache. Sie beriefen sich auf den Vertrag und die althergebrachte Übung: erst gestern hätten sie ein Fest gefeiert und keinen Fisch wie früher auf die Tafel bringen können. Die Gesandten aber wurden vor den Augen des Vaters von den Buben mit dem Schimpfworte: »Fort, ihr Wassermäuse!« hinausgejagt aus dem Schlosse, gestossen, geschlagen, und auf der Flucht fielen die armen Zwerge, und die Buben über sie hin.

Als sie endlich an's Wasser gekommen waren, kehrte sich der Zwerge Ältester, welcher auch das Wort geführt hatte, um, und fluchte den Buben, dass es ihnen nach ihrem Tode übel ergehen solle; sie sollten zu Wassermäusen werden, und in den Steinlöchern herumirren müssen, sie und Alle ihres Geschlechtes, bis einer käme, der sie erlöse.

So wurden diese und alle ihre Nachkommen zu Wassermäusen.

## 90 Der Müller und der Wassermann[18]

Auf einer Mühle im Walde hatte der Müller große Not mit dem Wassermann. Der kam jede geschlagene Nacht in die Stube und trug Fische auf und zu, und kochte und sott und briet, und fraß alle selber zusammen. Der Müller wusste sich nicht mehr zu raten und zu helfen. Nun sprach einmal ein Handwerksbursche zu, der hatte als Hunde drei Bären bei sich, und blieb über Nacht.

---

[18] „Der Wassermann . . . gilt dem Volke vorzugsweise als ein grausames Wesen, da er Kinder und Erwachsene in sein Element hinabzuziehen bemüht ist, somit dem Menschen feindselig gegenübersteht." *Sitten und Sagen*, Bd. 2: 185.

Now, however, other masters came to live there, who were ill-disposed toward the Little Water Men; in particular there were rude boys who, in their high spirits, drained the little pools of water, or spoiled the little fish. Whereupon the Little Water Men sent envoys to the noble lord to complain about the breach of faith. He, however, dismissed them with scornful laughter, and the rude boys made mischief even worse than before. Then a new delegation from the Little Water Men appeared before the lord of the manor, and this time carried a sterner message. They invoked the agreement and the long-established practice: only yesterday they had celebrated a festival but could bring no fish to the table, as in the past. But the emissaries were driven out of the castle by the knaves, before their father's eyes, with the insulting words, "Get out, you water mice!" The poor Little Water Men were pushed and beaten and falling down as they ran away, with the knaves falling upon them.

When finally they arrived at the water's edge, the eldest of the Little Water Men, who had also been their spokesman, turned around and cursed the boys as follows: they should suffer much evil after their deaths; they should become water mice, forced to wander around in the holes in the rocks, they and all their lineage, until one would come to redeem them.

That is how they and all their descendants become water mice.

## 90 The Miller and the Water Man[19]

At a mill in a forest, the miller had great trouble with a Water Man. He came into the living quarters each night like clock-work, and carried fish to and fro and cooked and boiled and fried and devoured [them], all by himself. The miller did not know any longer what to do or how to resolve this situation. Then one day, a journeyman who had with him three bears in the place of dogs, called [at the mill] and spent the night there.

---

[19] "The Water Man . . . is, in the first place, perceived as a cruel creature, since he is always trying to pull children and adults down into his Element, and is thus inclined to hostility toward humans." *Sitten und Sagen*, vol. 2: 185.

Wohl hatte er Hunger, aber der Müller konnte weder ihm noch den Bären in der Nacht etwas zu essen schaffen. Während dem kam auch der Wassermann, und war gar geschäftig, seine Fische zuzurichten und zu verzehren. Als er so an dem Tische saß und an seinen Fischen kaute, rochen die Bären die leckere Speise, und schlichen sich an den Tisch und schlugen mit ihren Tatzen auf die Schüssel. »Katsch Kodl!« schrie der Wassermann und schlug die ungebetenen Gäste auf die Bratzen. Diese aber wurden zornig und brummten und warfen den Tisch um, und fielen über den Wassermann her, den sie jämmerlich zerkratzten und zerbissen, bis er sein Heil in der Flucht fand. Er blieb nun im Mühlwasser, Tag und Nacht, und getraute sich nicht mehr in die Stube. Der Müller war dessen sehr froh, und tat, als sähe er seinen guten Freund gar nicht im Wasser sitzen. Über eine Weile hob der Wassermann seinen Kopf aus dem Wasser hervor und fragte den Müller, ob er noch die drei Katzen in der Stube habe? »Ja wohl,« sagte dieser, »noch mehr, ich habe deren sechs!« Da duckte sich der Wassermann und kam nicht mehr herauf.

## 91 Sage von der Meerfrau[20]

Einem Schiffe auf dem Meere waren die Leichen für die Meerfrau ausgegangen und es musste nun unter der Mannschaft das Los entscheiden, wer in die Fluten gesenkt werden solle. Es traf einen jungen schönen Mann. Doch erbarmte sich die Meerfrau seiner, weil die Braut schon an dem Ufer des nahen Landes mit Sehnsucht auf ihn wartete, und trug ihn an's Land und beschenkte ihn mit drei Säckchen, voll von Gold, Silber und Perlen. Dagegen musste ihr das Brautpaar das siebente Kind aus der Ehe versprechen.

Als dieses zur Welt kam, erschien die Meerfrau und nahm es in Empfang: denn jeden siebenten Tag der Woche ist es ihr vergönnt, die volle menschliche Gestalt anzunehmen; die trauernden Eltern tröstete sie damit, dass es dem Kleinen gut ergehen solle.

---

[20] „Die Seejungfrau war erst eine wunderschöne Prinzessin, dabei aber sehr böse und unruhig, weshalb sie der eigene Vater verfluchte und auf das Meer gehen hieß, wo sie tun könne, was sie wolle. So wurde sie halb Frau, halb Fisch, und lebt im Meere, wo sie durch einen ganz eigenen Gesang anzeigt, dass in 24 Stunden Sturm eintreten werde." *Sitten und Sagen*, Bd. 2: 192f.

The journeyman was indeed hungry, but the miller could not provide something to eat in the night for either him or the bears. Meanwhile, the Water Man also had arrived and was very busy preparing and eating his fish. As he sat at the table, chewing on his fish, the bears smelled the delicious food, sidled up to the table, and hit the bowl with their paws. "Shoo, tomcat!" shouted the Water Man, and whacked the uninvited guests on their claws. The bears, however, became angry and growled, and knocked the table over and fell upon the Water Man, whom they clawed and bit terribly until he saved himself by fleeing. Now he stayed in the mill stream, day and night, and no longer dared enter the living quarters. The miller was very happy about this, and pretended that he did not notice his good friend sitting in the water. After a while, the Water Man raised his head out from under the water and asked the miller if he still had the three cats in his room. "Yes indeed," the latter replied. "Even more; I have six of them now!" Whereupon the Water Man ducked down under the water and did not come out any more.

## 91 Legend of the Mermaid[21]

A ship on the ocean had run out of corpses for the Mermaid, and it had to be decided by lot who among the crew should be sunk into the waters. A handsome young man drew the lot. But the Mermaid had mercy on him because his bride was already waiting for him with longing on the shore of the country nearby, and she carried him to the shore, and gave him as a present three little bags full of gold, silver, and pearls. In return, the bridal couple had to promise [to give] her the seventh child born to them.

When that child came into the world, the Mermaid appeared and took delivery of it: for she is allowed to assume human form on every seventh day of the week; she comforted the grieving parents by assuring them that the little one would be treated well.

---

[21] "The Mermaid was once a fair and beautiful princess, but also very cross and fitful, whereupon her own father cursed her and banished her to the sea where she would be able to do whatever she wanted. Thus she became half woman and half fish, living in the sea, where she announces through a very distinct song that a storm will occur in 24 hours." *Sitten und Sagen*, vol. 2: 192f.

Es verging nun eine geraume Zeit: da wählte sich der älteste Sohn gegen der Eltern Willen ein armes Mädchen zur Frau und wurde von ihnen verstossen. Nun erschien die Meerfrau wieder, brachte das siebente Kind, zum schönen Jüngling erwachsen, zurück reiche Geschenke aber für das unglückliche Brautpaar gegen das Versprechen, dass wieder das siebente Kind der Ehe ihr angehöre.

So ist die Meerfrau auch jetzt noch der gute schützende Geist für diese Familie: bricht ein Unglück herein, kommt sie zu helfen; immer aber hat sie ein Kind aus deren Kreis bei sich in ihrem unterseeischen Glaspalaste, und ist dieses zum Jüngling erwachsen, stellt sie es zurück und holt sich ein neues.

## 92 Der Burgvogt und die Meerjungfrau[22]

Ein Burgvogt befragt, warum er so lange nicht heirate, gab zur Antwort, er habe einst geträumt und im Traume ein Mädchen gesehen, so schön und lieb, wie er noch keines bisher gefunden, sie stehe nun immer vor seiner Seele; er wisse noch alles ganz genau und würde selbst die Gegend erkennen, wo er im Traume sie gesehen.

Einmal musste er im Auftrage seines Herrn eine Reise unternehmen. Nachtherberge fand er auf einem Schlosse im Gartenhause. Es war eine schöne, mondhelle Nacht, und da er nicht schlafen konnte, ging er hinaus in den Garten. Am Ende eines Laubenganges befand sich ein Springbrunnen. In diesen schaute er eine Zeitlang hinein und glaubte plötzlich die Jungfrau, welche ihm im Traume erschienen war, im Wasserspiegel zu erkennen.

---

[22] „Man sieht sie zur Mittagsstunde oder um Mitternacht, bei Sonnen- oder Mondlicht, auf ruhigem Wasserspiegel, stets in verführerischer Stellung. Manchmal stehen sie auch mit einem Fuße auf dem Ufer . . . den andern halten sie ins Wasser. Ihre Haare sind teils hellblond, teils schwarz, blauschwarz, sehr reich und lang. Den Leib umhüllt ein Florschleier, leuchtend in Wasserfarbe. Dabei haben sie immer etwas zu tun: sie pflücken Blumen, flechten sich Kränze aus Wasserpflanzen. Gewöhnlich kämmen sie sich aber das Haar mit einem goldenen Kamm . . . mit sehr feinen Zähnen; sie lieben es dabei, den Kamm so zu halten, dass Sonne oder Mond darin widerstrahlt; dann blasen sie ihn aus ins Wasser, alles mit gewinnender Anmut." *Sitten und Sagen*, Bd. 2: 197.

A long time had passed, when the oldest son, against his parents' will, chose a poor girl for his wife, and they cast him out. Thereupon the Mermaid reappeared, brought back the seventh child, who had grown up to become a handsome young man, and brought rich presents for the unhappy bridal couple, but once again, in return for their promise that the seventh child of the marriage would belong to her.

To this day, the Mermaid is the kind and protective spirit for this family: when misfortune strikes, she comes to help; but always she has a child from the [family] circle with her in her palace of glass under the sea, and once this child has grown into a young man, she puts him back and takes another.

### 92 The Castellan and the Mermaid[23]

A castellan, asked why he had refrained from marrying for so long, replied that he had once had a dream, and in his dream he had seen a girl so lovely and sweet, like no other he had found so far, now she always stayed in his mind; and he still recalled every detail and would even recognize the place where he saw her in his dream.

One day, he had to undertake a journey on behalf of his lord. He found a place to stay for the night in the summer house of a castle. It was a beautiful, moonlit night, and because he could not sleep, he stepped out into the garden. At the end of a pergola, there was a fountain. He gazed into it for a long while and suddenly, he thought he spied the young woman who had appeared in his dream, reflected in the water.

---

[23] "They can be seen during the noon hour or at midnight, during sun- or moonlight, on the quiet surface of a body of water, and always in an enticing pose. At times, they plant one foot onto the shore . . . and the other is in the water. Their hair is sometimes fair, sometimes black, even blackish blue, and very thick and long. They are clad in a gauzy veil, iridescent in aquamarine. At the same time, they are always busy with something: they pick flowers, braid wreaths from aquatic plants. They usually comb their hair with a golden comb with very fine teeth, and they love to hold the comb so that either the Sun or the Moon is reflected in it; then they blow it into the water, and they do all of this with with a compelling air of grace." *Sitten und Sagen*, vol. 2: 197.

Nachdenklich kehrte er zurück, und es war ihm hierbei, als ginge
die Jungfrau vor seinen Augen einher. Er öffnete die Türe des
Gartenhauses, und war überrascht, dieselbe Jungfrau im Gemache zu erblicken. Nicht lange währte das Gespräch zwischen
den beiden, so trug ihr der Vogt seine Hand an, und sie blieb
sofort bei ihm, als wäre sie schon längst seine Frau. Am Morgen
aber hatte der Vogt Reue, dass er sie über Nacht bei sich behalten. Da lächelte sie und tröstete ihn. »Sei ruhig,« sprach sie,
»es hätte ja doch einmal sein müssen. Deine Formen sind nicht
die meinen; ich bleibe bei dir; doch frage mich nie um meine
Herkunft!« Dabei langte sie in die Falten ihres weiten Kleides
und reichte dem Erstaunten einen reichen Schatz an Perlen und
Edelsteinen daraus hervor. So lebten sie glücklich zusammen.
Das Glück erhöhten ihre Kinder, die sie ihm gebar. Als sie aber
mit dem siebenten Kinde schwanger ging, überkam sie große
Angst, und als der Knabe geboren war, wendete sie ihm eine
Sorgfalt und Zärtlichkeit zu, wie keinem der früheren Kinder.

Der Knabe war so zum jungen Mann von 25 Jahren gereift.
Da vernahm der Vater von ihrem Munde das Geheimnis, das
seither so schwer auf ihr geruht hatte. »Du musst wissen,« hub
sie an, »dass ich eine Wasserfrau bin. Sieben Kinder habe ich
geboren, sechs gehören dir, das siebente habe ich versprochen,
nach 25 Jahren dem Wasser als Tribut zu opfern, um die anderen sechse dir zu retten. Nun soll ich von meinem Sohne mich
trennen, der mir der liebste ist.« Da berieten sich die Gatten und
beschlossen, den Sohn auf Reisen zu senden, ihn aber vor dem
Wasser zu warnen.

Also verließ der Sohn die Heimat und ging hinaus in die weite
Welt, stets das Wasser vermeidend. Doch einmal vermochte er
es nicht, der Warnung der Mutter zu gehorchen; einem schönen
Mädchen zu Gefallen unternahm er eine Wasserfahrt. Heiter
und schön war der Himmel, ruhig wie ein Spiegel der See. Plötzlich aber begann das Wasser zu wogen und zu brausen; es warf
das Schifflein auf und nieder, so dass alle dachten, ihre letzte
Stunde sei gekommen. Wollte der Jüngling Hand anlegen, das
Schifflein zu lenken, tobten die Wogen noch unbändiger. Um
die anderen zu retten, sprang er hinaus in die stürmische Flut,

Deep in thought, he went back and it seemed to him that the young woman was walking along, right before his eyes. He opened the door of the summer house and was surprised to see the same young woman in his chamber. The conversation between the two had not gone on long when the castellan offered her his hand in marriage, and she stayed with him right away, as if she were already his wife. In the morning, however, the castellan was remorseful because he had kept her with him overnight. Thereupon she smiled and replied, "Be calm," she said, and comforted him. "It would have had to happen some day. Your customs are not mine; I shall stay with you, but never ask me about my origins!" She reached into the folds of her full dress and handed the astonished castellan a rich treasure of pearls and precious stones. So they lived happily together. The happiness increased with the children that she bore him. But when she was pregnant with the seventh child, she became very anxious, and when the boy was born, she lavished care and tenderness on him unlike with any of the earlier children.

The boy had matured into a young man of twenty-five. Then the father heard from her mouth the secret that had rested so heavily on her hitherto. "You must know," she began, "that I am a Mermaid. I have borne seven children; six belong to you, but I promised to give the seventh to the Water as a sacrifice, in order to save the other six for you. Now I am supposed to be separated from the son whom I love the most." Then the spouses discussed the matter and decided to send the son away traveling, but to warn him about the Water.

So the son left home and went out to the wide world, always avoiding the water. Once, however, he was unable to heed his mother's warning; he went on an excursion on the water to please a beautiful girl. The sky was bright and beautiful, and the lake was as smooth as a mirror. But suddenly, the Water began to heave and to foam; it tossed the little boat up and down so that everybody thought their last hour had come. When the young man tried to help steer the little boat, the waves raged even more vigorously. In order to save the others, he jumped into the stormy Waters,

und sogleich sah man ihn von einem schönen Frauenarm umschlungen und in die Tiefe gezogen. Er befand sich in den Armen einer schönen Wasserfrau und bedurfte keiner Überredung, bei ihr zu verbleiben; so sehr hatte ihn ihre Schönheit gefesselt. Doch mit Trauer gedachte er der Mutter zu Hause und erhielt das Versprechen, dass er sich ihr alle vier Wochen zeigen dürfe, indem er den Kopf über das Wasser erhebe. Zu gleicher Zeit sollte auch der Mutter Meldung geschehen, wo ihr Sohn sei, und dass sie ihn alle vier Wochen sehen werde, obwohl sie durch ihre Wortbrüchigkeit solche Gunst nicht verdient habe.

Der Sohn aber gedachte bald nicht mehr der Mutter, noch weniger der Zeit, wo er sich ihr zeigen könne; wohl mahnte den Liebetrunkenen die Wasserfrau. Doch er meinte immer, die Zeit sei noch nicht hiefür gekommen, wie denn die Zeit da unten eine ganz andere ist als bei uns. Erst als ihm ein Knabe geboren wurde, gedachte er seiner Pflicht, und wollte hinauf an den Wasserspiegel, um die Mutter zu sehen. Er vermochte es nicht mehr. So war ihm auch das siebente Kind geboren. Da wollte er sich nicht mehr zurückhalten lassen: er näherte sich der Wasserfläche und sah ein Schifflein fahren. Drinnen saß eine jugendliche Braut, mit den Zügen seiner Schwester. Da legte er sein Ohr an den Kahn, und vernahm, die Braut sei die Tochter seiner Schwester. Überwältigt von Sehnsucht nach den Seinigen auf der Erde, erhob er das Haupt über die Wasserfläche. Die Braut erkannte ihn. Er aber stieß einen Schrei aus und verschwand. An der Stelle zeigte sich eine Blutlache.

Eines Tages ging die Mutter, traurig über das unbekannte Schicksal ihres Sohnes, im Garten. Da lag die Leiche ihres Sohnes am Brunnen. Nun wurde ihr klar, was geschehen war. Auch ihre Zeit war um. Sie ergriff die teure Leiche und stürzte mit ihr in den Brunnen. Von beiden wurde nichts mehr gesehen.

So hatte die Wasserfrau sieben Kinder gewonnen, und durch den Wassertod des Siebenten für sich die Erlaubnis, auf neue drei Jahrhunderte schön und jung zu bleiben.

and immediately they saw a woman's beautiful arm clasping him tightly and pullling him down into the depths. He found himself in the arms of a beautiful Mermaid, and did not need any persuasion to stay with her, so much was he captivated by her beauty. But still he thought with sorrow of his mother back home, and was given the promise that he might show himself to her every four weeks by lifting his head above the water. At the same time his mother was to be told where her son was, and that she would see him every four weeks, even though because of her breach of faith she did not deserve such a favor.

But soon, the son thought no more about his mother, and even less about the times when he might show himself to her, though the Mermaid reminded the love-drunk youth. But he always replied that the time for that had not yet come, for the time down there is much different from ours. Only when a boy was born to him did he remember his duty, and he wanted to go up to the surface of the water to see his mother. He was no longer able to do so. And then his seventh child was born. He refused to be held back any longer; he neared the surface of the water and saw a little boat riding on it. In it sat a youthful bride, with the countenance of his sister. Thereupon he put his ear to the hull and learned that the bride was his sister's daughter. Overwhelmed by longing for his family above ground, he lifted his head above the surface of the water. The bride recognized him. He, however, let out a cry and disappeared. At that place a pool of blood appeared.

One day, the mother went about the garden, saddened over the unknown fate of her son. There at the fountain lay the body of her son. Now she understood what had happened. Her time also had come. She seized the cherished body of her son and plunged into the fountain with it. Nothing more was seen of the pair of them.

So the Mermaid had been allowed to bear seven children and, through the death by water of the seventh, was permitted another three hundred years to stay young and beautiful.

## 93 Der Graf und die Meerjungfrauen

Ein Ritter und seine Frau, sehr reich an Gütern dieser Welt, hatten nur ein Kind, einen Knaben. Als dieser zwölf Jahre zählte, starb der Vater, und die Mutter zog mit ihrem Kinde auf eine Burg, die in Mitte eines Sees stand, um von der Welt abgeschieden ganz ihrer Trauer leben zu können. Der Knabe aber wuchs und nahm zu an Schönheit und Verstand; doch war er immer so bleich und in sich gekehrt; er liebte es, allein zu sein, und hatte sich daher das Zimmer gewählt, welches am entlegensten die schönste Aussicht auf den See gewährte. Träumerisch schaute er immer hinaus in den See. Als er 24 Jahre alt war, drang die Mutter in ihn, sich eine Braut zu wählen; ihr war das Leben zu einsam geworden. Er aber wollte nicht. Eines Abends, nachdem die Mutter recht ernstlich in ihn gedrungen war, lehnte er sich betrübt an das offene Fenster und sah den Mond gar lieblich im Wasser sich spiegeln. Da gedachte er einer Braut und wie sie aussehen müsse, ihm zu gefallen. Ermüdet ging er zu Bette, vergaß aber, das Fenster zu schließen. Plötzlich bemerkte er einen lichten Schein am Fenster; er blickte auf, konnte aber nichts unterscheiden. Schon wollte er einschlummern, da rauschte der Vorhang des Bettes und ein weibliches Wesen mit Seidenhaaren und leichten Gewändern lag an seiner Seite. Der matte Schein des Mondes gestattete ihm so viel, dass er ein bleiches wunderschönes Frauenhaupt neben sich bemerken konnte. Sie schmiegte sich an ihn und in liebendem Spiel und Gespräche verging die Nacht. Am Morgen war das Frauenbild verschwunden. Kurz vorher hatte sie ihm eröffnet, dass sie wieder kommen werde: denn oft habe sie ihn gesehen, als er im Mondenlichte hinausgeblickt auf den See, und sie wäre schon früher zu ihm eingetreten, wenn die Fenster offen geblieben wären.

So lag jede Nacht ein Frauenbild an seiner Seite, und glücklich war er in dieser Liebe. Nun meinte er, es sei nicht immer dasselbe Wesen, welches mit ihm das Bett teile. Um so mehr bat er, sie möge sich bei Tage zeigen, seine Mutter dringe in ihn, dass er eine Frau nehme; möge sie auch arm sein, er werde sie zum Altare führen. Sie aber entgegnete immer: »Mein Lieber, das kann nicht sein; ich kann mich nicht trauen lassen nach deiner Weise;

## 93 The Count and the Mermaids

A knight and his wife, very rich in things of this world, had only one child, a boy. When he attained twelve years of age, the father died, and the mother moved with her child to a castle that stood in the middle of a lake, so that she could devote her life entirely to mourning, secluded from the world. The boy, however, grew up and increased in beauty and intellect; yet, he was always very pale and withdrawn; he loved to be by himself, and had therefore chosen the most remote room that granted him the most beautiful view of the lake. Dreamily, he kept looking out over the lake. When he turned twenty-four, his mother urged him to choose a bride; her life had become too lonely. But he did not want to. One evening, after the mother had urged him very seriously, he leaned on the open window, filled with sadness, and noticed how very lovely the moon was, reflecting in the water. Then he thought of a bride, and what she would have to look like to be pleasing to him. Tired, he went to bed, but he forgot to close his window. Suddenly, he noticed a bright glow at the window; he looked up, but he could not discern anything. He was just about to fall asleep, when the curtain of the bed rustled and a female being with silky hair and thin garments lay down at his side. The faint light of the moon allowed him only to be aware of a lovely pale-skinned woman's head beside him. She nestled up against him, and they passed the night in amorous play and conversation. In the morning, the ephemeral woman had disappeared. Shortly before that, she had disclosed to him that she would come back again, because she had seen him often looking down onto the lake in the moonlight, and that she would have entered his room before if the windows had stayed open.

So, every night an ephemeral woman lay by his side, and he was happy in this love. Then it occurred to him that it was never the same creature that shared the bed with him. More and more he implored her to appear in the daytime, because his mother was urging him to take a wife; he would walk to the altar with her, even if she were poor. However, she always replied, "My dear, that cannot be; I am not allowed to be married in your tradition;

lass mich deine Frau sein, wie ich es bisher war.« Indessen hatte sich die Mutter selbst um eine Braut für den säumigen Sohn umgesehen; doch sie ließ ihn kalt, und als er Abends zu Bette ging, seufzte das Frauenbild. Die Mutter aber eilte und bestimmte den Tag der Hochzeit. Er kam. Am ersten Tage wurde getanzt bis an den Morgen, den zweiten füllten Bankete aus, am dritten führten die Frauen die Braut in sein Gemach. Als sie eintraten, rauschten die Vorhänge an der Himmelbettstatt; die Braut erschrak. Sie sollte zuerst das Bett besteigen, und glaubte es schon besetzt zu finden. Lachend über ihre Ängstlichkeit folgte der Bräutigam nach. Aber zwischen beiden lag die Wasserfrau. Von eisigem Atem angeweht wich die Braut an den äußersten Rand. So war es jeden Abend. Der Ritter meinte seine Braut im Arme zu haben, die Braut aber härmte sich ab und starb noch vor Jahresfrist als Jungfrau.

In gleicher Weise erging es noch zehn Frauen, welche die Mutter dem Sohne gesucht: alle starben vor Jahresfrist. Die zwölfte Braut aber war klug, und erholte sich Rates bei einer Hexe. Von dieser erfuhr sie, wie Wasserfrauen Schuld seien an dem Unglücke der früheren Bräute: sie könne sich aber schützen, wenn sie am dritten Tage der Hochzeitfeier ihren Gatten nicht vor Ende der Geisterstunde begleiten würde; sie solle ihm nicht folgen, um ihn und sich zu retten; er werde zwar um die Mitternachtsstunde meinen, es ziehe ihn bei den Haaren hinaus in sein Schlafgemach: sie solle aber standhaft bleiben; ferner möge sie nicht unterlassen, das Fenster gegen den See schließen zu lassen, ja recht fest, damit die Geister nicht hereinkönnen. Der Gatte werde sich dann von klagenden Tönen angezogen fühlen, es werde ihn drängen hinauszuspringen in die Fluten. Dafür wurde sie mit einem Zauberspruche bewahrt, und mit Kräutern, welche sie unter das Bett werfen solle. Noch wurde ihr die Warnung, ja nicht vor ihrem Gatten die Vorhänge des Bettes auseinander zu ziehen und dieses zu besteigen, sowie alles, was sie gehört, für sich als Geheimnis zu bewahren, es würde sonst unfehlbar ihr Gatte sich wieder in die Gewalt der Wasserfrauen begeben.

Nun kam der dritte Hochzeittag. Es wurde Abend, dann Mitternacht. Immer unruhiger zeigte sich der Gatte; es hatte ihn

let me be your wife in the way I have been thus far." Meanwhile, his mother had herself looked for a bride for her procrastinating son; but that one left him cold, and when he went to bed that night, the ephemeral woman sighed. The mother, however, hastened and set the date for the wedding. On the first day, there was dancing until the morning, the second day was filled with banquets, and on the third the women led the bride into his room. When they entered, the curtains on the four-poster bed rustled; the bride became frightened. She was supposed to climb into the bed first and thought she found it already occupied. Laughing at her anxiety, the bridegroom followed. But the Mermaid lay between them. Touched by an icy breath, the bride gave way and moved to the very edge of the bed. Thus it was every evening. The knight meant to hold his bride in his arms, but the careworn bride died, still a virgin, within a year.

The same happened to ten other women who were sought out for the son by his mother; all died within a year. The twelfth bride, however, was clever, and sought the advice of a Witch. From her she learned that Mermaids were to blame for the misfortunes of the previous brides: she could protect herself, however, if she did not accompany her husband before the end of the witching hour, on the third day of the wedding celebration. To save both him and herself, she should not follow him; to be sure, he would feel as if he were pulled by his hair to his sleeping chamber at the midnight hour, but she should remain steadfast. Furthermore, she should not neglect to close the window facing the lake, really tightly, so that the spirits would be unable to enter. The husband would then be attracted by lamenting voices, and he might feel a compulsion to jump into the waters. For this she would have with her a secret magic spell, and herbs which she should throw under the bed. She should be warned also, under no circumstances to pull apart the curtains of the bed before her husband, nor to climb into it and, furthermore, to keep as a secret everything she might hear, otherwise her husband would inevitably be in the thrall of the Mermaids again.

Now came the third day of the wedding. It was evening, then midnight. The husband became increasingly agitated; he was

schon angewindet. Immer wollte er fort; die Braut hielt ihn
zurück, bis Mitternacht lange vorüber war. Im Schlafzimmer angelangt, öffnete er die Bettvorhänge: da seufzte es zwölfmal. Die
Braut sprach ihren Zauberspruch, und betete mit ihrem Gatten;
seit zwölf Jahren hatte dieser nicht mehr an Gott gedacht. Nun
vernahmen sie wilden Gesang und Brausen des Wassers. Der See
stieg, dass die Wellen an dem Fenster leckten. Aber die Nacht
war gewonnen und der Friede eingekehrt für immer.

Nach Umlauf eines Jahres gebar die Burgfrau; es war ein
Knabe und groß der Jubel. Die Hexe aber hatte geraten, die
Mutter solle das Kind vor dem zwölften Tage nicht aus der
Hand geben; die Zwölfzahl drohe dem Hause Gefahr. So wurde
das Kind am dreizehnten Tage getauft. Während der Taufe ver-
nahmen sie aus den Ecken des Zimmers Kinderstimmen und die
Worte: »Ich möchte es auch, ich möchte es auch.« Doch wurde
nichts gesehen. So gebar sie nach und nach zwölf Kinder. Bei
jeder Taufe aber ließen sich die Stimmchen hören. Als nun das
zwölfte Kind getauft wurde, ermannte sich die Mutter und rief:
»Wenn ihr wollt, so kommt hervor!« – und sogleich traten zwölf
Kinder, bleich, aber schön, mit Seidenhaaren, die Füße verbunden, hervor: sie sahen wasserfarbig aus. Der Graf erschrak, der
Priester taufte sie, und sowie eines die Taufe empfangen hatte,
fiel es zusammen und war tot. Das letzte der zwölf Kinder aber
sprach noch zuvor: »Ein Mensch ist unser Vater, zwölf Wasserfrauen aber sind unsere Mütter. Wir sind nicht Mensch, nicht
Geist, nun aber erlöst aus dem Banne, in dem wir lagen. Die
Wasserfrauen haben sich durch die Liebe zu unserm Vater auf
weitere dreihundert Jahre Schönheit und Jugend erkauft!«

## 94 Der schöne Tagelöhner und die Meerjungfrau

In einem Dorfe lebte ein schöner junger Tagelöhner, Veri,
und sein Liebchen war das schönste Mädchen weit und breit,
Anna Mayala mit Namen, aber arm. Die vielen Freier, die sich
meldeten, machten beiden Leutchen vielen Kummer, doch siegte
am Ende die Standhaftigkeit und der Tag zur Hochzeit wurde
bestimmt. Veri aber hatte von Natur etwas Wildes an sich: er
war so träumerisch und in sich versunken, und sang gar oft

already feeling the pull. Again and again, he wanted to leave; the bride held him back until midnight was long past. Having reached the bedchamber, he parted the curtains of the bed; there were twelve sighs. The bride recited her magic spell and prayed with her husband; for twelve years, he had not been thinking about God. Then they heard wild singing and the roaring of the Waters. The lake rose so high that the waves lapped onto the window. But the night had been won, and peace had returned forever.

Within a year, the lady of the castle gave birth; it was a boy and there was great rejoicing. However, the Witch had advised that the mother should not let the child out of her care before the twelfth day; the number twelve threatened danger to the family. So, they baptized the child on the thirteenth day. During the baptismal ceremony, they heard children's voices from all corners of the room, and the words: "I want it too, I want it too." Yet nothing was seen. By and by, she bore twelve children. But at every baptism, they heard the little voices. When the twelfth child was baptized, the mother plucked up courage and called out, "If you wish, come before us!"—and immediately, twelve children came out, pale-skinned, but beautiful, with silky hair and bound feet; they all looked like the color of water. The count became frightened, the priest baptized them, and as soon as each one received the sacrament, it collapsed and was dead. The last of the twelve children, however, said beforehand, "A human is our father, but twelve mermaids are our mothers. We are neither human nor spirits, but now we are released from the curse under which we lay. By means of the love of our father, the Mermaids have acquired another three hundred years of beauty and youth!"

### 94 The Handsome Day Laborer and the Mermaid

In a village there lived a young and handsome day laborer, named Veri, and his love was the most beautiful maiden far and wide; her name was Anna Mayala, but she was poor. The many suitors that offered themselves caused much misery for the two young people, but in the end their steadfastness prevailed and the date for the wedding was set. But Veri had a somewhat untamed nature; he was so dreamy and self-absorbed, and he often

gottlose Lieder von der Unterwelt. Davon hieß er der tolle Veri.
Tags vor der Hochzeit ging er in den Wald, um ein Wild für das
Fest zu erlegen. Mit einem prächtigen Rehbock auf dem Rücken
war er auf dem Wege nach Hause. Doch seine Gedanken irr-
ten wild umher, blieben nicht bei der Braut. Während er seinen wilden Träumen nachdachte, kam er an einen Steg. Schon
leuchtete der Mond. Da wurde er böse über sich, dass er sich
verspätet und versäumt habe, den Vorabend seiner Hochzeit bei
der Braut zu verbringen. Der Steg ging über ein helles flaches
Wasser, und der Mond spiegelte sich gar schön darin. Das zog
ihn wieder ab: es wehte ihn so wehmütig an. So legte er sein
Ohr, sich niederknieend, auf die Wasserfläche, ob er nichts höre.
Da vernahm er denn süßes Singen, je länger, desto schöner, je
schöner, desto bezaubernder. Immer mehr neigte er das Ohr den
wunderlieblichen Tönen, und gedachte, hinabzusinken in die
Fluten wäre gar so süß. Da schaute er hinein in die dunkle Tiefe;
es war, als ob schöne Beine, wie er sie nie gesehen, im Tanze
auf- und niederschwebten; er hob das Auge und sah Mädchen
schön und reizend, in leichter Bewegung nach den Tönen der
Musik einen Reigen beginnen. Alle waren schön, Eine vor allen. Er fragte sie, wie es da unten wäre. Sie näherte sich und
legte ihr bleiches Haupt auf seine Brust und sagte in Wehmut:
»Ach, es ist bei uns so schön, so ruhig, viel mehr Luft und Leben
als bei euch. Willst du mit mir?« Er bejahte es. Sie aber fügte
noch hinzu: »Sieh, ich war auch einst auf der Erde. Du hast eine
Braut. Kannst du sie vergessen? So du mit mir gingest, müsstest
du ihrer nicht mehr gedenken. Jedes Sehnen nach der irdischen
Braut würde dir Strafe zuziehen.« Bei diesen Worten schaute
sie ihm so gewinnend in die Augen, dass er sie umschlang.
Die Füße gleiteten ihm aus, er sank hinunter mit ihr in das
unbekannte Land.

Im Dorfe aber harrte die Braut umsonst des Geliebten: er
kam nicht. Man suchte aller Orten, und fand nichts, als auf
dem Stege sein Gewehr und den Rehbock. So vergingen viele
Jahre. An einem Dienstage sah man einen Hochzeitszug sich zur
Kirche bewegen, die Braut schön und anmutig wie eine Rose,
Anna Mayala genannt, hinter ihr Vater und Mutter. Letztere erschien bleich und leidend, an Jahren noch nicht vorgeschritten,

sang unholy songs about the Underworld. That is why he was called Wild Veri. The day before his wedding, he went into the forest to slay game for the feast. With a splendid roebuck on his back, he was on the way home. But his thoughts wandered about wildly, and did not stay on his bride. While thinking his wild dreams, he arrived at a bridge. The moon was already shining. Thereupon he became angry with himself for being late and having missed spending the eve before his wedding with his bride. The bridge led over clear, shallow water, and the moon reflected in it quite prettily. That distracted him afresh: it moved him to nostalgia. Kneeling down, he put his ear to the water's surface, to see if he couldn't hear anything. He heard then sweet singing, and the longer he listened, the more beautiful and hence more enchanting it became. On and on, he bent his ear to the wonderful and lovely melody, musing that it would be very sweet to sink down into the water. When he looked down into the dark depths, it was as if he saw beautiful legs such as he had never seen before, floating up and down in dance; he lifted his eyes and saw girls, beautiful and alluring, start a roundelay with gentle movements that followed the sounds of the music. All were beautiful, one in particular. He asked her what it was like down there. She came nearer and put her pale head against his chest, saying wistfully, "Oh, it is so beautiful in our place, so tranquil, much more air and life than in yours. Will you come with me?" He accepted. But she added, "Know that I too once lived above ground. You have a bride. Can you forget her? If you came with me, you would have to think of her no more. Any desire for your earthly bride would bring punishment upon you." But with these words, she looked him in the eye so seductively that he embraced her. His feet slid out from under him, he sank down with her into the unknown land.

In the village, though, the bride was waiting in vain for her beloved; he did not come. They looked for him everywhere and found nothing but his gun and the roebuck on the bridge. Many years went by. Then one Tuesday one could see a wedding procession approach the church, with the bride, named Anna Mayala, beautiful and dainty like a rose, followed by her father and mother. The latter looked pale and ailing, not very advanced in years

mit den Spuren hoher Schönheit. Der Zug ging über einen Steg. Tief auf seufzte die Mutter. Der Vater suchte sie zu trösten. »Ist die Gegenwart,« sprach er zu ihr, »nicht besser, als die Vergangenheit? Haben wir nicht in Frieden und Treue gelebt mit einander, und ist unsere schöne Tochter nicht dein sprechend Abbild?« Inniger lehnte sie sich an ihn. Plötzlich lief einer, die langen Haare wild in der Luft flatternd, in hastiger Eile den Bergabhang herunter, geradezu auf die Braut. Wie ein Rasender schlägt er sich vor die Stirne, wie ein Irrsinniger fasst er das Mädchen und nennt sie seine Braut: erst gestern habe er sie verlassen, sie müsse mit ihm zum Altare. Mit gewaltigem Arme schleudert ihn der Bräutigam hinweg, die Mutter bebt und meint zusammenzubrechen, der Zug geht weiter.

Nach zwei Tagen geht die junge Frau um Wasser an den Teich. Wieder kommt der wilde Mensch und umschlingt sie und will sie nicht lassen, und wieder wird er vom kräftigen Arme des Gatten hinweggeschleudert. Darauf sah man ihn im Dorfe herumgehen und nach Leuten fragen, die alle schon tot waren. Zuletzt ging er aus dem Pfarrhause heraus und seitdem sah und hörte man nichts mehr von ihm.

Später kam ein Franziskaner alljährlich in's Dorf, bleich und leidend, noch schön von Angesicht, und nirgends kehrte er lieber zu, als bei Anna Mayala. So oft er kam, befiel die Mutter ein Zagen, das sie nicht erklären konnte.

Nun starb der Vater. Der Mönch erschien zur Stelle, um die trauernde Witwe zu trösten. Er sprach folgende Worte zu ihr: »Gute Frau bedenkt, dass alles Leben hart ist: betrachtet mich und was ich gelitten, so werdet Ihr Euch weniger Euerem Schmerze hingeben.« Da sah ihn die Trauernde an, sie forschte, zagte, erschrak. Sie hatte den Veri erkannt, welcher in ihr schon längst seine Anna Mayala gefunden hatte. Nun kam die Reihe zu klagen an ihn; doch er ermannte sich und fuhr fort: »Ich habe da unten gelebt, in der Erde, in einem geisterhaften Reiche, gelebt mit einer Wasserfrau, schön und verführerisch, wie mit meiner Frau. Stets war sie um mich, nur an Freitagen blieb sie mir unsichtbar; ich wäre wohl glücklich gewesen in ihrer Liebe: doch blieb mir etwas zurück im Herzen, das keine Befriedigung fand. Zeitweise quälte mich eine Leere, die ich nicht auszufüllen vermochte;

and with the traces of great beauty. The procession passed over a bridge. The mother sighed deeply. The father tried to comfort her. "Is the present not better than the past?" he said to her. "Haven't we lived together in peace and faithfulness, and is our beautiful daughter not the very image of you?" She leaned in on him closer. Suddenly, a man, his long hair fluttering wildly in the air, ran down the side of the mountain in great haste, directly at the bride. Like a madman he pounds on his forehead; like a lunatic he seizes the maiden and calls her his bride; only yesterday had he left her; she must go with him to the altar. With powerful arms the bridegroom hurls him away; the mother trembles and thinks that she will faint; the procession moves along.

Two days later, the young woman goes to the pond for water. Again the wild man comes and embraces her and does not want to let go of her, and again he is hurled away by the strong arms of her husband. Later, he was seen walking around in the village and asking about people who already were all dead. Finally, he walked out of the presbytery, and after that he was neither seen nor heard of.

Later a Franciscan friar came to the village every year, pale and ailing, yet still with a handsome face, and he liked to visit nowhere more than at Anna Mayala's place. Whenever he came, the mother was afflicted with an apprehension that she could not explain.

Then the father died. The monk appeared on the scene to comfort the mourning widow. He said the following words to her, "Dear woman, consider that life is hard for everyone: look upon me and what I have suffered, and ye shall contemplate less thine own pain." So the mourning woman looked at him, she scrutinized, hesitated, became frightened. She had recognized Veri, who had long since already found his Anna Mayala in her. Now it was his turn to lament, but he took courage and continued, "I lived down below, in the Earth, in a land of phantoms, lived with a beautiful and alluring Mermaid, as with my wife. She was with me always, except that on Fridays she was invisible to me; I might have been happy in her love, yet always something remained in my heart that found no satisfaction. From time to time I was afflicted by an emptiness which I was not able to fill;

sie war eben doch keine rechte Frau. Besonders fiel mir auf, dass ihre Füße stets mit Schleifen gebunden und verhüllt waren. Sechs Kinder hatte sie mir geboren, und auch ihnen waren die Füße gebunden. Die Kinder wuchsen schnell zur vollen Grösse: so oft sie ein Kind gebar, war das vorhergehende schon vollkommen erwachsen. Das Geheimnis mit den Füßen peinigte mich aber immer mehr. Da löste ich, als sie einmal schlief, die Hülle der Füße, sie hatten Gänsefüße, Schwimmhäute zwischen den Zehen, an diesen kleine Krallerln. Ich erboste und fluchte und wünschte, dass doch das siebente Kind ein Mensch werden, mit menschlichen Füßen zur Welt kommen möchte. Und mein Wunsch wurde erfüllt. Die Wasserfrau aber, als sie das Kind zum ersten Mal sah, stieß einen Schrei des Entsetzens aus, dass sie einem solchen krüppelhaften Wesen zur Mutter werden musste und überhäufte mich mit Verwünschungen. Und nicht lange, so kamen die anderen Wasserfrauen, meine Frau zur Geburt Glück zu wünschen. Sie sahen aber nicht sobald die Menschenfüße des Kindes, als auch sie ergrimmten. Sie nahmen das Kind und zerrissen es in Stücke und begierig verschlangen sie die kleinen Glieder. Denn Kinderfleisch gewährt ihnen wieder auf dreihundert Jahre Schönheit und Jugend, und macht die Männer in Liebe zu ihnen entbrennen. Machtlos musste ich alles dieses über mich ergehen lassen.

Zuletzt tippte mich meine Frau an mit einem Stäbchen, ich verfiel in Schlaf, und als ich erwachte, befand ich mich an derselben Stelle, von welcher ich früher in das Wasser hinabgleitete. Ich sah den Hochzeitzug deiner Tochter; sie hielt ich der Ähnlichkeit halber für dich: denn es war mir alles wie ein Traum. Das Übrige weißt du. Erst der Pfarrherr klärte mich auf, dass seitdem schon mehr denn zwanzig Jahre verlaufen seien, und ich hatte gedacht, es wäre alles erst von gestern. Im Kloster büße ich für meinen Frevel. Deinen Enkeln habe ich Perlen und Edelsteine gebracht.«

Nicht lange und die Mutter kam zum Sterben. Wieder fand sich der Mönch ein; er kniete sich hin vor die Sterbende, und legte ihre Hände in die seinen: das Haupt sank ihm hernieder. Beide waren Leichen. Sogleich sah man zwei weiße Tauben zum Fenster hinausfliegen; die größere davon hatte aber an einem Fuße sieben schwarze Flocken hängen, welche bei der

she was, after all, not a real woman. I noticed, in particular, that her feet were always swathed and bound with bows. She had borne me six children, and their feet also were bound. The children grew quickly to full size; whenever she gave birth to another child, the previous one was already fully grown up. But the secret with the feet tortured me more and more. Therefore once, as she slept, I untied the wrappings over her feet, [and saw that] she had goose feet with webbing between the toes, which had little claws on them. I became very angry and cursed, and I wished for the seventh child, at least, to be human, and to come into the world with human feet. And my wish was granted. The Mermaid, however, when she saw the child for the first time, uttered a cry of horror that she had to be the mother of such a crippled creature, and she heaped malediction upon malediction over me. And then, not long after, the other Mermaids came to wish my wife happiness for the birth. However, no sooner had they noticed the human feet of the child, than they too became infuriated. They took the child and tore it into pieces and eagerly devoured the little limbs. For the flesh of children will confer upon them another three hundred years of beauty and youth, and it will make human men burn with love for them. Helpless, I had to let all of this happen to me.

At the last, my wife touched me with a little wand; I fell into a deep slumber, and when I awoke, I found myself at the very same spot from which earlier I had slid down into the water. I saw your daughter's wedding procession and, because of her similarity to you, thought she was you: for everything was like a dream to me. You know the rest. Only the presbyter explained to me that more than twenty years had passed since then, whereas I had thought it had all been just yesterday. In a monastery, I atoned for my sacrilege. For your grandchildren, I have brought pearls and precious stones."

Not long after that, the mother's last hour had come. Again the monk appeared; he knelt down by the dying woman and put her hands into his; his head sank down. Both were dead. Immediately, two white doves were seen to fly out the window; the larger of which had seven black flakes hanging from its foot which, upon

Berührung mit der kleinen fleckenlosen Taube am Fenster abgestreift wurden und weiß zur Erde fielen. Es waren Zettelchen, auf diesen standen die Namen der sieben Kinder des Wasserfräuleins: denn auch ihnen hatte der Vater durch sein späteres frommes Leben die Erlösung erwirkt, so dass auch sie in den Himmel eingehen durften.

Um die beiden Leichen abzuwaschen, ging eine der Enkelinnen hinaus an den Teich, um Wasser zu schöpfen, und schon war Avemaria vorbei, als sie zum Stege kam. Da begegnete ihr eine Freundin, welche sie fragte, warum sie zu so ungewöhnlicher Zeit Wasser hole. »Ach,« erwiderte sie, »es ist ja meine Großmutter gestorben, und ihr Geliebter, der Veri.« Da vernahm sie eine leise Stimme rufen: »Wer ist gestorben?« Und nun brauste der Teich, die Wellen hoben sich und wälzten sich auf das Haus zu und füllten die Stube, wo die Verblichenen lagen, und flötzten sie hin und her. Die Leute erschraken, gaben den Leichen Weihwasser und die Fluten zogen ab. Aber sie ließen sechs neue Leichen zurück, schöne Knaben und Mädchen, zwischen zehn und siebenzehn Jahren, die Füße verhüllt, in den herabhängenden Händen einen Zettel fassend, auf welchem geschrieben stand: »Wir sind erlöst.« Zuunterst an den Kinderleichen aber lagen zwei Füße eines Knaben, der dazugehörige Leib war in seinen Umrissen wie ein Schatten auf dem Boden gezeichnet. Daneben gab ein Zettelchen folgenden Aufschluss: »Der Leib ist verzehrt, die Seele währt.« Es war das siebente Kind der Wasserfrau, von welchem nur die menschlichen Füßchen übrig blieben. So oft der Jahrestag des Todes des tollen Veri kommt, bricht der Teich aus; an anderen Tagen schlägt er in seinem Gestade wilde Wellen. Seitdem scheint aber auch der Mond nicht mehr in seinen Spiegel.

## 95 Die gleichen Schwestern

Ein Fischer diente dem Grafen und war wohl gelitten, denn er brachte immer reiche Beute an köstlichen Fischen. Auf einmal aber vermochte seine Kunst nichts mehr, er fiel in Ungnade und wurde entlassen. So lebte er einige Zeit von seinem Ersparten, bis er nichts mehr hatte: da ging er hinaus auf das Wasser, um zu fischen,

touching the smaller spotless dove, were stripped off at the window and, turning white, fell down to the ground. They were little slips of paper on which were written the names of the seven children of the Mermaid, because as a consequence of his pious later life, the father had achieved their redemption also, so that they would be allowed to go to Heaven too.

In order to wash the two bodies, one of the granddaughters went down to the pond to scoop up water, and the evening prayer was already over when she arrived at the bridge. There she met one of her girlfriends who asked why she was fetching water at such an unusual hour. "Oh," she replied, "it is because my grandmother, and her beloved, Veri, died." Then she heard a quiet voice call, "Who died?" And then the pond began to roar, the waves rose up and rolled toward the house, filling the sitting room where the deceased lay, and they rocked them floating back and forth. The people were startled, sprinkled the corpses with Holy Water, and the Waters receded. But they left behind six new corpses, beautiful boys and girls between the ages of ten and seventeen, with their feet wrapped, and clutching in their hands that were hanging down, a slip of paper on which stood the words, "We are redeemed." But at the foot of the corpses they found two feet that belonged to a boy; the corresponding body had been outlined on the floor, like a shadow. Next to it, a little slip of paper explained, "The body has been consumed, the soul endures." It was the seventh child of the Mermaid, of which there remained only the little human feet. On every anniversary of Wild Veri's death, the pond floods, and on other days it makes wild waves upon its shore. Since that time, however, the moon no longer reflects from its surface.

## 95 The Identical Sisters

A fisherman was in the service of a count, and was well-liked because he always brought rich pickings of delicious fish. But there came a time when his skill was no longer sufficient; he fell from favor and was discharged. So he lived for a while on his savings, until he had no more: thereupon he went out on the water to fish,

fing aber wieder nichts und weinte bitterlich im Nachen. Plötzlich legte sich das Wasserfräulein heraus an den Wasserspiegel, und fragte ihn um sein Leid, und sagte ihm ihre Hilfe zu, wenn er ihr das verspräche, was er zu Hause nicht wisse: denn sie sei es, welche ihm die Fische erst zugetrieben, dann verjagt habe. Er gab das Versprechen, und tat einen reichen Fischzug und trug ihn heim. Als er aber der Frau sagte, um welchen Preis er glücklich sei, kam die Reihe zum Weinen an sie: denn sie trug ein Kind unter dem Herzen, wovon er nichts wusste. Doch trösteten sie sich mit dem Gedanken, dass sie das Kind Gott weihen wollten, und der Fischer fischte und fing wie früher die besten Fische, und brachte sie dem Grafen, der ihn wieder in Gnaden aufnahm. Zur bestimmten Zeit wurde ihm denn ein Sohn geboren, der gut gedieh an Leib und Geist, und für den geistlichen Stand bestimmt wurde. Doch als er fertig war, konnte er nicht Primiz halten: er gehörte ja der Wasserfrau. So gab er das Studium auf und wurde ein Bühner und ging in die Fremde. Auf dem Wege aber kam er zu mehreren Tieren, welche über einem Pferdeaas waren, und nicht wussten, wie sie es verteilen sollten: es war der Bär, der Fuchs, der Falke und die Ameise. Diese baten ihn, die Teilung zu übernehmen, und so teilte dieser und warf dem Bären die vier Viertel zu, damit könne er zufrieden sein, und dem Fuchsen das Rückgrad, und dem Falken das Ingeräusche und der Ameise den Kopf. Dann ging er seines Weges. Der Bär aber meinte, es wäre doch zu unbillig, wenn man den Mann so gar ohne Dank gehen ließe und befahl dem Fuchs, ihn zurückzurufen; und er kam und die Tiere gaben ihm die Gewalt, sich nach Wunsch in jede ihrer Gestalten zu verwandeln. Da lachte der Geselle und ging von dannen. Unter Weges bemerkte er in einem Kornacker eine Menge Rebhühner: um sein Geschenk zu prüfen, wollte er zum Fuchs werden, und sogleich war er Fuchs und fing sich soviel der Rebhühner, bis es ihm genug schien. Die nahm er in die nächste Stadt und ließ sich selbe in der Herberge zurichten zu einem Mahle. Während dessen traten vier Herren ein und setzten sich an den Tisch, und fingen zu karten an, wohl sehr rauh, denn es ging in

but again caught nothing and cried bitterly in his barque. Suddenly, a Mermaid poked above the surface of the water and asked him about his misery, saying she would help him if he promised her something that he did not know about in his home: for it was she who first had driven all the fish to him, and then had driven them away. He gave the promise, and made a rich catch, which he carried home. However, when he told his wife what the price of his happiness had been, it was her turn to cry because she carried a child in her womb of which he had known nothing. But they consoled each other with the thought that they would dedicate the child to God, and the fisherman fished and caught the best fish, as before, which he brought to the count, who restored him to favor. In due course, a son was born to him, who grew strong in body and spirit, and was destined for the clergy. But when he had finished [his ordination], he was unable to conduct First Mass; after all, he belonged to the Mermaid. So he gave up his studies, joined a theater, and went abroad. On his journey, however, he came across a number of animals who were standing over the carcass of a horse and did not know how they should divide it up: they were the bear, the fox, the falcon, and the ant. They asked him to take charge of the division, and so he cut it up and threw the four quarters of the body to the bear so that he could be satisified with it, and the backbone to the fox, and the innards to the falcon, and the head to the ant. Then he went on his way. But the bear opined that it would be too ungrateful to let the man go without any thanks, and asked the fox to call him back; whereupon he returned; and the animals bestowed upon him the power to assume each of their shapes at will. Thereupon the young fellow laughed and went away. Down the road, he noticed a flock of partridges in a cornfield: to test his gift, he wished to turn into a fox, and immediately he became a fox and caught as many partridges as he felt he needed. He took them to the next town, settled into an inn, and had them prepared for a meal. Meanwhile, four gentleman entered and sat down at a table and began to play cards, very raucously to be sure, because they played for

Kronentaler.[24] Der Geselle lag auf dem Stroh hinter dem Ofen, und sah, wie einer der Spieler schon einen großen Haufen Geldes gewonnen vor sich hatte: da machte er sich zur Ameise und kroch als solche unter den Spieltisch und hier wandelte er sich in einen Bären und richtete sich auf und warf den Tisch um mitsamt den Kronentalern, und erschreckte die Herren, dass diese eiligst davon liefen. Nun suchte er die blanken Stücke zusammen und legte sich wieder auf das Stroh und schlief und zahlte am Morgen seine Zeche und ging weiter.

Darauf geriet er in eine große Stadt: da war alles schwarz behangen und vom Turme wehte eine schwarze Fahne mit einem Totenkopfe. Er geht also in die Herberge und frägt den Wirt um die Ursache und erfährt, dass der König drei mannbare Töchter habe, alle gleich schön, und einander so ähnlich, dass man sie nicht auseinander kenne. Der König habe aber geschworen, dass nur die Mittlere das Reich erben solle: wer sie mit dem Reiche gewinnen wolle, müsse sie erraten: das aber misslinge jedem, und wer die Probe nicht besteht, verfalle dem Schwerte; so seien schon Viele umgekommen, und darum sei Trauer im Lande.

Da ging er hin zur Königsburg und sah in dem Garten, den ein tiefer Graben umgab, die Königstöchter lustwandeln, und er machte sich zum jungen edlen Falken und flog hinüber von Staude zu Staude und lockte die Mädchen, und ließ sich zuletzt von der einen fangen; er blieb ihr auf der Hand sitzen, wie früher auf der Staude und wurde von ihr in ihr Gemach getragen und auf eine goldene Stange gesetzt. Während sie nun schlief, nahm er seine Gestalt wieder an, jedoch in schönen, reichen Gewändern, und fasste die Prinzessin bei der Hand, dass sie erwachte, und erklärte ihr, wie er der Vogel sei und sie liebe.

---

[24] Der Kronentaler war eine Silbermünze von hohem Wert. Die meisten Münzen zeigen die Büste des habsburgischen Kaisers auf der Vorderseite und vier Kronen auf der Rückseite, daher der Name „Kronentaler." Nachdem die österreichischen Niederlande vom napoleonischen Frankreich besetzt wurden (1792), gaben einige deutsche Staaten (z.B. Bayern, Baden, Hessen-Darmstadt, und Württemberg) den Kronentaler als Zahlungsmittel aus, weil er zu einer oft benutzten Tauschmünze geworden war. (Siehe auch „FindMyCoin" <http://www.numismaster.com/ta/inside_numis2.jsp?page=PriceGuideInfoDenom>. Abgerufen 2 Sep 2012.)

Kronentalers.[25] The young fellow lay on a heap of straw behind the oven, and saw that one of the players already had a big pile of his winnings in front of him; thereupon he made himself into an ant and as such crept under the card table, then he changed himself into a bear and straightened up and overturned the table with all the Kronentalers on top, and terrified the gentlemen so that they ran away posthaste. Now he looked for the shiny coins and lay down on the straw again and slept, and in the morning he paid his reckoning and continued on his way.

Then he came to a large city: everything was covered in black hangings, and from the tower waved a black flag with a skull. So he goes into an inn and asks the host for the reason, and learns that the king has three marriageable daughters, all equally beautiful, and so much alike that one cannot tell them apart. However, the king had sworn an oath that only the middle daughter should inherit the kingdom: he who wants to win her, with the kingdom, has to guess her correctly; but everybody fails to do that, and he who does not pass the test is given to the sword; thus already many had perished, and because of that the land was in mourning.

Whereupon he went to the royal castle and saw the king's daughters strolling in the garden, which was surrounded by a deep moat, and he made himself into a young and noble falcon and flew across, from shrub to shrub, and enticed the maidens, and finally he allowed one of them to catch him; he stayed sitting on her hand, as earlier on the shrub, and was carried by her to her chamber and placed upon a golden perch. While she slept, he assumed his human form again, however this time in rich and beautiful garments, and took the princess by the hand so that she awoke, explained to her that he was the bird and that he loved her.

---

[25] The Kronentaler was a silver coin of high value. Most examples show the bust of the Austrian ruler on the front side and four crowns on the reverse, which gave it its name meaning "crown coin." After the Austrian Netherlands was occupied by Napoleonic France (1792), some German states (e.g., Bavaria, Baden, Hesse-Darmstadt, Württemberg) issued the Kronentaler, as it had become a popular trade coin. (See also "Find MyCoin," <http://www.numismaster.com/ta/inside_numis2.jsp?page=PriceGuideInfoDenom> Accessed 2 Sep 2012.)

Anfangs zu Tode erschrocken über den fremden Mann und seine Worte, fand sie doch bald Gefallen an ihm und bekannte sich als die Mittere der Prinzessinnen. Sie gab ihm auch den Ring vom Finger, und als Zeichen, woran sie zu erkennen, nannte sie einen roten Seidenfaden, den sie um den mittleren Finger der rechten Hand tragen werde, wenn er zur Wahl komme.

Nun machte sie das Fenster auf und der Falke entflog, und der Fremdling kam am Morgen, um die mittlere Königstochter zu werben, vor den König, der ihn mit dem ganzen Hofgesinde ob seiner Schönheit bedauert und bewegen will, abzustehen von dem gefährlichen Vorhaben. Er aber beharrt und wird aufgerufen, in den Saal zu treten, wo die drei Töchter sich befanden, und hinter ihn stellte sich der Scharfrichter mit blankem Schwerte. Da wurde ihm Angst und Bange und gerne willfahrte man seiner Bitte, das Fenster zu öffnen. So trat er vor die gleichen Schwestern: die eine trat mit dem Fuß vor, und trug am Finger den roten Faden; sie bezeichnete er als die mittlere und hatte die rechte getroffen. Große Freude herrschte nun am Hofe und in der Stadt: denn schon lange hatte der König Reue über seinen Schwur und das viele Blut, welches floss, und gerne gab er die Tochter dem glücklichen Freier.

Mehrere Jahre hatten sie glücklich gelebt, da zog er hinaus zur Jagd. Wohl riet ihm die besorgte Gemahlin ab, denn sie hatte üble Ahnung: aber er achtete es nicht; der Tag war heiß, er hatte lange einen Hirsch verfolgt, und ihn dürstete; nicht mehr gedachte er der Worte seiner Mutter, welche ihn so oft gebeten hatte, sich vor dem Wasser zu hüten. Er eilte dem Gefolge voraus, und fand eine Quelle, und bückte sich eben, um mit der Hand daraus zu trinken, als ihn die Wasserfrau erfasst und hinabzieht. Dem Volke aber, welches eben dazu kam, rief sie zu, sie habe ihn teuer erkauft.

Die traurige Mär wurde der Königstochter gebracht; diese hatte nicht Rast noch Ruhe, sondern eilte, zum Brunnen und zu ihrem Herrn und Gemahl zu kommen, und setzte sich hin an's Ufer und weinte. Da tauchte die Wasserfrau auf und tröstete sie damit, dass er es gut habe bei ihr. Die Königin aber war schon zufrieden, wenn sie ihren Gemahl nur zu sehen bekäme, und bot der Wasserfrau den goldenen Kamm vom Haupte.

At first she was frightened to death by the stranger and his words, but soon she took a liking to him and made it known she was the middle princess of the three. Also she gave him the ring from her finger, and as a sign by which to recognize her, she took a length of red silk thread which she would carry wrapped around the middle finger of her right hand, when he came to choose.

Then she opened the window and the falcon flew away, and in the morning the stranger appeared before the king to woo the king's middle daughter. The king, with all his courtiers, bemoans his handsomeness and tries to dissuade him from his dangerous plan. But he insists, and is called to step into the hall in which are the three daughters, and the executioner takes up his position behind him with his unsheathed sword. Thereupon he became frightened and they gladly obeyed his request to open the window. So he stepped up to the identical sisters; one put her foot forward, and wore the red thread on her finger; he declared her to be the middle one, and he had chosen right. Thereupon great joy ensued at the court and in the city, for the king had long regretted his oath and the much blood that had flowed, and he gave his daughter gladly to the happy suitor.

They had lived happily for several years, when he went out on a hunt. Despite that his concerned wife had counseled him against it, because she had had a premonition of evil, he did not heed her advice; the day was hot, and he had followed a stag for a long time and he was thirsty; he no longer kept in mind the words of his mother who so often had besought him to beware of the water. He hurried on ahead of his entourage and found a well and was bending down to drink from it using his hand, when the Mermaid seizes him and pulls him down. To the people who just arrived at the scene, she called out that she had paid for him dearly.

The sad story was related to the king's daughter, who reacted with neither rest nor calm, but rather hastened to the fountain to come get her lord and husband, and sat down at the water's edge and wept. Thereupon the Mermaid came up to the surface and consoled her, saying that he would have it good at her place. The queen, though, would be happy to merely see her husband, and offered the Mermaid the golden comb from her head.

Da hob ihn die Wasserfrau bis unter die Augen empor. Zum zweiten bot sie ihren Ring, und er stieg bis an die Hüften aus dem Wasser; zum dritten bot sie den goldenen Pantoffel vom Fuße, und die Wasserfrau stellte den Gemahl auf die Hand – und siehe, er entschwand als Falke und stand neben der Gattin. Da fährt die Wasserfrau in den Brunnen hinunter, dass es zischt und gischt, und wieder herauf, und wirft der Königin eine Hand voll blauen Sandes in das Angesicht, dass diese zum Drachen wurde.

Nun war wieder große Not. Der König bietet die Hälfte seines Reiches dem, der Hilfe brächte. Ein alter Zauberer ließ sich endlich melden und versprach zu helfen, wenn die hohe Frau es aushielte. Er lässt drei Öfen bauen und heizen, dass einer mehr glühte als der andere. Dann steckte er den Drachen hinein, und zog ihn heraus, als die Haut weich war, und kühlte ihn im Wasser; im zweiten Ofen barst die Haut, aber als er den Drachen in den dritten Ofen steckte, musste der unglückliche Gatte sich verbergen, um das Klagen und Winseln der Leidenden nicht zu vernehmen. Endlich steht die Königstochter nackt vor dem Gatten, der ihr seinen Mantel umwirft und sie im Triumph heimführt. Von nun an lebten sie froh und ohne weiteres Hindernis; die Wasserfrau hatte keinen Teil mehr an ihm.

## 96 Der Hüterjunge und die goldene Schuppe

Bei einem Grafen in den Bergen diente ein verlaufener Bube als Hirt. Der schlich eines Tages in den Baumgarten am Schloss und kam zu einem Brunnen. Da sah er was Glänzendes schwimmen und nahm es heimlich mit. Im Winkel des Stalles hielt er den Fund ans Spanlicht und es war nur eine kleine goldene Fischschuppe. Er wog und bog und rieb das schimmernde Ding, als auf einmal die junge Burgfrau vor ihm stand. Erschrocken fiel ihr der Hirt zu Füßen, denn sie war gar schön und stolz und hatte den hübschen Knecht noch keines Blickes gewürdigt. Jetzt aber erhob sie das Spanlicht und strich dem Jungen das Haar aus der Stirne und lächelte gar gnädig ihn an und nannte ihn einen schönen Jüngling, der ihr lieber wäre denn der alte Graf, ihr Gemahl.

Thereupon the Mermaid lifted him up and out to below his eyes. Second, the queen offered her ring, and he rose out from the water as far as his hips; third, the queen offered her a golden slipper from her foot, and the Mermaid put him onto her hand [above the water]—and lo and behold, he escaped in the shape of a falcon, and [then] was standing beside his wife. Thereupon the Mermaid departs down into the well, which hisses and froths, and back up again, and throws into the queen's face a handful of blue sand, which turned her into a Dragon.

Then there was great misery again. The king offers half of his kingdom to the person who brings help. Finally, an old Sorcerer presented himself and promised to help, if the noble lady could endure it. He had three ovens built and heated up, so that each one glowed hotter than the next. Then he placed the Dragon in the first, and pulled her out when the skin was soft, and then cooled her in water. In the second oven the skin burst, but when he placed the Dragon in the third oven, the unhappy husband had to hide away so that he could not hear the moaning and whimpering of the sufferer. Finally, the king's daughter stands naked before her husband, who places his cloak around her and leads her home in triumph. From this day on, they lived happily and without any further impediments; the Mermaid no longer owned a part of him.

## 96 The Shepherd and the Golden Scale

A lost young boy served as a shepherd for a count who lived in the mountains. One day, the boy sneaked into the orchard at the castle and came to a well. He saw something shiny floating on the water and secretly took it. In a corner of the stable, he held up his find to the light from a burning taper, and saw that it was only a small, golden fish scale. He cradled and turned and rubbed the shiny thing, when all of a sudden, the young lady of the castle stood before him. Scared, the shepherd fell at her feet, for she was quite beautiful and proud, and she had never given the handsome servant even a look. She then held up the burning taper and pushed the boy's hair from his forehead, smiling at him quite graciously and calling him a handsome young man, whom she would much prefer to the old count, her husband.

Das mochte dieser gehört haben: denn grimmig fuhr er herbei, packte den Buben und warf ihn den Felsen hinunter. Wer da hinunterfiel, vergaß das Aufstehen für immer bis zum jüngsten Tag.

Der Hirt aber fiel unten, wo sonst kein Wasser gewesen, in einen weichen Pfuhl und tat sich nicht weh. Eben kam ein Einsiedler des Weges; der trug einen schweren Sack und sagte zum Jungen: »Hilf mir den Brotsack in meine Hütte tragen!« Der hatte ein gutes Herz, trug den Sack, und diente fortan dem frommen Mann.

Einmal hatte der Knecht Langeweile und zog seine goldene Schuppe hervor und wollte sie glänzender haben; darum rieb er sie sachte. Wieder stand die Burgfrau vor ihm, der wie Espenlaub vor Angst zitterte, und sie bat, von ihm hinweg zu gehen, damit es ihm nicht noch übler ergehe wie vordem. Sie aber lächelte gar hold, nannte ihn ihren Schatz, und versprach, ganz ihm zu gehören, so er ihr ein Pfand geben würde. Der Junge aber merkte jetzt, was er für einen Fund getan und hatte Nichts, was er der Gräfin geben könnte. Diese fing nun zu seufzen und zu weinen an und setzte sich an seine Seite und umarmte und küsste den Knecht, dass ihm siedend heiß wurde. Die Frau berückte ihn so, dass ihm die Sinne schwanden und er nicht wusste, was er tat, und als er aus seinem Taumel erwachte, war er allein; er meinte, es wäre ein Traum gewesen: aber der Verlust der Schuppe belehrte ihn eines anderen. Da wurde der Knecht aus Liebe krank, und der Einsiedler pflegte sein wie ein Vater, dass er wieder genas. Doch wich das Bild der schönen Frau nicht aus seinem Herzen, er brütete Tag und Nacht und der Gram kam wieder über ihn. Da entdeckte er dem frommen Mann sein Leid. Der fragte ihn aus um seiner Kindheit früheste Tage – er hatte das eigene, lange verloren geglaubte Kind gefunden. Doch schwieg er hievon, denn er mochte nicht gestehen, dass er der Bruder des Grafen und durch dessen Zauberkünste um all sein Hab und Gut gekommen sei.

Den Knaben litt es aber nicht länger mehr im dunkeln Walde; er fühlte, wie es ihn anwindete, fortzog; so machte er sich auf und ging in der Irre herum und gelangte wieder zum Garten des Schlosses und zum Brunnen, der im trüben Mondlicht leise Wellen trieb. Er schaute hinein in die spielende Fläche,

The latter must have heard that because he rushed at them in a great rage, grabbed the boy, and tossed him down from the rock. Whoever fell down there forgot forever to rise again until Judgement Day.

But the shepherd fell down into a soft puddle, where there had been no water before, and did not get hurt. Just then, along came a hermit; he carried a heavy sack, and he said to the boy, "Help me carry this sack of bread to my cottage!" The boy had a good heart, carried the sack, and served the pious man from then on.

One day, the servant was bored and pulled out his golden scale and wanted to make it shinier, so he rubbed it gently. Again the lady of the castle stood before him; he shook like a leaf with fear, and asked her to go away so that he would not be treated even worse than before. But she gave him a very lovely smile, called him her sweetheart, and promised to be his alone if he gave her a token. However, the boy realized what kind of find he had made, and [replied] that he had nothing he could give to the countess. She then began to sigh and weep and, sitting down by the servant's side, embraced and kissed him so that he became boiling hot. The woman beguiled him so much that he lost his senses and did not know what he was doing, and when he awoke from his rapture, he was alone; he thought it had been a dream, but the loss of the scale taught him otherwise. Thereupon the servant became sick with love, and the hermit took care of him like a father, so that he recovered. The image of the beautiful woman, though, did not leave his heart; he brooded day and night, and he was grief-stricken again. Then he disclosed his grief to the pious man. He asked [the boy] about the earliest days of his childhood—he had found his own child, who for a long time he had believed to be lost. He kept quiet about this, however, for he did not want to confess that he was the count's brother and had lost all of his wordly goods through the former's magical skills.

But the boy could endure the dark forest no longer; he felt like [something] tugged on him and pulled him away, so he sallied forth and wandered about, disoriented, and arrived again in the castle's garden, and at the fountain, which made gentle waves in the dim moonlight. He looked down into the rippling surface,

schüchtern über den Rand des Brunnens gebückt. Da lag die
Gräfin im Bade, ruhig und still, und hatte die Augen geschlos-
sen, als ob sie schliefe, und bewegte nur den blendendweißen
Arm und die rosigen Finger der Hand, welche anstatt in Nägel,
in Schuppen sich endeten. Endlich regte sie sich; sie löste den
silbernen Gürtel vom Leibe und hielt ihn schwingend empor.
Der Jüngling, welcher die Wasserfrau erkannt hatte und nun
vermeinte, sie wolle ihm die Schlinge um den Hals werfen und
ihn erwürgen, griff hastig nach dem Gürtel und rannte mit der
Beute davon, wie von Hundert gehetzt, in langen Umwegen zur
Klause. Schon war es Tag. Da fand er den Grafen traulich beim
Alten sitzen. Jener aber hatte kaum den Gürtel in der Hand des
Knaben bemerkt, als er rasend aufsprang: »Ha, der Gürtel der
Gräfin,« rief er, und wollte den Jungen mit dem Schwerte durch-
bohren. Da rief der Alte: »Bruder, halt ein, es ist mein Sohn!«
Das Schwert entsank dem Grafen. Von beiden gefolgt, eilte er
zum Brunnen; da saßen die Meerwölfe und nagten noch an den
Knochen der Wasserfrau; sie musste sich alle Jahre einmal ba-
den, um die Fischhaut abzustreifen, die ihr alle Jahre wuchs; der
Gürtel schützte sie im Bade vor ihren Feinden, den Meerwölfen.

Der Graf verfiel in Wahnsinn und starb bald, nicht lange da-
nach auch der Einsiedler. So wurde der junge Knecht Burgherr;
unbeweibt endete er in Trübsinn das freudenleere Leben.

bending timidly over the edge of the fountain. There lay the countess in the bath, quiet and still, with her eyes closed as if she were sleeping, moving only her splendidly white arm and the rosy fingers of the hand that ended in scales rather than nails. Eventually she stirred, undid the silver belt from her body and held it up, swinging it. The youth, who had recognized the Mermaid, and now thought that she wanted to tie the noose around his neck and strangle him to death, hastily grasped the belt and ran away with his booty, as if hunted by dogs, on a long meandering path back to the hermitage. Already it was day. There he found the count sitting familiarly beside the old man. But hardly had the count noticed the belt in the boy's hand, when he jumped up in a frenzy: "Hah, the countess's belt," he called out, and wanted to run his sword through the boy. Then the old man shouted, "Brother, stop, it is my son!" The count's sword sank away. Followed by both, he hurried to the fountain; there sat the Seawolves, still gnawing on the Mermaid's bones; she had to bathe once every year to slough off the fish skin which every year grew [back again]; the belt protected her in the bath from her enemies, the Seawolves.

The count went insane and soon died; not long after that the hermit died too. So the young knight became the lord of the castle; wifeless, his joyless life ended in melancholy.

# THE ELEMENTS:
## EARTH II—CASTLES, MOUNTAINS, DWARVES, GIANTS, FORESTS & FOREST CREATURES

The Upper Palatinate landscape is characterized by lovely river valleys, rolling hills, and forests that stretch to the horizon, among them the Bavarian and Upper Palatinate Forests. In the legends of the Upper Palatinate, forests are the realm of the Forest Maidens and the "Hoymen," who help maintain and protect the forests, each in their own ways.[1]

The Upper Palatinate is the region with the most castles in Europe. There are almost 1,000 fortifications, and sadly, many of the castles now lie in ruins. Schönwerth collected many tales of castles shrouded in legend about mighty Giants, proud lords and spellbound damsels.

The area around Amberg, Schönwerth's birthplace, has become known as the "Ruhr Area"[2] of the Middle Ages. To this day, numerous metalworks in the Vils and Naab river valleys remain as evidence of the busy mining and smelting activity of past times. Many of the tales in Schönwerth's collection tell of Dwarves and other magical peoples of the Earth who wrest their treasures therefrom under cover of darkness.

---

[1] *Sitten und Sagen,* vol. 2: 337.

[2] The Ruhr Valley has been the most important industrial area in Germany since the beginning of industrialization, with large iron ore and coal mines which make it ideally suited for steel production.

This passage in Schönwerth's Introduction makes it clear that he sees Earth as the Element that connects all these legendary creatures, forests, castles, and the subterranean world, with the human people:

> Earth offers . . . a myriad of mythical creatures for discusssion; primarily on and inside of the mountains the Giants and Dwarves; in the forests the Forest Spirits with their unfortunate Forest Maidens; in the ancient castle ruins the damsels of the castle in a mythical background who await their redemption and offer rich treasures in return. Parallel to it a separate world developed beneath the Earth's crust . . . roads and alleys crisscross the terrain beneath its green cover, giving the impression that the present civilization had been built on the ruins of one long gone . . . [3]

---

[3] „[D]ie Erde bietet . . . eine Mehrzahl mythischer Wesen zur Besprechung, vorzugsweise auf und in den Bergen die Riesen und Zwerge, im Walde die Waldgeister mit den unglücklichen Holzfräulein, in den alten Burgruinen auf mythischem Hintergrunde die Burgjungfrauen, welche der Erlösung harren und dafür reiche Schätze bieten. Daneben entwickelt sich eine eigene Welt unter der Erdrinde. . . . Straßen und Gänge durchziehen den Boden unter der grünen Decke, damit es den Anschein gewinne, als habe die Gegenwart über den Trümmern einer vergangenen Kultur sich aufgebaut." *Sitten und Sagen.* vol. 2: 13.

## 97 Geschichte vom Ochsenkopf

Auf dem Ochsenkopf befindet sich nach der Sage eine Kapelle, die Geisterkapelle, gerade unter dem Felsen, welcher der Kirche von Bischofsgrün gegenüber liegt, gefüllt mit unendlichen Schätzen an Gold und Edelsteinen. Am Johannestage, wenn der Pfarrer von Bischofsgrün das Evangelium von der Kanzel herabverkündet, öffnet sich die Kapelle, um mit Ende des Evangeliums sich wieder zu schließen. Wehe dem, der dann die Frist übersieht: er wird zurückbehalten. Dagegen glücklich, der die kurze Zeit zu benützen wusste: er kehrt reichbeladen heim. – An diesem Tage wächst dort eine einzige Blume ihrer Art: sie ist der Schlüssel zum Öffnen der Kapelle. Vor vielen hundert Jahren glückte es mehreren Landleuten der Gegend, sie zu finden und die Kapelle zu öffnen: sie konnten sich nicht sattsehen an den Herrlichkeiten drinnen; Altäre und Kanzel waren von Gold, die Säulen von Silber, mit Edelsteinen besetzt. – Einst regnete es an diesem Tage, und der Köhler wollte seine Kohlen retten und war in den Wald geeilt, als die Glocken eben zusammenläuteten. Da sah er die Kapelle offen, trat ein, und der Glanz eines goldenen Altares trat ihm entgegen. Er lief nach Hause, um Leute zu holen, allein das Läuten nahm ein Ende und der Köhler vernahm nur mehr das Zusammenstürzen der Kapelle.

## 98 Der Teufelsfelsen[4]

Der Teufel war auf dem Wege nach dem Blocksberge in einer Walpurgisnacht müde geworden; so setzte er sich, um auszuruhen, auf das platte Dach des Kirchturmes zu Vilseck, das eben unter ihm lag. Davon brach der alte morsche Turm zusammen, und die Vilsecker mussten einen neuen bauen, den sie aber um so spitziger machten, als der erste stumpf war,

---

[4] „Besonders das Naabgebiet weist diese Steine auf; ein solcher steht an der Waldnaab im Waldrevier Reuth, ein anderer auch bei Diepoldsried. Es sind wohl alte Opfersteine; eigentümlich erscheint aber, dass gerade Teufel und Hexe mit Buttern zu tun haben." *Sitten und Sagen*, Bd. 2: 250f.

## 97 Tale from the Oxhead Mountain

According to legend there is a chapel on the Oxhead Mountain, the Chapel of the Ghosts, right beneath the rock opposite to the church in the town of Bischofsgrün, filled with boundless treasures of gold and precious stones. On Saint John's Day, when the priest of Bischofsgrün preaches the Gospel from the pulpit, the chapel opens its doors, [only] to close them again at the conclusion of the Gospel. Woe to those who miss that period of time, for they will be kept out. Happy is the one, however, who knows how to use the short timespan; he returns home, richly laden.— On this day grows a flower which is the only one of its kind: it is the key that opens the chapel. Many hundred years ago, several farming people from the region were lucky enough to find it and to unlock the chapel; they could not take their eyes off the magnificent treasures within; [the] altars and the pulpit were made of gold, the columns of silver, set with precious stones.—Once it rained on this day, and a charcoal maker, intending to save his coals, hastened to the forest just as the bells had begun to ring. He saw the chapel open, entered, and was greeted by the brilliance of a golden altar. He ran home to fetch some [other] people, however, the ringing of the bells came to an end, and all the charcoal maker could hear then was the sound of the chapel collapsing.

## 98 The Devil's Rock[5]

The Devil became tired on his way to the Block Mountain during Walpurgis Night; so he sat down on the flat roof of the church tower in the town of Vilseck, which was right beneath him, to rest there. This caused the old, rotten tower to collapse, and the people of Vilseck had to build a new one, but they made it as spiky as they could, unlike the first one that had been flat,

---

[5] "The Naab Valley in particular shows these types of rock; one of them can be found along the Waldnaab River in the Forest of Reuth, another one also near the village of Diepoldsried. They may well be sacrificial stones; what is peculiar, however, is that particularly here Devils and Witches are associated with churning butter." *Sitten und Sagen*, vol. 2: 250f.

damit der Teufel nicht wieder darauf rasten könne. So wurde der Vilsecker Turm der spitzigste in der ganzen Oberpfalz. Das verdross natürlich den Teufel; er nahm ein Felsenstück auf den Kopf und trug es gen Vilseck, um den Bau zu zertrümmern. Es war im Vilsecker Wald, wo er eine alte Frau, eine Schusterin und zugleich Vilseckerbotin, des Weges nach Hambach gehen sah. Diese fragte er, wie weit er noch nach Vilseck habe, er müsse dort den Turm einwerfen. Da öffnete die Alte ihren Sack voll alter zusammengebettelter Schuhe und erwiderte ihm: »So weit, dass ich alle diese Schuhe schon zugegangen habe; ich komme gerade von dort her.« »So weit kann ich den Stein nicht mehr tragen,« rief der Teufel voll Zorn und warf das Felsenstück mit solcher Gewalt hin, dass die Splitter, zentnerschwer, heute noch im Walde zerstreut liegen. Der Hauptstein aber, so groß wie ein Bauernhaus, fiel mitten im Walde auf eine Anhöhe; er zeigt noch die Spuren des Trägers, die Bratzen und den Kopf, letztern so groß wie ein großes Wasserschäffel. Es ist der Teufelsstein. Ringsum tönt der Boden hohl; daher stammt die Sage, dass hier eine Ortschaft untergegangen sei.

## 99 Der Zwergenschatz[6]

Eine von Eslarn ging am Weihnachtstage, eine Kürm auf dem Rücken, durch den Wald nach Hause. Da bemerkte sie einen Haufen Moos auf dem Schnee, ging hin, rührte darin herum und fand ein großes Hummelnest. Sie nahm es in ihre Kürm, um es ihren Kindern heimzutragen; da nahte sich ihr ein kleines Männchen, grün gekleidet, und fragte sie, was sie hier tue, und ließ sich das Nest im Korb zeigen. Sogleich fing er an, alles herauszuräumen;

---

[6] „Die edlen Metalle, besonders die gemünzten, welche sich bereits im Verkehre der Menschen befanden, aber durch Zufall oder mit Absicht demselben entzogen und unter die Erde geraten sind, so dass der Mensch kein Wissen mehr darum hat, können nicht ruhen und wollen wieder in den Besitz der Menschen gelangen. Ein solcher Schatz senkt sich neun Klafter tief und steigt dann alle sieben Jahre einen Fuß hoch zur Oberfläche empor. Wenn oben angekommen, gibt er von seinem Dasein durch ein über der Stelle schwebendes bläuliches Lichtchen Zeugnis. Dann heißt es: der Schatz blüht—und ist reif zum Heben. Wird er nicht oder unrecht gehoben, so sinkt er wieder . . . [A]uf vielerlei Weise gibt sich der Schatz dem menschlichen Auge kund, häufig als glühende Kohlen, oft aber auch in ganz unscheinbarer Gestalt." *Sitten und Sagen*, Bd. 2: 259f.

so that the Devil could not rest upon it again. Thus, the Vilseck Tower became the spikiest one in all of the Upper Palatinate. Naturally, that annoyed the Devil; he placed a piece of rock on his head and carried it toward Vilseck, to pound the structure to pieces. He was in the Vilseck Forest when he saw an old woman, a shoemaker and also the messenger of Vilseck, on the road to Hambach. He asked her how much farther he had to go to Vilseck, because he had to smash the tower. Thereupon the old woman opened her sack, filled with old shoes which she had accumulated by begging, and replied, "So far that I have already used up all of these shoes; I just came from there." "I cannot carry the stone that far," the Devil called out, enraged, and threw the rock with such violence that the very heavy fragments lie strewn about in the forest to this day. The main piece, however, as big as a farmhouse, landed on a hill in the middle of the forest; it still shows vestiges of the carrier; the claws and the head, the latter of which was as big as a large water tub. It is the Devil's Rock. All around it, the ground sounds hollow; thus the legend that a village had disappeared here.

## 99 The Dwarf's Treasure[7]

On Christmas Day, a woman went home through the forest from the town of Eslarn bearing a back carrier. She noticed a pile of moss on the snow, stirred around in it and found a big bumblebee nest. She placed it into her back carrier to take it home to her children; then a tiny little man clothed in green approached, and asked her what she was doing here and asked to be shown the nest in her basket. Immediately, he began to take everything out;

---

[7] "The precious metals, particularly those already minted, which had already been used by humans, but have been removed from them by accident or intent, and ended up buried in the Earth so that no human knows about it anymore, want to be back in the possession of humans. Such a treasure sinks down nine fathoms deep and then rises every seven years one foot toward the surface. Arrived at the surface, it gives testimony of its whereabouts with a blue little flame that hovers above the place where it is to be found. Then we say: the treasure is blooming—and ready to be unearthed. If it is not or is wrongly unearthed, it sinks down again. . . . The treasure reveals itself to the human eye in many ways, often as burning coals, but often also in quite insignificant looking forms." *Sitten und Sagen*, vol. 2: 259f.

mit dem Schlage zwölf verschwand es. Da fürchtete sich die Frau
und machte, dass sie heimkam.

Im Korbe lag ein neues Silberstück. Der Zwerg hatte ihr einen
Hummel darin gelassen, als ihn der Schlag der Glocke überraschte.

## 100 Der faule Riese und der Mond[8]

Ein Riese wurde mit dem Alter faul und ging nicht mehr gerne
zu Fuß. Da stieg er auf den Grat der Berge, als eben der Mond
aufging, und setzte sich wie ein Reiter auf den Mond und ritt
mit ihm bis dahin, wo die Sonne untergeht. Der Riese aber war
so schwer, dass nach jedem Ritte die Mondscheibe wie ein Sattel
eingedrückt war und etliche Zeit brauchte, um wieder rund und
voll zu werden. Der Mond geriet in große Furcht vor dem Riesen, dem er als Ross dienen sollte und ließ sich oft längere Zeit
gar nicht sehen. Daher das Auf- und Abnehmen des Mondes,
das Neulicht und der Vollmond. Noch jetzt sieht man die Strie-
men und Narben am Bauche des Mondes, welche der böse Riese
ihm geritten hat.

## 101 Das Riesenfräulein und die Menschen

An einem schönen Abende ging nun ein Riesenfräulein den Berg
hinunter, um sich die Gegend zu beschauen, und fand auf der
Fläche einen Bauer mit seinen Ochsen pflügen. Sie hatte noch
nie Menschen gesehen, und war also freudig erstaunt, so kleine
Dinger zu finden, welche sich immer bewegten, ohne gerade viel
vom Platze zu kommen. Während sie so ihre Neugier befrie-
digte, brach die Nacht herein: sie sollte zum Vater heim. Ohne
viel Besinnen raffte sie ein gut Stück des Ackerlandes in ihre
Schürze, legte ganz sachte das vom leisen Fingerdrucke schon
ohnmächtige Bäuerlein mit Gespann und Pflug darauf und
eilte, ihr neues Spielzeug auf die Burg zu bringen und dem Vater zu zeigen. In der Eile aber löste sich des Schurzes Band, die

---

[8] „Die Riesen sollen vor der Kreuzigung Christi in der ganzen Welt geherrscht haben . . .
Riesen waren die ersten Menschen." *Sitten und Sagen*, Bd. 2: 263.

on the stroke of twelve he disappeared. Thereupon the woman became scared and hastened home.

In the basket she found a brand new silver coin. The Dwarf had left behind one bumblebee when he was surprised by the striking of the clock.

## 100 The Lazy Giant and the Moon[9]

A Giant had grown lazy with age and did not like to walk anymore. So he climbed onto the crest of the mountain, just as the Moon began to rise, and sat on top of the Moon like a horseman and rode with him to the place where the Sun sets. The Giant, though, was so heavy that after every ride the disk of the Moon was dented like a saddle, and needed quite a bit of time to become full and round again. The Moon became very afraid of the Giant for whom he had to serve as a horse, and often could not be seen for a long time. That explains the waxing and waning of the Moon, the New Moon, and the Full Moon. To this day one can see the welts and scars on the belly of the Moon caused by the wicked Giant riding him.

## 101 The Maiden Giant and the Farmer

One beautiful evening, a maiden Giant walked down the mountain to look around the area and found a farmer plowing on the field with his oxen. She had never seen a human before and was thus happily astonished to find such small things that constantly moved about without ever gaining much distance. While she thus satisfied her curiosity, night fell; she had to return home to her father's house. Without thinking much, she gathered a piece of the farmland into her apron, very carefully placed the little farmer, who had already fainted from the soft touch of her fingers, on top with his harnessed team and plow, and hurried to take her new toy to the castle and show it to her father. In her haste, her apron strings came untied, the

---

[9] "Giants are said to have ruled all over the world before the crucifixion of Christ . . . Giants were the first humans." *Sitten und Sagen*, vol. 2: 263.

Last mochte doch etwas zu groß sein, und Erde, Bauer, Pflug und Ochsen fielen zu Boden. Die Erde ließ nun das Riesenkind liegen und sie liegt noch heute da, wo sie der Schürze entfiel; es ist der Kühkübel. Bauer, Ochsen und Pflug aber nahm sie wieder auf, trug sie hinauf und stellte sie dem Vater auf den Tisch. Doch dieser belehrte sein Kind in ernsten Worten, wie der Bauer auch Mensch sei gleich ihnen, nur kleiner, und wie diese Menschenkinder das Feld bebauten und Nahrung schafften, ohne welche sie auf der Riesenburg bei all ihrer Größe und Stärke verhungern müssten. Zugleich erteilte er dem betroffenen Kinde den Auftrag, den Bauer und seine Tiere gleichwohl für diese Nacht zu beherbergen und gastlich zu verpflegen, des folgenden Tages aber unfehlbar an den nämlichen Ort zurückzutragen, wo sie ihn genommen.

## 102 Die Riesen von Frauenberg

Etliche Stunden östlich von Bärnau in Böhmen haben die Riesen ein Schloss gebaut, Frauenberg genannt. Es waren ihrer zwölf Paare, und die Frauen trugen die Steine in ihren Schürzen auf den Berg. Als es vollendet war, feierten sie in der Hütte, welche sie seither[10] bewohnten, das letzte Fest. Einer der Riesen aber war so klug und reichte den anderen im Weine einen Schlaftrunk und zündete die Hütte an, und verbrannte diese mitsamt den elf Riesen und ihren Frauen. So gehörte das Schloss ihm und seiner Frau. Dieser Riesenstamm hat sich lange gehalten. Sie trieben dabei das Handwerk des Raubens und plünderten die Kaufleute, welche auf der Heer Straße von Hamburg über Nürnberg nach Böhmen hineinzogen. Denn die Straße ging unweit der Burg. Jetzt ist sie Wald, wie denn Böhmen nach Aussage des Holzfräuleins schon neunmal Wald und eben so oft Feld und Wiese gewesen ist.

---

[10] Der Kontext lässt vermuten, dass „bis dahin" angemessener wäre als das im Text verwendete „seither."

weight they carried might have been just a little bit too great, and soil, farmer, plow, and oxen all fell to the ground. The child Giant left the soil behind and it is still there to this day, where it fell out of the apron; the place is called the Cow's Pale. But she picked up the farmer, the oxen, and the plow again, carried them up and placed them on the table before her father. He, however, informed his child in stern words that the farmer was as much human as they were, only smaller, and how these human children cultivated the land and created food, without which those living at the Giant's Castle, notwithstanding their size and strength, would have to starve. At the same time he ordered the concerned child to provide accommodation for the farmer and his animals for the night nevertheless, and cater to them hospitably, and to take them back next day without fail, to the very same place whence she had taken them.

## 102 The Giants on Women's Mountain

Quite a few hours east of the city of Bärnau in Bohemia, Giants built a castle, called Women's Mountain. There were twelve couples, and the women carried the rocks up the mountain in their aprons. When it was completed, they celebrated their last feast in the cottage in which they had dwelt until then.[11] But one of the Giants was clever enough to offer the others a sleeping potion in their wine and set fire to the cottage, and burnt it down with the eleven Giants and their wives inside it. So the castle belonged to him and his wife. This dynasty of Giants was there for a long time. They took up robbing and pillaged the merchants who traveled on the army road from Hamburg to Bohemia via Nuremberg, for the road runs close to the castle. Now it is woodland, just as Bohemia has turned into woodlands nine times, and just as often into fields and meadows, according to the Forest Maiden.

---

[11] In the German source text, it reads "seither," which literally translates to "since then" or "subsequently." However, judging from the context, "until then" is the appropriate translation.

Der letzte Riese aber hat die Tochter eines Fürsten geraubt und den Kriegsleuten—im Schwedenkriege etwa—die Lebensmittel weggenommen. So gingen er und seine Burg im Sturme unter.

### 103 Der Hansl

Ein Bauer hatte zwei Söhne. Als er den letzten erhielt, sagte er zur Frau: »Lass ihn sieben Jahre saugen, den Hans!« Es geschah so, und als die Zeit um war, sendete der Vater den Hans aus, in den Wald, einen Baum auszureißen und heimzubringen. Der Bube ging hinaus und brachte einen Baum heim: der war dem Bauer aber zu klein und die Mutter musste ihn daher noch sieben Jahre an der Brust haben. Nach dieser Zeit sandte er den Hans wieder aus und der starke Bube brachte einen Sägbaum und der war recht. Da sagte der Bauer zur Frau: »Jetzt musst du ihn herabtun.«

Darauf spannt er seine zwei Söhne an den Pflug zum Ackern. Der Hans aber zog immer vor, weil er stark war, und stieß endlich voll Ungeduld seinen Bruder ganz hinweg, weil dieser immer hinten blieb; lieber zog er allein am Pfluge. Zur selben Zeit fuhr ein reicher Herr des Weges: der sieht den Hans und fragt sogleich den Bauer, ob der Bube ihm nicht feil wäre. Der Bauer aber wusste nicht, was er dafür bekäme. So bot ihm der Herr seine zwei Rosse vom Wagen und einen Sack voll Geld. Der Bauer war zufrieden, wenn es auch dem Hans recht wäre. Dem Hans war es recht, und der Herr spannt ihn sogleich vor den Wagen. Dann fragt er ihn, wie er heiße, Hans oder Hansl. Der Hans aber sagte drauf, es wäre gleich, er höre auf beides. Wieder fragt der Herr, ob er laufen könne. Der Hans erwiderte: »ein wenig,« und der Herr befiehlt ihm: »so lauf!« Da läuft der Hans und läuft immer stärker. Der Herr aber kriegt Angst und ruft ihm zu: »Hansl, stad!« Der Hansl geht aber immer geschwinder und hört nicht auf seinen Herrn, der ihn zurückhalten will, weil sonst alles hin wäre, und bald fliegt ein Rad, dann das andere, dann der Kasten, und der Hans geht nur mehr vor den zwei Rädern, zuletzt an der Deichsel allein. So musste der Herr ihm nachlaufen, der Hans aber war lange zur Stelle, als er ankam. Die Frau ging ihrem Manne jammernd entgegen, und zankte, dass er wieder einmal einen feinen Knecht eingestellt habe.

The last Giant, though, kidnapped a prince's daughter and stole provisions from the soldiers—for example in the Swedish wars. That is why he and his castle perished in the battles.

## 103 Little Hans

A farmer had two sons. When he received the second one, he said to his wife, "Let him suckle for seven years, that Hans!" And so it happened, and when the time was over, the father sent Hans out into the forest to uproot a tree and bring it home. The boy went out and brought back a tree, but it was too small for the farmer's taste, and the mother had to breastfeed Hans for another seven years. After that time, he sent Hans out again, and [this time] the strong boy brought back a tree ready to be cut down, and that was the right one. Then the farmer said to his wife, "Now you must wean him off."

After that, he yoked his two sons to the plow, to till the soil. But Hans always pulled ahead, for he was strong, and finally, full of impatience, pushed his brother away because he kept falling behind; he preferred to pull the plow by himself. At the same time, a rich lord came along; when he saw Hans, he immediately asked the farmer if the boy was not for sale. But the farmer did not know what to charge for him. So the lord offered him his two horses from the coach and a bag full of money. The farmer was happy over this, if Hans were all right with it too. Hans was fine with it, and at once the lord yokes him to the coach. Then he asks him what his name is, Hans or Little Hans. However, Hans replies that he doesn't care, it's all the same, he would listen to both. The lord asks another question, this time, is he able to run. Hans replied, "A little," and the lord orders, "Then run!" So Hans starts running and keeps running faster and faster. But the lord becomes scared and calls out to him, "Little Hans, go slow!" But Little Hans keeps going faster and faster, not listening to his master who wants to restrain him because otherwise everything would be broken, and soon one wheel flies off, then another, then the coach body, and then Hans is only pulling the two wheels, and finally only the drawbar. So his master is forced to run after him, but Hans had already been [waiting] there for a long time before the former arrived. The wife went to her husband complaining, and scolded him for having hired yet another fine servant.

Am Morgen befahl der Herr dem Hans, mit zwei Rossen ins
Holz zu fahren. Aber alle Knechte waren am Morgen schon aus,
nur der Hans blieb liegen und wollte auch nicht aufstehen, bis
man ihm einen Höhlhafen voll Knödeln brachte. Die verzehrte
er, den letzten wie den ersten, und fuhr dann aus. Auf dem Wege
sieht er die anderen Knechte schon heimwärts ziehen mit den
holzbeladenen Wägen. Da kam er in einen Hohlweg und das
war ihm recht: denn er verrichtete seine Notdurft ungesehen,
aber so stark, dass die Knechte, als sie hinkamen, stecken blieben. Hans fährt nun ein, holt die Klafter Holz, und zieht wieder heimwärts. Im Hohlwege aber können seine Rosse nicht
durch, so arg er auch antreibt. Voll Zorn schlägt er den einen
Gaul nieder, und weil der zweite jetzt noch weniger den Wagen hinüberbringen kann, auch diesen und wirft das Aas auf
den Wagen hinauf und zieht nun selber. Es waren aber Wölfe in
der Gegend zu Hause und einer kam herangesprungen, um das
Aas herabzureißen. Doch Hans schlägt den Wolf tot und wirft
auch ihn auf den Wagen und bringt den Wagen allein heim. Da
zankte die Frau noch mehr wie gestern mit dem Manne über den
dummen Knecht, und ruhte nicht eher, als bis er versprach, den
Hans fortzutun.

Der aber sagte zum Hans: »Weißt was, Hans, ich gehe in's
Wirtshaus zum Wein; wenn es Abend wird, kommst du und
leuchtest mir mit der großen Laterne heim.« Als es nun gegen
die Nacht zuging, zündete der Hans den Stadel an. Das Feuer
gab großen Schein und der Herr kam in Angst gelaufen. Weidlich wurde Hans ausgescholten über diesen neuen Streich: der
aber entgegnete ruhig, er habe den Befehl des Herrn getreulich
vollzogen; die Scheuer sei ja die große Laterne gewesen und
hätte dem Herrn recht gut geleuchtet, weil er so schnell habe
laufen können. – Nun wollte die Frau gar nichts mehr von Hans
wissen. Am Hause war ein tiefer Brunnen, der, lange nicht gebraucht, ohne Wasser stand. Diesen sollte Hans reinigen und
während er unten wäre, könnte man ihn totwerfen. Hans stieg
wirklich in den Brunnen, wie es der Herr befahl. Die oben geblieben waren, warfen ihm große Steine nach; aber der Hans rief
herauf: »Da müssen Hennen oben sein, die scharren und kratzen
Sand herunter.« Nun warfen sie einen großen Mühlstein hinab:

In the morning the master ordered Hans to go to the forest with two horses. But all the servants were already out in the morning; only Hans stayed in bed and did not want to get up until he was served a pot full of dumplings. Those he ate, the last just as the first, and then rode out. On the way he sees the other servants returning home with their carts loaded with timber. He arrived at a ravine, and that was all right with him because he had to relieve himself unseen, but it was so much that the servants got stuck when they tried to return through. Now Hans drives in[to the forest], fetches the cords of wood, and rides homeward again. In the ravine, however, his horses are unable to go through, regardless of how hard he presses them. In a rage, he strikes down one of the horses and, because the second one is now even less able to pull the cart, that one too, and then he throws the carcasses onto his cart and now pulls the cart himself. There were wolves in this area, however, and one jumped at him to pull down the carcasses. But Hans strikes the wolf dead and throws him onto the cart as well, then takes the cart home by himself. Thereupon the wife started bickering with her husband even more than the day before over the idiot servant, and did not rest until he promised to send Hans away.

So he said to Hans, "You know, Hans, I will go out to the tavern for a glass of wine; when it is evening, come and light me the way home with the big lantern." When night began to fall, Hans set fire to the barn. The fire gave plenty of light, and the master came running in fear. Hans was reproached thoroughly over this new prank; but he calmly replied that he had executed his master's order faithfully; the barn was the big lantern and it [must have] lighted the way for the master really well, since he was able to run so fast.—Now the wife wanted nothing more to do with Hans. By the house there was a deep well, which stood without water because it had not been used for a long time. Hans was supposed to clean it and, while he was down there, they could stone him to death. Hans really did climb down into the well, just as the master had ordered. Those staying on the surface threw big rocks at him, but Hans called up to them, "There must be hens up there; they scratch and scrape down sand." Then they threw down a big millstone:

der fiel gerade so, dass er dem Hans als Halskrause diente. Dieser machte seine Arbeit fertig und stieg unverletzt herauf.

Nun dieses nicht verhalf, sandten sie ihn auf eine Mühle, wo es niemanden litt; dort sollte er mahlen. Als es Mitternacht schlug, klopfte es. »Herein!« ruft Hans. Da kommen ihrer zwölf, einer um den anderen, und setzen sich an den Tisch und fangen zu karten an. Hans geht hin und schaut zu, und sieht, wie sie sich im Spiele betrügen; nicht faul nimmt er einen von ihnen bei der Mitte und trägt ihn in die Mühle hinunter und nimmt das obere Zeug herab und schleift dem Geiste den halben Hintern zu. So trägt er ihn wieder hinauf und setzt ihn wieder hin. Wie das die anderen sahen, liefen sie alle fort, der mit dem halben Hintern hintendrein. Am Morgen aber bringt der Hans sein Mehl richtig heim.

In Verzweiflung, dass sie seiner nicht loskommen können, schicken sie ihn zur Hölle: er solle dort ein Achtel Geld, das die Teufel schuldig wären, holen. Der Hans geht zur Hölle und verlangt für seinen Herrn das Geld. Die Teufel aber weigerten sich dessen, und stritten sich lange herum, bis der mit dem halben Hintern herangelaufen kam und den anderen abbot: mit diesem sei nichts zu machen. So ging Hans mit dem Gelde heim. Ein pfenziger Teufel aber konnte es nicht verwinden, dass der Hans mit dem Gelde fortging, und lief ihm nach, und hielt ihn auf dem Wege an und sagte: »Hier habe ich einen Sack voll Geld; wollen wir wetten; wer auf meinem Höllhorn am stärksten blasen kann, dem soll alles, was dein und mein ist, gehören.« Dem Hans war dies recht. Da blies der Teufel in das Höllhorn, dass die ganze Welt erzitterte. »Tropf du!« sagte Hans, »kannst du's nicht besser? Gib her das Hörnl, aber lass mich's erst mit einer Rute umwinden, dass es nicht zerreißt, wenn ich blase.« Da wurde dem Teufel bange. »Halt!« schrie er, »das gilt nicht, ohne Horn dürft' ich ja gar nicht mehr in die Hölle hinein!« Er lief mit dem Horn davon und ließ dem Hansen das Geld.

Der Hans trägt nun das Geld heim zur Frau; die aber schickt ihn fort zu seinem Vater mit sammt dem Gelde, damit er nur ging.—Und so war der Große Hans wieder zu Hause.

it fell straight down onto Hans so that it served him as a ruff. He completed his work and climbed back up unharmed.

After this did not help, they sent him to a mill where nobody could bear to work; he was to grind there. When midnight struck, there was knocking. "Come in!" Hans called out. Twelve men come in, one after another, and they sit down at the table and start to play cards. Hans joins them and watches, and sees how they cheat each other in the game. Without further ado, he picks up one of them around the waist, carries him down to the mill, removes the Ghost's outer garments, and grinds down half of its buttocks. Then he carries him back up and sets him down again. When the others saw that, they all ran away, the one with the halved buttocks behind the rest. But in the morning, Hans brings home the flour as instructed.

In despair because they cannot get rid of him, they send him to Hell, telling him to go bring them one eighth of the money that the devils owe them. Hans goes to Hell and demands the money for his master. However, the devils refused and they argued until the one with the halved buttocks came running and told them to stop arguing: there is nothing that could be done with this one. So Hans returned home with the money. But a penny-pinching devil could not abide the fact that Hans was making off with the money and ran after him, and stopped him on the way and said, "Here I have a bag full of money, let's make a bet: he who is able to blow my Hellhorn the loudest shall get all of what's yours and mine." Hans agreed to that. Then the devil blew into the horn, so loud that the whole world started to shake. "You poor devil" Hans said, "can't you do better? Give me the little horn, but first let me entwine it with a rod so it won't burst when I blow it." Thereupon the devil became very fearful. "Stop!" he cried out. "The bet is off because without a horn I wouldn't be allowed back into Hell!" He ran off with the horn and left Hans with the money.

Now Hans carries the money home to the wife, but she sends him away to his father, with all the money, just so that he would leave.—And so Great Big Hans was home again.

## 104 Der Hirt und die Riesen

Ein Bauer hatte einen Sohn, der war groß und stark, schickte sich aber nicht recht zu Pflug und Wagen. Da brachte er ihn zu einem Schmid in die Lehre, da könne er das harte Eisen schlagen. Der Junge schlug aber gleich das erstemal so gewaltig auf den Amboss, dass das Horn wegflog. »Weißt was,« sagte der Meister, »du schlägst mir gar ein wenig zu grob drein; für dich wüsste ich einen anderen Platz, droben auf dem Berg beim Grafen, der braucht starke Leute wider die Riesen, welche seine Herden plagen. Hier, da hast du ein altes Schwert, dort kannst du es brauchen.«

Der Bube ging auf's Schloss und ließ sich dingen als Viehhirt, und trieb sogleich aus auf einen Berg. Als er es sich kaum versah, stand ein Riese da, und wollte auf Vieh und Hirten einhauen. Der Hirt aber rannte auf ihn zu, und schlug ihm mit seinem rostigen Schwerte beide Hände ab. Da heulte der Riese wie ein Wetterhorn, fiel dem Hirten zu Füßen, und flehte: »Dein Knecht will ich sein, dein Vieh will ich hüten, stets will ich dir helfen, wenn du mir meine Hände wieder ganz machst.« »Dass du aber auch Wort hältst,« sagte der Hirt. »Ein Riese lügt nie,« erwiderte dieser, und der Hirt schlug rückwärts mit seinem Schwert, und der Riese hatte seine Hände wieder.

Der Hirt trieb heim und wieder aus und kam in ein Tal weit hinein. Kaum war er da, so lief das Vieh zusammen und brüllte, und ein Riese, größer als der gestrige, lief hinterher. Der Hirt lachte sich in die Faust und richtete sein Schwert her. »Was willst du hier,« brüllte der Riese, »in meinem Gehege!« »Du trauriger Wicht,« entgegnete der Hirt, »mach', dass du weiter kommst, sonst ergeht es dir, wie gestern deinem Gesellen!« Da wollte der Riese auf den Hirten los, der aber zuckte sein Schwert, und schlug dem Riesen die Arme weg, wie Nichts. Der sang dasselbe Lied, wie der gestrige, und erhielt seine Arme.

Der Hirt trieb heim und wieder aus, und kam in eine andere Gegend, in einen tiefen, finsteren Wald. Schon meinte er, heute ohne Strauß durchzukommen. Aber plötzlich kam ein

## 104 The Shepherd and the Giants

A farmer had a son who was tall and strong, but was not well suited for the plow and oxcart. He gave him to a blacksmith as an apprentice, because there he could pound the hard iron. The first time, however, the boy pounded so forcefully on the anvil that the top flew off. "You know what," his master said. "You are pounding just a little too hard even for my taste; I know of another place for you, up on the mountain at the count's place; he needs strong people [to protect] against the Giants who plague his herds. Here, now you have an old sword; you may well need it there."

The boy went up to the castle and hired on as a shepherd, and at once drove his herd out onto a mountain. Before he knew it, a Giant had appeared who wanted to hack at the animals and the shepherd. However, the shepherd ran at him and cut off both the Giant's hands with his rusty sword. Thereupon the Giant howled like a weather horn, fell at the feet of the shepherd and implored: "I will be your servant, tend your animals, and always help you if you make my hands whole again." "I hope you will keep your word," the shepherd said. "A Giant never lies," the former replied, and the shepherd swung backwards with his sword, and the Giant had his hands again.

The shepherd drove his herd home and out again, deep into a valley. He had hardly arrived there when the animals all ran together and bellowed, chased by a Giant, bigger than yesterday's. The shepherd laughed into his fist and adjusted his sword. "What do you want here," roared the Giant, "in my preserves!" "You poor wretch," the shepherd replied. "Go, get out of here, or you will fare as badly as did your friend yesterday!" Then the Giant wanted to attack, but the shepherd unsheathed his sword and cut off the Giant's arms, as if it were nothing. That one sang the same song as the one yesterday and received his arms back.

The shepherd drove his herd home and out again, and came to a different place in a deep, dark forest. He was just thinking that the day would pass without a fight, when suddenly there came a

Riese, so groß wie ein Tannenbaum: der trappte daher und hätte das Vieh zertreten wie Flöhe. »Lümmel,« schrie ihm der Hirt zu, »reiß aus oder ich lasse dich auf den Knieen tanzen!« Da beugte der Riese sein Haupt und sah herunter und brummte: »Gibt es da auch Frösche? Wart, die fresse ich erst gerne.« »Halt!« schrie auch der Hirt, »ich will dir eine Brühe dazu richten,« und schlug mit seinem Schwerte darein wie ein Holzhauer, und fällte den Riesen, dass er ohne Beine lag. Der Riese bat jetzt um schön Wetter und wurde, wie die anderen, mit dem Hirten gut Freund.

Der Hirt trieb heim, und schon wartete seiner, gnädigen Blickes, der Graf. »Mir scheint es,« sprach er, »du kannst mehr als schwarzes Brot essen; so wie du, hat mir noch keiner die Herde heimgebracht. Ich will dir was sagen. Unser Land verwüstet ein Lindwurm mit neun Köpfen; er will nicht eher ablassen von seinem Gräuel, als bis ihm der König seine Tochter zur Speise gibt. Wer den Drachen erlegt, erhält von ihm Reich und Tochter zum Lohne.«

Der Hirt nahm also Abschied vom Grafen und ging zum Riesen mit der Hand, und sagte ihm, er solle einstweilen für ihn seine Herde hüten, vorerst aber eine Rüstung und ein weißes Ross bringen. Der Riese gehorchte und der Hirt ritt von dannen. Da kam er zu einem Gerüste, das war errichtet, um die Prinzessin darauf zu stellen, wenn der Drache käme, sie zu holen. Dieser kam auch in Dampf und Rauch wie ein Backofen heran, und der Hirt sprang auf das Gerüste. Kaum war er oben, als das Untier schon nach ihm schnappte. Doch mit einem Streiche schlug er diesem drei Köpfe ab, und schnitt sich die drei Zungen aus dem Rachen und steckte sie zu sich. Der Drache entwich heulend und der Hirt stieg auf sein Ross und sprengte davon in solcher Eile, dass die Rüstung barst und der Gaul erlag.

Des anderen Tages ging der Hirt zum zweiten Riesen und verlangte den Dienst und eine andere Rüstung und ein braunes Ross – und wieder trabte er auf den Kampfplatz. Der Drache kam, der Hirt harrte schon seiner und schlug ihm drei andere Köpfe ab und steckte die Zungen zu sich: rechtshin entwich der Drache, links der Hirt so spornstreichs, dass die Rüstung barst und der Gaul tot niederfiel.

Giant as tall as a fir tree: he clumped along, and he would have crushed the animals under his feet like fleas. "Ruffian," the shepherd shouted at him, "get out of here, or I will have you dancing on your knees!" Thereupon the Giant bent down his head and looked down and mumbled, "Are there also frogs? Wait, I like to eat them the most." "Stop!" the shepherd shouted then. "I will prepare for you a broth for that," and he struck with his sword like a woodchopper, and felled the Giant so that he lay without legs. The Giant now asked for mercy and, like the others, became good friends with the shepherd.

The shepherd drove his herd home, and the count was already waiting for him, with a gracious demeanor. "It seems to me," he said, "you can do more than eat black bread; no one has ever brought the herd home [intact] as you have. I'll tell you what. Our land is being ravaged by a Lindworm with nine heads; he won't stop his atrocities until the king gives him his daughter for a meal. He who slays the Dragon shall receive his kingdom and daughter as a prize."

So the shepherd took leave from the count and went to see the Giant with the [restored] hand, and told him he should tend his herd for the time being, but before that, bring him a suit of armor and a white horse. The Giant obeyed and the shepherd rode away. Thereupon he came to a scaffold, which had been erected to place the princess upon it when the Dragon would arrive to claim her. The latter also arrived, steaming and smoking like a baking oven, and the shepherd jumped onto the scaffold. He had hardly made it up there when already the monster snapped at him. But with one stroke he cut off three heads, and cut from the mouths the three tongues, which he tucked away. Howling, the Dragon escaped; the shepherd mounted his horse and raced away in such a hurry that the armor burst and the horse perished.

The next day, the shepherd went to see the second Giant, and asked for his service and another suit of armor and a brown horse—and again he rode to the battle ground. The Dragon arrived with the shepherd already waiting for him, and he cut off three other heads and tucked the tongues away; the Dragon escaped to the right and the shepherd to the left, so hastily that the armor burst and the horse fell down dead.

Am nächsten Morgen ging der Hirt zum dritten Riesen und verlangte den Dienst, und erhielt eine goldene Rüstung und einen Rappen. So ritt er davon auf den Kampfplatz; doch ließ der Drache heute den ganzen Tag auf sich warten; erst abends schoss er, wütend von Schmerz, heran, und bäumte sich und schlug das Gerüst in Trümmer. Zu gleicher Zeit mit den Balken flogen aber auch die letzten drei Köpfe von seinem Rumpfe und der Hirt nahm die Zungen und ritt heim. Ein Hoflakai aber kam, und nahm die neun Köpfe mit sich.

Der Hirt hütete nun wieder seine Herde: es war Ruhe im Lande. Auf der Straße aber wurde es lebendig. Ein Zug Ritter um den anderen, in vollem Schmucke, zog heran, er wusste nicht warum. Und als er heimwärts trieb, kommt auch sein Graf des Weges mit stattlichem Gefolge und rief ihm zu: »Wärst du weniger dumm und faul, als du stark bist, könntest du jetzt mein Gebieter sein!« Der Hirt verstand den Sinn der Worte nicht, und lief zu seinen Riesen, sie zu fragen. Diese sagten ihm, dass die Königstochter, welche er vom Drachen befreit hatte, dieser Tage Hochzeit halte. Er soll nur auch hingehen, sie würden getreulich der Herden warten.

»Der Teufel mag die Herden hüten,« rief der Hirt. »Auf! und rüstet mich und euch: wenn sonst zu nichts, zu Musikanten kann man uns dort wohl noch brauchen.« Die Riesen gingen nun zu Fuß neben ihm her, denn kein Ross ist stark genug, auch nur ein Riesenkind zu tragen.

Der Hirt aber saß im schönen Wams und Zeug auf einem hohen Rappen und fort ging es zur Königsburg. Der Einlass hielt aber gar schwer, denn der Bräutigam, ein Herr von Hof, hatte befohlen, nur Vertrauten und Herren, nicht aber Unbekannten und Abenteurern, die Tore zu öffnen. – Im Burgsaale aber saß der König auf seinem Throne, zur Seite die Prinzessin, ringsum die Herren und Vasallen ohne Zahl. Da öffneten sich die Flügeltüren und neun Pagen trugen auf neun goldenen Schüsseln die neun Häupter des erschlagenen Drachen, und der Herold blies in die Trompete und rief aus: »Wer das Schwert gegen den Drachen gezückt, trete vor, und empfange des Königs Dank mit der Hand der Prinzessin!«

The next morning, the shepherd went to see the third Giant and asked for his service, and he received golden armor and a black horse. He rode away to the battle ground, but today the Dragon made him wait the whole day; not until the evening did he dash up, raging with pain, and, rearing up, he smashed the scaffold to pieces. But at the same time as the timber flew, the last three heads flew off his torso, and the shepherd took the tongues and then rode home. But a footman arrived and took the nine heads away with him.

Now the shepherd again herded his animals; there was peace in the land. But on the road, traffic was picking up. One after another, many knights passed by in full armor, and he did not know why. And as he drove the herd homeward, his count also comes his way with a large entourage and called out to him, "If you had been less stupid and lazy, as much as you are strong, you could be my lord now!" The shepherd did not understand the meaning of these words and ran to ask his Giants. They told him that the king's daughter, whom he had liberated from the Dragon, would get married soon. He should go there also, as they would take care of his herds faithfully.

"May the Devil herd the animals," the shepherd shouted. "Let's go! Get armor for me and for you: if nothing else, we shall make some music." The Giants then escorted him on foot, because no horse is strong enough to carry even a Giant's child.

The shepherd, however, sat in his fine doublet and finery on a tall, black horse and off they went to the king's castle. Entering proved difficult because the bridegroom, a gentleman from the court, had ordered the gates opened only to familar people and gentlemen, but not to strangers and adventurers.— Meanwhile, in the castle's main hall, the king was sitting on his throne with the princess at his side, and surrounded by countless gentlemen and vassals. Then the double doors opened, and nine pages carried the nine heads of the slain Dragon on nine golden plates, and the herald blew his trumpet and called out: "He who drew his sword against the Dragon, come forward and receive the princess's hand as a sign of the king's gratitude!"

Geschmückt wie ein Prinz trat ein Hoflakai hervor aus der Menge und kniete sich nieder vor dem Throne und sprach gebeugten Hauptes: »Mein ist der Lohn, denn mein sind die neun Drachenköpfe,« – und der König führte ihm seine Tochter zu und ließ ihm huldigen.

Aber schon krachte das Burgtor, von den drei Riesen zerbrochen, Treppen und Gänge zitterten unter ihren Füßen, es flogen die Türen des Saales auf, und herein trat der Hirt, hinter sich die Riesen, und er fragte, wer der sei, der ihm die Drachenköpfe gestohlen. Der Lakai trat vor. Da höhnte ihn der Hirt und sprach: »Wohl habe ich die Köpfe weggeworfen gleich tauben Nüssen; hier sind die Zungen, seht zu, ob sie den Köpfen passen!« Und es fand sich so und der Hirt wurde der Gemahl der Prinzessin und der Herr des Landes; der freche Lakai aber von vier Pferden zerrissen.

## 105 Der Schneider und die Riesen

Es war einmal ein Schneider, klein von Gestalt, der auf der Welt in der Fremde herumwanderte. Wie er eines Tages so dahin ging, kam er in einen Wald und in diesem zu einer Quelle, neben welcher er ein rotseidenes Band fand, auf dem die Worte standen: »Sieben auf einen Schlag, wer macht es mir nach.« Der Schneider hob es auf und band es sich um den Leib.

Da er schon lange weiter gewandert war, kam ihm plötzlich ein Riese entgegen, der ihn hart anfuhr und ihm fürchterlich drohte. Der Schneider aber gedachte seines Bandes und der Worte, die darauf standen, und machte sich nicht viel aus den Drohungen des Riesen. So zankend und streitend kamen sie zu einem Kirschenbaum, der voll reifer Kirschen hing. Da sagte der Riese höhnisch: »Halt, ich will dir die Äste des Baumes herabbiegen, damit du von den Kirschen essen kannst. Lass es dir noch schmecken, denn wenn du gegessen hast, will ich dich umbringen.«

Der Riese bog also den Baum hernieder, und der Schneider hielt sich fest an dem Gipfel desselben, um bequem die üppigen Kirschen verspeisen zu können. Aber zu gleicher Zeit ließ der Riese den Baum wieder los und der gute Schneider wurde hoch in die Luft hinaufgeschleudert. Er hatte es dem Bande zu danken,

Adorned like a prince, the footman stepped from the crowd and kneeled down before the throne and said, with his head bent: "The prize is mine, for mine are the nine Dragon heads,"—and the king led his daughter to him and had him rendered homage.

However, in the same instant, the castle's gate came crashing down, broken by the three Giants, and the stairways and hallways shook under their feet; the doors of the hall flew open and in stepped the shepherd, with the Giants behind him, and he asked who it was that had stolen the Dragon heads from him. The footman stepped forward. Thereupon the shepherd scoffed at him, saying, "Indeed I did throw away the heads, like empty nuts; here are the tongues; see if they fit the heads!" And thus it turned out, and the shepherd became the princess's husband and the lord of the land; the insolent footman, however, was torn apart by four horses.

## 105 The Tailor and the Giants

Once upon a time there lived a tailor, who was short in stature, and he wandered about in the world in foreign places. Walking about one day, he came to a forest and in it to a well, beside which he found a red silk sash on which there were written the words, "Seven with one stroke; who can match that?" The tailor picked it up and tied it around his waist.

After he had been walking for a long while, a Giant suddenly came up to him, yelling at him and uttering dreadful threats. The tailor, however, remembered his sash and the words that were written on it, and therefore did not worry much about the Giant's threats. Thus bickering and arguing, they came to a cherry tree full of ripe cherries. Scoffingly, the Giant then said, "Stop, I will bend down the branches of the tree for you, so that you may eat of the cherries. May you enjoy them because when you have finished eating, I shall slay you."

So the Giant bent the tree down and the tailor held on tightly to its top, so that he could eat the luscious cherries in comfort. At the same time, however, the Giant let go of the tree again, and the good tailor was catapulted high into the air. He had his sash to thank,

dass er unversehrt auf der anderen Seite wieder zur Erde kam. Da bekam der Schneider Mut, der Riese aber geriet in Erstaunen und ließ den kleinen Mann von nun an neben sich herziehen.

Wie der Schneider nun so hinter dem Riesen einherging, lief ihm ein Spatz unter den Füßen herum; er bückte sich, ergriff den Vogel und trug ihn, ohne dass der Riese es sah, fortan in der Hand.

Auf diese Weise waren sie eine bedeutende Strecke gegangen, da hob der Riese einen Stein auf und sagte zu seinem Gefährten: »Nun wollen wir um die Wette werfen, und sehen, wer weiter wirft.« Und er warf und der Stein flog so weit, dass ihn die Augen des Schneiders gerade noch ersehen konnten.

Da bückte sich auch der Schneider, als wolle er einen Stein aufheben, ließ aber den Vogel fliegen: dieser flog so weit, dass der Riese gar nicht bemerken konnte, wo der Stein zur Erde fiel.

Nun bekam der Riese schon eine bessere Meinung von seinem kleinen Reisegefährten, und bot ihm an, ihn in seine Höhle zu nehmen, wo ihrer zwölf beisammen wären: er selber aber sei König.

Wieder gingen sie einige Zeit des Weges, da lag ein Käslaibchen auf der Straße, welches der Schneider gleichfalls aufhob und in der Hand behielt. Bald darauf hob der Riese einen Stein auf und drückte ihn in seiner gewaltigen Faust so fest, dass Wasser heraus trat. Der Schneider bückte sich nun auch, tat, als nähme er einen Stein von der Erde auf und drückte dann das Käselaibchen, das er in der Hand trug, so fest, dass Milch herausdrang. Neckisch fragte er den Riesen, ob er es auch so könne. Dieser war nun voll Erstaunen über die Kraft des Zwerges, wie er meinte.

So kamen sie in die Höhle, und der Riese erzählte seinen Genossen, was der Erdwurm bisher alles getan habe. Sie hießen ihn daher willkommen und behielten ihn bei sich, ohne ihm etwas Leides zu tun. Sie gingen oft auf Raub aus; manchmal nahmen sie ihn auf ihren Streifzügen mit, meistens aber musste er zurückbleiben, wo sie ihn dann einsperrten. Alle Abende aber mit dem Schlage sechs Uhr verfielen sie in Schlaf, aus welchem sie nicht zu wecken waren, bis sie nicht volle zwölf Stunden geschlafen hatten.

for that he landed on the ground on the other side, without coming to any harm. That gave the tailor courage, but the Giant was astonished and, from then on, allowed the little man to walk with him.

While the tailor was walking behind the Giant, a little sparrow hopped around under his feet, so he bent down, picked up the bird and carried him in his hand from that time on, without the Giant noticing it.

In this manner they had walked for a considerable distance, when the Giant picked up a rock and said to his companion, "Let us have a throwing contest to see who is able to throw farther." And he threw, and the rock flew so far away that the tailor's eyes could just barely still make it out.

Then the tailor bent down as well, pretending to pick up a rock, but instead he let the bird fly; the latter flew so far that the Giant was completely unable to perceive where the rock had fallen to the ground.

After that, the Giant had a much better opinion of his little travel companion, and offered to take him to his cave where there were twelve of his kindred living together; he himself was their king.

Again, they had been walking for some time, when the tailor saw a little chunk of cheese on the road which he, as before, picked up and kept in his hand. Soon after that, the Giant picked up a rock and squeezed it so hard in his enormous fist that water began to drip from it. Then the tailor bent down also, pretended he was picking up a rock from the ground and squeezed the little chunk of cheese which he had been carrying in his hand so hard that milk began to drip from it. Whimsically, he asked the Giant if he could do that as well. The Giant became filled with amazement over the strength of the little man, as he thought.

So they arrived at the cave, and the Giant told his Giant comrades about all that the earthworm had done so far. Thereupon they welcomed him and kept him in their company without doing him any harm. They often went out to go on robberies; sometimes they took him along on their forays, but more often than not he had to stay behind, where they locked him up. Every evening at the stroke of six, they fell into a slumber from which they could not be awoken until they had slept a full twelve hours.

So hatte er zwar zu leben, aber auch viele Langweile. Als daher einmal die Riesen wieder ausgezogen waren, besah er sich die Höhle recht genau, ob denn kein Entkommen möglich wäre. Da entdeckte er eine Türe, welche in einen langen dunklen Gang führte. Er ging hinein und mehrere Stunden in großer Finsternis fort, bis endlich Helle ihn umfloss und er sich wieder oben auf freier Erde sah.

Vor seinen Augen lag eine Stadt; er ging also auf sie zu. Unterdessen waren die Riesen nach Hause gekommen; sie fanden den kleinen Mann zwar nicht, bekümmerten sich aber auch nicht viel um sein Verschwinden: denn sie dachten, der Erdwurm werde sich irgendwo verkrochen haben, und schon wieder zum Vorschein kommen, wenn ihn hungere.

Dieser aber war in die Stadt getreten, wo er alle in Bestürzung und Trauer fand. Alle Fenster waren mit schwarzen Tüchern verhangen. Er erkundigte sich daher, was die Ursache solcher Trauer wäre, und erfuhr, dass Riesen in der Nähe wohnten, welche die Stadt immer in Angst und Schrecken hielten; und dass sieben Drachen in einer nahen Höhle hausten, welchen sie jeden Tag einen Menschen opfern müssten, – und endlich sei eine Schlange nicht weit auf einem Baume, welche alle Menschen verzehre, die unglücklicher Weise in ihr Bereich kämen. Niemand aber wäre zu finden, welcher die Stadt von diesen Ungeheuern befreien wollte.

Nun sei das Los auf die Königstochter gefallen, dass sie des übermorgigen Tages den Drachen geopfert werden solle. Der König habe zwar verkünden lassen, dass wer diese Ungeheuer erlegen würde, die Königstochter zur Ehe und später das Königreich als Erbe haben sollte; aber niemand finde sich, der ein so gefährliches Unternehmen wagen wollte.

Da meinte der Schneider, er wäre nicht abgeneigt, das Wagestück zu unternehmen: man möge ihn nur zum Könige führen. So wurde er denn zum Könige geführt und dieser versprach ihm auf's neue seine Tochter und sein Reich als Lohn, wenn ihm die Tat gelingen würde.

Der Schneider ließ sich nun ein Schwert geben, welches er leicht handhaben konnte, und legte den Harnisch zur Seite, womit man ihn bekleiden wollte. Denn das Zeug war sehr schwer und hinderte ihn am Gehen. Darauf ging er der Riesenhöhle zu, welche er eben verlassen hatte. Da er auch die Zeit wusste, wann die Riesen in

So he was able to stay alive, but he also experienced much bore-
dom. So one day after the Giants had gone out and away, he
inspected the cave thoroughly to see if it were possible to escape.
Then, he discovered a door which led into a long and dark passage. He entered it and continued several hours in great darkness, until finally he was surrounded by light again and found
himself back on open ground.

Before his eyes lay a city, and so he walked toward it. Meanwhile, the Giants had returned home; when they did not find the
little man, they did not care much about his disappearance for
they thought the earthworm had hidden somewhere and would
surely emerge again once he was hungry.

But the latter had gone into the city, where he found everybody in great trepidation and sorrow. All of the windows were
hung with black cloth. He inquired what the cause of such grief
was and learned that there were Giants living close by who were
keeping the city in fear and terror, and that there were seven
Dragons living in a cave nearby to which they had to make a
human sacrifice each day—and finally, that there was a Serpent
in a tree not far from there which would eat all humans who,
by misfortune, entered that area. But nobody could be found to
volunteer to free the city from these monsters.

Now the princess had fallen by lot to be sacrificed to the Dragons the day after tomorrow. Indeed, the king had announced
that he who would slay these monsters would get the hand of
the princess in marriage and subsequently inherit the kingdom;
yet nobody had been found who wanted to undertake such a
dangerous mission.

Thereupon the tailor opined that he would not be disinclined
to undertake the daring deed; if they would only lead him
before the king. So he was taken before the king, who promised
anew [to give] his daughter and his kingdom to him if he were
successful.

Then the tailor had them give him a sword which he could eas-
ily handle, [but] he put aside the armor in which they wished to
suit him up. For the suit was very heavy and hindered his movements. After that, he went to the Giants' cave which he had left just
a little while earlier. Since he knew also the time when the Giants

ihren festen Schlaf versenkt wären, so betrat er nach sechs Uhr die Höhle und schlug ihnen Allen den Kopf ab: die Augen und die Zungen schnitt er ihnen heraus und brachte sie als Wahrzeichen dem Könige, welcher große Freude darüber hatte.

Des anderen Tages ließ der Schneider ein großes Fass machen, außen voll eiserner Spitzen, nahm sein Schwert, und kroch in das Fass. Dieses Fass ließ er dann unter den Baum bringen, welcher der Schlange als Wohnung diente. Wie die Schlange den Geruch von Menschenfleisch in die Nase bekam, stürzte sie vom Baume herab, und zu dem Fasse hin, in welchem der Schneider ein Loch gelassen hatte. Die Schlange bog eben ihren Rachen über diese Öffnung. Da nahm der Schneider die Gelegenheit wahr und stieß ihr das Schwert bis in den Hals hinein, dass sie sich in Schmerz und Wut um das Fass in vielen Ringen herumwand, sich aber an jedem eisernen Zacken spießte und bald tot war. Da stieg der Held aus dem Fasse, schlug der Schlange den Kopf ab und brachte ihn dem Könige als Siegeszeichen, welcher heute eine viel größere Freude hatte als gestern.

Nun waren die Drachen noch übrig zu erlegen – wohl die schwerste und gefährlichste Arbeit. Der Schneider ließ sich nun einen eisernen Wagen machen, der bis auf eine kleine Öffnung ganz verschlossen war. In diesen stieg er am dritten Tage, und ließ sich zur Höhle der Drachen fahren. Kaum war er dort angekommen, so fuhr einer der Drachen heraus, zerfleischte die beiden Rosse vor dem Wagen und stürzte den Wagen um. Da indessen der Kopf des Drachen in die Nähe der Öffnung gekommen war, so stieß ihm der Schneider sein Schwert bis an das Heft hinein und tötete so das Untier. Da sah er auf sein rotes Band, welches er um den Leib hatte, und siehe, die Worte waren verschwunden, statt deren aber stand geschrieben: »Gehe nur in die Höhle hinein, die übrigen sechs Drachen können dir nichts mehr anhaben, weil du den ersten davon erschlagen hast.« Er stieg daher aus dem Wagen und trat in die Höhle und tötete die sechs Drachen, welche sich wirklich nicht bewegen konnten. Die Köpfe aber brachte er dem Könige, welcher ihm nicht Dank genug zu beweisen wusste und ihm noch an selbigem Abende die Königstochter zur Ehe gab, wobei es gar herrlich und fröhlich herging, weil jeder Einwohner an der Freude über die Rettung aus Not und Gefahr den innigsten Anteil nahm.

were sunk in deep sleep, he entered the cave after six o'clock and severed all of their heads: he cut out their eyes and tongues, and brought them, as proof, back to the king, who was overjoyed by this.

The next day, the tailor ordered a big barrel be made that was spiked with iron barbs on the outside, took his sword, and crept inside the barrel. He had the barrel tied at the bottom of the tree which served as the dwelling place for the Serpent. When the Serpent got a whiff of human flesh into its nose, it rushed down the tree, to the barrel wherein the tailor had left a hole. The Serpent opened its mouth and closed it over this opening. Thus the tailor seized the opportunity, thrusting his sword down into its throat, whereupon, filled with pain and rage, it wound itself around the barrel many times, but skewered itself on each of the iron barbs and was soon dead. Then our hero climbed out of the barrel, severed the Serpent's head and took it to the king as a proof of his victory; and the king was in much greater joy than the day before.

Now only the Dragons remained to be hunted down—indeed the most difficult and most dangerous task. So then the tailor had an iron carriage made which was completely closed except for a small opening. On the third day, he entered it and had it taken to the Dragons' cave. No sooner had he arrived there when one of the Dragons darted from it, mauled the two horses that had been drawing the carriage, and rolled it over. Meanwhile, the head of the Dragon had appeared close to the opening, so the tailor thrust his sword up to the hilt into the Dragon and thus slew the beast. When he looked upon his red sash which he had slung around his body, the words had disappeared, and instead he saw written, "Go now into the cave; the other six Dragons will be unable to hurt you because you slew the first of them." Therefore he climbed out of the coach and entered the cave, then he slew the six Dragons which were indeed unable to move. The heads, however, he took to the king, who could not thank him enough and gave him the hand of the princess in marriage that same evening. And there was much merriment and happiness because every inhabitant shared in the most heartfelt way the happiness over having been saved from misery and peril.

Da nun der Schneider Beilager mit der Königstochter hielt und eingeschlafen war, träumte ihm von seinem Handwerk, von Nadel, Schere, Bügeleisen, und da er laut träumte, hörte die Prinzessin, welche wach war, alles, und geriet in große Besorgnis, es möge ihr Gatte doch wohl nicht mehr als ein Schneider sein. Kaum war es Morgen, so ging sie zu dem Könige und klagte diesem ihren Argwohn, und erklärte ihm, nie und nimmer die Schande ertragen zu können, als Königstochter die Frau eines Schneiders zu sein.

Der König aber tröstete sie und sagte, er wolle ihn zum Feldherrn machen und gegen die Feinde schicken und ihn an die äußerste Spitze stellen, damit er gleich im Anfange zu Grunde gehe. Sein Wort aber, das er ihm gegeben, und wodurch er sein Eidam geworden, könne er nicht zurücknehmen, mithin auch die Ehe nicht lösen. Der Schneider wurde inne, dass ihn die Königstochter hasse und den Grund warum. Wie er daher wieder zu Bette ging, stellte er sich, als träume er wieder, und diesesmal von lauter Schlachten und Siegen.

Da wurde die Königstochter noch trauriger und ging am Morgen wieder zum Könige und meldete ihm, was ihr Gatte heute Nacht geträumt habe. Worüber aber ihr das Herz brechen wollte, das erfüllte das Herz des Königs mit Freude. Er erteilte noch am nämlichen Tage dem Eidam den Befehl, das Heer gegen den Feind zu führen, ließ ihm aber doch, seiner Tochter zu Gefallen, die schlechteste Rüstung und das schlechteste Pferd geben; zugleich befahl er ihm, stets an der Spitze des Heeres zu bleiben.

Der Schneider aber machte sich nicht viel daraus, sondern band sein rotes Band um den Leib, und wie er es betrachtete, las er die Worte: »Du wirst Sieger sein!«

Er zog also getrost aus. Da sein Pferd aber sehr matt ging, so blieb er häufig zurück, und so auch in dem Augenblicke, wo die Feinde, lauter Heiden, an der Seite herankamen. Eben strauchelte das Pferd und riss im Fallen ein Kreuz um, welches an dem Wege stand. Das Kreuz aber fiel auf den Schneider, welcher es fasste, und weil es nicht schwer war, in der Hand behielt. So ging es gegen den Feind. Dieser aber wurde kaum des Kreuzes ansichtig, welches der Schneider an der Spitze des Heeres trug, als sie

After the tailor had enjoyed marital bliss with the king's daughter and fallen asleep, he dreamed of his craft, of needles, scissors, and flat iron, and since he dreamed very loudly, the princess heard everything because she was awake, and she became very worried that her husband might indeed be nothing more than a tailor. Morning had hardly broken, when she went to the king and relayed her suspicions, declaring that she, being a king's daughter, would never ever bear the disgrace of being married to a tailor.

But the king comforted her and said that he was going to appoint him a general, and then send him against his enemies, placing him at the very front [of the army], so that he would perish right at the beginning. He had given his word, though, which had made him his son-in-law, and he was unable to take that back, and thus could not dissolve the marriage either. The tailor learned that the princess hated him, and the reason why. Therefore, when he went to bed again, he pretended that he was dreaming, and this time entirely of battles and victories.

Whereupon the princess became even sadder and again in the morning went down to see the king and report to him what her husband had dreamed last night. What threatened to break her heart, though, filled the king's heart with joy. That very day, he gave his son-in-law the order to lead the army against the enemy but, to please his daughter, had him given the worst suit of armor and the worst horse; at the same time, he had ordered him to stay at the head of the army, at all times.

The tailor did not worry much about this, but instead tied his red sash around his waist and, when he looked at it closely, read the words, "You shall be the victor!"

So he marched out with confidence. Since his horse was staggering, he slowed down frequently, and that was so in the moment when the enemies, all of them heathens, approached from the side. At that very moment, his horse stumbled and, falling, took down with it a crucifix that had been standing by the wayside. However, the cross fell onto the tailor who caught it and, because it was not very heavy, held it in his hand. Thus they advanced toward the enemy. No sooner did the enemy see the cross which the tailor carried at the head of of the army than they

in wilder Flucht umkehrten und dem Schneider den vollstän-
digsten Sieg überließen. Sie hatten nämlich geglaubt, dass der
Gott der Christen mit diesen streite, und gegen einen Gott könnten Menschen nicht kämpfen.

So wurden die Feinde geschlagen und ihnen ein großer Teil
ihres Landes abgenommen. Der Schneider aber kehrte wohlbe-
halten, an Ehren reich, zurück, und wurde auch von dem Könige
mit allen Ehren, von der Königstochter aber mit Liebe empfangen; denn diese hatte nun ihren Gatten achten gelernt.

Von da an lebten sie noch lange und glücklich.

## 106 Die Zwerge vom Giebenberg[12]

Der Giebenberg, Gaýmberg, etwa eineinhalb Stunden von Rötz
entfernt, ist seit undenklichen Zeiten Aufenthaltsort der Strazeln.
Ganz öde und ohne Ruine, aber durch Geister und Sagen gleich
dem Untersberg[13] verrufen, ist er fast ganz ausgehöhlt von den
Schrazen, welche hier ihren Sammelplatz hatten; die Gänge,

---

[12] „Unter Erdzwergen [auch Strazeln, Fankerln, oder Razeln genannt] sind jene kleinen
Wesen verstanden, welche . . . unter oder auf der Erde leben und bis in die jüngere Zeit
herab mit den Menschen in gesellschaftlichen Verkehr traten . . . [Sie] machen sich durch
ihre Liebe zur Haus- und Feldwirtschaft bemerklich . . . Doch bleiben sie nur bei guten
Leuten und bringen durch ihre Anwesenheit dem Hause Glück. . . . Indessen dürfen die
Menschen ihnen dafür nicht danken, besonders nicht mit Geschenken, es wären denn
Speisen, die man für sie übrig läßt. Sie glauben in ihrer großen Empfindlichkeit damit
bezahlt worden zu sein für ihre Arbeit und den Abschied erhalten zu haben. Ihre Arbeit
verrichten sie bei Nacht, wenn alles schläft, denn sie wollen sich nicht sehen lassen,
selten bei Tag." *Sitten und Sagen*, Bd. 2: 288–291.

[13] „Der Untersberg ist ein Bergmassiv der Nördlichen Kalkalpen, an der Grenze von Bayern (Deutschland) und Salzburg (Österreich). Die Sage geht, dass Kaiser Friedrich Barbarossa, von den ‚Untersberger Mandln' umsorgt, im Untersberg auf seine Auferstehung
warte. Alle hundert Jahre wacht er auf und wenn er sieht, dass die Raben immer noch
um den Berg fliegen, dann schläft er ein weiteres Jahrhundert. Sein Bart wächst um einen
runden Tisch. Bis jetzt reicht er zweimal herum. Doch wenn er die dritte Runde been-
det hat, beginnt das Ende der Welt. Und wenn der Kaiser erwacht und den Untersberg
verlässt findet die letzte große Schlacht der Menschheit auf dem Walserfeld westlich von
Salzburg statt." (Siehe auch „Kaiser Karl im Untersberg," <http://www.sagen.at/texte/
sagen/oesterreich/salzburg/div/kaiserkarlimuntersberg.html>. Abgerufen 8 Sep 2012.)

turned around in a wild rush to escape, leaving the tailor with the completest victory. For the enemies had assumed that the God of the Christians was fighting on their side, and against a god humans cannot fight.

So the enemy was beaten, and a large part of their land taken away from them. The tailor, however, returned safe and sound, rich with honor, and was received by the king with all honors, and by the princess with love because now she had learned to respect her husband.

From that time on, they lived long and happily.

## 106 The Dwarves in Mount Gieben[14]

Mount Gieben or Mount Gaym, about an hour and a half from the town of Rötz, has been the domicile of the "Strazel" Dwarves from time immemorial. Completely barren and without a castle ruin, but notorious for Ghosts and legends, like the Untersberg;[15] it was almost completely gutted inside by the "Schrazen," who had their meeting place here; the tunnels

---

[14] "Earth Dwarves, also 'Strazeln,' 'Fankerln' or 'Razeln,' are those little creatures which live under or above ground, and up until very recently they conducted social business with humans . . . They stand out because of their love for domestic and agricultural work and they approached humans . . . However, they only stay with good people and bring happiness to the house with their presence. Humans, though, are not allowed to thank them for their work, particularly not with presents, except for food which can be left for them. In their great sensitivity, they believe that they are being paid up for their work and dismissed. They complete all their work at night, when everybody is asleep, and rarely during the day, for they don't want to be seen." *Sitten und Sagen*, vol. 2: 288–291.

[15] "The Untersberg is a mountain massif of the Berchtesgaden Alps that straddles the border between Berchtesgaden, Germany and Salzburg, Austria. According to legend, Emperor Frederick Barbarossa (of the Holy Roman Empire) is asleep inside the Untersberg, looked after by dwarf-like creatures. His beard is said to be growing longer and longer around a round table and to have grown around it two times. When the beard has grown three times around the table, the world will come to an end. The emperor awakes every hundred years and when he sees the ravens still flying around the Untersberg, he goes back to sleep for another hundred years. When Frederick leaves the mountain, the last battle of humankind will be fought on the Walserfeld, west of Salzburg." (See also "Kraftort Untersberg," <http://www.kraftort.org/Osterreich/Salzburg/Untersberg/untersberg.html>. Accessed 8 Sep 2012.)

die ihn durchziehen, tragen noch die Spuren von den kleinen Leuten, welche hin und wieder gingen: an den Stellen, wo sie mit den Ellenbogen anstreiften, ist die Wand ganz glatt. Wo diese Gänge zu Tage gehen, sind sie etwa 3 Fuß hoch, 2 Fuß breit, oben halbrund.

Aus diesem Berge führt ein langer, unterirdischer Gang bis in den Keller eines Wirtes in Heinrichskirchen: er soll von den Strazeln gebaut sein. Da dieser Keller auch zur Aufbewahrung von Esswaren diente, bemerkten die Wirtsleute gar oft einen Abgang daran und ließen daher die Dienstboten nicht mehr allein hinunter gehen. Gleichwohl fehlte ungeachtet dieser Vorsicht nach wie vor Manches an den Vorräten, weshalb sich der Wirt einmal nachts hinter einem Fasse versteckte. Da sah er gegen den Morgen hin die Strazeln in großer Menge aus der Öffnung, durch welche das zusammengesessene Wasser ablaufen sollte, herauskommen und weil sie von ihm ungestört blieben, auf die Speisen zugehen und heißhungrig davon verzehren; als sie satt waren, nahm jeder noch mit, so viel er eben tragen konnte. Das war dem guten Wirte denn doch zu unbescheiden, und er rief ihnen ein ernstes »Halt« zu. Mit jämmerlichem Geschrei drängten sich die Kleinen durch das Loch hinaus, ohne Etwas von dem, was sie einmal eingepackt, fallen zu lassen. Der Wirt ließ es gutwillig geschehen, verwahrte sich aber gegen die ungebetenen Gäste für die Zukunft durch ein Gitter, welches er vor die Öffnung stellte. – Nicht lange darauf fand man aber das Gitter eingeschlagen.

Man hatte ihnen später Mehl gestreut, um zu sehen, was sie für Füße hätten: es drückten sich natürliche Kinderfüße ab, denen je eine Zehe fehlte.

### 107 Die Zwerge in der Klostermühle

Seit uralter Zeit geht die Sage von den Razen in der ehemaligen, nun zu einer Tabakfabrik umgewandelten Klostermühle Schöntal. Sie wird von der Schwarzach getrieben, welche oft aus den Ufern tritt und die Arbeit des Müllers auf längere Zeit verhindert.

which crisscross it still carry the marks of the little people who walked back and forth here—at the places where their elbows brushed, the wall is entirely smooth. Where these tunnels come up to the surface, they are about 3 feet high, 2 feet wide, and semi-circular at the top.

From this mountain, a long, underground tunnel leads to the cellar of an inn in the town of Heinrichskirchen; it is said to have been built by the "Strazel" Dwarves. Because this cellar was used for food storage, the innkeepers very often noticed that some of it was missing and didn't allow their servants to enter the cellar by themselves. Regardless of this precautionary measure, quite a few of their provisions still went missing, whereupon one night the innkeeper hid behind a barrel. Toward morning, he saw a large number of "Strazel" Dwarves emerge from an opening through which the accumulated water was supposed to drain, and since he did not disturb them, they went up to the food, ate of it with a ravenous appetite and, when they were full, each took away with them as much as they could possibly carry. The good innkeeper thought this a bit too brazen, and so he called out a commanding "Stop!" to them. Wailing and whining, the little ones squeezed out through the hole, without dropping any of what they had packed. The innkeeper allowed this to happen in good humor, but deterred the unwelcome guests from returning again, by placing an iron grille before the opening.—Not long after that, however, they found the grille had been broken through.

Later, they strewed flour about to see what kind of feet they had; as expected, they found footprints that looked exactly like children's, with each footprint missing a toe.

## 107 The Dwarves in the Monastery Mill

From time immemorial the legend tells of the "Razen" who lived in the former monastery mill of Belle Valley, which is now a tobacco factory. It is powered by the Schwarzach River, which often overflows its banks, and so prevented the miller from working for long stretches at a time.

In grauer Vorzeit nun war der Fluss auch einmal überge-
treten, die Mühle stand. Das Gemalter mehrte sich mit jedem
Tage und damit der Ungestüm der Mühlgäste. Endlich fiel das
Wasser. Der Müller voll freudiger Hoffnung nahm sich vor, die
ganze Nacht über recht fleißig zu schaffen, und legte sich, um
seine Kräfte beisammen zu halten, schon bei Tag zu Bette, ver-
schlief aber ermattet von den seitherigen Sorgen und erwachte
erst gegen Morgen. Ganz betrübt ging er in seine Mühle hinunter an sein Geschäft, welchem trübe Wolken am Himmel keinen
günstigen Erfolg versprachen. Wie groß aber war sein freudig
Erstaunen, als er dort sämtliches Gemalter gemahlen, die Säcke
nach Abzug der Maut gehörig gefüllt, die Kleie abgesondert und
alles nach den Gesetzen der Mühlordnung bestellt fand. Zugleich gedachte er, wie vortrefflich es sein müsse, durch fremde
Knappen sein Mehl mahlen zu lassen und versuchte es daher,
noch einmal das Gemalter sich ansammeln zu lassen, vielleicht
würden die dienstfertigen Knappen wiederholt für ihn arbeiten. Doch stach ihn die Neugierde, zu erfahren, wer ihm denn
so gar zu Gefallen stehe, ging auf den Dachboden der Mühle,
hob ein Brett aus und legte sich dann nieder, um nachts sicher
bei Händen zu sein und die sonderbaren Helfer belauschen
zu können.

Um Mitternacht sah er denn auch in seiner Mühle ganz kleine,
noch kleiner als Zwerge gebaute Männchen kommen, in der Zahl
unter zwölf; denn mehr als elf konnte er nicht zählen, obwohl ihn
die Anzahl bald größer, bald kleiner schien. Ihre grauen Bärte
wallten lang herab, ihre Röckchen schienen zerrissen. Diese kleinen Dingerchen arbeiteten nun so geschäftig, wie emsige Ameisen,
banden die Getreidesäcke auf, indem einer den andern hinauf-
schob, brachten das Getreide in die Gosse, verrichteten überhaupt die Arbeit mit einer Genauigkeit und Schnelligkeit, dass
der Müller über ihre Kunstfertigkeit und Stärke nur so staunen
musste.

Er ließ sie daher ohne Unterbrechung fort arbeiten, fasste aber
den Entschluss, den guten Männlein seine dankbare Gesinnung
kund zu geben, indem er ihnen statt der abgetragenen neue
Röckchen machen ließe. Nach geschehener Arbeit verschwanden
endlich die Razen in einer Ecke der Mühle, oder es schien ihm
vielmehr, dass sie sich dort in einem Loche verkröchen.

One time in the dim and distant past, the river had been flooding again, and the mill stood still. The amounts of grain to be milled grew every day and with it the impatience of the mill's clients. Finally, the water level dropped again. The miller, filled with joyous expectation, had planned to work quite busily all night, and lay down to sleep early when it was still daylight. However, exhausted from all his previous troubles, he overslept and awoke only after the day had already dawned. Deeply saddened, he went down to the mill to start his daily business, which didn't promise to be successful because of the overcast sky. He was greatly and pleasantly surprised to find all of the grain which he had planned to grind was already ground, and the sacks, after the deduction of his charge for grinding, were appropriately filled, the bran separated out, and everything had been done according to the laws of the milling regulations. At the same time he pondered how excellent it might be to have the flour milled by independent apprentices, and thus tried again to gather up grain; maybe the obliging apprentices would do the work for him again. But, piqued by curiosity to find out who those very obliging fellows were, he climbed up to the top floor of the mill, removed a floor board and lay down so that he would be ready at hand to eavesdrop on his strange helpers during the night.

Around midnight, he saw tiny men arrive in his mill, of a stature even smaller than average Dwarves, numbering less than twelve; for he was unable to count more than eleven, though their number sometimes seemed larger, and then again smaller. They had long flowing gray beards, with coats that seemed tattered. These tiny little creatures then worked as busily as hard-working ants; they untied the sacks of grain by one little man push another next up and over, emptied the grain into the hopper and, throughout, completed their work with such alacrity and speed that the miller could not help but be amazed at their skill and strength.

Thus, he allowed them to work without interrupting them, but decided to express his feelings of gratitude toward the little men by having new little coats made for them, in the stead of their tattered ones. Finally, after they had completed their work, the "Razen" disappeared into one corner of the mill or, rather, it looked to him as if they were hiding out in a hole there.

Als nun der Müller wieder ein ansehnliches Gemalter beisammen und in der Mühle aufgestellt hatte, legte er neue Röckchen auf den Wassertrog, das Schlafbrett in der Mühle, und begab sich wieder auf den Boden, um zu lauschen. Wieder kamen die kleinen Leutchen und arbeiteten unverdrossen, wie sonst: doch schienen sie nicht so heiter und fröhlich wie vordem. Der Müller meinte, es wäre ihnen der Lohn zu geringe und nahm sich vor, das nächstemal mehr zu tun. Doch tröstete er sich wieder, als er sah, dass die Zwerglein die alten Röckchen aus- und die neuen anzogen: aber wieder erschrak er zu Tode, wie er sah, dass sie die alten Kleidchen unter den Arm nahmen und mit herzzerreißendem Weinen und Wehklagen abzogen.

Das nächstemal hoffte der Müller seine Sache vortrefflich zu machen, wenn er viel schönere Wämschen mit Hütchen auf das Gemalter ausbreitete. Aber die Männchen kamen nicht und holten auch ihr Geschenk nicht ab; sie waren für immer verschwunden.

Später erst erfuhr er, wie man ihnen keinen höheren Lohn reichen dürfe, als drei Stückchen Brot auf die Bank hingelegt, damit sie nicht glauben sollen, man habe ihnen den Dienst aufgesagt und zahle sie aus.

## 108 Röschen und die Zwerge

Der Blaubauer hatte einen Sohn, den er einem reichen Mädchen verheiraten wollte; dieser aber hatte schon gewählt, ein hübsches und frommes, aber armes Kind. Der Vater drängte immer mehr, und die Lage der Liebenden wurde immer unerträglicher. Eines Abends hatte Röschen, so hieß das Mädchen, noch am Brunnen zu tun; auf einmal vernahm sie ein Seufzen; neugierig sah sie auf und erblickte einen Zwerg, der mit aller Anstrengung sein Krügerl Wasser nicht aus dem Brunnen hervorzuheben vermochte. Röschen lachte darüber, fühlte aber doch Mitleid, und hob auf einen bittenden Blick des Kleinen das Krügerl heraus und gab es ihm in die Hand. Da sagte das Zwerglein: »Was willst du zum Dank für deinen Dienst?« »Mir kann niemand helfen, denn Gott allein,« war die Antwort. »Warte ein wenig,« rief der Zwerg, »ich muss das Krügerl hineintragen, meine Frau

When the miller had again accumulated a large amount of grain to be milled and stacked in the mill, he placed the new little coats onto the water trough, the sleeping board in the mill, and then climbed up to the top floor again to eavesdrop. And again the little people came and worked assiduously as usual; however, this time they did not seem as happy and joyful as before. The miller thought that to them [perhaps] the pay seemed too small, and planned to do more for them the next time. But he felt reassured again when he saw that the little Dwarves took off their old little coats and put on their new ones; however, he was frightened to death when he saw that they took their old little garments under their arms and left, while wailing and whining heartbreakingly.

The miller hoped to do an excellent job the next time, when he would spread out even nicer looking little doublets, including little hats, onto the grain to be milled. But the little men did not come, and also they did not fetch their presents; they had disappeared forever.

He learned later that one was not supposed to give them a reward more valuable than three little pieces of bread placed onto the bench, so that they would not think they had been dismissed and paid out.

## 108 Little Rose and the Dwarves

The proprietor of the Blue Farm had a son whom he wanted to marry to a rich girl; the son, however, had already chosen a pretty and pious, but poor maiden. The father urged more and more, and the situation of the lovers become increasingly unbearable. One evening Little Rose, which was the name of the maiden, still had work to do at the fountain, when suddenly she heard sighing. Curious, she looked up and saw a Dwarf who was trying hard to lift his little pitcher out of the water, but was not able. Little Rose laughed at this, though she did feel pity for him and, when the little one looked at her imploringly, lifted the little pitcher out of the water and handed it to him. Thereupon the little Dwarf said, "What do you wish for in return for your service?" Her reply was, "Nobody can help me but God alone." "Wait a little," the Dwarf called out. "First I have to carry the little pitcher inside because my wife

hat Durst, ich bin gleich wieder da.« Derweil setzte sich das
Mädchen auf den Brunnenring und weinte. Der Zwerg aber
kehrte schnell zurück und setzte sich ihr auf den Schoß und ließ
sich von ihrem Kummer erzählen, und wie er alles vernommen,
begann er: »Dein Vater war ein reicher Mann; sein Geld aber hat
der Geizhals vergraben, und das Geheimnis ist mit ihm zu Grabe
gegangen. Geh nun heim und hebe vom Herd in der Küche . . .
Doch nein, heute Nacht um 11 Uhr will ich deiner in der Küche
warten und dir zu den Schätzen verhelfen, damit du nicht mehr
eine arme Dirne bist.« Als nun Röschen etwas vor Mitternacht
in die Küche trat, wartete ihrer schon lange der Zwerg und
zankte sie, dass sie so spät komme. »Du hast lange geschlafen,«
sagte er, »und unser Viere haben zu schütteln gehabt, um dich
zu wecken.« Sie musste nun die obere Decke des Herdes herabtun und mehrere Steine herausnehmen: es zeigte sich eine Öffnung, die abwärts ging. Der Zwerg sprang hinein, das Mädchen
ihm nach, ein Gang führte sie zu einem Gewölbe. Der Zwerg
zog einen verrosteten Schlüssel heraus und öffnete es. Da standen die Schätze in großen und kleinen Häfen. Nun war Röschen reicher, als die dem Geliebten vom Vater bestimmte Braut.

Am andern Tage ging sie heiter und hüpfend dem Geliebten
entgegen, der aber traurig den Kopf hing und nicht begreifen
konnte, warum das Liebchen heute gar so lustig sei; er selber
habe keinen Grund, sich zu freuen: er sei auf des Vaters Befehl
hier, um ihr zu entsagen. Röschen aber lachte und erzählte ihm
von ihrem Glücke und so war der Vater gewonnen.

Der Zwerg verließ die junge Hausfrau nicht; sie arbeitete zwar
selbst sehr fleißig, aber der kleine Freund hatte seine Genossen
mitgebracht und ging ihr mit diesen immer zu Händen und half,
wo er konnte, die Arbeit fördern. Das Geschäft ging immer besser,
die Kunden mehrten sich, der Reichtum wuchs zusehends an.
Die Zwerge fegten und putzten, reinigten das Vieh im Stalle, gaben ihm Futter vor, sie halfen der jungen Frau bei ihren Gebur-
ten, warteten der Kinder, spielten mit ihnen. Als Lohn erbaten
sie sich täglich dreimal warme Kuhmilch.

Später brachten sie auch ihre Frauen auf Besuch und ihre
Kinder; diese lernten sogar lesen von der Bäuerin. Kamen die

is thirsty; I will be back at once." Meanwhile, the maiden sat down on the rim of the fountain and cried. The Dwarf quickly returned, sat down on her lap and had her tell him of her misery, and when he had heard everything, he began, "Your father was a rich man, but the miser buried all his money and took the secret with him to the grave. Now go home and take from the stove in the kitchen . . . But no, I will wait tonight at 11 o'clock in your kitchen and restore the treasures to you, so that you will be a poor maiden no more." When Rose entered the kitchen a little before midnight, the Dwarf had already been waiting a long time for her and scolded her for being so late. "You slept a long time," he said, "and four of us had to shake you so that you would wake up." She then had to remove the lid on the top of the stove and take out several stones; thereupon an opening appeared that led downwards. The Dwarf jumped into it, and the maiden followed him; a tunnel led them to a domed chamber. Then the Dwarf pulled out a rusty key and unlocked [the door]. And there were the treasures, in large and small pots. Now Little Rose was much wealthier than the bride that her beloved's father had chosen for him.

On the following day, she skipped and walked merrily toward her beloved, who let his head hang sadly, however, and couldn't understand why his sweetheart was so very happy today. He himself had no reason to be merry; he was here at his father's orders to renounce her. However, Little Rose laughed and told him about her fortune, and thus the father was won over.

The Dwarf did not leave the young wife; although she was working very hard, her little friend had brought along all his companions, and they came to help her with her work, as did he, as much as he possibly could. Business improved more and more, the number of customers grew, and their wealth increased visibly. The Dwarves swept and cleaned, brushed the animals in the stable, fed them, helped the young woman in childbirth, attended to the children, and played with them. For pay, they asked for warm cow's milk three times a day.

Later, they also brought their wives and children to visit; the latter even learned to read with the help of the farmer's wife. In turn,

Zwergenweiblein hinwieder in's Kindbett, so besuchte sie die Bäuerin und gab den Kindern ihren Namen her. Dabei gingen die Zwerge in den kleinsten Gängen voran, die Bäuerin ohne Beschwernis hintennach. Es war das innigste Verständnis zwischen beiden Teilen. Die Bäuerin bat daher einst die Zwerge, sie möchten auch ihren Kindern zur Seite bleiben, und erhielt zur Antwort: »Wohl, aber nur so lange sie gut bleiben.« – Wollte sie die Kleinen auf Besuch haben, so rief sie nur: »Mannla, kumts, d'Manna han furt!«[16] und die Zwerge schlüpften sogleich aus den Spalten des Bodens hervor.

## 109 Evchen und die Zwerge

Auf einem Edelhofe meldete sich einst spät Abends eine schöne Jungfrau, ärmlich aber reinlich gekleidet, bei der Verwalterin, welche wegen ihres gestrengen Regimentes weit und breit verschrieen war und eben jetzt einer Dirne bedurfte. Sie erbat sich, bei ihr sogleich in Dienst treten zu wollen und bedang sich Lohn, so viel oder so wenig man ihr geben wollte, wenn sie nur eine Kammer für sich allein erhielte. Die Verwalterin hatte kundigen Blickes die feinen Händchen des Mädchens bemerkt und hielt sie nicht eben geeignet für rauhe Arbeit. Doch behielt sie Evchen bei sich, um die Probe mit ihr zu machen.

Evchen ließ sich aber gut an; sie war ernst, lachte nie, tat ihre Arbeit. Doch die Frau forderte gar so viel, besonders gab es viel Geschirr zu spülen, und man konnte ihr damit nicht früh genug zu Ende kommen. Darüber musste Eva einmal harte Worte hören: statt zu essen, stellte sie ihr Töpfchen mit Hirsebrei unter die Bank und setzte sich hin, um recht von Herzen zu weinen. Als sie genug geweint hatte, wollte sie das Töpfchen unter der Bank hervornehmen, war aber sehr verwundert, zwei kleine Zwerge dort unten zu sehen, welche erschrocken die Reste des Hirsebreies von ihrem Munde abzuwischen sich bemühten. Als Eva kein böses Gesicht machte, wurden sie zutraulich und erboten sich ihr bei der harten Arbeit zu helfen, wenn sie ihnen von ihrer kleinen Mahlzeit täglich etwas mitteilen wollte. Das Mädchen

---

[16] Oberpfälzisch für: „Männlein, kommt, die Männer sind fort!"

when the little Dwarf women gave birth, the farmer's wife visited them and named their children. On these occasions, the Dwarves walked ahead in the smallest tunnels and the farmer's wife followed without difficulty. Between them there was the most heartfelt understanding. Once the farmer's wife thus asked the Dwarves to stand by her children also, and the reply was, "Very well, but only if they remain good."—If she wanted the little ones to visit her, all she had to do was to call out, "Little men, come to me, the men are gone!" Whereupon the Dwarves slipped out from between the floorboards.

## 109 Little Eve and the Dwarves

On a big estate one evening a beautiful maiden, dressed humbly but cleanly, called on the stewardess, who was notorious far and wide for her strict rule, and was just now in need of a maidservant. The maiden expressed an interest in entering immediately into service with the stewardess and agreed to work for any wages, no matter how much or how little they wanted to pay her, [but] only if she could have her own chamber. The stewardess, with an expert look, had noticed the maiden's smooth hands and did not think her fit for rough work. However, she took Little Eve on to test her out.

But Little Eve made a promising start; she was serious, never laughed, and always did her work. But the stewardess asked for quite a lot, and there were especially a lot of dishes to be done, and she never thought it was completed early enough. About this Eve was once given hard words; instead of eating her food, she placed the little pot with millet gruel under the bench and sat down to cry with all her heart. When she was done crying, she wanted to pick up the little pot under the bench, but was quite astonished to see two little Dwarves down there who, frightened, tried to wipe the remains of the millet gruel from their mouths. When Eve did not make an angry face, they became trusting and offered to help her with the hard work if she were to give them a share of her small meal every day. The maiden

ging den Vertrag mit Freunden ein, und nun brauchte sie zum
Spülen nicht einmal jene Zeit, welche die Verwalterin ihr gesteckt
hatte. – Die Beziehungen zu den Zwergen wurden so immer inniger; sie entdeckte ihnen den Kummer, der ihr Herz bedrückte,
dass sie mit einem Kinde schwanger sei, und die Kleinen gaben
ihr etwas in die Suppe, dass dem Menschenauge ihr Zustand
verborgen blieb. In ihrer Kammer hatte sie hinter dem Bettvor-
hange eine Wiege mit Zubehör versteckt. Als nun ihre Zeit um
war, gebar sie, und die Zwerge leisteten Hebammendienste und
gaben ihr einen stärkenden Trank, damit sie sogleich aufstehen,
und um allen Verdacht abzuwenden, ihrer Arbeit nach wie vor
nachgehen konnte. Die Furcht, das Kind möge schreien und alles
verraten, benahmen ihr die kleinen treuen Freunde mit der Ver-
sicherung, sie würden es während der Abwesenheit der Mutter
wohl warten und verhüten, dass es schreie. So trugen ihrer sechs
das Kind im Büscherl herum und wiegten es in Schlaf, indem
sich je drei an die Wiegenbänder rechts und links hingen. Das
machte die Mutter immer heiterer. Es kam der dritte Sommer
und die Herrschaft wollte ihn auf dem Edelhofe zubringen. Da
wurde alles zum Empfange hergerichtet. In einem Prunkzimmer
hing eine Laute. Diese nahm Eva und setzte sich hin und spielte
und sang wundervoll dazu; die Verwalterin, in Angst, es möchte
die Herrschaft ohne ihr Wissen bereits im Schlosse sein, eilte
hinauf und sah – die Magd. Sie schüttelte den Kopf und behan-
delte von nun an Eva aufmerksamer.

Bald darauf fuhr ein Wagen vor. Sechs Zwerge hüpften heraus,
machten den Schlag auf, und ein junger, hübscher Mann stieg
aus. Eva lag ihm im Arme. Versteinert schaute die Verwalterin
drein. Eva aber beruhigte sie und sprach: »Ich bin die einzige
Tochter reicher Eltern; zur Waise geworden, wollte ein habsüch-
tiger Vormund mein Vermögen durch meine Hand gewinnen,
ich wollte nicht; da drang er in mich, den Schleier zu nehmen:
ich hatte aber schon einen Bräutigam gewählt und entfloh. Seitdem bin ich bei Euch. Nun ist der Vormund tot und ich bin frei.
Doch jetzt muss ich nach meinem Kinde schauen.«

Sie eilte hinauf in ihre Kammer. Die Zwerge hatten reiche Gaben an Perlen und Edelsteinen ausgelegt. Sie führten das Kind ihr
entgegen.

happily agreed to the deal, and now she did not even use up the time the stewardess had allotted her for doing the dishes.—The relationship with the Dwarves became more and more heartfelt; she even disclosed her sorrow over being with child, which distressed her heart greatly; and the little ones put something in her soup which prevented a human eye from noticing her condition. In her bedchamber, she hid a cradle and accessories behind the bed curtain. When her time came, she gave birth, and the Dwarves served as midwives and administered an invigorating potion that helped her to rise up immediately, to avert any suspicion and still allow her to attend to her work. The loyal little friends took away her fear that the child might cry and give away her secret by assuring her that they would, in the mother's absence, tend it well and prevent it from crying. Therefore six of them carried the child around on a bed of flowers and lulled it to sleep by hanging onto the ribbons of the cradle, three on the left and [three on] the right. That made the mother increasingly happy. The third summer came, and the lord and lady of the estate planned to spend it there. Everything was made ready for their reception. In one of the staterooms, a lute was hanging. Eve took it, sat down and played, and sang along with it wonderfully; the stewardess, fearing that her lord and lady had already arrived at the castle without her knowledge, hurried upstairs and saw—the maidservant. She shook her head over this and from now on treated Eve more considerately.

Soon after that, a coach drove up. Six Dwarves jumped out, opened the door, and a young handsome man emerged. Eve was taken in his arms. The stewardess looked on, petrified. But Eve reassured her, saying, "I am the only daughter of rich parents. When I became an orphan, a covetous guardian tried to seize my fortune by marrying me. I did not agree to that, thereupon he urged me to take the veil. However, I had already chosen a bridegroom and fled. Since that time, I have been with you. Now the guardian has died and I am free. But now I have to look after my child."

She hurried upstairs to her bedchamber. The Dwarves had laid out rich presents of pearls and jewelry. They carried the child to her.

Nun war nicht mehr länger ihres Bleibens an diesem Orte der Dienstbarkeit. Als sie abfuhr, weinten die Zwerge. Sie beschied sie zu sich auf das Schloss ihres Bräutigams, und nicht mehr trennten sie sich. Wie früher leisteten sie auch da Hebammendienste und pflegten und warteten der Kinder. Ein Mädchen davon war schon zur schönen Jungfrau geworden und hatte das Herz eines Zwerges so entzündet, dass dieser um ihre Hand anhielt. Wohl wurde ihm statt dieser ein Korb gegeben. Doch störte dieses die Freundschaft nicht und das Glück blieb mit den Zwergen beim Hause, bei Kindern und Kindeskindern.

## 110 Die Mär von Woud und Freid[17]

Es war einmal ein Herrscherpaar, mit großem Gebiete, in der Zauberkunst wohl erfahren; selbst die Elemente waren ihnen untertan. Er hieß Woud, sie Freid. Der König war ein gewaltiger Mann mit langem wallenden Barte, sein Auge so feurig blitzend, dass Menschen, welche hineinblickten, darob erblindeten; gewöhnlich ging er nackt, nur an der Hüfte bekleidet; gehalten wurde das Hüftenkleid durch einen endlosen Gürtel, an diesen war die Herrschergewalt gebunden: so lang er ihn trägt, herrscht er. Doch kann er ihm nicht entwendet werden, denn Hüften und Schulter sind so breit, dass der Gürtel sich nicht abziehen lässt. – So oft er zum Herrschen ging, hing er einen Mantel um, der ihn ganz einhüllte.

Seine Gemahlin war das schönste Frauenbild; sie trug ein Hüftenkleid gleich ihrem Gatten, aber die Haare so reich und lang, dass sie sich darin ganz verhüllen konnte. Sie trank nur Wasser aus der Quelle, ihr Gatte eine Art Wein. Wenn sie sich bückte über der Quelle, um mit der hohlen Hand Wasser zu schöpfen, erglänzte ihr Haar im Sonnenglanze und ihr Arm wie Schnee.

Doch wurde sie eifersüchtig, sie fürchtete, dem feurigen Gatten nicht zu genügen; in ihrer Leidenschaft ging sie zu kunstreichen Zwergen. Diese arbeiteten ihr einen Halsgürtel, der die Kraft hatte, dass wer ihn trug, alle Herzen bezauberte und den

---

[17] „Die Zwerge sind kunstfertige Schmiede; davon eine Sage, welche in die Göttersage hinübergreift." *Sitten und Sagen*, Bd. 2: 312.

She did not want to remain in this place of servitude any longer. When she departed, the Dwarves cried. She then told them to come to her bridegroom's castle, and so they were separated no more. Just as before, they provided midwife services to her there also, and tended and cared for the children. When one of the girls had grown into a beautiful young woman, she moved the heart of one of the Dwarves so much that he asked for her hand in marriage. As expected, instead of [receiving] her hand, he was turned down. However, that did not disturb their friendship, and together with the Dwarves, happiness stayed in the house for generations.

## 110 The Legend of Wodan and Frija[18]

Once upon a time there was a royal couple who ruled over a large area; they were well-versed in magic; even the Elements were their subjects. His name was Wodan, and hers was Frija. The king was a powerful man with a long flowing beard, and his eyes were so fiery that the humans who looked into them turned blind. He usually walked naked, only his waist was clad; his waist garment was fastened with a cast belt buckle to which his ruling power was tied—as long as he wears it, he will rule. However, one cannot steal it from him, for his hips and shoulders are so broad that the belt cannot be pulled over them.—Every time he went about the business of ruling, he put on a coat which covered him completely.

His queen consort was the most beautiful woman ever seen; like her husband, she wore a waist garment, but her hair was so rich and long that she could cover herself with it entirely. She drank only water from a well; her husband, some kind of wine. When she bent over the well to scoop water into her hand, her hair shone in the light of the sun, and her arms [shone as white] as snow.

However, she grew jealous, she feared she no longer satisfied her fiery husband; in a fit of passion she went to see the skilled Dwarves. They fashioned a necklace for her which had the power to turn the hearts of all toward the bearer, and made

---

[18] "The Dwarves are skilled blacksmiths; here is a tale that touches on the legends of the Germanic deities." *Sitten und Sagen*, vol. 2: 312.

Geliebten nie in seiner Treue wanken ließ. Doch musste sie sich den Zwergen zum Lohne ergeben.

Mit dem Schmuck angetan, fesselte sie den Gatten in Liebe. Doch erfuhr er, um welchen Preis sie den Schmuck erworben. Da entwich er von ihr. Als Freid am Morgen im Bette erwachte, streckte sie den Arm aus nach dem Gatten. Er war nicht da; sie fuhr mit der Hand an den Hals, das Halsgeschmeide fehlte. Namenlos unglücklich machte sie der Verlust des Schmuckes erst recht in Liebe zu Woud entbrennen. Sie eilte dem Flüchtigen nach in viele Länder lange Jahre. Wenn sie abends ermüdet von der Fahrt sich niedersetzte, weinte sie in ihren Schoß, und jede Träne wurde zur kostbaren Perle.

Endlich als die Zeit um war, traf sie ihn und klagte ihm ihr Leid und wies auf die Perlen, die sie geweint um ihn. Und er zählte die Perlen, und ihrer waren gerade so viele, als der Steine im Halsgeschmeide. Da wurde er erweicht, und reichte ihr zur Versöhnung den Schmuck. Weit sei er herumgewandert, aber keine habe er gefunden, ihr gleich an Schönheit: so habe er ihr die Treue bewahrt.

## 111 Die Zwergenburg

Nicht weit vom Orte Fichtelberg ist eine verfallene Burg, Zwergennest oder Zwergenburg genannt. Aus diesem Orte ging ein Weber in die Fremde; als er heimkehrte, waren die Eltern tot; er wollte sein Geschäft beginnen, seinen Webstuhl aufschlagen. Niemand nahm ihn auf, denn seine Mutter war als böse Hexe bekannt gewesen. Sie wiesen ihn hinaus mit seinem Webstuhle in die Schafhütte am Zwergenneste. Diese hatte der Schäfer verlassen müssen, weil die Zwerge nachts die Schafe versprengten und zu Falle brachten.

So ging er denn hinaus und richtete sich die Hütte zurecht und schlug seinen Webstuhl auf. Als er nun die erste Nacht zu Bette lag, erwachte er plötzlich und sah einen Zwerg beim Lichte des Vollmondes hereinkommen in die Kammer, der, ein Hütchen auf dem Kopfe, in Frack und kurzen Höschen, mit Schnallenschuhen und einem Stöckchen in der Hand, mehre Male auf- und abging und sich neugierig alles besah; er schien vergnügt zu sein, alles so wohlgeordnet zu finden. Zuletzt sprang er

the [bearer's] beloved never waver in his loyalty. However, as payment she had to give herself to the Dwarves.

Adorned with the jewels, she captivated her husband's love. He learned, however, at what price she had acquired the jewelry. Thereupon he fled from her. When Frija awoke in bed in the morning, she reached out her arms for her husband. He was not there; when she quickly reached to her neck, the necklace was gone. Sad beyond words, she began to burn with love for Wodan more than ever. She rushed after the fugitive, traveling to many countries over the course of many years. When she sat down in the evening, weary from the journey, she cried [tears] into her lap, and each of the tears turned into a precious pearl.

At last, when the time came to an end, she encountered him, and told him her woes and showed him the pearls she had cried for him. And he counted the pearls, and there were as many as there were jewels in the necklace. Thereupon he softened and gave her [back] the jewels in reconciliation. [He told her] he had traveled far and wide, but had found no other equal to her in beauty; so he had remained faithful to her.

## 111 The Dwarves' Castle

Not far from the village of Fichtelberg are the ruins of a castle called Dwarves' Nest or Dwarves' Castle. From this village, a weaver left to go abroad. When he returned home, his parents had died, and he wanted to start his own weaving business and set up his weaving loom. Nobody wanted to take him in because his mother had had a reputation for being an evil Witch. They cast him out with his weaving loom to the shepherd's cottage at the Dwarves' Nest. The cottage had been abandoned by the shepherd because the Dwarves had scattered his sheep at night and driven them to fall [off the mountain].

So he went out there, fixed up the cottage, and set up his weaving loom. When he had gone to bed on his first night there, he awoke with a start and saw a Dwarf enter his bedchamber in the light of the full moon. Sporting a dress coat and shorts, with buckled shoes and a cane in his hand, he paced up and down the room several times, inspecting everything curiously; he seemed to be in a jolly mood to find everything so neatly arranged. At last he jumped

auf den Tisch, setzte sich – er war nur spannlang – auf den Brot-
laib, der noch dort lag, und schnitt sich ein Stückchen ab, das
er aß. Da redete er den Gesellen an, dass so er hier wohnen
wolle, Mietlohn gezahlt werden müsse. Er verlange nicht Silber
noch Gold, denn er wisse ja, dass er arm sei, aber drei Bedin-
gungen setze er, welche genau zu erfüllen wären. Das erste sei,
dass an jedem Vollmonde der Webstuhl abgeräumt sein müsse,
das zweite, dass der Weber niemals bei Nacht in die Werkstätte
hineinsehe, das dritte, dass er schweigsam bleibe. Damit war der
Geselle zufrieden und der Zwerg ging.

Nun hatte er in Bayreuth einen Kaufherrn gefunden, der ihm
Arbeit gab, und richtete es so ein, dass mit nächstem Vollmonde
der Stuhl abgeräumt war. Als er daher am Morgen darauf in
die Werkstatt trat, war er nicht wenig erstaunt, am Stuhle einen
Streifen seidenen Gewebes, ein Muster, zu finden, welches seines
Gleichen nicht fand. Damit ging er zum Kaufherrn und bat um
Seide, um nach dem Muster zu wirken. Er erhielt so viel er deren bedurfte, und schon am nächsten Vollmonde brachte er ein
wunderschönes Stück Seidenstoff, welches dem Herrn so gefiel,
dass er dem tüchtigen Gesellen sogleich neue Arbeit gab.

So hatte der Geselle Brot, und öfter traf es sich, dass er am
Morgen nach der Vollmondsnacht ein neues schönes Muster am
Stuhle fand, was ihm stets neue Bestellungen verschaffte. Darüber wurden aber die anderen Handwerksgenossen voll Neid,
besonders der Werkmeister; die bemühten sich auf alle Weise,
ihm sein Geheimnis zu entlocken; er schwieg.

Da führten sie ihn öfter zum Weine und machten ihn trunken;
aber auch so hielt er sein dem Zwerge gemachtes Versprechen.
Doch einmal kehrte er berauscht heim: Neugier hatte ihn erfasst,
die Werkstätte zu besehen. Schon hatte er den Griff der Tür in
der Hand, als sein guter Geist ihn noch zurückhielt. Am Morgen
fand er zwar ein Muster am Stuhle hängen, aber ganz verworren.
Gleichwohl machte er es nach, und die Arbeit gefiel mehr als alle
früheren.

Indessen wurde ihm stets mehr und mehr mit Wein zugesetzt:
er verfiel in Trägheit und schlechte Sitte, das Geschäft blieb
zurück. Umsomehr wollte er sehen, wie es die Zwerge machten,
hatte aber kaum die Tür geöffnet, als er ohnmächtig zu Boden fiel.

onto the table and sat down—he was only a hand's breadth in height—on a loaf of bread that was still there, cut off a little piece and ate it. Then he addressed the craftsman, telling him that he needed to pay rent if he planned on staying there. He would ask neither for silver nor for gold, for he knew that the craftsman was poor, but he gave him three conditions with which he had to comply to the letter. The first one was that, on every full moon, the weaving loom had to be completely cleared; the second that the weaver should never peek into the workshop at night; and the third that he remain silent [about it]. To these conditions, the craftsman agreed and the Dwarf left. It happened that he found a client in Bayreuth who gave him work, and he arranged for the weaving loom to be cleared at the next full moon. When he entered the workshop on the next morning, he was quite surprised to find on the loom a patch of silk fabric, a sample, which was unique. Taking it along, he went to see his client and asked for silk in order to produce fabric matching the pattern. He received as much as he needed, and already by the next full moon, he delivered a magnificent piece of silk cloth which the client liked so much that instantly he offered the competent craftsman new work.

Thus the craftsman was able to earn a living, and now and then it happened that he found a new and beautiful pattern on his loom the morning after a full moon night, which always provided him with new orders. Thereupon the other craftsmen became envious, the master craftsman in particular, and they tried to pry away his secret from him; but he remained silent.

Then they took him out to buy wine for him and make him drunk, but even then he kept the promise he had made to the Dwarf. Once, however, he returned home drunk; he was seized by curiosity to inspect the workshop. Already he had the door handle in his hand when his common sense managed to hold him back. Indeed, he found a pattern on the loom the next morning, but it was very confused. Nevertheless, he copied it and the work pleased [people] even more than his earlier pieces.

Meanwhile, they pressed him more and more with wine; he began to succumb to idleness and bad habits, and his business diminished. All the more he wanted to see how the Dwarves worked, but hardly had he opened the door when he fell to the floor, senseless.

Am Morgen war der Webstuhl zerbrochen und die Hütte in ihrem vorigen zerfallenen Zustande.

Da nahm er seine Arbeit, um sie zum Kaufherrn zu bringen und alles dort zu entdecken. Auf dem Wege legte er sich unter einem Baume nieder; zufällig sah er nach dem Gewebe, es war in Asche zerfallen. In höchster Verzweiflung machte er sich auf den Weg, um in die weite Welt zu gehen; er kam in einen Wald, und hier dachte er, wie gut es für ihn wäre, wenn ihm der Teufel helfen wollte; jetzt habe er ja doch nichts mehr zu verlieren und dem Teufel wäre er ja ohnehin schon verfallen. Wie er nun so vor sich hinging, sah er ein zwei Schuh hohes Männchen auf einem Steine sitzen, welches einen Stiefel ausgezogen hatte und zu schmieren begann. Der Weber dachte, das könne nur der Teufel sein und ging auf ihn zu. Das Männchen aber kannte des Gesellen Herz und rief ihm entgegen: »Ich bin nicht der Teufel, aber ich suche, was du suchest, Rache an den Zwergen. Willst du mit mir gehen, um dich zu rächen, so tue, was ich dir sage. Hole mir da unten zwei Binsen herauf.« Der Weber brachte sie. Sie setzten sich nun rittlings jeder auf eine Binse und flogen weithin durch die Luft. An einem steinigen Platze hielten sie an und gingen dann, das Männchen voraus, der Weber hintendrein, in das Steingesprenge und zuletzt durch eine Kluft, welche so enge wurde, dass der Geselle vermeinte, er müsse zu einem Kartenblatte werden, um durchzukommen. Endlich machten sie Halt. Da sagte das Männlein zum Weber: »Hörst du nicht Musik; sie kommt von den Zwergen, welche Hochzeit halten; sieh durch diese Öffnung hinunter, und wenn die Braut dir nahe kommt, hole sie mir herauf!«

Da schaute der Weber hinunter durch eine Spalte in einen Saal, in welchem die Zwerge bei süßer Musik fröhlich auf und abgingen und tanzten. Die Braut trug nebst allen Gästen seidene Kleider: die Stoffe waren dieselben, deren Muster einst an seinem Webstuhle hingen; im Bräutigam erkannte er den Zwerg, mit dem er einst verkehrt hatte. – Köstlicher Speisengeruch stach ihm in die Nase: schon näherte sich die Braut; er wollte sie herauf langen: doch zog er die Hand wieder zurück; dem ungeduldigen Begleiter, der ihn darüber zankte, entschuldigte er sich, dass ihm ein Schweißtropfen von der Stirne in das Auge gelaufen sei. So auch das zweite Mal: immer überkam ihn eine gewisse Furcht, die Braut zu stehlen. Da fuhr das Männchen

In the morning, the weaving loom was broken and the cottage was in its former state of disrepair.

He then took his work to bring it to his client and confess to everything. On his way there, he lay down under a tree. When he happened to look at the fabric, it had disintegrated into ashes. In extreme despair, he went on his way out into the world; he came to a forest and thought how good it would be for him if the Devil helped him; he had nothing more to lose at this point, and anyway he was already lost to the Devil. While he was walking along, he noticed a little man, two feet high, sitting on a rock, who had taken off one boot and had begun to polish it. The weaver thought that this could only be the Devil and approached him. The little man, however, knew the craftsman's heart and called out to him, "I am not the Devil, but I am looking for what you are looking for, to take vengeance on the Dwarves. If you want to come along to seek vengeance, do as I say. Go fetch two rushes from down there." The weaver fetched them. Then each sat astride a rush, and flew through the air, far away. They stopped on a rocky place and then walked, with the little man leading the way, the weaver following behind, across the rocky area and finally through a crevice that became so narrow that the craftsman thought he had to turn into a playing card in order to pass through it. At last they stopped. Then the little man said to the weaver, "Don't you hear the music; it's coming from the Dwarves who are celebrating a wedding. Look down through this opening, and when the bride comes close, seize her and fetch her up to me!"

Then the weaver looked down through the gap into the hall where, to a sweet tune, the Dwarves walked to and fro and danced. Like all the guests, the bride wore a silk dress; the fabric was the same as those whose patterns had been draped over his weaving loom, and in the bridegroom he recognized the Dwarf with whom he had been in contact.—The smell of delicious food stung his nose, and the bride was getting closer to him. He was about to pull her up, but then pulled back his hand again. To his impatient companion, who scolded him for that, he apologized, saying that a drop of sweat from his forehead had run into his eye. And so it happened again the second time; each time he was overcome by a definite fear of stealing the bride. Whereupon the little man

zornig auf seinen Nacken und drohte ihn zu erwürgen, so er nicht zugriffe. Zum drittenmale streckte der Geselle die Hand aus nach der Braut, da nieste sie, und er rief ihr unversehens ein »Helf Gott« hinunter. Nun brach alles zusammen mit fürchterlichem Getöse: der Weber lag von einem Schlage des Männchens getroffen ohnmächtig da. Als er erwachte, standen die Zwerge um ihn und der Bräutigam dankte ihm für die Rettung seiner Braut, ermahnte ihn aber, von nun an ein besseres Leben zu führen; mit Silber könne er ihm nicht lohnen, aber zu Arbeit wolle er ihm helfen, wie früher.

So ging der Weber heim, die Hütte war wieder ganz und der Webstuhl ordentlich aufgestellt. Er fing wieder zu wirken an, hatte stets der Arbeit genug und lebte fortan glücklich.

## 112 Die schöne Bertha, der rote Schuh und die goldene Nadel

Ein Graf im Fichtelgebirge hatte Frau und Kind, Herden und Hirten, war aber rauh und hart. Da schwur ihm der Hirt Rache und stahl einst dem Vater das Kind und vertauschte seine Tochter dagegen. Hylde, des Hirten Kind, war aber garstig und böse, schön und gut hingegen Bertha, das edle Kind. Als nun der Hirt alt und schwach wurde und nicht mehr lange zu leben hatte, warf er der jungen Gräfin einen Stein in's Auge, dass sie erblindete, und der Graf befahl, ihn dafür zu hängen. Fortan mussten die Hirtin und Bertha die Herden hüten. Da kam ein schmucker Geselle und sprach bei der Hirtin vor und blieb bei ihr, um statt ihrer den Dienst zu tun. Das war dem Grafen gerade recht: denn nun musste Bertha als Magd in's Schloss. Weil sie aber schön war und klug und den Neid des hässlichen Burgfräuleins vermeiden wollte, verunstaltete sie ihr Gesicht mit Ruß und ihre Gestalt durch plumpe alte Kleider. Nicht lange, so gefiel dem Grafen der junge Hirte und er nahm ihn als Knappen in's Schloss. Seine schöne Gestalt gewann gar schnelle das Herz der hässlichen Hylda, aber auch das der bescheidenen Bertha. Doch tat der Knecht stolz gegen Beide. Als aber einmal Bertha am Brunnen Wasser holte und mit dem Krug fiel, hob er sie auf und tat ihr schön. Das sah die Gräfin vom Fenster und voll Eifersucht und Rache ließ sie der schönen Magd die schönsten Kleider anziehen,

quickly jumped at his neck, angrily, and threatened to strangle him to death if he didn't grab her. For the third time, the crafts-man reached for the bride, when she sneezed and, without think-ing, he called out a "Bless you!" down to her. Then everything collapsed with a terrible roar, and the weaver lay unconscious, struck down by a blow from the little man. When he awoke, the Dwarves stood around him and the bridegroom thanked him for saving his bride, but admonished him to lead a better life hence-forth; he was unable to reward him with silver, but was willing to help him get work, as before.

So the weaver returned home. The cottage was again intact and the loom properly set up. He took up weaving again, always had enough work, and henceforth lived happily.

## 112 Beautiful Bertha, the Red Shoe, and the Golden Needle

A count in the Fichtel Mountain Range had a wife and child, herds and shepherds, but was rough and hard. So the shepherd swore revenge, and one time stole the child away from the father and put his own daughter in her place. Hylde, the shepherd's child, was very mean-spirited and evil, whereas the noble child, Bertha, was beautiful and virtuous. When the shepherd had grown old and did not have long to live, he threw a rock into the young countess's eye, so that she went blind, and the count ordered him hanged for that. Henceforth, the shepherd's wife and Bertha had to herd the animals. A handsome young lad arrived, called on the shepherd-ess, and stayed with her to do service in her stead. This suited the count very well, for now Bertha had to be a maidservant in the castle. But because she was beautiful and clever, she sought to evade the envy of the ugly damsel of the castle; she made her face ugly with ashes, and her form ugly with shapeless old dresses. Soon the count took a liking to the young shepherd and took him into the castle as a servant. His comely shape swiftly won the heart of the ugly Hylda, but also that of modest Bertha. But the servant acted aloof toward both. Once, when Bertha was fetching water from the well and fell with her pitcher, he helped her up and flirted with her. The countess saw this from her window and, full of jeal-ousy and spite, she had the maid dress in the most beautiful clothes

und in diesen allen zum Spotte die niedrige Arbeit verrichten. Darüber härmte sich Bertha und weinte im Stillen; der Stallknecht aber schlich ihr nach und tröstete sie. Einmal wagte er es, sie zu küssen. Das sah aber die alte Hirtin, die hinter der Burgmauer stand, und der Maid nun in harten Vorwürfen drohte. Sie zu begütigen, zog die erschrockene Tochter die goldene Nadel aus dem Haare und steckte sie in den roten Schuh und warf beides ihr zu. Aber auch die Gräfin hatte den Vorgang gesehen und ließ aus Zorn und Wut die Magd in den Turm werfen.

Alle Jahre ritt der Graf einmal aus und kehrte erst am nächsten Morgen wieder. Das reizte den Knappen und er ging der Hufspur nach, welche in einer engen Bergschlucht sich verlor. Da trat er zur alten Hirtin und fragte sie um den Weg, und diese gab ihm ein Stäbchen und ein Päckchen; jenes werde ihm das Bergtor, dieses den Eingang in die unterirdische Burg eröffnen. Er ging nun wieder vor den Berg und schlug mit dem Stäbchen daran, und der Berg ging auseinander und der Knecht hindurch. Da arbeiteten Zwerge gleich Goldschmieden, und mehrere davon waren eben daran, dem Rosse des Grafen goldene Hufeisen anzuschlagen. Er drang weiter vor und gelangte auf eine schöne Au; hier stand ein großes weißes Schloss: ein großer Hund mit eines Mannes Kopfe hütete des Einganges. Der Knecht warf ihm das Päckchen vor und kam ungehindert in das Schloss und in den Saal. Da saßen alte graue Herren am langen Tische, und junge Leute tanzten zur Seite. Der Knappe trat an den Tisch und brachte damit die Ritter in Bewegung. Der Älteste aber befragte ihn: »Wer bist du?« – und der Knappe rief voll Entsetzen ihm zu: »Mein Ahnherr!« – Da wurde alles finster um ihn, er sank ohnmächtig nieder; am Bergtor erwachte er, eben ritt sein Graf vorüber.

Bald darauf hieß es, ein junger Fürst durchreise das Land, sich eine Braut zu wählen. Mit Ungeduld harrte seines Besuches die Gräfin: aber der junge Fürst zog an dem Schlosse vorüber. Da ließ sie ihre Wut gegen alle im Schlosse aus: besonders hatte es die Magd im Turm zu fühlen, dass sie so schön sei.

Eben hatte sie wieder die Unbilden der boshaften Gräfin zu ertragen, da erbebte die Burg, und Zwerge traten herein und brachten den roten Schuh und die goldene Nadel und sagten, jene sei des Fürsten Braut, welcher beides gehöre. Da griff die Gräfin darnach.

and perform menial chores in them, to ridicule her before all. Bertha was worn down over this and secretly cried; the stable servant sought and consoled her. Once he dared kiss her. Standing behind the castle wall, the old shepherdess saw this and reproached the maiden harshly. To appease her, the frightened daughter pulled the golden needle out of her hair, stuck it into the red shoe and threw both to her. But the countess saw this also and, furiously angry, had the maidservant thrown into the tower.

Once every year the count rode out and did not return until the next morning. This piqued the servant's curiosity and he followed the horse tracks which ended in a narrow mountain gorge. He then went to the old shepherdess and asked her for directions, and she gave him a little stick and a sachet; the former would open the gate to the mountain, and the latter the door into the underground castle. He went back to the mountain and struck it with the little stick, whereupon the mountain opened up and the servant entered. There were Dwarves there working as goldsmiths, and several of them were about to shoe the count's horse with golden horseshoes. He pressed on and arrived in a beautiful meadow where he saw a large white castle; a large dog with a man's head guarded the entrance. The servant threw the sachet in front of it, and entered the castle and the hall unobstructed. There he saw old gray gentlemen sitting at a long table, and young people were dancing at the side. The servant stepped up to the table, thus stirring the knights into action. The eldest asked him, "Who are you?"—And the servant called out to him, horrified, "My forefather!"—Then everything turned dark around him, and he sank down, unconscious; he awoke at the mountain gate just as his count rode past him.

Soon thereafter, it was said that a young prince was traveling the country to choose a bride. The countess waited impatiently for his visit. However, the young prince passed the castle by. Thereupon she took out her rage on everybody in the castle; the maidservant in the tower in particular had to suffer for being so beautiful.

As she endured the harassment of the wicked countess, the castle shook and Dwarves entered, bringing with them the red shoe and the golden needle, and said that she to whom both belonged would be the prince's bride. The countess reached for them.

Zu gleicher Zeit aber traten der Fürst und die Hirtin ein, mit großem Gefolge; die Hirtin verkündete, dass Bertha des Grafen rechtes Kind sei, Hylda sei ihr eigenes, das sie ausgewechselt habe, um sich zu rächen. Zum Zeichen trage ihre Tochter Schafhaare auf den Armen, wie sie, die Alte, selber. Da stürzte sich die Gräfin vom Turm, der Graf enteilte auf seinem Hengst und Bertha wurde des jungen Fürsten, des früheren Knappen, schöne Gemahlin.

## 113 Der Zwarglberg[19]

Zwischen Aschach und Raigering, bei Amberg, liegt ein kleiner Berg, der Zwarglberg, ganz zerklüftet. Durch die Klüfte hin führt ein unterirdischer Gang bis Aschach in das Haus eines Bauern. Diesem halfen die Zwargl in der Hausarbeit, backten Brot im Backofen, rührten aus, molken die Kühe, reinigten den Stall. Ihrer kleinen Gestalt zu spotten und der zerrissenen Röckchen, legten böse Leute ihnen einmal lange neue Kleider hin. Da fingen die Kleinen zu weinen an und ließen sich seitdem nicht mehr sehen.

## 114 Die Zwerge und die Klöße

Zu Kircheneidenfeld bei Velburg waren in einem Bauernhause auch Zwerge, ein Paar, Männlein und Frauchen, und so klein, dass ihrer sechs in einem Backofen dreschen konnten. Sie gingen allen Leuten sichtlich aus dem Weg und ein kochten sich selbst, ohne dass man wusste, woher sie die Lebensmittel nahmen. Das Wasser hiezu holten sie sich im Hollenberge, damit sie kein Salz brauchten: denn es war selbst salzig.

Fleißig und unbemerkt verrichteten sie die schwersten Arbeiten im Hause für die Bauern. Einmal aber kochte die Bäuerin Klöße, und weil sie Verdacht nahm, dass ihr durch die Zwerge manches abhanden gekommen,

---

[19] „Zwargl" ist umgangssprachlich für „kleiner Zwerg."

But at that moment, the prince and the shepherdess entered, followed by a large entourage; the shepherdess proclaimed that Bertha was the count's rightful child; Hylda was her own, which she had switched to take revenge. Proof of this was that her daughter had fleecy hair on her arms, as did she, the old woman. Thereupon the countess threw herself from the tower, the count fled on his stallion, and Bertha became the beautiful wife of the young prince, the former servant.

## 113 Little Dwarves Mountain

Between the towns of Aschach and Raigering, close to Amberg[20] you can find a small mountain, called Little Dwarves Mountain, which is riddled with fissures. Through the fissures, a subterranean passage leads to the town of Aschach, straight into the house of a farmer. The Dwarves helped him with housework; they baked bread in the oven, shelled [peas], milked the cows, cleaned the stable. Once, evil people laid out tall new clothes for them, to mock their little size and their tattered coats. The little ones began to cry and have not been seen since.

## 114 The Dwarves and the Dumplings

In the town of Kircheneidenfeld, close to Velburg, there lived a pair of Dwarves on a farm, a little man and a little woman, and they were so small that six of them would have been able to thresh corn in a baking oven. They went out of their way to avoid contact with humans and even cooked their own meals, and nobody knew whence they took their food. The water for it they fetched from Hollen Mountain so they wouldn't need salt; for the water was already salty.

Working diligently and unnoticed, they performed the hardest work in the house for the farmers. One time, the farmer's wife cooked dumplings, and since she became suspicious that the Dwarves were responsible for quite a few things going missing,

---

[20] Schönwerth's hometown

zählte sie dieselben. Das verdross die Kleinen so sehr, dass sie ausblieben, worüber die Leute heute noch jammern.

## 115 Der neckende Venezianer[21]

Als einmal einer von Ebnat auf seine Wiese am Naabranger ging, sah er am Ufer des Flusses ein kleines Männchen mit dreispitzigem Hute, Schurzfell und Waidtasche, auf einem Felsenstücke sitzen und auf einem Stein in seiner Hand mit dem kleinen Hammer loshämmern. Wie es den Fremden bemerkte, verschwand es, kam aber gleich auf einer andern Sandwelle in der Naab wieder zum Vorschein, und so äffte es den Mann so lange, als dieser ihm nachging. Es war ein Venetianer.

## 116 Der einäugige Venetianer[22]

Es wurde einmal Heu heimgefahren. Da erhob sich das Windgespreil. Ein Bube, der neben dem Wagen ging, warf sein Messer hinein. Dieses wurde nicht mehr gefunden und die Sache vergessen.

Der Bube wuchs zum Manne und musste eine Reise nach Venedig unternehmen. Wie er nun herumgeht, die Wunderstadt zu beschauen, sieht von einem Hause einer zum Fenster heraus, der ihn hinaufruft und gastlich bewirtet. Als er ihn entließ, sagte er: »Ich habe nur ein Auge. Das verdanke ich dir.« Der Fremdling war hierüber umsomehr betroffen, als er den Mann gar nicht kannte. Da ging der Wirt hinaus und kam nach einiger Zeit als Venetianer gekleidet herein und zeigte dem Gaste ein Messer, ob er es nicht kenne.

---

[21] „Zu den erzgewinnenden Bergmännchen gehören die rätselhaften Venetianer; sie kommen und gehen in der Windsbraut, das oft turmhoch steigt; in weiter Ferne, gegen Süden, ist ihre Heimat; sie suchen nach edlen Erzen in den oberpfälzischen Bergen ... und kehren reichbeladen zurück ... Größe und Aussehen ist wie bei den Bergmännchen." *Sitten und Sagen*, Bd. 2: 332f.

[22] „Doch nicht immer sind diese Venetianer zwergartig; oft sind es Menschen, welche mit dem Bösen im Bunde stehen, mehr können als unsereins und gleichfalls ... edle Metalle in der Oberpfalz suchen: sie kommen geraden Weges von Venedig in der Luft durch die Windsbraut hergetragen." *Sitten und Sagen*, Bd. 2: 333.

she counted them. This annoyed the little ones so much that they stayed away, which people lament to this day.

## 115 The Mocking Venetian[23]

When a man once walked from the town of Ebnat to his meadow along the Naab River, he saw a little man wearing a three-pointed cocked hat, a leather apron, and a hunting bag, sitting on a piece of rock on the embankment, pounding a rock in his hand with a little hammer. When he noticed the stranger, he disappeared, but almost instantly reappeared on a different sand bank in the Naab River, and thus he teased the man as long as he followed the little one around. He was a Venetian.

## 116 The One-eyed Venetian[24]

One time, people were making hay when a Whirlwind arose. A boy who was walking next to the wagon threw his knife into the Whirlwind. They were unable to find it anymore, and the incident was forgotten.

The boy grew into a man and had to go on a trip to Venice. When he is walking around to do some sightseeing in the miraculous city, a man is looking out from a window and calls him in to treat him to a meal. When he bade him farewell, he said, "I have only one eye. That is thanks to you!" The foreigner was very concerned about this, all the more because he did not know the man at all. Then his host left the room and returned after some time, dressed like a Venetian, and showed the guest the knife, asking him if he did not recognize it.

---

[23] "The enigmatic Venetians belong to the Little Mountain Men, who are in the ore mining business. They use Whirlwinds, which often rise as high as a tower, for traveling. Their home is far away, toward the south. They look for precious metals in the mountains of the Upper Palatinate . . . and return, weighed down with riches . . . Their size and shape equals those of the Little Mountain Men." *Sitten und Sagen*, vol. 2: 332f.

[24] "However, the Venetians are not always the size of Dwarves. Sometimes they are humans in league with the forces of Evil, who have more powers than we do, and are likewise looking for precious metals in the Upper Palatinate. They arrive directly from Venice, carried through the air by the Whirlwind." *Sitten und Sagen*, vol. 2: 333.

Nun gingen diesem die Augen auf: er erkannte den Venetianer, den er als Knabe gar oft in seiner Gegend nach Goldsand suchen gesehen hatte.

## 117 Die sprechenden Buchen

In einem alten Buchenwalde standen zwei riesige Buchen nebeneinander. Es war Abend, und traurig hing die eine die Zweige, weshalb die Nachbarin fragte, was sie habe, dass sie das Haupt so senke. Jene aber hub an, dass gestern der Förster hier gewesen sei und sie auf morgen zum Fällen bestimmt habe: sie werde nun bald das Leben lassen. Wehe mir, erwiderte die Nachbarin, da wirst du auch mich im Falle verletzen, und die Erste schwieg, noch mehr betrübt durch diesen Ausbruch der Selbstsucht. Am andern Tage aber kam der Förster mit dem Herrn des Waldes, und sie fingen darüber zu streiten an, welche von den beiden schönen Buchen gefällt werden solle. Da beugten sich beide Bäume seufzend hin und her. »Wer hat geseufzt?« rief der Herr. Es war aber niemand da, der Antwort gab. Furcht trieb sie von dannen, und die herrlichen Bäume blieben verschont.

## 118 Der „Hoymann"[25]

Ihrer Drei aus Bärnau, sie leben noch, gingen nachts auf das Holzstehlen und nahmen ein Mädchen mit zum Aufpassen. Sie fangen an, eine Buche abzusägen, und wie sie in Mitte der Arbeit sind, kommt das Mädchen gelaufen und meldet, vom Berge da oben komme etwas herunter. Die Männer aber richten sich zum Kampfe. Da hörten sie das Geschrei: »Hoy Mann, Hoy Mann!« immer näher kommen, sie schauen auf und sehen einen Mann, so groß wie ein Baum, den Berg in Riesenschritten, von denen einer gleich zehn der Ihrigen war, herniedersteigen. Er trug einen Stecken.

---

[25] „Der Hoymann ist ein geisterhaftes Wesen, welches an bestimmten Stellen allein geht und seine Gegenwart durch Rufen kund gibt . . . Von seinem Ruf: hoy, hoy . . . helfts, den er zeitweise mehrere Male nacheinander ausstößt, und so starktönend gibt, dass man ihn Viertelstunden weit vernimmt, hat er den Namen. Die Leute halten ihn für den Teufel, auch für eine Arme Seele, die nicht zum Erlösen ist, oder einen verwunschenen Geist." *Sitten und Sagen*, Bd. 2: 342f.

Now the man's eyes were opened, and he recognized the Venetian whom he had seen often searching for gold sand in the area where he lived when he was a boy.

## 117 The Talking Beech Trees

In an ancient beech tree forest, two gigantic trees were standing next to each other. It was evening and one of them sadly let her branches droop, whereupon her neighbor asked what was wrong with her, and why she hung her head like that. The former replied that the forest ranger had been here yesterday and had earmarked her to be felled tomorrow, and so soon she would have to give up her life. Woe is me, her neighbor replied, for you will hurt me too when you fall, and the former one fell silent, even more saddened by this selfish outburst. The next day the forest ranger arrived with the lord of the forest, and they started arguing which of the two beautiful beech trees should be felled. Thereupon both trees flexed back and forth, sighing. "Who sighed?" the lord asked. However, there was nobody there to answer. Fear drove them away, and the magnificent trees were spared.

## 118 Tale of the "Hoyman"[26]

Three men from the town of Bärnau, who live to this day, went out to steal timber one night, and took a maiden along as a lookout. They begin to cut down a beech tree, and just as they are in the midst of their work, the maiden comes running and announces that something is coming down the mountain. Thereupon the men get ready for a battle. Then they hear "Hoy Man, Hoy Man!" being shouted nearer and nearer; they look up and see a man, tall as a tree, descending the mountain in gigantic leaps, each one of them as big as ten of theirs. He carried a stick.

---

[26] "The 'Hoyman' is a ghost-like creature which dwells in certain places, alone, and makes its presence known by shouting . . . His name is derived from his call, 'Hoy, hoy . . . help!' which he repeatedly utters, in a kind of staccato style; it is so loud that you can hear it from fifteen minutes [distance] away. He is sometimes taken for the Devil, at other times also for a Poor Soul that cannot find redemption, or even a bewitched spirit." *Sitten und Sagen*, vol. 2: 342f.

Gehen hörte man ihn nicht. Seine Kleider waren weiß und schwarz gescheckt, und Hosen und Goller wie zusammengenäht. Das Gesicht konnten sie nicht unterscheiden. Als er auf sie zutrat und keine Antwort erhielt – der Schrecken hatte sie gelähmt – ging er rechts ab, immerfort schreiend. – Die Furcht trieb die Diebe noch in derselben Winternacht nach Hause.

### 119 Geschichte vom Waldzwerg[27]

Im Pfarrdorf Hausen bei Kastl ist ein Gütler-Anwesen, zum Spitzbartlweber genannt. Davon erzählt man sich Folgendes:

In uralter Zeit war ein Weber darauf, der ganz arm war, aber desto mehr Kinder hatte. Einmal hatten sie gar nichts mehr zu essen; da nahm er die Axt und ging hinaus in den Wald, um Holz zu stehlen, an eine wegen Geisterspukes verrufene Stelle, um desto sicherer zu sein. Da traf er aber auf einen grün gekleideten Zwerg, der ihn anredete, und als er des armen Mannes Kummer erfuhr, in eine Felsenhöhle führte, voll aufgehäufter Schätze. Diese zeigte er ihm und gab ihm zugleich zu verstehen, dass sie alle ihm gehören sollten, so er seinen Namen binnen drei Tagen erraten könnte: er sei vom ewigen Richter verdammt, diese von Räubern mit Blut erworbenen Schätze so lange zu hüten, bis ein armer Vater seinen Namen errate und laut ausrufe. Damit verschwand Zwerg und Felsenhöhle. Tiefsinnig kehrte der Weber heim und erzählte der Frau, was er gesehen und gehört. Diese aber riet ihm ab, den Zwerg wiederum aufzusuchen; es wäre sicher der Böse gewesen. Doch Hunger tut weh, und so ging das Paar am dritten Tage vor der Sonne in den Wald. In einer Feldkapelle am Wege beteten und weinten sie lange; am Saume des Waldes aber blieb die Frau zurück, während der Mann zur Stelle einwärts ging: sie kniete an einem Gebüsche nieder und betete noch inniger um des Himmels Schutz. Im Dickicht aber saß der grüne Zwerg und wehklagte mit betrübter Stimme,

---

[27] „Verschieden von jenen Zwergen, welche gleich Menschen gelten und ein Volk bilden, sind die Zwerge, so einsam lebend, mehr den Charakter des Geisterhaften aufweisen, und durch Menschen erlöst werden." *Sitten und Sagen*, Bd. 2: 353.

No one could hear his movements. His clothes were checkered black and white, and the pants and collar looked sewn together. They were unable to distinguish any facial features. When he stepped up to them and did not get a reply—fear had paralyzed them—he veered right, shouting without end.—Fear drove the thieves home that same winter night.

### 119 Tale of the Forest Dwarf[28]

In the parish village of Hausen close to the town of Kastl, there is a little farm named the Little Pointed Beard Weaver's Place. The following [tale] is told about it:

In ancient times a weaver owned it, who was very poor, but had all the more children. One time they had nothing left to eat; so he took his axe and went into the forest to steal wood, to a place with a reputation for being haunted, to be all the more safe. There he came upon a Dwarf clad in green, who started talking with him and, when he learned of the man's misery, led him to a cave heaped full of treasures. The Dwarf showed him these, while disclosing that they would all be his if he were able to guess the Dwarf's name within three days; he had been damned by the Eternal Judge to guard these treasures, which had been acquired by robbers through bloodshed, until a poor father would guess his name and call it out loud. Having said this, the Dwarf and the cave vanished. Deep in thought, the weaver returned home and recounted to his wife what he had seen and heard. She advised against seeking out the Dwarf again; he surely was the Evil One. But hunger hurts, and so the couple went into the forest before sunrise on the third day. In a wayside chapel en route, they prayed and shed tears for a long time; at the edge of the forest the wife stayed behind while the husband continued on to the place; she knelt down by a bush and prayed even harder for Heavenly protection. In the thicket, though, the green Dwarf was sitting, lamenting in a doleful voice

---

[28] "The Dwarves who live alone show more of the qualities of ghost-like creatures and need to be redeemed by people; thus they are different from those Dwarves who are similar to people and live together as a community." *Sitten und Sagen*, vol. 2: 353.

dass auch dieses Erdenkind keinen Mut habe, und es wäre doch so leicht, aus seinem »Spitzbärtl« seinen Namen zu wissen. Das hörte die Frau und freudig eilte sie ihrem Manne nach, und war schon nahe, als auch der Zwerg kam. Da bat sie, statt des Mannes das Rätsel lösen zu dürfen, und der Zwerg gestattete es um ihrer Treue willen. Sie rief nun den Namen »Spitzbartl« weit in die Luft hinaus und sogleich flog eine weiße Taube von der Stelle auf, wo soeben der Zwerg gestanden hatte, und der Felsen spaltete sich und ließ das Geld erscheinen, welches die glücklichen Gatten sammelten und zu ihren Kindern heimtrugen.

## 120 Die Schöne und die Hässliche[29]

Zwei junge Dirnlein, die eine schön, die andere hässlich, säten Lein, jene auf dem Berge, diese im Tale. Die Schöne aber sang, während sie vor dem Pfluge ging und gedachte dabei der vielen Freier um ihre Schönheit, die andere hingegen, weil garstig und nicht begehrt, arbeitete gar fleißig darauf los, und warf nur hier und da ein Körnlein in die Büsche des nahen Waldes für das Holzfräulein.

Als die Leinsaat aufgegangen war und üppig emporwuchs, kamen die Mädchen wieder, um das Unkraut zu jäten. Die Schöne aber dachte mehr an ihre Freier als an die Arbeit, und die Garstige war um so emsiger, das Unkraut auszureißen, und versäumte nicht, am Ende des Feldes dem Holzfräulein aus Flachsstengeln ein kleines Hüttchen zusammenzubinden. Dann rief sie noch in den Wald: »Hulzfral, dau is dàñ Dal, gib an Flachs an kräftinga Flaug, nau hob J und Du gnaug«[30] – und ging nach Hause.

So verkam aber der Flachs auf dem Berge, und der im Tale schoss ellenlang auf. Beide brachten ihre Ernte ein und spannen im Winter und trugen im Frühlinge die Leinwand auf die

---

[29] „Es . . . gehört zu den Waldgeistern, weil es sich besonders am dichten Walde aufhält . . . Sie sind ganz klein, haben auf dem Ofen, auf einem Baumstocke Platz, und gelten als Arme Seelen, welche von den Holzhetzern gar oft gehetzt, gefangen und zerrissen werden . . . Da sie geheime Kräfte der Natur kennen und ärztlichen Rat erteilen, sind sie auch kluge Frauen." *Sitten und Sagen*, Bd. 2: 358–362.
[30] Oberpfälzisch für: "Holzfräulein, hier ist dein Teil, gib dem Flachs einen kräftigen Flug, dann haben ich und du genug."

that this child of the Earth also lacked courage, and it would be so easy to deduce his name from his "little pointed beard." This the wife overheard and, joyfully, hurried after her husband, and she was already close by when the Dwarf also arrived. Thereupon she asked to be allowed to solve the riddle in her husband's stead, and the Dwarf agreed to it because of her devotion. Then she called out the name "Little Pointed Beard!" loudly to the skies, and right away, a white dove flew up from the place where the Dwarf had stood only a moment before; and the rock split and the money appeared, which the fortunate spouses gathered up and carried home to their children.

## 120 The Pretty and the Ugly Maidens

Two young maidens, one pretty and the other ugly, were sowing flax; the former on the mountain and the latter in the valley. The pretty one sang while thinking of her many suitors and walking before the plow; the other one, though, because she was ugly and not desired, worked away very diligently and now and again threw a little flax seed into the bushes on the edge of the nearby forest for the Forest Maiden.[31]

When the flax seed had sprouted and grown abundantly, the maidens returned to pull the weeds. The pretty one thought more about her suitors than her work, while the ugly one worked all the more diligently pulling up the weeds, and after she was done did not fail to make a little house for the Forest Maiden by tying together the flax stalks. Then she called out into the forest, "Forest Maiden, here is your share; give the flax a big boost, then you and I will have enough"—and went home.

So the flax on the mountain withered, while the flax in the valley shot up incredibly tall. Both brought their harvest home and spun it in the winter, and in spring they carried the linen cloth onto

---

[31] "[Forest Maidens] belong to the family of forest spirits because they live most often in dense forests. . . . They are very small and fit onto a stove or a tree stump and are regarded as Poor Souls who are frequently hunted, captured, and torn asunder by the evil Wood Hunters . . . Since they have knowledge of the secret powers of nature and give medical advice, they are also wise women." *Sitten und Sagen*, vol. 2: 358–362.

Bleiche in die Wiese, und siehe, die Leinwand der Schönen war
grob und wenig, die der Hässlichen fein und viel. Da erzürnte
die Schöne und schalt ihre Freundin und rief: »Ich weiß schon,
wie du es gemacht hast, du Nachteule, eine Hexe bist du und
hast es mit dem schäbigen Holzfräulein zu tun; darum bist du
aber auch so garstig und bekommst ebenso wenig einen Mann,
wie die alte Waldjungfer.«

Da rollte es plötzlich auf dem Waldwege heran und ein schöner Prinz, auf einem goldenen Wagen, kam mit vier Schimmeln
gefahren und hatte einen Mohren hinten auf dem Sitze.

An der Wiese hielt er an und stieg aus. Er nahm die Schöne bei
der Hand und fragte sie: »Ich will dich heiraten; ist deine Leinwand fein?« – Das Mädchen schwieg, der Wiederhall vom Walde
her aber rief: »Nein!« Der Prinz ließ ihre Hand los und ging zur
Garstigen, und nahm sie bei der Hand und fragte: »Ich will dich
freien, ist dieses deine Leinwand da?« – Sie aber schwieg errötend;
und vom Walde kam der Wiederhall mit der Antwort: »Ja!«

Nun umarmte und küsste er sie als seine Braut und von seines
Mundes Hauch wurde sie so schön wie ein Engel und stand da
in die reichsten Gewänder gekleidet. Dagegen wurde die Schöne,
als sie dieses sah, giftig vor Neid, und so garstig, dass der Mohr,
der sie für seines Gleichen hielt, auf sie zusprang und ihr seine
Hand anbot, die sie voll Ärgers wegstieß.

Der Prinz fuhr mit seiner glücklichen Braut von dannen, die
Schöne, nun hässlich geworden und unglücklich aus Neid, kehrte
in's Dorf zurück. Seitdem singt kein Mädchen mehr beim Säen
des Leins, und vergisst auch nicht, dem Holzfräulein ein Hüttchen von den Restchen der Flachsstengel zu bauen.

## 121 Der Ritter und das Holzfräulein

Ein Ritter fand auf der Jagd im Walde einen Knaben, der ganz
verlassen unter einem Baume saß. Er nahm ihn mit heim, weil
ihm seine Schönheit gefiel und ließ ihn auf seiner Burg heran-
wachsen. Doch der Bube lernte nichts und wollte auch keine
knechtische Arbeit tun, obwohl er groß und kräftig geworden
war. Das verdross den Edelmann, und einmal im Zorn ließ er
den Burschen kommen und trug ihm auf, den großen Holzstoß

the meadow, to bleach it, and behold, the pretty one's linen was coarse and sparse, while the ugly one's was smooth and abundant. Thereupon the pretty one become angry and scolded her friend, saying, "I know exactly how you have managed to do that, you night owl; you are a Witch and are in league with the sordid Forest Maiden; that is why you are so ugly and just as unlikely to find a husband as the old forest spinster."

Suddenly something rolled down the forest path, and a handsome prince in a golden carriage drawn by four white horses appeared, with a Moor riding on the back of the seat.

At the meadow, he stopped and alighted. He took the pretty one by the hand and asked, "I want to marry you; is your linen smooth?"—The maiden fell silent, but the echo from the forest called out, "No!" The prince let her hand go and approached the ugly one, took her by the hand and asked, "I want to marry you; is this your linen over here?" —But blushing, she fell silent; and from the forest came the echo with the reply, "Yes!"

He then embraced her and kissed her as his bride, and from his breath she became as beautiful as an angel and stood there, clad in the most luxuriant garments. The pretty one, however, on seeing this became green with envy, and so ugly that the Moor, who took her for one of his own kind, rushed at her and offered her his hand, which she brushed away in anger.

The prince rode away with his happy bride, and the pretty one, who now had turned ugly and unhappy with envy, returned to the village. Since that day, no maiden sings anymore when sowing flax, and also, [no maiden] forgets to build a little house for the Forest Maiden from the leftover flax stalks.

## 121 The Knight and the Forest Maiden

While hunting, a knight once found a boy in the forest, who sat all alone under a tree. He took him home with him because he liked his beauty, and let him grow up in his castle. However, the boy did not learn any trade, and neither did he want to do the work of a servant, although he had grown tall and strong. The noble man was annoyed at this and once, in his wrath, had the boy appear before him and ordered him to split the big pile of wood

im Burghofe klein zu spalten oder das Schloss zu verlassen. Der Junge aber setzte sich auf den Holzstoß und tändelte mit der Axt. Da öffnete sich ein Fenster der Burg und das schöne Burgfräulein, die Pflegetochter des kinderlosen Grafen, welche schon lange die schöne Gestalt und das furchtlose Wesen des jungen Knechtes angezogen hatte, rief bittend herunter, er möge doch dem Befehle gehorchen, sonst müsste er fort aus ihrer Nähe.

Da sprang der Knecht hurtig herab und schwang seine Axt und schlug und hieb sich in das Bein. Das Fräulein aber hatte es gesehen und eilte hinab und verband ihm die Wunde.

Nun wollte der Junge noch weniger seiner Arbeit pflegen, und damit ihm der verhasste Holzstoß aus den Augen käme, nahm er zwei Hölzer, rieb sie so gewaltig gegeneinander, dass sie in Brand gerieten, und wollte damit den Holzstoß anzünden. Aber plötzlich kroch ein Holzfräulein daraus hervor und fragte ihn, was er wolle. Er meldete ihr sein Anliegen, dass er wie ein Knecht arbeiten solle, aber nicht möge, und sie bot ihm ihre Hilfe an, wenn er tun würde, was sie ihn heiße. Er sagte es zu. Über Nacht entstand Lärm im Zwinger, und als man am Morgen hinabsah, war alles Holz klein gespalten. Da stieg auch der Graf hinunter, den Knecht seines Fleißes zu loben; dieser aber hatte schnell nach den Worten des Holzfräuleins ein kleines Feuerchen angemacht, und als der Edelmann herantrat, sprang das Fräulein in die Flamme. In diesem Augenblicke stand eine schöne junge Frau dem Ritter vor Augen; es war die Waldfrau, die er einst gefreit hatte. »Der Knecht ist dein und mein Kind!« rief sie dem Erstaunten zu, und verschwand. Da nahm er den Jungen zu sich und behielt ihn für seinen Sohn, und ließ ihn nach Ritterart erziehen, und als dieser siegreich aus mehreren Fehden heimkehrte, gab er ihm auch noch die Pflegetochter zur Frau und die Burg zur Aussteuer.

## 122 Die Bäuerin und das Holzfräulein

In einem Dorfe heiratete ein junges Paar, konnte aber, weil arm, keine Dienstboten halten, und musste alles selber tun. Am beschwerlichsten fiel, dass die Äcker und Wiesen gar so weit weg

in the courtyard into small pieces, or leave the castle for good. The boy, however, sat down on the pile and played around with the axe. Then one of the castle windows opened and the pretty damsel of the castle, the childless count's foster daughter, who had been attracted to the handsome form and the fearless character of the young servant for quite a while, implored him to obey the orders, otherwise he would have to leave her company.

So the servant quickly jumped up and swung his axe, and struck and cut into his leg. But the damsel saw this, rushed down to him, and bandaged his wound.

Now the young man was even less inclined to do his work, so to get the detested pile of wood out of his sight, he took two pieces of wood and rubbed them together so forcefully that they caught fire, and was about to set the wood pile alight with them. All of sudden, however, a Forest Maiden crawled out from it and asked him what he wanted. He told her of his wish, that he was supposed to work like a servant but did not want to, and she offered him her help if he did as bidden. He agreed to that. During the night, a commotion ensued in the courtyard and when they looked down into it in the morning, all the wood had been split into small pieces. So the count also went down to the courtyard, to commend the servant for his diligence; the latter, however, on the Forest Maiden's advice, had quickly lit a small fire and, when the nobleman approached, the Maiden jumped into the flames. Instantly, a beautiful young woman appeared before the knight's eyes; it was the Forest Woman whom he had married long ago. "The servant is your child and mine!" she called out to the surprised man and disappeared. Thereupon he took the boy in and kept him as his son, had him trained as a knight and, after he returned as the victor of several feuds, gave him also his foster daughter as wife and the castle as dowry.

### 122 The Farmer's Wife and the Little Forest Woman

In a village a young couple got married, but because they were poor, were unable to afford servants and had to do everything themselves. It was hardest for them that their fields and meadows

am Saume des Waldes lagen. Die junge Frau hielt sich daher, wenn die Zeit es erforderte, oft im Walde in einer Bretterhütte mit ihren Kühen und Ziegen auf, und kochte dort dem Manne, der die Äcker bestellte.

Einmal kam der Mann vom Felde heim und sagte: »Ich weiß nicht, was das Holzmannl hat, es läuft immer winselnd um unsere Hütte, es muss ihm was fehlen.« Tags darauf sollte die Frau hüten, sie ging aber schon zur Entbindung und bekam in der Nacht ein Kind und musste daher zu Hause bleiben, und da hörte sie, wie alle Abend das Holzmannl winselnd um die Hütte herumlief. Als das Kind getauft war, ging sie mit ihrem Kinde in den Wald hinaus, setzte sich auf einen Stock und ließ es trinken. Das sah der Holzmann und lief eiligst fort. Die Mutter hing aber das Kind, um zur Arbeit zu kommen, in dem Tuche an einer Birke auf. Da läuft der Holzmann, ein winzig kleines Kindlein, in Bast gewickelt, auf den Armen tragend, quer herüber zur Frau, und fragt sie, ob ihr Kind schon genug habe. Die Mutter erwiderte ihm freundlich: »Ja überflüssig, und habe noch eine Brust frei.« Da bat das Männchen, sein Kleines an die Brust zu nehmen, denn seine Frau habe sich den Fuß gebrochen und dadurch die Milch verloren, und nun müsse das Kind verhungern, wenn sich kein Mensch darüber erbarme. Da fühlte die Bäuerin Mitleid mit dem kleinen Wesen und stillte es sechs Wochen lang, wobei sie das haarige Ding, um sich nicht zu ekeln, in ihren Schurz einschlug. Nach dieser Zeit kam das Holzmannl und sein Frauchen, das Kind im Arme, zu der Bäuerin in's Haus, fielen auf die Knie vor ihr nieder und dankten ihr von Herzen für die erwiesene Wohltat, und machten ihr ein Näpfchen voll kleiner Nüsse und Äpfel zum Geschenke. »An solchen Sachen haben wir genug, aber anderes fehlt uns,« sagten sie. Die Bäuerin lächelte zwar über die sonderbare Gabe, hob sie aber doch auf für ihr Kind zum Spielen. Später sah sie wieder darnach und es war eitel Gold. Nun waren die Leutchen reich und kauften sich in der Nähe einen artigen Bauernhof. Aber auch da kam das Holzfräulein noch gar oft auf Besuch, und wenn sie ins Kindbett kam, musste noch öfter die junge Bäuerin aushelfen.

Einmal gaben die Kühe wenig Milch; die Bäuerin melkte die Kühe gleichwohl nicht aus, damit das Holzfräulein auch noch etwas habe, und so ging ihr die Milch nie mehr aus.

were so far away on the edge of the forest. Therefore, when the times required it, the young wife often stayed in a simple wooden hut in the forest, with her cows and goats, and prepared meals for the husband, who tilled the fields.

One time, the husband returned from the field and said, "I don't know what's wrong with the Little Forest Man; he is running around our hut wailing; something is wrong with him." The next day, the woman was supposed to herd the animals, but went into labor instead and delivered a child during the night, and since she had to stay in she heard the Little Forest Man run around the hut, wailing all evening. After the child was baptized, she took it to the forest, sat down on a tree stump, and nursed it. The Forest Man saw this and ran off in a hurry. But the mother, to get [back] to work, hung the child in a piece of cloth from a beech tree. Across the meadow and up to the woman, here runs the Forest Man with a tiny little child wrapped in bast fibers in his arms, asking if her child was already full. The mother replied cordially, "Yes, more than full, and I still have a breast free." Thereupon the Little Forest Man asked that she put his little one to the breast, for his wife had broken her foot and thus lost all her milk, and now the child would have to starve to death if no human had mercy upon it. So the farmer's wife took pity on the little creature and nursed it for six weeks, wrapping the little hairy thing in her apron so as not to be disgusted by it. After this time, the Little Forest Man and his little wife with the child in her arm appeared at the farmer's wife's house, fell down on their knees before her, and thanked her with all their hearts for the good deed done for them, and they gave her a little pot full of little nuts and apples as a present. "We have plenty of such things, but others we lack," they said. Though the farmer's wife smiled at this strange gift, she still kept it for her child to play with it. Later she took another look and found that it was pure gold. Now the good people were rich and acquired a sizeable farm nearby. But the Little Forest Woman still visited often, and when she delivered a child, once in a while the young farmer's wife had to help her out.

Once the cows gave little milk; even so the farmer's wife did not milk them completely, so that the Little Forest Woman also would have some, and so she never ran out of milk again.

Wieder einmal hat der Fuchs arg unter den Hennen aufgeräumt. Die Bäuerin aber zwackte dem Holzfräulein doch nichts ab; im Gegenteil stellte sie ihr eine kräftige Suppe, d.h. Milch mit Eiern hinaus, denn es war ja gar so kalt, und von dieser Zeit bekam der Fuchs keinen Hühnerbraten mehr.

Wenn die Bäuerin in den Wald ging und ihr Kind im Tuche, wie in einer Hängmatte, an einer Birke aufhing, kam das Holzmännchen und schaukelte es, damit es bald einschlief.

### 123 Der Ritter, die schöne Maid und das Holzfräulein

Es war ein Ritter, schön von Gestalt, aber wilden Gemütes und lockeren Wandels. Keine Dirne der Umgegend konnte sich für sicher erachten, so er in der Nähe war, und die Holzfräulein verfolgte er mit wütendem Ingrimm. Da ging er einmal in den Wald, um diese armen Wesen in gewohnter Weise zu quälen, verirrte sich aber und kam an einen großen Baum, unter welchem das schönste Mädchen des Dorfes eingeschlafen war. Der Anblick der holden Maid entzündete in ihm das wilde Feuer; er schlich sich näher und fasste die Dirn in seine Arme und wollte eben auf den im Traume lächelnden Mund einen Kuss drücken, als aus dem Dickicht das Holzfräulein in gellendem Tone hervorrief:

> Liebes Kind,
> So geschwind,
> Wie der Wind,
> Kommt die Sünd'.
> Sei bedacht,
> Nimm dich in Acht,
> Liebes Kind.

Da erwachte das Mädchen aus ihrem süßen Traume; sie hatte geträumt, es stehe ein schöner Ritter vor ihr und werbe um ihre Hand; aufgeschreckt aus ihren Traumgebilden, entfloh sie dem bestürzten Ritter.

Dem Mädchen lag aber der schöne Ritter immer im Sinne, sie dachte stets an ihn und wollte des andern Tages wieder in den Wald, um an der glücklichen Stelle ihren schwärmerischen Gedanken

Another time, the fox killed a lot of the hens. However, the farmer's wife did not deprive the Little Forest Woman of her share; on the contrary, she set out for her a strong soup, i.e., milk with eggs, because it was so very cold, and from that time on, the fox received roast chicken no more.

When the farmer's wife went into the forest and put her child up on a birch tree in a piece of cloth, as in a hammock, the Little Forest Man came and rocked it, so that it soon fell asleep.

## 123 The Knight, the Beautiful Girl, and the Forest Maiden

There was a knight who was handsome, but had a fierce temper and loose morals. When he was nearby, no girl in the area could think herself safe, and he pursued the Forest Maidens with raging vengeance. Once he went into the forest to torture these poor creatures in the usual way; however, he got lost and came to a large tree under which the most beautiful girl of the village had fallen asleep. A the sight of the lovely maiden, the fire of wild passion ignited in him; he crept up close and took the girl in his arms, and was about to plant a kiss onto her mouth which was smiling in her dreams, when the Forest Maiden called out from the thicket in a shrill voice:

> Dear child,
> As fast
> As the wind
> Sin creeps up
> Be careful!
> Watch out!
> Dear child!

Thereupon the girl awoke from her sweet dream; she had dreamt that a handsome knight was standing before her and asked for her hand in marriage; frightened out of her dreamscape, she fled from the astounded knight.

However, the maiden always had the handsome knight on her mind; she kept thinking about him and wanted to go back to the forest on the following day, to indulge in romantic thoughts at that

nachzuhängen. Aber kaum setzte sie den Fuß über die Schwelle der Hütte, so tanzte das Holzfräulein gegen sie her und sang:

Schau, schau,
Des Ritters Frau!
Lass dir nur Zeit!
Nicht zu bereit!
Schau, schau,
Du wirst des Ritters Frau.

Darauf warnte sie in ernsten Worten vor dem Verführer, versprach aber ihre Hilfe, wenn das Mädchen auch als Rittersfrau jede Woche ihr einen Aschenkuchen mitbacken und ihren Gemahl von Verfolgung der Holzfräulein abbringen wollte. Und das Mädchen sagte zu.

Der Ritter ging aber alle Tage in den Wald, in der Hoffnung, seine böse Absicht zu erreichen. Wie er nun einmal so herumirrte, stand das Holzfräulein auf einem Stocke und rief ihm zu, er möge herantreten. Sie wisse, was ihm fehle, wolle ihm aber raten, von seinem bösen Treiben abzulassen; nur wenn er das Mädchen zu seiner ehelichen Gemahlin mache, werde er sie besitzen. Da erkannte der Ritter reuevoll seine Schuld und bat das Holzfräulein, für ihn um die Hand der Geliebten zu werben.

Als der Zug zur Trauung in die Kapelle ging, zeigte sich das Holzfräulein zum letzten Male; es erinnerte die Braut ihres Versprechens: so lange sie es halten werde, solle Glück in der Burg herrschen.

## 124 Die Schäferin und das Holzfräulein

Ein Mädchen hütete die Schafe, da kam auch das Holzfräulein und sagte zu ihr: »Deine Mutter bäckt heute Brot, sage ihr, sie solle mir einen Kuchen mitbacken.« Das Mädchen ging heim und hinterbrachte es der Mutter und erhielt den Kuchen. Das Holzfräulein nahm ihn freundlich an, höhlte ihn aus und tat Steinchen hinein, und gab ihn dem Kinde zurück. Zu Hause fand die Mutter statt der Steinchen lauter Goldstücke.

happy place. But no sooner had she stepped over the threshold out of the cottage, when the Forest Maiden danced up to her, singing:

> Behold, behold,
> The knight's wife!
> Just take your time!
> Don't be too eager!
> Behold, behold,
> You shall be the knight's wife.

Whereupon she warned the girl against the seducer in stern words, but offered her help if the girl, even after she was the knight's wife, would bake a ring cake in ashes for her every week, and dissuade her husband from persecuting the Forest Maidens. That the girl promised.

The knight, though, went out into the forest every day, hoping to fulfill his evil intentions. As he was roaming about one day, he saw the Forest Maiden standing on a tree stump and calling out to him to step closer. She said that she knew what ailed him, but advised him to cease pursuing his evildoing; only if he made the girl his lawful wife, would he be able to possess her. The knight, remorseful, became aware of his guilt and begged the Forest Maiden to ask for the girl's hand on his behalf.

When the wedding procession entered the chapel for the marriage ceremony, the Forest Maiden showed herself for the last time; she reminded the bride of her promise, as long as she kept it, happiness would rule in the castle.

### 124 The Shepherd Girl and the Forest Maiden

A girl was herding sheep; then came the Forest Maiden and said to her, "Your mother is baking bread today, ask her to bake a cake for me also." The girl went home and told the mother about it and received the cake. In a friendly manner, the Forest Maiden accepted it, hollowed it out and placed little rocks into it, and gave it back it to the child. At home, the mother found gold coins in place of the little rocks.

### 125 Der Untergang des Schlosses in Amberg I

Auf diesem Platze stand nach alter Sage ein Schloss, welches zuletzt von zwei Jungfrauen bewohnt war, so reich, dass sie das Geld in Metzen[32] maßen. Sie kamen zuletzt überein, ihren gemeinsamen Reichtum zu teilen. Nun war die eine davon blind, und sah nicht, dass die andere beim Abmessen sie betrog, indem sie für sich den Metzen hoch anhäufte, für die Blinde umkehrte. Diese aber wollte sich doch überzeugen, ob ihr Recht geschehen sei und griff mit den Händen um: da merkte sie, dass ihr Teil gegen den ihrer Schwester sehr klein sei, und entbrannte in Zorn, und verwünschte das Schloss, dass es versank.

### 126 Der Untergang des Schlosses in Amberg II

Vom Untergange des Schlosses geht aber noch eine andere Sage. – Der letzte Besitzer war ein Raubritter, der den Landleuten die Ernte wegnahm, und weit und breit Schrecken verbreitete. Ihm war eine schöne Tochter erwachsen, frommen Gemütes, welche in seiner Abwesenheit den Beraubten Gutes tat, um das Unrecht zu sühnen, und den Vater selber gar oft eindringlich bat, seinem wüsten Treiben ein Ende zu machen, da ihn sonst des Himmels Rache treffen würde. Der Ritter aber blieb verstockt. Da überzog den Himmel einmal ein furchtbares Gewitter, welches den Tag zur Nacht machte, und am Morgen sah man nur die Stätte, wo das Schloss gestanden. Es war versunken.

Seitdem sieht man eine Jungfrau in weißem Schleier auf einem Steine dort sitzen und betrübten Blickes den Vorübergehenden winken. Doch niemand nähert sich: denn ihr zur Seite hält ein schwarzer Hund mit feurigen Augen, im feuerspeienden Rachen den goldenen Schlüssel, welcher demjenigen die Schätze der versunkenen Burg öffnet, der Mut genug besäße, ihm den Schlüssel aus dem Rachen zu nehmen. Regelmäßig zeigt sich die Jungfrau am Sonnwend-Abende.

---

[32] Metze: altes Hohlmaß 1 Metze = 35 Liter.

## 125 The Sinking of Amberg Castle I

According to an old legend, there once stood a castle in this place, which was last occupied by two spinsters who were so rich that they measured their money by the barrel.[33] At last they agreed to divide up their shared fortune. One of them was blind and did not see that the other cheated her when measuring off, allotting big heaps to herself, reversing that for the blind one. But the latter wanted to make sure that she had been given her rights, and felt around with her hands; that was when she noticed that her share was very small compared to her sister's, and she flew into a rage and cursed the castle, so that it sank into the ground.

## 126 The Sinking of Amberg Castle II

Another legend circulates about the sinking of the castle.—Its last lord was a robber baron who carried off the harvests of the country people and spread terror near and far. He had a beautiful grown-up daughter of pious disposition who, in his absence, did good to those he had robbed, to atone for the injustices, and often implored the father to put an end to his wild deeds, otherwise Heaven's revenge would strike him down. However, the knight remained stubborn. One day the sky was lit up by a terrible thunderstorm that turned the day into night, and in the morning one could see only the place where the castle had stood. It had sunk into the ground.

Since that time, one can see a young woman in a white veil, sitting there on a rock and beckoning to passersby with a sorrowful look. But nobody approaches her; because at her side a black hound with fiery eyes holds in his fire-breathing mouth the golden key which unlocks the treasures of the sunken castle unto whomever is courageous enough to take the key out of his mouth. At regular intervals, the young woman shows herself on the evening of the solstice.

---

[33] Metze: ancient measure of capacity. 1 Metze = 35 liters = 9 gallons.

### 127 Der Untergang des Schlosses in Amberg III

Eine Bäuerin von Raigering ging einst in der Christnacht hier vorbei, um aus der Stadt den Arzt zu holen. Sie wurde aber vom rechten Wege durch ein Licht zum Brunnen geführt. Da winkte ihr eine Jungfrau gar freundlich und führte sie durch eine Tür neben dem Brunnen in den Berg, und in einen Saal, wo ein Ritter mit reichem Haare und fleischfarbenem Goller an einem Tische saß und sich auf sein Schwert lehnte: vor ihm stand eine Zofe mit ausgebreiteten Armen, wie wenn ihr der Teller, der auf dem Boden lag, so eben entfallen wäre. An einem anderen Tisch saßen Ritter in dunklen Kleidern, aus großen Humpen zechend; einer davon aber schlief im Stuhle, das Haupt in die Hand gelegt. Aus einem anstoßenden düsteren Gemache vernahm sie männliche Klagetöne. Als die Jungfrau eintrat, kniete sie sich vor dem ersten Ritter in flehender Stellung nieder, und zeigte dann der Frau die Schätze. Doch diese konnte vor Schreck nicht reden und ging unverrichteter Dinge hinaus.

### 128 Schloss Rosenberg

In dem Felsen, auf welchem das zerstörte Schloss Rosenberg bei Sulzbach steht, ist am Ostertage der Eingang offen, und tritt man ein, so kommt eine Jungfrau entgegen, weiß gekleidet, welche winkt. Aber man wagt es nicht, an sie zu kommen: denn eine ungeheure Schlange ringelt sich an ihr empor und sperrt, so oft sie winkt, den zahnreichen Rachen auf. In der Burg selber fand man einen großen steinernen Sarg, und diesem gegenüber in der Ecke lehnte ein Gerippe.

Eine Dirne ging nachts des Weges und erblickte auf dem Felsen das Schloss hell erleuchtet und das Tor geöffnet. Sie trat unbefangen ein und wurde von einer schönen Jungfrau empfangen, welche sie durch Gänge und Zimmer in einen großen herrlichen Saal geleitete und da mit köstlichen Speisen bewirtete. Zuletzt eröffnete sie der Dirne, dass sie verwünscht sei und hier gehen müsse: eben sei wieder eine Reihe von hundert Jahren um, und damit die Zeit gekommen, wo sie ein Mensch erlösen könne. Der Lohn wäre groß,

## 127 The Sinking of Amberg Castle III

A farmer's wife from the village of Raigering once walked by there on Christmas night, to fetch the doctor from the town. However, she was led off the path, [and] to a fountain, by a light. There a young woman beckoned to her in a friendly way, and led her through a door beside the fountain into the mountain, and into a hall where a knight with thick hair and a flesh-colored toby collar sat at a table and leaned on his sword; before him stood a chambermaid with her arms outspread, as if the plate that lay on the floor had just slipped from her grasp. At another table there were knights sitting in dark clothes, drinking from big tankards; one of them slept in his chair, with his head in his hand. From an adjacent, dark chamber she heard sounds of wailing from a male voice. When the young woman entered, she knelt down before the first knight, beseeching him, and then she showed the treasures to the farmer's wife. But the latter was terrified and unable to speak, and left empty-handed.

## 128 Rosenberg Castle

On the rock on which stand the ruins of the castle of Rosenberg, near Sulzbach, on Easter Sunday the entrance gate stands open, and if one enters, a young woman clad in white approaches and beckons. However, nobody dares to step close to her, for a monstrous Serpent curls itself up around her and opens its mouth full of teeth each time that she beckons. Inside the castle, a large stone sarcophagus was found, and in the opposite corner there leaned a skeleton.

A maiden walked by there one night and saw the castle on top of the rock, ablaze with light, with the gate open. Without trepidation, she entered and was greeted by a beautiful young woman who led her through hallways and chambers into a large and magnificent hall, where she was entertained with a delicious meal. Finally, the young woman disclosed to her that she had been cursed and had to haunt this place; now another hundred years had passed, and so the time had come [again] when she could be released from the curse by a human. There would be a large reward:

Alles, was im Schlosse an Schätzen sich finde. Dabei bat sie das Mädchen, sich ihrer zu erbarmen und sie zu erlösen: sie vermöge es; doch dürfe sie nicht erschrecken, wenn sie einen Drachen kommen sähe, der im feurigen Rachen den Schlüssel zu den Schätzen trage; den müsse sie ergreifen, um damit zu den Schätzen zu gelangen. Das Mädchen sagte zu, die bleiche Jungfrau aber bat sie noch einmal, ja nicht den Mut zu verlieren, und lieber einen Priester mitzunehmen. In der folgenden Nacht kehrte die Dirn wieder, aber allein: denn sie mochte dem Priester keinen Anteil an dem Lohne vergönnen. Die Jungfrau empfing sie wie gestern und bewirtete sie, bedauerte aber sehr, dass der Priester fehle. Als es gegen Mitternacht ging, entfernte sich die Jungfrau, nachdem sie noch recht innig gebeten hatte, ja das Werk der Erlösung zu vollenden: der Drache könne nicht schaden. Mit dem Schlage zwölf vernahm nun die Dirn fürchterlichen Lärmen, und das Rasseln des Drachen; schweifringelnd brach er in den Saal herein, im geöffneten Rachen den Schlüssel. Die Dirn erbebte und entfloh durch eine Seitentür hinaus in's Freie. Da stürzte das Schloss zusammen und zerschneidendes Wehklagen folgte der furchtsamen Dirne.

### 129 Die Grube in Hirschau[34]

In der Nähe von Hirschau befindet sich ein Abgrund; wirft man einen Stein hinab, hört man ihn nicht fallen; hier stand früher eine Burg. Noch sieht man an heiligen Zeiten drei Jungfrauen auf drei Haufen Geldes sitzen. Kommt ein Mensch zu ihnen hin, will ihn jede zu ihrem Haufen haben. Da nun alle drei sehr schön, und dem Menschen die Wahl wehe tut, versäumt er sich und kehrt leer zurück. Einer hatte schon zweimal von einer Jungfrau genommen, das drittemal sich verspätet; da musste er Jahr und Tag bei ihnen bleiben, hatte aber genug zu essen und zu trinken und wurde liebevoll von den Jungfrauen bedient. Von da an schlief er, so oft er auch kam, vor der Höhle ein, und versäumte damit die gebotene Zeit.

---

[34] Diese Grube, bekannt als „Alte Grube," wird heute als Badeweiher genutzt. (Siehe auch „Alte Grube," <http://www.mein-badesee.de/alte-grube-114219>. Abgerufen 29 Okt 2012.)

all the treasures to be found in the castle. Also, she asked the girl to have pity on her and release her, she would [surely] be able to do it; but she should not be frightened if she saw appear a Dragon who carried the key to the treasures in his fire-breathing mouth; she had to seize that [key] to get to the treasures. The maiden agreed, and the pale young woman warned her again, not to lose courage under any circumstance, and [it would be] better to have a priest accompany her. The following night, the maiden returned, but alone, because she begrudged the priest a share of the treasure. Just as the day before, the young woman greeted her and entertained her with a meal, but greatly regretted that a priest was not present. When midnight drew close, the young woman withdrew after beseeching the maiden to complete the work of redemption; the Dragon would not do any harm. When the clock struck twelve, the maiden heard a terrible commotion and the clattering of the Dragon; it rushed into the hall with its tail curling, the key in its open mouth. The maiden shook with terror and fled out to the open through a side door. Then the castle collapsed and heartrending wailing followed the fearful maiden.

### 129 The Hirschau Pit[35]

Close to Hirschau there is an abyss; if a rock is dropped into it, one cannot hear it hit the bottom. In olden times, a castle stood there. On Holy Days, one still sees three maidens sitting on three heaps of money. When a man approaches, each of them wants to draw him to her heap. Since all three are very beautiful and choosing among them pains a man, he misses [his opportunity] and returns empty-handed. One man already had taken a share from one of the maidens twice, the third time he was too late; he had to stay with them for a year and a day. However, he had enough to eat and drink and was tended to lovingly by the maidens. From then on, whenever he came back, he fell asleep on the edge of the hole, and thus missed the proper time.

---

[35] This pit, known as "Alte Grube" [Old Pit], is a former claypit that is used nowadays for recreational swimming. (See also "Alte Grube," <http://www.mein-badesee.de/alte-grube-114219>. Accessed 29 Oct 2012.)

## 130 Schloss Reuth

Auf Schloss Reuth, bei Burggrub, war einst ein Vehmgericht;[36] während die Verurteilten in einem Turm das Muttergottesbild küssten, wurden sie hinabgestürzt. Ein Herr von Reuth klagte vor den Vehmrichtern seine Ehefrau der Untreue an, und erhielt die Erlaubnis, sie zu töten, wenn er sie für schuldig halte. Die Frau aber beteuerte ihre Unschuld auch da noch, als sie schon den Dolch im Herzen hatte; da warf der Mörder, von Reue ergriffen, den Dolch weg, und bat dieselben Richter um sein Urteil, wenn er ein solches verdiene, und sie verurteilten auch ihn zum Tode. – Seitdem ging die Burgfrau um, in weißem Gewande, die Wunde sichtbar, besonders bei besonderen Ereignissen in der Familie. Einmal sollte Hochzeit sein; der Vater hatte die Erbtochter wider ihren Willen verlobt; denn sie liebte schon, und als sie sich beharrlich weigerte, an den Altar zu treten, warf er sie in den Turm. Hier erschien ihr die weiße Frau und tröstete sie, indem sie ihr Hilfe versprach. Darauf zeigte sich der Geist dem harten Vater und drohte ihm, wenn er seine Tochter unglücklich mache. Er schlug nach ihr, sie verschwand. Nun ging er in sich, und ließ der Tochter ihren Willen.

## 131 Burg Leuchtenberg[37]

Eine böhmische Fürstentochter, dem Christentum gewonnen, wendete sich von dem heidnischen Hofe des Vaters und zog in die Wildnis des Waldes. Da traf sie ein Ritter, und von ihrer Schönheit gefesselt bot er ihr seine Hand, welche sie unter der

---

[36] Die Ursprünge des Vehmgerichts gehen auf das Jahr 772 AD zurück; es war anfänglich als Geheimtribunal konzipiert, um die Sachsen und native heidnische Religionen auszurotten. Die Vehm soll auch Verbindungen zum „Waldgericht" and zum „Baumgericht" gehabt haben und keltischen Ursprungs sein. Während des 15. Jahrhunderts wurde es der Inquisition angeglichen. (Siehe auch Karl Christian Hütter, *Das Vehmgericht Des Mittelalters: Nach Seiner Entstehung, Einrichtung, Fortschritten Und Untergang (1793)*, Charleston, SC: Nabu Press, 2011.)

[37] „[D]ie berühmteste der oberpfälzischen Burgen, von welcher daher auch mehrere Sagen gehen." *Sitten und Sagen*, Bd. 2: 442.

## 130 Reuth Castle

At Castle Reuth close to the town of Burggrub, there was once a vehmic court;[38] while the condemned, in a tower, were kissing an image of the Mother of God, they were thrown off it. A lord of the castle denounced his wife to the judges of the vehmic court, accusing her of infidelity, and was granted the right to kill her if he thought her guilty. But the wife continued to protest her innocence, even when the dagger was already in her heart; upon which the murderer, seized with remorse, threw the dagger away and asked the same judges for his sentence, should he deserve such; and they sentenced him to death also.—Since then, the lady of the castle, in a white dress, the wound showing, has haunted the castle, particularly at special family events. One time a wedding was planned; the father had betrothed the daughter who would inherit, against her will; and when she tenaciously refused to walk down the aisle because she already loved [another], he had her thrown into the tower. There the white woman appeared to her, comforting her by promising help. The Ghost appeared to the harsh father and threatened him [with punishment] if he made his daughter unhappy. He swatted at her and she vanished. But then he reconsidered and allowed the daughter to have her way.

## 131 Leuchtenberg Castle[39]

A Bohemian prince's daughter who had been won over to Christianity turned her back on her father's heathen court and settled in the wilderness of the [Bavarian] Forest. There she met a knight and, captivated by her beauty, he offered his hand in marriage,

---

[38] Dating back to 772 C.E., initially, the vehmic court was a secret tribunal intended to remove the Saxons and native pagan religion. The vehmic court may have been connected to the "Forest Law" or "Tree Law" and be Celtic in origin. During the fifteenth century, it was brought in line with the the Inquisition. (See also Karl Christian Hütter, *Das Vehmgericht Des Mittelalters: Nach Seiner Entstehung, Einrichtung, Fortschritten Und Untergang (1793)*, Charleston, SC: Nabu Press, 2011.)

[39] "The most famous of the castles of the Upper Palatinate; hence there are several legends about it." *Sitten und Sagen*, vol. 2: 442.

Bedingung annahm, dass auch er sich taufen lasse. An der Stelle, wo sie sich gefunden, bauten sie eine Burg und nannten sie, dem Christentume als der wahren Glaubensleuchte zu Ehren, Leuchtenberg.—Der Vater aber, erzürnt über die Flucht der Tochter, entsendete überallhin seine Boten, sie zu suchen. An einem Berge angelangt, sahen sie von einer Höhe im Walde her Licht schimmern, gingen darauf zu und kamen zur Burg, wo sie in der Schlossfrau die Tochter des Herrn erkannten. Davon, dass sie von der Burg her Licht schimmern sahen, benannten sie diese Leuchtenberg, den Berg aber, von dem aus sie das Licht zuerst gesehen, also den Aufenthalt der Flüchtigen erfahren hatten—Fahrenberg, eine etwas holperige Deutung[40] der Namen. Mit seinen Reisigen zog nun der Fürst aus, sein Kind zu holen und den Räuber zu züchtigen. Am Burgtore begegnete ihm der Priester, welcher eben die heilige Wegzehrung zu einem Kranken trug. Den Heiden übermannte die Nähe des wahren Gottes, versöhnt umarmte er seine Kinder.

## 132 Der kalte Baum

In der Burg zeigt man eine Mauernische; der Landgraf ließ da die eigene Tochter einmauern, weil sie von einem Knappen zu Falle gekommen war; den Buhlen aber hingen sie an der Stelle auf, wo jetzt der kalte Baum steht, gerade gegenüber dem Fenster, hinter welchem das Fräulein seiner Ehre Verlurst beweinen musste. Der kalte Baum wurde nach der Strafvollziehung gepflanzt: seitdem geht dort der Wind bei Tag und Nacht.

## 133 Die Landgräfin auf dem Igel

Eine Landgräfin war gar vorwitzig und quälte ihren Gemahl häufig mit der dringlichen Bitte, ihr auch doch von seinen Geheimnissen zu vertrauen. Der Graf willfahrte ihr einmal, sie aber vermochte es nicht zu bewahren und wurde daher zur

---

[40] „Entfahren," z.B., kann auch die Bedeutung „fliehen" haben.

which she accepted on the condition that he too be baptized. On the place where they found each other, they built a castle and called it "Leuchtenberg,"[41] in honor of Christianity as the true shining light of faith.—The father, however, enraged by his daughter's escape, sent messengers out everywhere to search for her. Having arrived on a mountain, they saw a light shine from a hill in the forest, walked toward it and came to a castle where they recognized their lord's daughter as the lady of the castle. Upon seeing the light shining from the castle, they called it Leuchtenberg; but the mountain from which they had first seen the light and thus discovered the whereabouts of the escapee, they called Fahrenberg,[42] a somewhat clumsy interpretation of the name. The prince and his warriors set out to bring his child home and punish the kidnapper. At the castle gate, he encountered a priest who was about to administer the last rites to a sick man. The heathen was overcome by the presence of the True God and, thus reconciled, he embraced his children.

## 132 The Cold Tree

In the [Leuchtenberg] Castle, an alcove in the wall is shown, where the Landgrave had his own daughter walled in because she had given herself in love to a young squire; but the lover they hanged in the place where the Cold Tree now stands, just opposite the window behind which the damsel had to bemoan the loss of her honor. The Cold Tree was planted after the sentence was carried out, and from that time on, the wind has blown there day and night.

## 133 The Countess on a Hedgehog

A very meddlesome countess often pestered her husband, urging him to share his secrets with her. One time the count complied with her request, but she was unable to keep his secret and, as a

---

[41] Leuchtenberg, English "Shining Mountain."

[42] "Fahren." German for "drive" or "ride." When combined with the prefix "ent-" as in "entfahren," means "to escape."

Strafe, auf einem Igel zu sitzen, verurteilt. Man sah über diesen
Vorfall ein Gemälde an der Wand in einem Zimmer, und drunter
den Reim:

»Das macht mein Fürwitz,
Dass ich auf dem Igel sitz.«

punishment, was sentenced to sit on a hedgehog. One can see this incident still, captured in a painting on the wall of one of the rooms, and beneath it you can read the verse:

"My penance now is writ,
On a hedgehog I must sit."

# THE DEVIL AND DEATH,
# HEAVEN AND HELL

An important motif and often even the central plot in many fairy-tales, Schönwerth notes that in the tales of the Upper Palatinate Death is usually personified: "For the people, Death represents a person, the pale or black man with a scythe who mows everything down . . . " But Death was not the most feared figure in life's landscape; in comparison with his female counterpart, Plague, she appeared even more terrifying to the people of the Upper Palatinate: "Though female, she is even more cruel than the male Death."[1]

Hell is a place of torment that delivers retribution for evil deeds. For the people of the Upper Palatinate the way to Hell was a broad and enticing path, sloping downwards, and access to Hell was to be found in the dense forests with their massive boulders and steep-walled canyons.[2] (The word "Hell" has its origin in the Germanic word "hel" or "hal" which means to hide or conceal.) Many a place in the Upper Palatinate bears the name "Hell," as in "Höllmühle," "Oberhöll," "Mitterhöll," or "Unterhöll."[3]

In Schönwerth's tales, the Devil's attempts to corrupt humans often fail. The folk of the Upper Palatinate, accustomed to life's

---

[1] „Obgleich Weib, ist sie noch grausamer als der männliche Tod." *Sitten und Sagen,* vol. 3: 15f.

[2] *Sitten und Sagen,* vol. 3: 25.

[3] Anton Schlicksbier, „Bezirk Oberpfalz: Verzeichnis aller Orte," 16 February 2011, <http://www.afo-regensburg.de/download/Oberpfalzorte.pdf>. Accessed 21 Nov 2012.

hardships, resist the Devil's temptations, and often trick even that master of trickery himself.

Heaven, as imagined in the Upper Palatinate, was of course the opposite of Hell. As Schönwerth puts it:

> Heaven is a garden, and Hell is an abyss . . . One may assume the common people fashioned the vision of its new Heaven, as well as of Hell, after . . . the same archetype, the Germanic Heaven. Equipped with pagan elements, Heaven aims at the satisfaction of the senses, alternating between meals, play, and dance.[4]

---

[4] „[D]er Himmel ist ein Garten, die Hölle ein Abgrund. Man . . . könnte . . . vermuten, das Volk habe sich das Bild seines neuen Himmels sowie der Hölle, nach . . . demselben Urbild, dem germanischen Himmel, geschaffen. Der Himmel ist mit heidnischer Ausstattung auf sinnlichen Genuß berechnet. Mahlzeit, Spiel und Tanz wechseln miteinander ab." *Sitten und Sagen*, vol. 3: 288.

## 134 Der Tod als Herrscher der Welt

Im Anfange, ehe Sonne und Mond waren, herrschte der Tod auf der Welt. Als aber diese beiden Gestirne erschienen und herangewachsen waren, vertrieben sie den Tod unter die Erde. Doch nun erwürgte er von da aus alles, was Sonne und Mond erzeugten, worüber es zum Streite kam, dass fast die ganze Welt zu Grunde ging und die Sintflut hereinbrach. Nun trugen die Riesen steinerne Stühle auf den Bergen zusammen, setzten sich darauf und hielten Rat. Und sie fanden kein Ende, bis nicht das weiße Wiesel aus dem Berge hervorkroch und ihnen die Augen beleckte. So wurden sie einig, Sonne und Tod vor sich zu entbieten. Der letztere aber wollte dem Spruche sich nicht fügen, denn als Mann habe er ohnehin Recht gegenüber einer Frau. Darüber entbrannte der Streit auf's neue. Die Riesen aber erzürnten und ergriffen den dickleibigen Tod, und rissen ihm fast alles Fleisch vom Leibe. Seitdem ist er so mager. Darüber erbarmte sich die Sonne und warf ihm ihren dunkeln Schleier zu, sich zu bedecken und vor den Riesen zu verbergen. Seitdem aber trägt der Tod den Schleier der Sonne und wirft die Sonne dunkle Schatten.

## 135 Die Pest und der Tod

Als die Bärnauer vom Christentume zum Heidentume zurücktraten, strafte sie der Herr mit Seuche. Man sah den Tod auf der Kirche und dem Friedhofe stehen und seine Sense schwingen, worauf eine gespenstische Frau, die Zusammenrecherin kam und mit dem Rechen alles zu Haufen sammelte, was so der Tod gemäht hatte. Es war die Pest. In ein paar Tagen darauf brach das Sterben aus, und nur ein alter Hutmacher blieb übrig, der sich mit seiner gleichbejahrten Ehehälfte in der Radstube an der Stadtmühle von einer Geiß fortbrachte. Die Gestorbenen wurden auf dem Friedhof in eine große Grube verscharrt, noch jetzt Pestgrube genannt, und mit Steinen zugedeckt. Später einmal wollte man nachsuchen und öffnete einen Teil davon: da stieg bläulicher Rauch auf und tötete den Totengräber.

## 134 Death as the Ruler of the World

In the beginning, before there were the Sun and the Moon, Death ruled the world. But after those two celestial bodies had appeared and grown to size, they drove Death under the Earth. From there, however, he choked everything the Sun and the Moon created, whereupon a battle ensued which brought the world to the brink of collapse and resulted in the Great Flood. Then the Giants brought together stone chairs on the tops of the mountains, sat down on them, and held a council. And they were unable to come to a conclusion until the White Weasel crept from inside the mountain and licked their eyes. So they agreed to summon the Sun and Death to come before them. But the latter did not want to comply with their edict for, as a male, he was entitled to more rights than a female anyway. Thereupon, the fight broke out anew. The Giants, however, became very angry, seized the corpulent Death, and tore almost all the flesh from his body. Since then, he has been very rawboned. Because of this, the Sun took pity on him and tossed her dark veil to him, that he may cover himself and hide from the Giants. Ever since, Death has borne the Sun's veil, and the Sun casts dark shadows.

## 135 Plague and Death

When the people of Bärnau reverted from Christianity to heathenism, the Lord punished them with an epidemic. Death was seen standing in church and in the graveyard, swinging his scythe, whereupon appeared a ghostly woman, known as the One Who Rakes Up, and, with her rake, piled everything that Death had cut down, into a heap. She was the Plague. Within a few days, the dying had begun, and only an old hatmaker remained who, together with his better half, equally advanced in years, survived on [milk from] a goat in the wheelhouse of the city mill. The deceased were buried in a large pit in the graveyard, known to this day as the Plague Pit, and covered with stones. At a later time, they wanted to inspect it, and opened up a part of it; bluish smoke rose up and killed the gravedigger.

## 136 Des Bauern Höllenfahrt

Ein Bauer, jung und kräftig, besaß ein schönes Hofanwesen, das seinem Herrn und Grafen gewaltig in die Augen stach. Der Graf wusste es mit Hilfe seines Büttels auch dahin zu bringen, dass der Bauer von einem Rechtsstreite in den anderen und damit in Schulden geriet, zuletzt an den Bettelstab kam. Nur mehr ein paar schlechte Ochsen hatte er, und diese sollte er nun verkaufen, um Gilt und Zehent zu bezahlen. Das ging ihm zu Herzen, doch half alles Klagen nichts: er verkaufte sie und machte sich auf den Weg in's Schloss, seine letzten Pfennige dem harten Zinsherrn zu bringen. Er musste durch einen Wald: ermüdet setzte er sich auf einen Baumstock, um auszuruhen. Nicht lange saß er da, so stand ein Jägersmann vor ihm: seine Augen blitzten, sein Bart war rot. Dieser sprach: »Ich will dir helfen, wenn du mir eines versprichst.« Der Bauer war zu allem bereit und der Jäger gab ihm ein Beutelchen. Damit könne er seine Schuld bezahlen: zuletzt aber solle er des Müllers Rappen kaufen und den Wagen, und Ross und Wagen in gutem Stand erhalten. Der Bauer aber schüttelte den Kopf: denn in dem ledernen Beutelchen war nur ein Groschen: damit konnte er ja nicht zahlen, viel weniger kaufen. Doch kehrte sich der Jäger nicht an seine Zweifel und hieß ihn gehen, und tun, wie er befohlen: sie würden sich wieder sehen.

Der Bauer ging und kam auf's Schloss und nahm sein schweres Beutelchen herfür und zahlte aus dem Erlöse seiner Ochsen Zins und Gilt. »Das ist noch nicht genug,« sagte der Büttel, »einen Groschen macht es mehr für mich.« Der Bauer griff verlegen in seine andere Tasche und holte das leichte Beutelchen heraus, und nahm den Groschen drinnen und legte ihn hin. – So wollte er zur Tür hinausgehen: da rief ihm aber der Wächter zu: »Einen Groschen bekomme ich für Gebühr!« Voll Schrecken warf der Bauer das Beutelchen dem Wärtl vor die Füße. Der hob es auf, fand darin seinen Groschen und warf dem Bauer das leere Beutelchen nach. Nun wusste der Bauer, woran es stehe: schnell hob er das Beutelchen auf, sah hinein und fand wieder ein Gröschlein darin. Flugs ging er in's Wirtshaus, und zechte nach Belieben, und zahlte am Schlusse Groschen um Groschen eine artige Zeche.

## 136 The Farmer's Journey to Hell

A farmer, young and able-bodied, owned a sizeable farm, for which his overlord and count envied him mightily. With the help of his bailiff, the count managed to have the farmer embroiled in one legal battle after another and, as a consequence, he fell into debt, and finally was reduced to poverty. He was left with only a couple of poor oxen and he was going to have to sell them in order to settle his debt and the interest. This weighed heavily on his heart, but all his complaining was to no avail; he sold them and set off walking to the castle, to take his last pennies to his harsh creditor. He had to walk through a forest and, fatigued, sat down on a tree stump to take a rest. He had not been sitting there for long when a hunter appeared before him with fiery eyes and a red beard. He said, "I shall help you if you promise one thing." The farmer agreed to everything and the hunter gave him a small pouch. With this, he would be able to pay off his debt; he was instructed to buy the miller's black horses along with the wagon and to take good care of both horses and wagon. Thereupon the farmer shook his head, for in the little leather pouch there was only one penny; with that he would be unable even to pay [his debt], let alone make a purchase. Yet, the hunter did not care about his doubts and told him to go and do as he was told; they would meet again.

The farmer went ahead and, arriving at the castle, took his heavy little pouch out and paid off principal and interest from the proceeds of the sale of his oxen. "This is not enough," the bailiff said. "I demand one more penny." Embarrassed, the farmer reached into his other pocket for the light little pouch, took out the penny and set it down.—He was about to leave through the door, when the guard called out to him. "I demand a penny as a fee!" Terrified, the farmer threw the little pouch at the guard's feet. The latter picked it up, found his penny therein and threw the empty little pouch at the farmer. The farmer realized now what was going on: quickly, he picked up the little pouch, peered into it, and found another little penny. Swiftly, he went to the next inn and ate and drank as much as he desired, and at the end he settled his sizeable bill, penny by penny.

Drauf ging er fort und kaufte sich Müllers Rappen und Wagen, und fuhr mit reichem Mundvorrat heim. Nun zahlte er alle seine übrigen Schulden und baute sogleich einen Stall für seine Rappen. Als die Zimmerleute zur Stelle kamen, foppten sie das Bäuerlein, weil kein Holz auf dem Platze lag. Dieser aber befahl ihnen, einstweilen die alte Hütte mit Stall und Stadel niederzureißen, er wolle indessen in den Wald um Holz. Schnell waren die Rappen eingespannt und fort ging es in den Wald: da traf er den Jäger, welcher schon Holz in Menge hatte fällen lassen. Er half ihm auch den Wagen beladen, dass dieser halb versank. Das Bäuerlein schlug die Hände über den Kopf zusammen, aber der Jäger tat einen Pfiff und die Rappen gingen wie leer dahin.

So baute der Bauer alles vom Grund neu auf, schöner denn zuvor, und gab es groß, und seine Bäuerin putzte sich heraus, dass die Gräfin und selbst die Frau des Büttels sich darüber ärgerten, und Tag und Nacht ihren Männern anlagen, dem stolzen Bauer Eines zu versetzen. »Was tun,« sagte der Graf zum Büttel, »der Bauer ist mir hörig, ich könnte ihn zum Knechte machen; bring ihn her!« Der Büttel ging, der Bauer kam. – »Du wächst mir über den Kopf,« fuhr ihn der Gebieter an, »du musst es mit dem Teufel haben! Lass sehen, was du weiter kannst; drei Dinge setze ich dir, vermagst du es nicht, so geht es um deinen Kragen. Zuerst fährst du mir mit Ross und Wagen draußen am Hag die große Eiche her in der Hof!« »Soll geschehen,« nickte der Bauer, »schickt nur Leute, Herr Graf, den Baum zu fällen und zu laden.« So gingen dreißig Mann hinaus und schlugen die Rieseneiche nieder. Und als der Bauer mit dem Wagen kam, luden sie den Stamm auf und der Wagen sank zur Achse in den Boden. Aber der Bauer tat einen Pfiff und die Rappen gingen wie leer dahin, und so fuhren sie in den Schlosshof hinein, dass Tor und Schupfen in Trümmer ging. Darüber erboste der Graf noch mehr und grimmig befahl er dem Bauer, den großen Stein beim Brunnen zu bringen, sonst gehe es ihm an den Kragen. »Soll geschehen, Herr Graf,« lachte der Bauer, »schickt nur Leute, ihn aufzuladen!« Die dreißig Mann brauchten einen Tag, den großen Steinblock zu laden, und der Wagen sank wieder zur Hälfte ein.

Then he went and bought the miller's black horses and wagon, and returned home with rich provisions. Then he settled all his remaining debts and immediately went about building a stable for his black horses. When the carpenters arrived at the spot, they mocked the little farmer, for they did not find any lumber there. He, however, ordered them for the time being to tear down the old cottage, including the stable and the barn; meanwhile he would go out to the forest to fetch timber. Quickly, the black horses were yoked and [they] went out into the forest; there he met the hunter who already had a large amount of timber cut down. He helped the farmer also to load the wagon, so that it halfway sank into the ground. The little farmer threw up his hands, but the hunter let out a whistle and the black horses moved off as if pulling an empty load.

So the farmer rebuilt everything from the ground up, much nicer than before, throwing his money around, and his wife spruced herself up so much that the countess and even the bailiff's wife became irritated by this and nagged their husbands day and night to teach the proud farmer a lesson. "What's to be done?" the count said to the bailiff. "The farmer is my serf, I could make him my servant; bring him before me!" The bailiff went away, the farmer came. "You are rising above your station," his overlord threw in his face. "You must be in league with the Devil! Let's see what else you can do: I am laying three tasks on you; if you cannot accomplish them, you will be strung up by the neck. First, with horse and wagon, you will bring the tall oak tree from the grove out there to my castle!" "It shall be done," the farmer nodded. "Just send some men to cut down and load the tree, my lord." Whereupon thirty men went out to cut down the gigantic oak. And when the farmer arrived with his wagon they loaded the trunk, and the wagon sank into the ground down to the axle. But when the farmer whistled, the black horses moved off as if pulling an empty load, and so they drove into the castle courtyard, turning the gate and shed into ruins. Whereupon the count became even more furious and, grim-faced, ordered the farmer to bring him the large rock by the fountain, otherwise he would be strung up by the neck. "It shall be done, my lord," the farmer said laughingly. "Just send some men to load it!" It took the thirty men one day to load the large rock and, again, the wagon sank halfway into the ground.

Aber der Bauer tat nur einen Pfiff, und die Rosse gingen wie leer, und als die Männer die Last vom Wagen warfen, bebte das Schloss, und Mauer und Fenster zersprangen.

Darüber ergrimmte der Graf noch mehr und hieß nun zum Dritten, ihn und den Büttel zur Hölle zu fahren. »Soll geschehen, Herr Graf,« lachte der Bauer, »sorgt nur um Mundvorrat für den Weg!«

So fuhren sie, und in der ersten Nachtherberge verzehrte der Graf mit seinem Büttel den Imbiss, ohne dem Bauer davon mitzuteilen. Der Wirt aber sagte zum Bauer: »Nimm dir bei mir, was du brauchst, denn morgen in der Herberge bekommt Ihr nichts.« Und der Bauer tat so. Als sie des anderen Abends zur Nachtherberge kamen, war nichts zu haben.

Der Bauer aß; Graf und Büttel aber hungerten. Diese baten ihn nur um etliche Brocken; der Bauer aber teilte seinen Vorrat mit dem Jäger, der in die Herberge nachkam.

Am dritten Tage ging der Weg durch lauter Wildnis, über Stock und Stein, durch Sumpf und Wald. Schon hörte man die Teufel singen, und roch den Höllenrauch und Gestank. Der Bauer fuhr darauf zu. Die Rappen wieherten und tanzten voll Freude, und sprangen auf einen großen breiten Stein, der dalag wie eine Kellertür. Der Bauer wusste schon, was das für eine Tür wäre; flink sprang er vom Wagen auf die Rappen vor und schnitt die Stränge ab, und sprengte in einem Satze über den Stein hinweg. Dieser aber brach zusammen, und Feuer fuhr heraus und verschlang den Graf und seinen Schergen.

Langsam ritt der Bauer heim und sah sich nach einem anderen Wagen um. Da ließ ihn die Gräfin zu sich bescheiden und fragte ihn nach ihrem Herrn, und erhielt die Antwort, der wäre ganz sicher in der Hölle, wohin er gewollt habe. »Das lügst du,« zürnte die Gräfin, »das ist nicht wahr, so wenig als der dürre Rosenstock dort Rosen trägt.« Aber kaum gesagt, stand der Stock über und über voll Rosen. Da entsetzte sie sich und stieß sich das Messer in den Leib, und als die Frau des Büttels davon vernahm, erhängte sie sich an einem Stricke.

Auf der Rückkehr vom Schlosse setzte sich der Bauer im Walde wieder auf denselben Stock wie früher. Da stand der Jäger

But, the farmer whistled only once, and the horses moved off as if pulling an empty load, and when the men pushed the load off the wagon, the castle shook, and wall and window shattered.

Thereupon the count became yet more enraged and ordered, as a third task, to take him and the bailiff to Hell. "It shall be done, my lord," the farmer said laughingly. "Just provide the provisions for the journey!"

So they went on their way, and at their first overnight inn, the count and the bailiff ate their small repast without sharing with the farmer. But the innkeeper said to the farmer, "Take from me whatever you need, for you won't receive anything at the inn tomorrow." And so the farmer did. When they arrived at their overnight inn next evening, there was nothing to be had.

The farmer ate, but the count and the bailiff went hungry. They asked him only for a few scraps; however, he shared his rations with the hunter, who had arrived at the inn later.

On the third day, their path led through a wilderness, over sticks and stones, through marsh and forest. Already they heard the Devil singing and smelled the smoke and stench of Hell. The farmer drove toward it. The black horses neighed and pranced with joy, and jumped onto a large, wide rock which lay on the ground like a cellar door. The farmer already knew what kind of door this was; nimbly he jumped off the wagon onto the black horses, cut the traces and, in one big leap, jumped over the rock. It broke apart, though, and flames rose up and swallowed the count and his henchman.

Slowly, the farmer rode home and looked for a new wagon. Then the countess summoned him and asked where her lord and master was, and received the reply that he was surely in Hell where he had wanted to go. "You are lying," the countess said angrily. "That is not true, as surely as the shriveled-up rose tree over there does not carry roses." No sooner had that been said than the rose tree stood covered all over with roses. She became horrified and thrust a knife into her body, and when the bailiff's wife heard of this, she hung herself with a rope.

On the way back from the castle, the farmer sat down on the same stump in the forest, just like before. Whereupon the hunter

vor ihm und sprach: »Den Beutel kannst du samt dem Groschen behalten, du hast mir den Dreier mit Vieren vergolten!
Leb wohl!«.

## 137 Der unrechte Höllenkandidat

Ein Maurer starb und kam vor die Tür des Himmels. Der Pförtner
St. Peter aber nahm ihn nicht auf, weil er auf Erden auch nichts von
Gott hätte wissen wollen. Der Geselle ging daher an die nächste
Tür, welche in die Hölle führte, und trat ein. Da er niemanden in
dem großen Saal sah, setzte er sich in den schönen rotgepolsterten
Armsessel, der unbenützt dastand: denn er war sehr müde von
dem langen Wege. Nicht lange saß er, so kam ein Teufel daher
und auf ihn zu, um ihn zu fragen, wer er wäre. »Ich bin der Maurer, den St. Peter nicht in den Himmel einließ; deshalb bin ich da
herein gegangen,« sagte der Gefragte. Da gab ihm der Teufel eine
Ohrfeige und fuhr ihn hart an: »Mach, dass du hinkommst, wo
du her bist; dieser Stuhl gehört dem Amtsvogt von Kolmberg!« So
kehrte des Maurers Seele wieder in ihren Leib zurück.

## 138 Das Teufelsbündnis der Hexe[5]

Eine alte Hexe hatte es mit dem Teufel; schon zweimal war ihre
Zeit aus und immer wieder wusste sie den Bösen zu bereden, ihr
auf's neue hundert Jahre zuzulegen: dafür hatte sie ihm versprochen, die Kinder im Mutterleibe zu töten oder in der Wiege, und
mit deren Blute bösen Zauber zu üben zum Schaden der Menschen: und es gelang ihr gar oft: denn das Blut diente ihr nicht
nur selbst zur Nahrung für ihren ausgetrockneten Leib, sondern
auch dazu, sich unsichtbar zu machen.

---

[5] „Es genügt dem von Gott abgewendeten Menschen nicht, dass er den Teufel bewegt,
ihm Schätze zu bringen: er will auch seiner sonstigen Hilfe zu jeder Zeit seines Lebens
teilhaftig sein. So tritt er in die innigste Gemeinschaft mit dem Teufel. Mit seinem Blute
unterzeichnet er den förmlichen Vertrag, in welchem er seine arme Seele dem Bösen für
seine Hilfeleistung verschreibt und ihm fortan zu Gefallen und zum Verderben seiner
Mitmenschen leben muß. Gewöhnlich wird eine bestimmte Zeit bedungen, auf welche
der Teufel dem Menschen zu dienen hat, nach deren Umlauf dann dieser mit seiner Seele
jenem verfällt." *Sitten und Sagen*, Bd. 3: 51.

appeared and said to him, "You may keep the pouch, including the penny, for you have rewarded me with four instead of three! Farewell!"

## 137 Hell's Unsuitable Candidate

A bricklayer died and arrived at Heaven's door. However, the gate-keeper, St. Peter, did not take him in since he had wanted nothing to do with God when he was on Earth, either. Thereupon the fellow went to the next door, which led to Hell, and entered. Since he saw nobody in the great hall, he sat down in the beautiful, red upholstered armchair that was standing there unoccupied, for he was very tired from his long journey. He had not been sitting there for long when a devil arrived and [came up] to him to inquire who he was. "I am the bricklayer whom St. Peter did not allow into Heaven. Therefore, I entered here," the man replied. Thereupon the devil slapped him in the face and snarled at him, "Go back to where you are from; this chair belongs to the Steward of Kolmberg!" Thus the bricklayer's soul returned into his body.

## 138 The Witch's Pact with the Devil[6]

An old Witch had made a pact with the Devil; already her time had come twice, and she always managed to talk the Evil One into adding another hundred years; in return she had promised to kill children in the womb or in the cradle and practice black magic using their blood, to the detriment of humanity: and she succeeded in doing this quite often, for the blood served not only as a nourishment for her dried-up body, but also to render her invisible.

---

[6] "For the individual who turned away from God it does not suffice that he moves the Devil to bring him treasures; he also wants to have his help at all other times in his life. He thus enters into the most intimate alliance with the Devil. With his blood he signs a formal treaty in which he signs over his Poor Soul to the Evil One in exchange for the latter's helps, and from this time on he has to live to please him and cause the downfall of his fellow men. Usually there will be a certain agreed upon time in which the Devil has to serve a human being and, at its end, the latter forfeits his soul to the former." *Sitten und Sagen*, vol. 3: 51.

So war sie denn nach Umlauf der jüngsten Frist auf dem Berge in Gesellschaft anderer Schwestern beim nächtlichen Tanze, als der Teufel zu ihr trat und ihr ankündete, heute noch müsse sie mit ihm, er wolle nicht länger mehr zuwarten. Die Alte aber versprach ihm die schöne Tochter zur Ehe, welche sie zu Hause habe, und bestellte ihn für die dritte Nacht mit dem Auftrage, ja als schmucker Geselle zu erscheinen.

In der Hütte aber führte zu selber Zeit das Mädchen ihren Geliebten durch die schönen Zimmer, welche sich eines an das andere reihten: im letzten Gemache wurde es beiden unheimlich: denn hier waren schwarze Katzen, welche bei ihrem Eintreten die Köpfe aneinander legten, und sonderbare Vögel, welche ganz ungebärdig taten und verschiedenes Zaubergeräte mit Flaschen und Gläsern: schon wollten sie zurückweichen, da stand die alte Hexe zornerfüllt vor ihnen. Der junge Förster fasste sich schnell und hielt um die Hand der Tochter an, wurde aber mit Hohn abgewiesen, denn schon habe sich ein reicher Graf gemeldet.

Für die dritte Nacht musste sich das Mädchen gleich einer Braut schmücken. Um Mitternacht kam der gefürchtete Freier und bedeckte den Tisch mit den kostbarsten Geschenken. Die Braut bückte sich etwas, sie zu beschauen: da schob sich das Kreuzchen hervor, welches ihr am Halse hing und der Teufel entwich bei diesem Anblicke. Auf sein Drohen bestellte den Wütenden die alte Hexe für die nächste Nacht: während die Tochter schlief, nahm sie ihr das Kreuzchen weg. Diese aber merkte es am Tage und verschaffte sich heimlich ein anderes. Als nun der Böse wieder kam und sie umfassen wollte, vermochte er es nicht: das verborgene Kreuz schützte die Jungfrau. Dafür wollte er die Alte mit sich führen.

Diese aber stellte sich und setzte ihm drei Dinge, die er bis zum ersten Strahle der Sonne vollendet haben müsste: das Steinfeld vor der Hütte in ein Saatfeld umzuwandeln, den nahen Teich auszuschöpfen und zur grünen Wiese zu gestalten, drittens, den Berg mit der Kapelle abzutragen: denn sie habe sich bei ihren Nachtfahrten immer daran gestossen. – Da hörte sie es rauschen, wie wenn tausend Sensen durch Steine gingen und Funken sprühten und knisterten. Schon war das Saatfeld und die Wiese grün, und der Teufel hatte eben den Turm der Kapelle im Arme, als die

So, when her latest deadline had expired, she was in the company of other sisters at a midnight dance when the Devil approached her and announced that she had to come with him that very instant; he did not want to wait any longer. The old hag then promised to give him her beautiful daughter to marry, whom she had at home, and instructed him to arrive at her house on the third night, [and] to appear without fail in the guise of a handsome fellow.

At the same time, however, at her home the girl led her beloved through the beautiful rooms that were lined up one behind the other: in the last chamber, both began to feel spooked, for there were black cats which, upon their entry, leaned their heads together, and strange birds that acted in unruly ways, and a variety of magical tools with bottles and glasses: they were about to back out when the old Witch stood before them, filled with rage. The young woodsman quickly recovered and asked for the daughter's hand in marriage, but was rejected with scorn, [and was told that] a rich count had already come forward.

On the third night, the maiden had to adorn herself like a bride. At midnight, the dreaded suitor arrived and covered the table with the most precious gifts. The bride bent down slightly to inspect them, when the little crucifix which she wore around her neck became visible, and the Devil escaped upon seeing it. The Witch, because of the threats the enraged Devil made, invited him for the following night: while the daughter was sleeping, she took away the little crucifix. The maiden, however, noticed this and secretly acquired another one. When the Evil One arrived again and tried to embrace her, he was unable to do so: the hidden crucifix protected the maiden. So, in her stead he wanted to carry the old Witch off with him.

The latter, however, resisted and set him three tasks which he had to complete before the first rays of the Sun: turn the rocky field before her house into a freshly seeded plot; scoop out the nearby pond and turn it into a grassy meadow; and third, remove the mountain with the chapel on its top, for she always bumped into it on her nightly rides.—Then she heard a clattering as if a thousand scythes were cutting through stone, and sparks flew and crackled. Already, the seed plot had appeared and the meadow turned green, and just when the Devil had the chapel tower in his arms, the

Hexe, um den Teufel zu berücken, zu krähen anfing, und augenblicklich krähten alle Hahnen der Gegend nach und die Sonne sendete ihren ersten Strahl hinter dem Berge hervor. Da warf der Teufel den Turm auf die Hütte und riss die Alte samt ihren Zaubertieren mit sich fort durch die Luft. Das Mädchen aber blieb verschont: es war die geraubte Tochter eines Edelmannes.

## 139 Das Mädchen und der Teufel

Es war einmal ein armer Taglöhner, der hatte viele Kinder und wenig Brot für sie. Einmal als die Not gar bitter über ihn kam, ging er in den Wald hinaus und setzte sich auf einen Stock und weinte heiße Tränen. Da trat ein Mann zu ihm heran und fragte ihn, was ihm fehle, und wie er hörte, dass er nicht Brot habe für seine hungrigen Kinder, erbot er sich, ihm zu geben, dass er genug daran habe für sich und Frau und Kind, wenn er ihm eines seiner Mädchen überlassen wolle; sie solle es bei ihm gut haben. Der arme Vater war des Handels froh und zeichnete seinen Namen in das dargebotene Buch. Mit einem großen Sack Geldes ging er heim und der Not war ein Ende. Zum Mädchen aber sagte er: »Geh mit mir in den Wald.« Sie gingen, und im Walde angekommen, hieß er sein Töchterlein auf dem Stock, wo er gestern gesessen, niedersitzen und warten, bis ein Herr komme, der sie mitnehmen werde; sie solle es gut bei ihm haben.

So blieb das Mägdlein sitzen und wartete. Da kam eine schöne, große, milde Frau, – es war U.L. Frau – und sagte zu ihr: »Kind, es wird jemand kommen und dich mitnehmen wollen; erst aber wird er drei Fragen an dich stellen: die Antwort darauf will ich dir sagen, du könntest es nicht wissen. Zum Ersten wird er dich fragen: ›Was ist süßer als Zucker? darauf antworte: ›Die Brüste meiner Mutter, an denen ich getrunken.‹ Die zweite Frage wird sein: ›Was ist linder als Federflaum?‹ Darauf sage ihm: ›Der Schoss meiner Mutter, auf dem ich gesessen.‹ Das drittemal sollst du ihm Bescheid geben: ›Was ist härter als Stahl und Eisen?‹ Die Antwort sei: ›Das Herz meines Vaters, der mich dem bösen Feinde verkaufen will.‹«

Witch, to ensnare the Devil, started to crow and, instantly, all the roosters in the area crowed too, and the sun began to send out her first rays from behind the mountain. Thereupon the Devil threw the tower onto the house and swept away the old Witch, as well as her enchanted animals, with him through the air. The maiden, however, was spared; she was the kidnapped daughter of a nobleman.

### 139 The Maiden and the Devil

Once upon a time there was a day laborer who had many children and little bread for them. One day, when poverty hit him particularly hard, he went out into the forest, sat down on a tree stump, and cried hot tears. Thereupon a man approached and inquired what was wrong with him, and when he learned that he lacked food for his hungry children, he offered to give him enough for himself and his wife and children if he let him have one of his daughters; she would have a good life. The poor father was happy over the deal and signed his name in the Book presented to him. With a big sack of money he went home, and their poverty ended. To the girl, however, he said, "Go into the forest with me." They went away and, upon their arrival in the forest, he asked his little daughter to sit down on the tree stump on which he had sat yesterday and wait for a gentleman who would take her with him; she would have a good life there.

So the little maiden sat and waited. Thereupon a beautiful, tall, and mild-mannered woman appeared—it was Our Dear Lady—and said to her, "My child, a man will come wanting to take you away with him, but first he will ask you three questions: I will tell you the answers, for you would not know them. First, he will ask you, 'What is sweeter than sugar?' [and] thereupon answer, 'My mother's breasts from which I drank.' His second question will be, 'What is softer than downy feathers?' Whereupon tell him, 'My mother's lap on which I sat.' The third time you must give him an answer to: 'What is harder than steel and iron?' The answer shall be, 'The heart of my father who wants to sell me to the Evil Enemy.'"

Damit verschwand U.L. Frau und gleich darauf erschien der fremde Herr und fragte sie die drei Fragen, und erhielt vom Kinde die Antwort, wie sie gelernt hatte.

»Das hat dir die Blaue Frau geraten, dass du mir so antwortest,« schrie der Herr, »sonst wärst du mein eigen gewesen!« – und verschwand.

## 140 Der Teufel und der Besenbinder

Es war einmal ein Förster, der hat seinen Wald nicht mehr überkommen können, es ist ihm allzuviel Holz gestohlen worden. Darüber hat er so geflucht, bis der Teufel kam und ihn fragte, was ihm fehle. »Kommst mir gerade recht,« antwortete ihm der Förster, »den Wald übergebe ich dir und all Leute, die da stehlen.«

Der Teufel ging nun in den Wald wie der Förster und erwischte sogleich und zunächst einen Besenbinder, der Birkenreiser schnitt. »Halt, du gehörst mir,« schrie der Teufel, und packte den Besenbinder beim Schopf. Der aber fiel auf die Knie, und bat, ihn nur diesesmal laufen zu lassen, Frau und Kind zu Hause müssten sonst verhungern. Da sagte der Teufel: »Weißt was, in drei Dingen musst Du mit mir eine Wette eingehen; gewinnst du sie, sollst du frei von dannen gehen. Zuerst musst du mit mir in die Wette laufen.« »Recht,« sagte der Besenbinder, »aber meinen Alten musst du auch mitlaufen lassen.« Zunächst in der Staude saß aber ein Hase. Der Teufel lief, der Besenbinder klopfte auf die Staude und der Hase sprang heraus und lief dem Teufel voraus.

»Jetzt,« sagte der Teufel, »musst du mit mir auf einen Baum steigen: wer zuerst oben ist, der gewinnt.« »Recht,« erwiderte der Besenbinder, »aber meinen Jungen musst du auch mitsteigen lassen.« Da standen zwei dürre himmelhohe Bäume: im Busche aber saß ein Eichhörnchen.

Der Teufel fing zu steigen an, der Besenbinder stieß in den Busch und das Eichhörnchen sprang flugs zu höchst auf den dürren Baum, dem Teufel weit voraus.

»Jetzt,« sagte der Teufel zornig, »musst du diese Eisenkugel höher werfen als ich.« Er nahm nun die Kugel und warf sie so hoch,

Whereupon Our Dear Lady disappeared and soon thereafter the stranger appeared and asked her the three questions, and received from the child the answers as she had learned.

"That is what the Blue Lady advised you to say," the gentleman snarled. "Otherwise you would have been mine!"—and disappeared.

## 140 The Devil and the Broom Maker

Once upon a time there was a woodsman who was unable to manage his forest properly; too much theft of timber occurred. Whereupon he started cursing hard, until the Devil arrived and asked what was wrong with him. "You arrived in the nick of time," the woodsman replied. "I hand over to you the forest and all the thieving people in it."

Then the Devil went into the forest [acting] like a woodsman, and right there and then caught a broom maker cutting brushwood from a birch shrub. "Stop, you belong to me," the Devil yelled out, and grabbed the broom maker by his hair. The latter, though, fell to his knee and asked to be let off just this one time, otherwise his wife and children would have to starve. Thereupon the Devil said, "You know, you will have to make a bet with me about three things; if you win all, you shall walk away a free man. First, you must race me." "All right," the broom maker replied, "but you must allow my old father to race along with us." In the shrub closest to them, however, there sat a rabbit. The Devil ran, the broom maker knocked on the shrub, and the rabbit jumped out and sprinted ahead of the Devil.

"Now," the Devil said, "you must climb a tree with me: he who reaches the top first, shall be the winner." "All right," the broom maker replied, "but you must allow my young son to climb with us." There stood two dried-out trees, tall as the sky: but in the bush sat a squirrel.

The Devil began to climb, the broom maker poked in the bush, and the squirrel jumped quickly to the top of the dried-out tree, far ahead of the Devil.

"Now," the Devil said angrily, "you must throw the iron ball higher than I do." He took the ball and threw it up so high that

dass sie über die Wolken hinauf fuhr, und als sie niederfiel, ein Loch in den Boden schlug. Der Teufel grub sie heraus und gab sie dem Besenbinder in die Hand, damit er werfe. Der aber konnte sie kaum in der Hand halten, so schwer war sie. »Heiland der Welt,« rief er voll Angst, »hilf, dass die Kugel über den Wolken hängen bleibt!« »Halt,« schrie der Teufel voll Entsetzen, »gib mir meine Kugel wieder, ich dürfte ohne sie nicht mehr in die Hölle,« und lief davon.

## 141 Der Mühlknappe und der Teufel

Bei Ebnat ist eine Mühle, wo kein Knecht mehr bleiben konnte; denn wenn sie bei der Nacht mahlen wollten, jagte sie ein Geist davon.

Da kam ein Mühlknecht mit Violin und Klarinette auf die Mühle, und bat um Arbeit, und der Müller behielt ihn, weil er stark war. Schon die erste Nacht mahlt er; um 11 Uhr kommt ein grüner Jäger zu ihm herein. Er fragt ihn: Woher? Der Jäger schweigt. Da fängt der Knappe zu geigen an, und gibt dann dem Jäger die Violine und heißt ihn auch geigen. Der Jäger schwieg und seine Hand war steif. Da nimmt der Mühlknecht den Schraubstock und steckt dem Jäger die Finger hinein.

Dieser fing nun erbärmlich zu schreien an. Doch der Mühlknappe ließ ihn nicht los, bis er versprach, die Mühle von nun an in Ruhe zu lassen. »Wo willst du hin,« fragte er den Teufel. »In den Weiher!« Nein: der gehört dem Müller. »In den See!« – So fuhr der Teufel in den See.

Zum Lohne bekam der mutvolle Mühlknappe des Müllers artiges Töchterlein zur Frau.

Einmal fuhren sie auf dem See. Da sieht er an einer Stelle das Wasser aufwallen und schäumen. Er gedachte nun des Teufels, nimmt seine Frau, stellt sie auf den Kopf, und schreit zur wogenden Stelle hin: »Wart nur, hier ist mein Schraubstock.«

it flew above the clouds and, upon falling back down, punched a hole in the ground. The Devil dug it out and handed it to the broom maker to throw it up [into the sky]. The latter, however, could hardly hold it in his hand, for it was so heavy. "Savior of the World," he cried out in fear, "help me keep the ball above the clouds!" "Stop!" the Devil cried, filled with horror. "Give me back my ball; without it, I would never be allowed back into Hell," and ran away.

## 141 The Miller's Servant and the Devil

Close to the town of Ebnat there is a mill where no servant could stay any more, for if they wanted to grind corn at night, a Ghost would chase them away.

One time a mill servant arrived at the mill with his fiddle and clarinet, and asked for work, and the miller retained him because he was strong. Already on the first night, he grinds; at 11 o'clock a hunter dressed in green comes inside to him. He asks the hunter, "Where do you come from?" The hunter remains silent. The mill servant begins to play the fiddle, then hands it to the hunter, calling on him to play it also. The hunter remained silent and his hand was rigid. Then the mill servant takes the vise and puts the hunter's fingers into it [and tightens it].

The latter began to scream miserably. But the mill servant did not let him go until he promised to leave the mill in peace from now on. "Where would you like to go?" he asked the Devil. "Into the pond!" No, that is the miller's. "Into the lake!" So the Devil dove into the lake. As a reward, the courageous mill servant received the miller's lovely daughter as his wife.

One day they were boating on the lake when he saw the water bubble up and foam in one place. Thinking of the Devil, he takes his wife, turns her on her head, and shouts in the direction of the bubbling spot, "Just wait, here is my vise!"

## 142 Der Teufel und der Förster[7]

Nun lebte auf dem Schellenberge ein Förster recht einträchtig mit seiner Frau: er war aber sehr gestreng im Dienste, und misshandelte einst eine alte Frau, welche Holz stahl. Voll Rache ging sie heim und überlegte schon auf dem Wege, was sie dem rohen Manne antun solle. Da bekommt ihr ein Jäger: der fragt sie, was sie denke. Sie offenbarte ihm ihren Zorn. Der Jäger gab ihr Recht und versprach ihr, wenn sie ihre Rache gut ausgeführt hätte, ein paar Pantoffel zum Lohne. Die Alte nimmt nun ein langes Messer und legt es dem Förster unter das Kissen ins Bett; als er von der Schenke betrunken heimkehrte, passte sie ihn ab, und sagte ihm, seine Frau wolle ihn heute Nacht umbringen: schon habe sie das Messer unter das Bett versteckt. Er will es nicht glauben, findet aber das Messer. Nun ging die Alte zu seiner Frau und meldete ihr, der Mann wolle sie heute Nacht erstechen: schon habe er das Messer unter das Bett versteckt. Wie die Frau ins Bett geht, sucht sie nach dem Messer: der Mann glaubt nun wirklich, sie wolle ihn umbringen, springt heraus und rauft sich mit seiner Frau herum. Von nun an hausen sie nicht mehr gut. Die Alte aber war noch nicht zufrieden: sie verschaffte dem Förster ein Blendwerk, in welchem er seine Frau in Untreue zu überraschen glaubte; wütend jagt er dem Scheinbilde den Hirschfänger durch den Leib. Zu Hause aber findet er seine Frau tot im Bette.

Nun ging die Alte in den Wald an den bestimmten Platz, um ihren Lohn zu holen. Der Teufel aber hielt sich ferne von ihr und reichte ihr die Pantoffel an einer Stange über den Bach hinüber: sie war ihm zu schlecht.

## 143 Teufels Dank[8]

Wieder einmal reisten U.L. Herr und der Teufel mitsammen. Die Leute des Weges taten vor Unserem Herrgott ehrfurchtsvoll den

---

[7] „Den Teufel verdrießt bekanntlich nichts mehr, als wenn zwei Eheleute glücklich miteinander leben." *Sitten und Sagen*, Bd. 3: 86.

[8] „Der Teufel kann es niemanden . . . recht machen: auch für den Fall, wo er warnend oder helfend auftritt, erntet er nur Undank." *Sitten und Sagen*, Bd. 3: 87.

## 142 The Devil and the Woodsman[9]

There was a woodsman who lived with his wife in harmony on Mount Schellen, but he was very stern in his duties, and one time he mistreated an old woman who was stealing timber. Full of revenge, she went home, and all the way pondered what she could do to the ruffian. Then a hunter comes up to her, who asks what she is thinking about. She reveals her anger to him. The hunter agreed that she was right, and promised her a pair of slippers as a reward, for exacting her revenge well. Then the old woman takes a long knife, and puts it under the woodsman's pillow in the bed; as he returned home drunk from the tavern, she intercepted him and told him that his wife intended to kill him that night: already she had hidden the knife under the bed. He does not want to believe it, but finds the knife. Then the old woman went to his wife, and reported to her that her husband wanted to stab her to death that very night; already he had hidden the knife under the bed. When the wife goes to bed, she searches for the knife: the man now truly believes that she wants to kill him, jumps up and wrestles with his wife. From that time on, they no longer live together in harmony. But the old woman was not yet satisfied: she created an illusion which led the woodsman to believe that he was catching his wife in an act of unfaithfulness: furiously, he drives his hunting sword through the phantasm. But at home, he finds his wife dead in bed.

Then the old woman went into the forest, to the specified place, to fetch her reward. The Devil, however, kept far away from her and handed her the slippers across the stream with a pole; she was too evil [even] for him.

## 143 Thanks for the Devil[10]

One day Our Dear Lord and the Devil were again traveling together. Along the way, the people took off their hats before the Lord,

---

[9] "Nothing annoys the Devil more than when two spouses live together happily." *Sitten und Sagen,* vol. 3: 86.

[10] "The Devil is unable to please anybody. Even in such cases where he appears to warn or to help peope, he reaps only ingratitude." *Sitten und Sagen*, vol. 3: 87.

Hut ab, und jedesmal bleckte der Teufel die Zähne dazu. U.L. Herr aber ermahnt ihn seiner Bosheit gegen die Menschen, worauf der Teufel sich entschuldigte mit der Bosheit der Menschen gegen ihn, welche vor ihm noch niemals den Hut abnehmen würden. Wieder bedeutet ihm der Herr, er möge gegen die Menschen freundlich sein: so er ihnen Gutes erwiesen, würden sie auch ihm dankbar sein. Der Teufel aber widersprach geradezu und ließ es auf eine Probe ankommen.

Auf dem Wege sahen sie einen Bauer seine Kühe auf der Wiese weiden. Da vermochte der Teufel U.L. Herrn, die Kühe in den Graben zu werfen. Sogleich schrie der Bauer: »Was für ein Teufel muß hier wieder seine Hand im Spiele haben« – und lief fort, um Leute zu holen, welche ihm die Kühe aus dem Loche brächten. Mittlerweile half aber der Teufel ihnen heraus, und wie der Bauer zurückkehrte und seine Kühe auf der Wiese grasen sah, rief er: »O du lieber Herrgott, wie danke ich dir!«

So hatte der Teufel bewiesen, dass er es bei den Menschen nie zu Ehren bringen könne.

## 144 Der Bauer, seine Frau und der Teufel

Ein anderer Bauer wettete mit dem Teufel, dass er doch nicht alle Vögel kenne, die Gott erschaffen habe: es wäre ein Vogel, den er gewiss nicht kenne. Der Teufel erbat sich, den Vogel bis zur nächsten Morgenlichte auf einem Baume zu sehen. So legte der Bauer Mehlteig über seine Frau und drauf Federn, dass sie ganz befiedert aussah und setzte sie auf den Baum. Und wie der Teufel kam, sah er oft und lange hinauf, aber diesen Vogel hatte er noch nie gesehen. So verlor er die Wette.

## 145 Salomo und der Teufel

Salomo wollte dem Teufel nicht glauben, dass was zusammengehört, zusammen muss, d.h. dass die Ehen im voraus bestimmt seien. Der weise König aber unterhielt große Waisenhäuser und übergab daraus dem Teufel, der ihm untertan war, ein Mädchen mit dem Auftrag, sie auf eine unbewohnte Insel im Meere zu bringen und dort zu bewachen: das Essen könne er aus der Hofküche holen.

and each time the Devil bared his teeth. Our Dear Lord rebukes him for his malice toward people, whereupon the Devil used the malice of the people toward him as an excuse, saying they would never take off their hats off before him. Again the Lord advises him to be kind to people; if he acted kindly to them, they would be grateful to him in return. The Devil, however, disagreed with this adamantly and [said that he] would take his chances.

On their way, they saw a farmer who let his cows graze in the meadow. The Devil succeeded in persuading Our Dear Lord to throw the cows into the ditch. Immediately, the farmer shouted, "What sort of devil must have had a hand in this again?"—and he ran off to fetch people to help him pull the cows from the hole. Meanwhile, however, the Devil helped the cows out [of the ditch], and when the farmer returned and saw his cows grazing in the field, he called out, "Oh my Dear Lord, how much I thank you!"

Thus the Devil had proven that he would never achieve honor amongst people.

### 144 The Farmer, His Wife, and the Devil

Another farmer made a bet with the Devil that he did not know all the birds that God had created; there was one bird which certainly he did not know. The Devil asked for the bird to be shown to him in a tree at the next dawn. So the farmer covered his wife in dough, with feathers on top of it so that she looked as if she had plumage all over, and placed her into the tree. And when the Devil arrived, he looked long and hard at the bird, but had to admit that he had never seen such a bird before. So he lost the bet.

### 145 King Solomon and the Devil

King Solomon did not want to believe the Devil, when he said that what belongs together must come together, meaning that marriages are preordained. But the wise king maintained large orphanages and from one of these he gave to the Devil, who was his subject, a young girl, with orders to take her to an uninhabited island in the ocean and take care of her there; he would be permitted to take food for her from the royal kitchen.

Da führte der Teufel das Mädchen hinaus und baute ihr, die ganz nackt war, ein artiges Häuschen auf einen Baum und wartete ihrer nach Pflicht. Als sie aber mannbar wurde geschah es, dass ein Schiff an der Küste scheiterte und sich nur der Herr desselben retten konnte. Als dieser das Häuschen sah, stieg er auf den Baum, wurde aber von dem Mädchen abgetrieben. Da kleidete er sich wie sie war und wurde nun eingelassen, und beide lebten nun zusammen wie Mann und Frau und bekamen nach und nach drei Kinder. Der Koch aber beschwerte sich bei Salomo, dass er dem Teufel seit geraumer Zeit nicht genug Essen reichen könne. Ließ also der König den Teufel kommen. Der aber fuhr statt der Antwort ab und holte das Häuschen, und stellte es mit seinem Inhalte zu Füßen seines Herren. So hatte er seinen Ausspruch bewiesen und es heißt noch jetzt: »Wer zusammengehört, muss zusammen, und sollte sie der Teufel auf seinem Schubkarren zusammen fahren.«

## 146 Der Affe im Kloster

Zu Kloster-Zeiten zeigte sich einmal ein Affe im Garten des Norbertinerklosters zu Speinshart; der Gärtner hinterbrachte es und erhielt den Auftrag, das Loch, durch das er käme, zu suchen, und wenn der Affe sich wieder zeige, es sogleich zu verstopfen. So hatte der Gärtner dem fremden Gaste den Ausgang verrammelt und 29 Väter kamen ganz freudig herab, Jagd auf ihn zu machen. Der Affe aber wich immer aus und so ihm ein Mönch nahe kam, drohte er mit dem Finger. Da wussten sie, wie es um den Affen stände und holten ihre Bücher und wollten den bösen Geist verlesen. Der aber lachte sie nur aus und höhnte sie: denn nicht einer von ihnen Allen hatte einen sauberen Brustfleck. Die Herren schickten nun um einen frommen Mann in der Nachbarschaft, den Pfarrer von Schlammersdorf, einen ehemaligen Jesuiten, der weithin berühmt war durch seine Gewalt über die Geister. Der las den Affen zusammen, und zwang ihn zur Rede. Es war ein Mönch des Klosters, dem alle Sünden vergeben waren bis auf Eine: er hatte nämlich Messgelder für sich verwendet, ohne die hl. Messen für die Ruhe der Armen Seelen zu lesen. Darum sei er verdammt. Schließlich bat er, ihn nur nicht ins

Thereupon the Devil led away the completely naked girl, and built for her a pretty little hut in a tree and took care of her as was his duty. But when she reached marriageable age, it happened that a ship stranded on the coast, and only its master was able to save himself. When he saw the little hut, he climbed the tree, but was driven away by the maiden. Then he clothed himself as she was, and now was allowed in, and both lived together as man and wife, and eventually had three children. The cook, however, complained to King Solomon that for some time now he had been unable to provide the Devil with enough food. The king summoned the Devil. Instead of a reply, he went away and fetched the little hut and placed it at his Lord's feet, together with all its contents. Thus he had proven his dictum, and to this day people say, "Those who belong together will come together, even if the Devil has to gather them in his wheelbarrow."

## 146 The Monkey in the Monastery

During monastic times, there once appeared a monkey in the garden of St. Norbert's Monastery in the town of Speinshart; the gardener brought the news and received orders to look for the hole through which the monkey had entered and, if he reappeared, to plug it at once. So the gardener had barred the exit for the strange guest, and 29 Holy Fathers gathered joyfully to chase it. But the monkey was able to elude them again and again and, whenever a monk came close, wagged its finger at him. Thus they knew how matters stood with the monkey and fetched their books and wanted to exorcise the Evil Spirit. But the monkey simply laughed and sneered at them, for not one amongst them had a clean conscience. Then the fathers sent for a pious man nearby, the pastor of Schlammersdorf, a former Jesuit, widely known for his power over spirits. The latter exorcized the monkey and forced him to speak. He had been a monk at the monastery, absolved from all his sins but one, that is to say: he had used the collection money on himself, without having Mass said for the peace of the Poor Souls. Therefore he was damned. In the end, he pleaded not to be

Wasser zu setzen. So kam er als Rabe an einen Bach bei Zettlas, wo er sich alle Mittage baden muss. Die Leute kennen ihn, und kein Tier naht sich der Stelle.

## 147 Bestrafte Hoffart

Eine Bauerntochter war jung, schön und reich, aber so voll Stolz, dass sie alle Menschen verachtete und jeden Freier mit Hohn abwies. Als sie starb, befahl sie, ihr die neuen Schuhe mit ins Grab zu geben. Nun war einer aus ihrem Orte, der sie bei Lebzeiten kannte, des Weges und das Nachtgload kam, und da sah er die Bauerntochter im Zuge und dass ihre Schuhe ganz zerrissen waren. Das erzählte er den Eltern. Man ließ das Grab öffnen, und die neuen Schuhe waren wirklich zerrissen und bis an die Waden hinaufgeschoben. – Nach dem Erzähler gelten die Nachtgloater[11] als Arme Seelen, und dürfen auf einem Stock mit drei Kreuzen ausruhen.

## 148 Der Zauberer und der Bettelbube

Ein Zauberer dingte einen Bettelbuben, der in Lumpen herumlief und seinem Vater Brot zutrug. Er hatte bei ihm nichts zu tun, als die Bücher abzustauben, sollte aber beileibe nicht darin lesen. Der Bube tat den Dienst, las aber auch fleißig in den Büchern und lernte daraus, wie man sich in Tiere und andere Dinge verwandeln könne. Als nun seine Zeit aus war, ging er heim und sagte zum Vater: »Jetzt soll es anders gehen bei uns. Ich habe gelernt, mich in ein Pferd umzuwandeln; als solches führst du mich morgen auf den Markt, nimmst dir aber beim Verkaufe

---

[11] „Nachtgload, auch bekannt als die wilde ‚Jagd,‘ die in stürmischen (Rauh-)Nächten durch die Luft braust. Nach altem Volksglauben reitet da Gott Wotan mit Gefolge, unter Blitz und Donner im tosenden Sturm durch die Nacht. Bedrohliche Wölfe, heulende Hunde Katzen, Krähen usw. geben ihm das ‚Geleit' (Gload). Unsere Ahnen glaubten, dass das Nachtgload auch Menschen gefährlich werden konnte. Wer sich in so einer Nacht im Freien befand, legte sich am besten mit gekreuzten Armen, mit dem Gesicht nach unten, flach auf den Boden und verrichtete ein Stoßgebet." („Mundart-Eckerl," *Eichendorfer Rathausfenster*, Bd. 10 (Juni 2009): 9, <http://www.markt-eichendorf.de/documents/Infoblatt_Jun09.pdf>. Abgerufen 1 Nov 2012.

put into water. So, in the shape of a raven, he was banished to a stream near Zettlas, where he has to bathe every day at noon. The people know of him, and no animal goes near the place.

### 147 Pride Will Be Punished

A farmer's daughter was young, beautiful, and rich, but so full of pride that she despised everybody and rejected all suitors with scorn. When she died, she ordered that her new shoes be put into the grave with her. But a local man who had known her when she still lived came along when the Wild Hunt passed by, and he saw the farmer's daughter in the procession and that her shoes were all torn up. This he told her parents. They opened the grave and indeed found the shoes torn and pushed up to her shins.—According to the narrator, these Wild Hunters are regarded as Poor Souls,[12] and they are allowed to rest upon a staff with three crosses.

### 148 The Sorcerer and the Beggar Boy

A Sorcerer had hired a beggar boy who ran about in tatters and supplied his father with bread. The boy was given nothing to do but dust the books, but under no circumstances was he to read them. The boy performed his duties, but also studied the books diligently, learning from them how to change himself into animals and other things. When his time was up, he returned home and said to his father, "Now things at home shall be different. I learned how to change into a horse; and as such you shall take me to the market tomorrow morning; however, exclude

---

[12] "The 'Night Entourage,' known also as the 'Wild Hunt,' roars through the air during stormy (Robbing) Nights. According to ancient and popular beliefs, the God Wotan then rides through the night with his entourage, in the midst of a raging storm with thunder and lightning. Charging wolves, howling dogs, cats, crows, etc. are his 'entourage' (German, 'Gload' or 'Gloat'). Our ancestors believed that the Night Entourage can be dangerous for humans also. If you find yourself outside during such a night, lay flat on the ground face down with your arms crossed and say a quick prayer." „Mundart-Eckerl," Eichendorfer Rathausfenster, vol. 10 (Juni 2009): 9, <http://www.markt-eichendorf.de/documents/Infoblatt_Jun09.pdf>. Accessed 1 Nov 2012.

den Zaum aus: denn der Zaum bin ich.« Da führte der Vater ein prächtiges Pferd auf den Markt und alles lief zusammen, es zu sehen. Einer aber drängte sich durch und kaufte das Pferd um den Preis, ohne zu handeln, und setzte sich auf und ritt eiligst davon. Es war der Zauberer, und der Vater hatte auf den Zaum vergessen bei dem Anblicke des vielen blinkenden Goldes. Als das Ross nahe daran war, vom Hetzen zusammenzusinken, stieg der Zauberer ab und band es an einen Baum. Da verwandelte sich das Pferd schnell in eine Krähe, und der Zauberer in einen Habicht. Nicht lange rauften sie herum, so fiel die Krähe zu Boden; flugs war sie in einen goldenen Ring verwandelt, der Habicht vermeinte nach der Krähe zu beißen und schluckte den Ring und erstickte. So wurde der Bettelbube wieder frei und trieb von nun an das Handwerk des Zauberns.

### 149 Der Prinz und die blinde Prinzessin

Ein Prinz, durch die Feinde aus seinem Lande vertrieben, irrte in der Fremde herum, und kehrte zuletzt nur in Höhlen und Wäldern zu. Er hatte eben in einer Höhle geschlafen und war erwacht, als er einen garstigen Zwerg neben sich liegen, einen Esel draußen stehen sah. Der Zwerg bot dem müden Prinzen sein dürres Tier zum Reiten an und so ging es fort bis zu einer Hütte, wo sie einkehrten. Kaum waren sie aber da, brach eine Schar Räuber herein und wollte den Prinzen mit dem Zwerge töten. Der Esel aber erhob solches Geschrei in allerlei Stimmen, dass die Räuber eiligst entwichen und selbst ihr Geld zurückließen. Der Zwerg lud das Geld dem Esel auf, und nun ging es in die Stadt. Hier war große Trauer, denn die schöne Prinzessin war erblindet; wer ihr das Augenlicht wieder gäbe, sollte sie zur Frau erhalten. Da ließ der Zwerg den Prinzen sich fürstlich kleiden, und führte derweilen seinen Esel an eine Staude, wo er so lange naschen durfte, bis er einige Kotbollen fallen ließ. Diese steckte er dem Prinzen zu und gab ihm den Auftrag, sich bei Hof als Arzt zu melden: er solle die Bollen der Prinzessin auf die Augen legen, und sogleich werde sie sehend sein. – Der Prinz in stattlichem Gewande und schön von Gestalt wurde auch als

the bridle from the sale: for I shall be the bridle." The father then led a splendid horse to the market and everybody gathered to inspect it. One man pushed through the crowd and bought the horse at the [asking] price without bargaining, mounted it, and rode away in the greatest of haste. It was the Sorcerer, and the father had forgotten about the bridle when seeing the many flashing gold coins. When the horse was close to collapse from the hard ride, the Sorcerer dismounted and tethered it to a tree. Thereupon the horse quickly changed into a crow, and the Sorcerer into a hawk. They had not fought long when the crow fell to the ground; swiftly, it changed into a golden ring; the hawk meant to eat the crow, but swallowed the ring and choked to death. Thus the beggar boy won back his freedom, and from this time on practiced the craft of Sorcery.

### 149 The Prince and the Blind Princess

A prince who had been driven out of his country by enemies strayed in foreign lands and eventually dwelt only in caves and forests. He had just woken from sleep in a cave, when he found an ugly Dwarf lying next to him and saw a donkey standing outside. The Dwarf offered the tired prince a ride on his scrawny animal, and thus they arrived at a cottage where they stopped for a meal. No sooner had they arrived when a band of robbers stormed in and wanted to kill the prince along with the Dwarf. The donkey, however, began to scream so loudly in sundry voices that the robbers fled in the greatest haste and even left their money behind. The Dwarf loaded the money onto the donkey, and off they went to the city. Here there was great sadness, for the beautiful princess had been struck blind; he who restored her eyesight would receive her hand in marriage. Then the Dwarf had the prince dressed richly, and meanwhile led his donkey to a herb bush where he was allowed to nibble until he dropped some dung balls. These he gave to the prince with the instruction to present himself at court as a physician; he should lay the dung balls onto the princess's eyes, and immediately she would be able to see [again].— Clad in rich clothes and cutting a handsome figure, the prince

bald zur Blinden gelassen, er tat, wie ihm der Zwerg geraten und
die Prinzessin war geheilt und auf der Stelle seine Braut. Da wollte
er nach dem Zwerge schauen, um ihm zu danken: der war aber
verschwunden und damit das einfache Mittel, Blinde sehend zu
machen, verloren.

### 150 Der Weg zum Himmel

Ein einfältiger Bauer hatte in der Predigt vernommen, wie der
Weg in den Himmel ein gerader sei. Da macht er sich auf, und
geht fort über Berg und Tal, durch Wald und Wasser, immer geraden Weges, und wo es nicht anders anging, stieg er auch über
die Häuser hinweg. So gelangt er vor eine schöne Kirche: und
als er fragte, wie sie heiße, und ihm zur Antwort wurde: »Himmelreich« – trat er ein, vermeinend, es sei hier der Himmel, und
legte sich hin in eine Ecke, um für immer da zu bleiben. Die
Mönche des nahen Klosters wollten ihn zwar forthaben, aber
die fromme Einfalt siegte. Sie reichten ihm sogar jeden Tag etwas Nahrung, da er alle seine Zeit mit Gebet hinbrachte. Es war
ein hoher Festtag, da erhielt er bessere Speisen: erfreut darüber
blickt er auf und schaut an der Wand den Heiland am Kreuze. Sogleich bittet er U.L. Herrn, herabzusteigen und bei ihm zu Gaste
zu sein; und der reine Sinn fand seinen Lohn: denn der Heiland
stieg vom Kreuze hernieder und setzte sich zu ihm hin, und teilte
sein Mahl, und als sie gegessen hatten, lud ihn der Herr zu sich
ins Himmelreich. Der Arme aber lehnte es ab, denn er war ja
schon im Himmel, bis er des Besseren belehrt wurde. Da meldete
er den Vorgang dem Klosteroberen, der seinerseits nun bat, auch
ihn mitzunehmen, wenn Unser Herr komme, ihn zu holen. Nun
lud der Fromme den Heiland wieder zu Gaste und trug ihm seine
Bitte für den Oberen vor und wurde erhört. Und als der nächste
Sonntag kam, und beide während der heiligen Messe vor dem
Altare knieten, sanken sie um, und zwei weiße Tauben flogen
zum Himmel auf.

was soon led before the blind maiden; he did as advised by the Dwarf, and the princess was healed and became his bride there and then. Then he wanted to look for the Dwarf to thank him: but he had disappeared, and with him was lost the simple cure for restoring eyesight to the blind.

## 150 The Road to Heaven

A simple-minded farmer had heard in a sermon that the road to Heaven was a straight one. Thereupon he leaves, and walks over mountains and valleys, through forests and water, always in a straight path and, when there was no other way to go, he even climbed over houses. Thus he arrived at a beautiful church, and when he asked what its name was, and was given the answer "The Heavenly Kingdom"—he entered, taking this place to be Heaven, and lay down in a corner to remain there forever. The monks of the nearby monastery wanted to have him removed, but his pious simple-mindedness prevailed. They even gave him some food every day, for he spent all his time in prayer. It was on a High Feast Day that he received better food: pleased by this he looks up and on the wall, notices the Savior on the Cross. Immediately, he asks Our Dear Lord to step down to be his guest, and his pure spirit was rewarded, for the Savior stepped down from his Cross and sat down with him and shared his meal, and when they had finished eating, the Lord invited him to join Him in the Heavenly Kingdom. But the poor man refused this, because [he thought] he was already in Heaven, until he learned otherwise. Then he reported this encounter to the monastery Superior, who asked to be taken with him when the Lord would come to fetch him. Now the pious man invited the Savior to be his guest again, and also presented the Prior's request, and [it] was granted. And when the next Sunday came, and during Holy Mass both men were kneeling before the altar, they fell to the ground, and two white doves flew up to Heaven.

# TRANSLATOR'S PROFILE

A native of Germany, M. Charlotte Wolf has lived in the United States for almost 20 years. Before coming to the U.S., she conducted her undergraduate work in American Studies and German language and literature at two German universities. In the U.S., she completed an M.A. in German, a Ph.D. in Interdisciplinary Studies (Literature & Women's Studies), and a graduate degree program in Education Administration.

Since 1985, she has worked as a freelance translator and editor for English and German. Her expertise is in Literature, Linguistics, Women's Studies, and Technology. In addition, she has had a successful career in education as an administrator, consultant, coach, teacher, and trainer for German, English, ESL, Women's Studies, and Yoga.

In her free time she is a passionate reader of multilingual literature, watches movies (foreign and film noir), travels, and writes poetry. She is happily married to Martin Tobias, who, after a long career in electrical engineering, has now turned to photography.